FOUNDATIONS
OF
Landscape
Architecture

FOUNDATIONS
OF
Landscape
Architecture

INTEGRATING FORM AND SPACE
USING THE LANGUAGE OF SITE DESIGN

Norman K. Booth

WILEY

John Wiley & Sons, Inc.

Library of Congress Cataloging-in-Publication Data:

Booth, Norman K
  Foundations of landscape architecture : integrating form and space using the language of site design / Norman Booth.
     p. cm.
  Includes index.
  ISBN 978–0–470–63505–6 (pbk.), ISBN 978–1–118–12727–8 (ebk.); ISBN 978–1–118–12728–5 (ebk); ISBN 978–1–118–12945–6 (ebk); ISBN 978–1–118–12946–3 (ebk); ISBN 978–1–118–12947–0 (ebk)
  1. Landscape architecture. I. Title.
  SB472.B564 2012
  712—dc23

                                                                    2011018370

This book is dedicated to Professor Emeritus George Curry and the late Professor George Earle, of the Department of Landscape Architecture, SUNY College of Environmental Science and Forestry at Syracuse University. The design knowledge and skills they taught me in a sophomore design class have been ever present throughout my career and have served as a foundation for my own teaching. I owe my love of landscape architecture and a broader appreciation of the arts to both. This book would not be possible without them.

Contents

Preface

Landscape architectural design is a complex and multitasked journey that seeks to create environments that are acclimated to their site and surrounding context, accommodate users' characteristics and needs, incorporate cultural heritage, embody sustainability, and integrate functional requirements. In addition to all these principal intentions, landscape architectural design also endeavors to forge space as a stage for human activities and enjoyment. Space is the invisible entity in the landscape that people occupy and use whenever they are in the landscape. The process of creating space, whether it be in a backyard garden or grand public space, distinguishes landscape architectural design from other environmental and garden design vocations.

Among the numerous devices and techniques employed to create space in the landscape, one of the most important is form. Form is the two- and three-dimensional armature that frames landscape space and gives is organizational structure. Well-conceived form is essential to a landscape design because it is the underlying armature for almost aspects of design. Like an animal skeleton or the steel structure of a building, form affects the overall size, proportion, and massing of a landscape architectural design as well as the relationship among individual components.

The sense of structure is most pronounced in highly architectonic landscapes that employ orthogonal forms and least evident in designs that emulate natural patterns. Structural form is often established with fundamental geometric shapes like the square, triangle, circle, and their component elements. Forms may also be organic and be derived from naturally occurring objects and shapes. Whatever its source, form is typically seen in the landscape by edges between spaces, elements, and ground materials. Form is further expressed in the third dimension by a building footprint, walls/fences, steps, plant masses, and the contour of the ground plane.

Most important, form is the foundation for space in the landscape. The scale, proportion, orientation, use, and meaning of outdoor space are profoundly dependent on the ground plane footprint and its three-dimensional expression, just as architectural volume is decidedly associated with a building's floor plan, associated walls, and ceilings. In essence, how people experience and move through space corresponds to how it is structured. Form likewise establishes the feel and temperament of a landscape. Heroic, poetic, serial, exploratory, and so on are all potential landscape dispositions affected by the underlying configuration. Finally, style is explicitly associated with form as well. Classic, romantic, modern, postmodern, and other styles are each based on a particular set of forms and their arrangement.

Although a well-composed organization of forms is necessary for an admired landscape architectural design, it is only one ingredient. By itself, form does not ensure that an effective landscape design will be achieved. Adroit form composition in the landscape must be fused with a respect for the site, sensitivity to potential site users, incorporation of sustainable techniques, and an intelligent and creative vision. Further, form must serve as a foundation for three-dimensional spatial volumes. It is easy, especially for novice designers, to become focused only on plan pattern and to forget that the spatial experience is the most engaging quality of the landscape. Finally, form is only an underpinning and must ultimately be expressed with the proper choice of elements and materials. A landscape design with a sound structural framework can be captivating and memorable with the correct palette of materials but a visual misadventure if a poor selection of materials is used. So, a design's forms must be combined with sound judgment in all phases and deliberations of the design process. In the end, form is simply one of the many tools used to fashion a design, not an end unto itself.

This book offers a written and graphic description of the interrelationship between form and space, two reciprocal entities that each rely on the other for articulation. The focus is on the use of form to delineate space in landscape architectural site design, a genre that encompasses such projects types as parks, urban plazas, courtyards, entry spaces, gardens, residential sites, and the like. Site design is the pedestrian scale of landscape architecture where meaning, art, and craft coalesce to forge environments that are directly experienced with all our senses.

This text first presents the concepts, typologies, and rudimentary principles of form and space as the foundation of design. Subsequent chapters focus on fundamental form typologies starting with orthogonal shapes, the most architectonic and humanly influenced geometry, and progressing to organic forms, the genre of shapes most informed by nature. Individual chapters describe and illustrate the elements, unique characteristics, landscape uses, and design guidelines for each type of form. While an attempt is made to discuss the most commonly employed forms in the landscape, it is by no means meant to recognize and categorize all. The book is intended to provide the core concepts of the most prevalent form typologies with the awareness that all designers are continually seeking and creating new ways to shape the landscape. Thus, this book is meant as a point of departure, not a definitive prospectus.

A quick note for the beginning designer about the graphic style used in the illustrations throughout the book. The graphics used here have been employed to convey landscape designs in a clear, legible manner. As a consequence, many of the designs can be interpreted as employing a simplistic palette of materials, especially plant materials where, for example, only one tree symbol is applied throughout a design. However, the designs should be understood as being schematic and not being a final design proposal. Thus, most designs, if and when studied more at a larger drawing scale, would in fact use a wider variety of plant species within the established structure for both visual interest and sound sustainable practice.

It is hoped that the reader will be informed by the variety of form and spatial typologies that can be used to structure the landscape. Ultimately though, it is the reader's own imagination and inspiration that should shepherd a design's organization. Enjoy.

Acknowledgments

I wish to thank a number of individuals for their help and support throughout the development and production of this book. First, thanks go to Shelley Cannady, Lorn Clement, Bradley Goetz, and Jason Kentner who reviewed a draft manuscript of this book. Their feedback and suggestions were instrumental in shaping the underlying intent of the book and the inclusion of the first two chapters. Their comments provided a touchstone throughout the remainder of the book as well.

I am grateful to Walter Schwarz for his invaluable and concise technical advice in working with Adobe InDesign and Photoshop. His input was critical in making sure all the digital pieces would ultimately come together in a seamless whole. Thanks also go to Nancy Cintron, Senior Production Editor at John Wiley & Sons, for her support and earnest willingness to work through various issues related to my layout of the book.

I also owe much to Margaret Cummins, Senior Editor at John Wiley & Sons, who has provided experienced guidance, advice, inspiration, and enthusiastic support throughout. In addition, Margaret gave me the freedom to compose the layout of the book and the help needed to fulfill my vision of what this book should be. Margaret has been an immeasurable asset at all stages.

Finally and most important, I owe boundless gratitude to Gail, whose ever-present challenges and questions have continually pushed me to seek a higher standard. I am also deeply indebted to her for assuming almost all the duties of managing our household, allowing me the time and freedom to devote to this book. I could not have completed this project without her help. THANK YOU from the bottom of my heart.

Landscape Form

One principal objective of landscape architectural site design is to impart a spatial organization for human use and enrichment by orchestrating a broad palette of elements in an inspiring and coordinated manner. A primary means for choreographing this potpourri of elements is "form," an armature for assembling the many landscape elements that define landscape space. Without form, space exists as an amorphous void that lacks clarity and legibility (top 1.1). Form is the cornerstone for forging landscape site design and provides the most elemental means for coherently aligning elements so that space is discerned (bottom 1.1). Form is inherent to how landscape architects think and express themselves.

This chapter examines form as the basis for molding space in landscape architectural site design. The definition, typologies, ways for modifying, and techniques for organizing form in the landscape are all examined as the foundation for subsequent chapters. The sections of this chapter include:

- Form
- Primary Shapes
- Form Transformation
- Organizational Structures
- Unifying Principles

NO FORM PRESENT

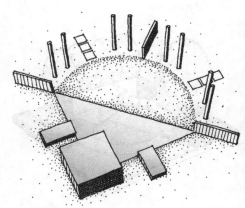

FORM PRESENT

1.1 Form organizes and delineates space.

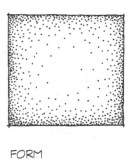

FORM   SHAPE

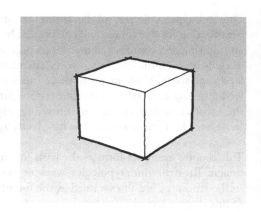

1.2 Right: Comparison between form and shape.

1.3 Below: Form is the overall arrangement of a design.

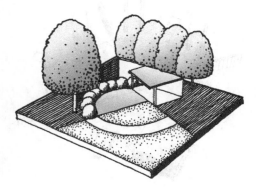

Form

Form is defined as the "structure of a work—the manner of arranging and coordinating the elements and parts of a composition so as to produce a coherent image" (Ching 2007, 34). Form is analogous to physique, anatomy, figure, formation, format, and arrangement. The term "form" is often interchanged with "shape" although "form" more accurately refers to the three-dimensional expression of volume while "shape" refers to a two-dimensional edge or outline (Bell 1993, 50; Ching 2007, 34). Shape is the silhouette of a form juxtaposed against a contrasting background or material (1.2).

The term *form* is used in this text to mean both the defining edge and internal area of each individual design element as well as the overall arrangement of the design (1.3). The notion of form is not limited to the shape of areas on the ground plane but is the totality of a design that encompasses both flat planes and three-dimensional volumes. Form may be simple or complex, controlled or spontaneous, human or organic, repetitive or variable, symmetrical or asymmetrical, and so on (1.4).

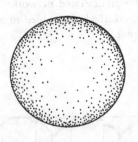

SIMPLE

COMPLEX

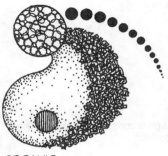

ORGANIC

Form is articulated in the landscape by edges and shape. The silhouette of form is easiest seen around structural elements that have mass and extend upward from the base plane like walls, fences, steps, decks, planters, and so on (left 1.5). Similarly, the outline of form is seen around voids that are recessed into the ground like pools, sunken spaces, descending steps, and the like. Less obvious, although just as important, are the perimeters exhibited by softer landscape elements like a line of trees, mass of shrubs, water bodies, and topography.

Form is also evident on the ground plane where different materials meet one another to establish a line (middle 1.5). The greater the contrast between the juxtaposed materials, the more clearly an edge is perceived. A complete form is defined when this boundary encircles an area, thus suggesting the floor of a space. Finally, the boundary of form is forged by elements above the ground like canvas awnings, trellises, and tree canopies (right 1.5). The junction of three-dimensional elements with one another expresses form as well.

1.4 Form is highly variable in complexity and character.

1.5 Examples of form in the landscape.

EDGES in VERTICAL PLANE

EDGES on GROUND PLANE

EDGES in OVERHEAD PLANE

3

In summary, form is created any time a line circumscribes an area whether it be on the ground or in the third dimension. Consequently, a landscape site design is composed of a multitude of lines and forms, all intertwined in a carefully orchestrated network (1.6). During the design process, these edges are thoughtfully and creatively assembled to mold outdoor space as discussed more thoroughly in the next chapter.

1.6 A design is composed of multiple lines and forms.

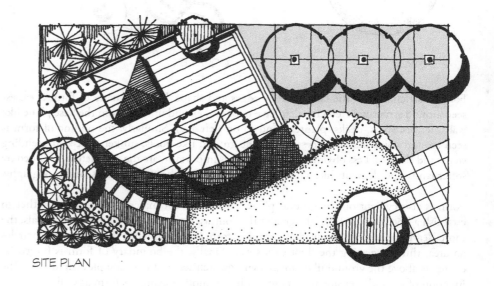

SITE PLAN

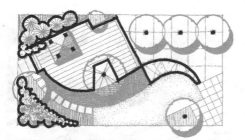

EDGES in VERTICAL PLANE

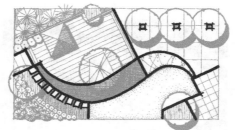

EDGES on GROUND PLANE

EDGES in OVERHEAD PLANE

4

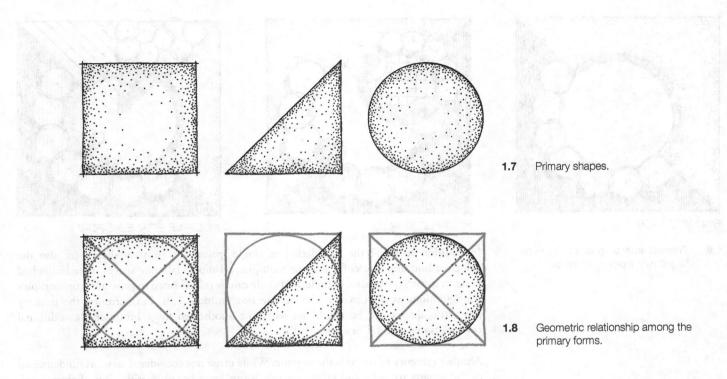

1.7 Primary shapes.

1.8 Geometric relationship among the primary forms.

Primary Shapes

There are innumerable forms that the landscape architect can employ to mold exterior space. Some are human fabrications while others are abstracted from natural elements. Among the many possibilities, the most rudimentary shapes are the square, triangle, and circle (1.7) (Reid 2007, 17). Simple polygons like pentagons and hexagons are sometimes also considered among the basic geometric shapes (Ching 2007, 38). These primary shapes are composed of the least number of sides and therefore are the most pure. Similarly these shapes are the easiest to recognize and typically the first learned by an infant.

The triad of the square, triangle, and circle also possess an intrinsic geometric relationship. Each can be defined within and/or generated from the others (1.8). No other family of shapes manifests this unique interrelationship. There is an almost mystic association among the primary shapes that gives them special significance in design.

The square, triangle, and circle can each serve as the underpinning for a simple, single landscape space (left 1.9). Such spaces are fitting for an individual function, a place of restrained emphasis, and/or as one space among others. Their simplicity makes them easily recognized and understood, thus providing a feeling of familiarity and comfort.

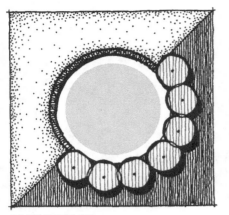

SINGLE SPACE

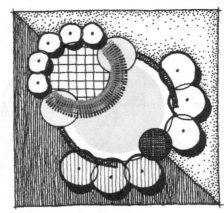

MULTIPLE SPACES

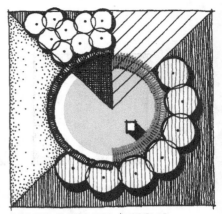

MULTIPLE SPACES & FORMS

1.9   Potential array of spaces that can be forged with the primary forms.

In addition to being the foundation of single spaces, the primary shapes are also the principal building blocks for forging multiple and more elaborate spaces. Like individual notes in music, the square, triangle, and circle can be transformed to generate more complex configurations as discussed in the next section (middle 1.9). Furthermore, the primary geometric shapes can be combined with one another to forge innumerable additional compositional possibilities (right 1.9).

Another category of forms is the organic. While often not considered to be as fundamental as the square, triangle, and circle, organic forms are a broad classification of shapes that are derived from elements and patterns found in nature. Vegetation, landform, geological formations, water, the sky, insects, animals, and so on all provide copious sources that can be emulated or abstracted as the basis of landscape space (1.10). It should be noted that the square, triangle, and circle are themselves found in nature or extracted from nature. Thus, the natural world is the true origin of all forms (see Chapter 16).

1.10   Examples of organic forms.

The square, triangle, polygon, and circle along with organic forms are the basis for Chapters 3–16 of this text. Each primary shape and its constituent parts are more thoroughly examined in their ability to serve as the foundation of landscape space along with their fundamental design qualities, potential uses, and associated design guidelines.

Form Transformation

In addition to being used by themselves as pure forms, the primary shapes are the origin for the evolution of other more elaborate forms. The process for forging altered forms is referred to as *transformation* or the mutation of one shape into another. The purpose of transformation is to generate forms that are appropriate to the particular circumstances of each design setting and to be a vehicle for creatively molding landscape space. The extent of metamorphous a primary form undergoes can be minimal or extensive depending on site circumstances and program requirements. There are five fundamental strategies for transformation discussed in the following paragraphs: subtraction, addition, rotation, intervention, and synthesis of the others (1.11).

1.11 Typology of transformation processes.

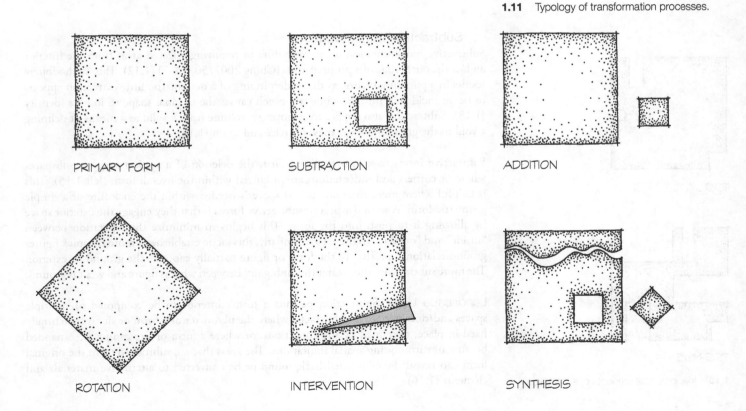

PRIMARY FORM   SUBTRACTION   ADDITION

ROTATION   INTERVENTION   SYNTHESIS

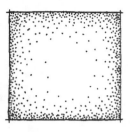

ORIGINAL FORM

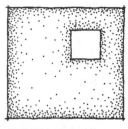

SUBTRACTION from
INTERIOR

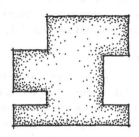

SUBTRACTION from
EXTERIOR

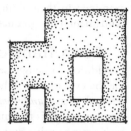

SUBTRACTION from
INTERIOR & EXTERIOR

1.12 Alternative strategies of subtraction.

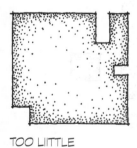

TOO LITTLE

TOO MUCH

1.13 Inappropriate amounts of subtraction.

Subtractive Transformation

Subtractive transformation is the procedure of removing selected areas from the interior and/or the outer edge of a primary form (Ching 2007, 50, 54–7) (1.12). This methodology results in a punctured fabric as the underpinning of a design. Too little extraction appears to be an incidental mistake while too much causes the original shape to lose its identity (1.13). Subtraction also applies to removing a volume from a solid as a means of defining a void in the ground plane, a mass of trees, and so on (1.14).

Subtractive forms have two qualities. First, the deletion of a section suggests subspaces wherever corners and indentations are produced within the overall form (left 1.15). This is helpful where more than one use or space is needed within the enclosure of a simple geometric form. A second aspect of subtractive forms is that they engage the exterior space by allowing it to push into the form. This begins to minimize the separation between "inside" and "outside" (right 1.15). Similarly, this tactic establishes a more complex figure/ground relationship. That is, the form or figure partially captures the ground or exterior. The more subtraction, the greater the ambiguity between what is figure and what is ground.

Landscape Uses. Subtraction permits a form's interior to be composed of multiple spaces and/or materials, a viable tactic where the perimeter of a form or site is structurally fixed in place, restrained by site conditions, or where a form or site cannot be expanded because of surrounding spatial limitations. The areas that are subtracted from the original form can reveal the contextual background or be converted to alternative materials and elements (1.16).

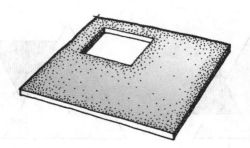

SUBTRACTIED FORM in the
GROUND PLANE

SUBTRACTIED FORM from a
TREE MASS

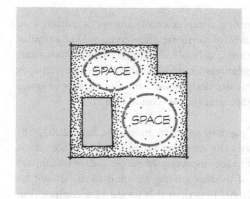

SUBSPACES WITHIN a
FORM

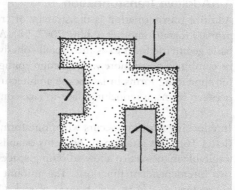

SUBSPACES ALONG the
EDGES of a FORM

1.14 Above: Subtraction of a volume.

1.15 Left: Subtraction can create subspaces within a form.

1.16 Example of a site design created via subtractive transformation.

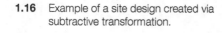

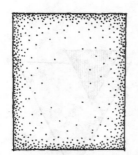
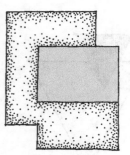
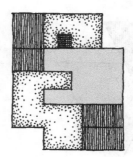

TRANSFORMATION PROCESS

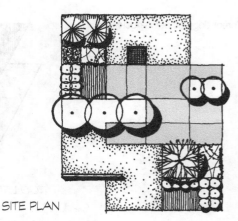

SITE PLAN

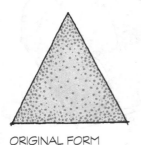
ORIGINAL FORM

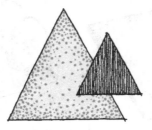
INTERLOCKING

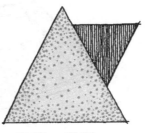
FACE-to-FACE

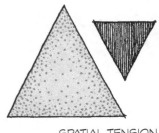
SPATIAL TENSION

1.17 Alternative strategies of addition.

Additive Transformation

Additive transformation is the strategy of creating complex compositions by adding one primary form to another (Ching 2007, 58). Additive forms are often composed of a similar basic geometric form to assure overall cohesiveness, although dissimilar primary forms can be combined when more varied design configurations are desired. There are three methods for appending forms in landscape architectural site design based on the amount of space between forms: interlocking, face-to face-contact, and spatial tension (1.17).

Interlocking addition occurs when one form partially overlaps another (Ching 2007, 58) (left 1.16). This attachment of forms establishes the strongest visual bond possible and is a suitable maneuver to allow adjoining spaces to inconspicuously merge and/or to support two interdependent functions. The amount of overlap among merging forms should be approximately 1/4 to 3/4 the area of each (1.18). Less than this produces a composition that appears more accidental than intentional. Too much overlap causes the initial forms to be visually absorbed and lost in one another.

1.18 Different degrees of interlocking.

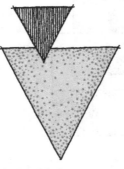
TOO LITTLE

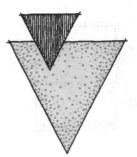
APPROPRIATE OVERLAP

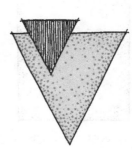
TOO MUCH

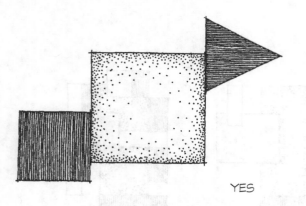

YES

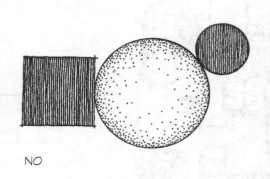

NO

Face-to face-contact is the connection of one form to another along a common side (middle right 1.17). This technique of addition requires the affiliated forms to have planar or flat sides like squares, rectangles, triangles, and polygons (Ching 2007, 58) (left 1.19). These forms are able to join along a common uniform face, resulting in a stable and compositionally strong relationship between the attached forms. Circles and other curved forms do not lend themselves to face-to-face contact because a rounded face is able to connect to a planar face only at a single point, thus creating an unstable point of visual tension (right 1.19).

Spatial tension is the tactic of additive transformation that places forms near each other without touching or overlapping (Ching 2007, 58) (right 1.17). This is a viable concept where there is a need to have spaces and uses in relative close proximity while maintaining their individual identity. However, spatial tension creates the weakest compositional connection of all the alternative strategies for additive transformation because the intervening space visually separates the forms from each other. As the distance of this interstitial space increases, the less association there is between neighboring forms (1.20).

1.19 Face-to-face addition should be undertaken with flat-sided forms.

1.20 Different degrees of spatial tension.

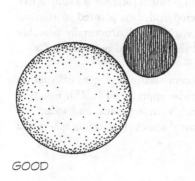

GOOD

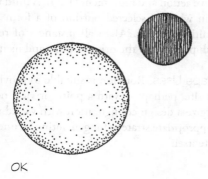

OK

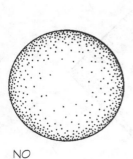

NO

11

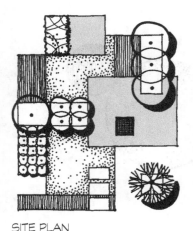

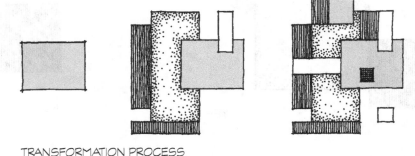

SITE PLAN

TRANSFORMATION PROCESS

1.21 Above: Example of a site design created via additive transformation.

1.22 Below: Rotation of original form.

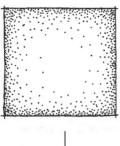

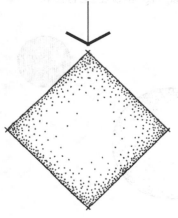

Landscape Uses. Additive transformation is appropriate when the exterior of the initial form is not dimensionally constrained, when space around it is available for expansion, and when multiple spaces are required, each within its own identity. Furthermore, additive transformation is a viable means of expanding into an adjoining landscape from an existing space (1.21). Similarly, the technique is good for embellishing a simple space to give it greater visual intrigue.

Rotation

Rotation is the transformation process of pivoting a primary geometric form around an axis or point in one of several ways. First, the entire form can be turned to a new orientation in relation to its original position (1.22). A second means of rotation is to treat it as additive process in which each new component is turned in relation to the first, thereby suggesting cumulative action and movement (1.23). A third tactic is to consider rotation as a subtractive process in which a selected portion of a form is extracted and then pivoted in relation to the initial form (1.24) In all instances of rotation, visually and structurally unstable relationships between the original form and its modified version should be avoided.

Landscape Uses. Rotation is suitable to provide an accent and/or divergent orientation within a site, perhaps toward a point or view not otherwise appreciated (1.25). Rotation can energize a design configuration with varied relationships among spaces and areas. It is also an appropriate strategy for generating an unconventional association among spaces and to the site itself.

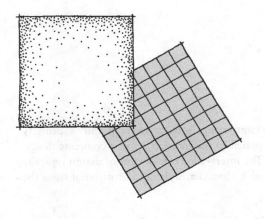

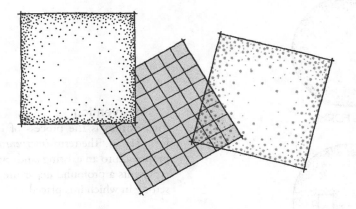

The intent of matching a form ...
... Since the program's also explic-...
... and to a certain extent, use the. The interventi-...
... is a recombin-ation to produce the entire theorem...
... form in which this g-real...

Landscape Here the super-... over-look is to take place resulting in the intersection-...
of the site's design to connect the ... de-sign corresponding at each axis, as an area the right-...
of a certain interest, the problem is the resultant axes by virtue of the obtaining differences...
... (1.23)

1.23 Above: Additive rotation.

1.24 Left: Rotation of a selected area within the original form.

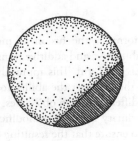 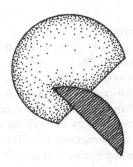

The last ... rotation that create form ...
another ... decisive it is ... it is a selected... resolution ... transformation process...
can be appreciated ... ... each design ... this ... will humanize the general...
... ... and give the ... ... designs in continuously and by...
... ... match different ... ... is by that available to...
... one ... decomposition or its ... ... combination while within a...
... of an ... component ... add. That ... ... that the resulting composition will have...
... in comprising make ... so ... that is ... the ... resultant de-...

1.25 Example of a site design created via rotation.

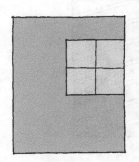 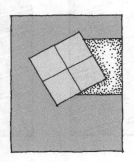 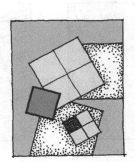

TRANSFORMATION PROCESS

SITE PLAN

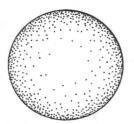

ORIGINAL FORM

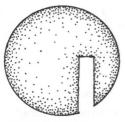

INTERVENTION

1.26 Intervention.

1.27 Example of a site design incorporating intervention.

Intervention

Intervention is the process of inserting a contrasting form or element into a primary form (1.26). The term *intervention* is also applied to the interjection of a complete design proposal into an existing landscape setting. The intervening component or design typically represents a profound departure in form, order, character, style, and/or material from the setting in which it is placed.

Landscape Uses. The purpose of intervention is to energize a design by the juxtaposition of dissimilar design structures. The intervening component can serve as an area of emphasis or it can accent the unique qualities of the original setting by virtue of the obvious differences (1.27).

Synthesis

The last category of transformation of forms is the fusion of more than one type of modification (1.28). For example, both subtractive and additive transformational processes can be applied to the same or different areas of a form. This approach furnishes the greatest freedom for creative expression and gives the designer the ability to simultaneously apply independent design tactics to accomplish different design objectives. It is often advisable to use one means of transformation as the primary method of modification while others are used in a supplementary role. This helps to ensure that the resulting composition will have one prevailing quality that consolidates the overall design.

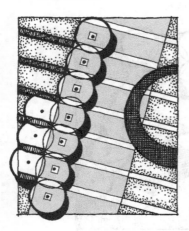

SITE PLAN

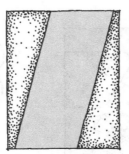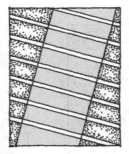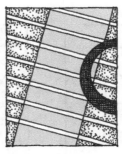

TRANSFORMATION PROCESS

TRANSFORMATION PROCESS

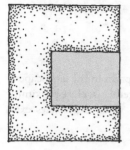 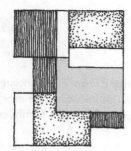 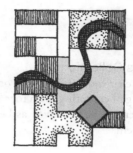

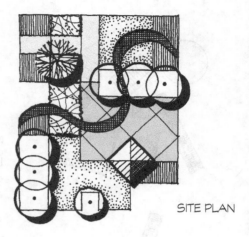

SITE PLAN

Organizational Structures

All the transformation processes discussed in the previous section are dependent on an organizational structure that governs where all the constituent design components are located in relation to one another. This applies equally to subdivision, addition, rotation, or intervention within a single form or in an assemblage of multiple forms. In essence, an organizational structure is the underlying skeleton or infrastructure of a composition and is akin to a tree's trunk and branch configuration or to a building's wood/steel frame. It defines the overall configuration of a design. The purpose of an organizational structure is to provide compositional order and to give a design a sense of legibility for people who experience it. The use of an organizational structure is essential for landscape architectural site design; without it, a design is likely to be a chaotic collection of forms and elements that have little or no relationship to one another. The most common organizational structures are (1.29): mass collection, line, grid, symmetry, and asymmetry.

1.28 Example of a site design created via a synthesis of transformation processes.

1.29 Typology of organizational structures.

 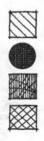 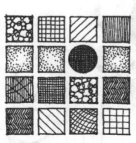 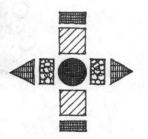 

MASS
COLLECTION　　　　LINE　　　GRID　　　　　　　SYMMETRY　　　　　　ASYMMETRY

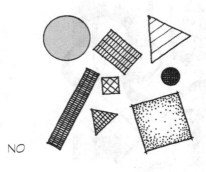

NO

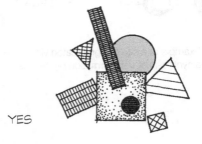

YES

1.30 Mass collection groups design components together.

1.31 Mass collection requires close spacing among elements.

Mass Collection

The most elementary method for organizing forms and associated spaces in the landscape is by massing or clustering them together (1.30). Placing elements together in close proximity causes them to be perceived as being members of a family even when differences exist among them.

Mass collection is the easiest and most rudimentary method of organization. It requires no special design skill other than to assemble component elements together. However, successful mass collection does require that the constituent design elements be located relatively close to one another if not touching or overlapping. As previously discussed, proportionally broad interstitial space segregates a design composition and so needs to be avoided. Therefore, one of the most fundamental organizational design guidelines is to group spaces and the elements that define them together with little or no intervening space (1.31).

Landscape Uses. Mass collection is the foundation and beginning point for all the other design organizations discussed in the following paragraphs. That is, they too aggregate constituent elements together, although in more elaborate ways. Because these other organizational typologies go beyond mass collection, it is typically not used as the sole design framework unless there are no functional or aesthetic requirements beyond grouping (1.32). While this design structure appears chaotic and thrown together to many eyes, it is nevertheless ordered by the fact that the design elements are gathered together.

NO—ELEMENTS are NOT MASSED

YES—ELEMENTS are MASSED

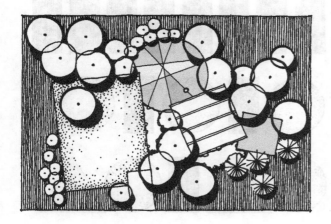

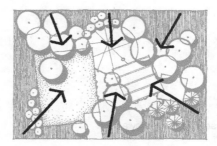

1.32 Example of a site design incorporating mass collection.

Line

Stretching a single form along one dimension or assembling several forms next to one another in a chainlike configuration is the next level of organization (Ching 2007, 62) (1.33). Rather than simply being randomly heaped together as they are in mass collection, multiple design elements are intentionally assembled next to one another in succession. An actual line can be, but does not necessarily have to be, delineated to produce a linear organization. A linear organization may be straight, angled, curved, and so forth, depending on the design context and the desired disposition of movement along it. All linear organizations regardless of alignment emphasize extension, directionality, and movement. Cadence or rhythm is established when multiple elements are spaced in a recurring pattern within the serial construct (1.34).

1.33 Alternative strategies for creating a linear organization.

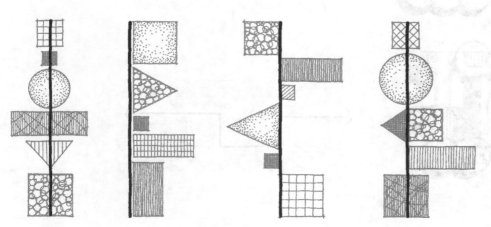

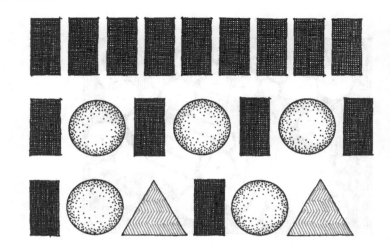

1.34 Right: Examples of cadence created by a linear organization.

1.35 A linear organization can establish a direct or indirect path of movement between spaces.

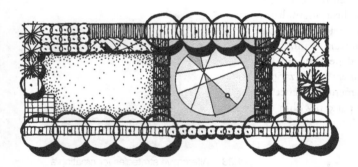

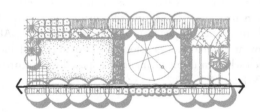

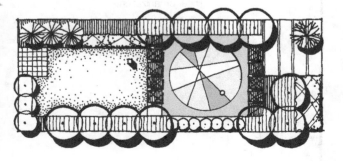

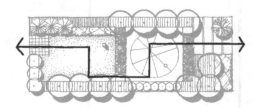

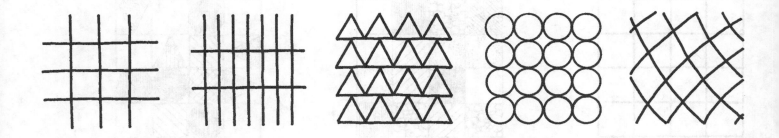

Landscape Uses. One application of a linear organization is to establish a sequential series of spaces, one experienced before and after another. This forges a chronological progression through the landscape that intentionally choreographs movement, a particularly effective design structure in an elongated site. The sequence can be arranged on an axis (see Symmetry) or a straight spine that is located next to or through the spaces (top 1.35). This concept provides an obvious route of travel. An alternative strategy is to organize the spaces so that path of travel is not direct or even explicitly expressed (bottom 1.35). This establishes a more explorative progression that has an aspect of mystery.

Grid

A grid is an assemblage of elements arranged in contiguous parallel lines, a more advanced organizational structure than the previous two (1.36). The intersecting lines establish points and interstitial spaces that are the basis of the four primary types of grid: line, mesh, point, and modular (1.37) An orthogonal grid (see Chapter 6) is the most conventional, although other forms and directions of lines can create grids as well.

1.36 A grid is formed by repeating forms and lines in sets of parallel rows.

1.37 Grid typologies.

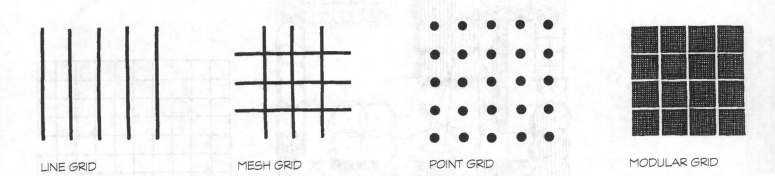

LINE GRID   MESH GRID   POINT GRID   MODULAR GRID

19

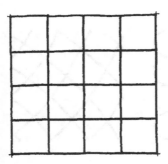

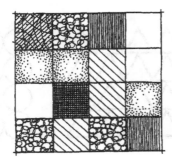

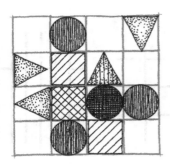

1.38 A grid is an armature for organizing different content.

A grid organization represents a systemized, rational approach to design. It is a non-hierarchical field of equal components; each line, point, or module is the same as the others. A grid has no inherent points of emphasis or dominant areas. Similarly, a grid is a neutral, nondirectional configuration. In essence, a grid is a standardized template that similar or varied design elements can be inserted into in a predictable and regular fashion (1.38).

Landscape Uses. A grid organization is an armature for orchestrating various landscape design elements and spaces along its lines, at the intersection points, and/or in the interstitial modules (1.39). The static dimensions, orientation, and position of the grid lines assures that all the design elements will align with one another and be unified by the common size of the area in which they are placed. A grid can be limitlessly added onto or subtracted from, thus permitting it to acclimate to either a site with uniform conditions or one with numerous impediments. Finally, a grid potentially provides choices of movement along its lines, a distinct difference to a linear organization.

1.39 A example of a site design based on a grid.

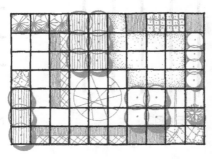

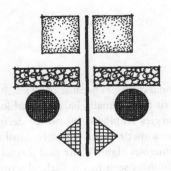

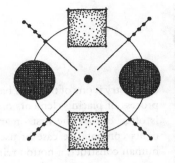

1.40 Left: A symmetrical composition is organized around a line or point.

1.41 Below: All elements in a symmetrical composition are mirrored around a dominant axis.

Symmetry

Symmetry is the balanced distribution of equivalent forms and spaces around a point, line, or plane (Ching 2007, 339) (1.40). The centering element or plane is called an axis and may be a line such as a walk or road, or it may be an elongated element like a pool, panel of lawn, bed of plants, and so forth (Simonds 1997, 223). Compositional elements are located directly on the axis or adjacent to it so that each side of the axis is the mirror image of the other, a phenomenon that is sometimes referred to as reflective symmetry (1.41). Thus, members of a symmetrical design exist as singular elements, pairs, or multiples of pairs.

The axis has several other traits. First, the axis is *the* dominant feature, whether explicitly or implicitly expressed, that governs the use, form, and character of all elements on or near it (Simonds 1997, 224) (left 1.42). The consequence of the axis's supremacy is a clear sense of hierarchy within a design; not only does the axis demand authority for itself, but also for spaces and elements placed on it. Second, as a line, the axis concentrates movement and views along its length toward the termini or to any element placed on it (right 1.42).

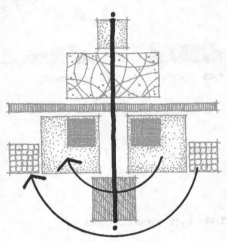

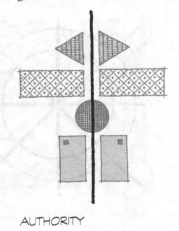

AUTHORITY

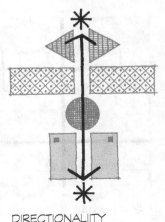

DIRECTIONALIITY

1.42 Left: The axis dominates the composition and creates directionality along its length.

21

1.43 Examples of symmetry in nature.

Symmetry is one of the most basic organizational strategies because of its relatively simplistic process of placing elements on or near an axis in an equally balanced fashion. Symmetry is often one of the first organizational strategies employed by novice designers because of its comparative ease of use. Symmetry is sometimes inaccurately considered to be a human construct, a notion reinforced by numerous highly controlled formal gardens. Yet, symmetry is a naturally occurring phenomenon as seen in the skeletal structure of most animals, flowers, crystals, and so on (1.43). However, it should be noted that these forms of symmetry primarily exist as individual elements, not as a broad organizing system within the landscape. There are three fundamental symmetrical typologies: bilateral, cross-axial, and radial.

Bilateral Symmetry. Bilateral symmetry is the organization of spaces and elements along one dominant axis, thus producing two distinct sides (bilateral) (left 1.44). The arrangement of design components on one side of the axis is typically the mirror image of the opposite side. This organizational structure establishes a heroic, autocratic power that concentrates energy along the axis and toward the termini.

Cross-Axial Symmetry. Cross-axial symmetry is the organization of spaces and elements along multiple axes (middle 1.44). The axes may intersect one another at any angle, although they commonly do so at a right angle. The multiple axes and paths of movement can provide numerous routes for navigating through this design structure and permit the landscape experience to be varied.

1.44 Symmetrical typologies.

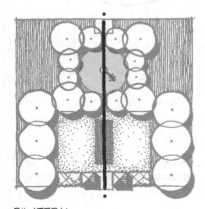

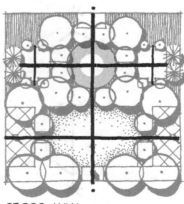

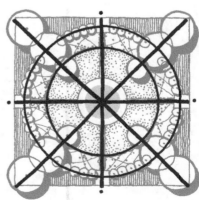

BILATERAL

CROSS-AXIAL

RADIAL

Radial Symmetry. Radial symmetry is the organization of spaces and elements along radii and/or concentric circles around a single center point (right 1.44). The compositional authority of radial symmetry lies almost entirely in the center point. Everything else in the design extends from or around it in a subservient manner. To furnish symmetry, the component elements and spaces are placed on the radii or concentric circles in an equally balanced fashion.

Landscape Uses. A symmetrical organization is appropriate to impose human authority on the landscape, especially when the constituent design elements like plant materials are precisely manicured. Symmetry is also apropos for establishing selected elements or areas as being absolutely supreme in relation to the surrounding landscape (1.45). Similarly, symmetry directs attention and movement toward selected points and/or spaces in a persistent and relentless manner. The movement is typically highly controlled along predetermined routes of travel. Symmetry is best used on open, uniform sites where there are few restrictions or existing elements that need to be incorporated into the design. Symmetry demands consistency and does not easily acclimate to site variation.

1.45 Example of a site design based on a symmetrical organization.

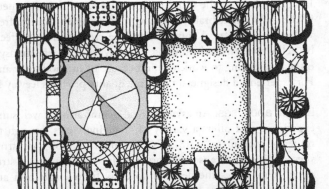

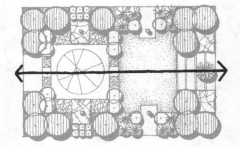

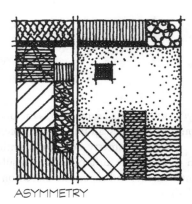

SYMMETRY   ASYMMETRY

1.46 Right: Comparison of asymmetry with symmetry.

1.47 Below: An asymmetrical organization places elements by feel and intuitive balance.

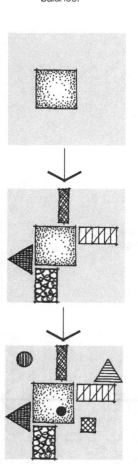

Asymmetry

Asymmetry is an organizational structure that intuitively orchestrates and balances constituent design elements to achieve overall compositional order (1.46). The feeling of equilibrium is created by subjectively distributing design elements so that one area of the composition appears to equate to another in terms of visual weight. There is typically no definitive center point in an asymmetrical organization although hierarchy is frequently created with a commanding element or space.

An asymmetrical organization creates visual balance by instinctive placement of diverse design components (1.47). It does not require that constituent design elements be the same or be paired with one another. Varied design elements and spaces are easily incorporated into the design. In addition, asymmetry lacks the ever-present and domineering axis of symmetry. There may be multiple points or spaces that garner attention without being slavishly located in a predetermined position.

In comparison to the other design constructs, the asymmetrical organizational structure is the most right-brained, giving the designer relative freedom and latitude to work within. Asymmetrical compositions are created more by feel and perceptive insight than by deliberate, rational thinking. For novice designers, an asymmetrical design structure is often challenging to work within because its methodology and "rules" are not self-evident. For experienced designers, this same quality provides leeway for pushing one's creativity.

Landscape Uses. An asymmetrical organization is well suited to creating an exploratory experience that offers a variety of changing views through the landscape and alternative routes of movement (1.48). The asymmetrical design construct easily acclimates to varied site conditions because it is not rigidly tied to a preset structure. Finally, asymmetrical design encourages the designer to draw from inspiration and emotion, thus facilitating inventiveness.

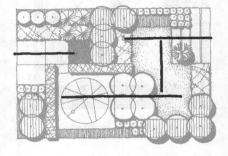

1.48 An example of a design based on an asymmetrical organization.

Unifying Principles

There are a number of unifying principles for landscape architectural site design that should guide how forms and spaces are assembled within the organizational structures just discussed. These principles are universal to all design expressions including architecture, graphic design, sculpture, painting, photography, and clothing design. Unifying principles inform the appearance, material, and size of all elements in a composition. The most essential unifying principles are similarity, dominance, interconnection, and compartmentalization.

Similarity

Similarity is the concept of making all the forms and spaces of a design like one another in shape, size, and/or material (1.49). This is the simplest and most elementary method for establishing design unity. An easily applied strategy to forge unity is to use the same family of forms as the underpinning throughout a landscape design. For example, creating a design entirely with straight lines and squares, or arcs and circles, and so on assures a unified design foundation.

1.49 Repetition of a similar form establishes design unity.

NO UNITY

UNITY via SIMILARITY of TONE

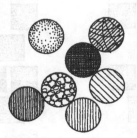

UNITY via SIMILARITY of FORM

25

SIMILAR GROUND FORMS

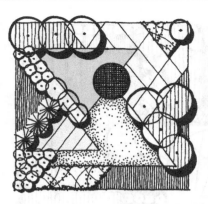

VARIETY via DIFFERENT FORM

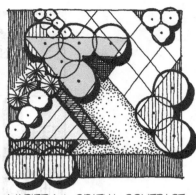

VARIETY via SPATIAL CONTRAST

1.50 Similarity and variety.

However, too much similarity can be monotonous (left 1.50). So, there normally needs to be a balance in a landscape design so that some qualities vary while others remain the same. This can be accomplished in several ways. One is to carefully interject different forms into a design (middle 1.50). The dissimilar forms are usually few in quantity and are skillfully added to fit the prevailing forms with common alignment and careful attention to how one form connects to another. Often the contrasting forms serve as accents to call attention to notable areas or spaces within the design.

Another means of interjecting variety is in the treatment of the spaces themselves. Even though all the spaces in a design might have similar forms as their foundation, they can each be distinctly individual with its own size, degree of enclosure, and palette of materials. One space might be relatively large, open to the sky and have a prevalence of lawn while the next is intimate in scale, shaded, and enveloped by dense planting of shrubs and trees (right 1.50). Thus, it is important to understand that similar forms throughout a design unifies its underlying structure, but not necessarily the appearance and feel of the spaces that result from them (also see Spatial Sequence, Chapter 2).

1.51 Different techniques for establishing dominance in a composition.

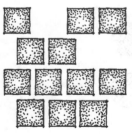

NO DOMINANCE

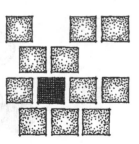

DOMINANCE via
CONTRAST of TONE

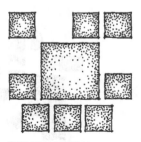

DOMINANCE via
CONTRAST of SIZE

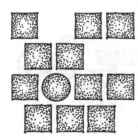

DOMINANCE via
CONTRAST of SHAPE

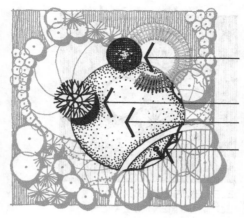

WATER FEATURE

SPECIMEN TREE

DOMINANT SPACE

SCULPTURE

Dominance

Dominance is the visual authority of one point or area of a composition over others. This is commonly described as being an accent or focal point, a place that readily attracts the eye. The predominance of an element or area of a design is usually established by contrast in size, orientation, material, color, and/or texture (1.51). The greater the apparent difference, the more the authoritative element stands out.

Dominance is desired in a design because it provides a place for the eye to rest. Without an accent, the eye wanders aimlessly and becomes bored. Furthermore, a focal point establishes unity in a composition by visually standing out, thus making the dissimilarity among the other constituent elements seems less noticeable.

In organizing forms as the basis of a landscape design, it is often advisable to create a dominant form or space by making it unique in character, enclosure, size, and/or orientation. A good site design frequently possesses one space that is more significant than the others. This provides a place to pause and remember, a critical factor in way finding through the landscape. A sequence of spaces that appear and feel too similar is more difficult to understand than one that varies and has at least one distinct space.

At a more detailed level, dominance can be established by numerous objects such as sculpture, distinctive building, specimen plant, a bed of perennials, water feature, framed, and so on. It is important to realize that there can be, and often should be, a hierarchy of dominance within a landscape with multiple accents, some being more important than others. It is desirable to create one predominant focal point in a design that prevails over the entire composition and simultaneously establish other accents that exercise control over smaller sections of the design (1.52).

1.52 Left: Alternative means for creating dominance in a site design.

1.53 Below: Interconnection links otherwise separate elements.

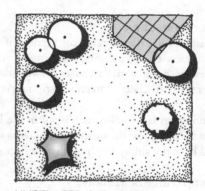

UNRELATED ELEMENTS

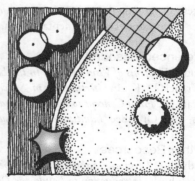

ELEMENTS UNIFIED VIA INTERCONNECTION

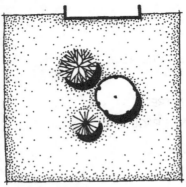
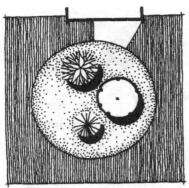
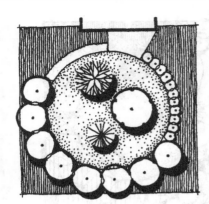

UNRELATED ELEMENTS

ELEMENTS UNIFIED VIA
COMPARTMENTALIZATION

1.54   An example of compartmentalization.

Interconnection

Interconnection is the physical connection of one design element to another. Linking what are otherwise separate design components permits the eye to move among them in a continuous fashion, thereby causing individual pieces to be perceived as one. It will be recalled from previous discussions that space between design elements segregates them into isolated fragments. The more space, the more the design elements seem unrelated. Interconnection serves to overcome the potential isolating effect of interstitial space by bridging across it.

Interconnection is typically established in the landscape by linking detached elements with a third. The additional element is a physical link that literally joins the other two elements together into one formation. A pavement surface, ground cover bed, line of trees, wall, and so on all have the ability to physically connect separated areas and unify a design (1.53).

Compartmentalization

Compartmentalization unifies a design composition by encircling selected elements of a design within one enclosure (1.54). In essence, compartmentalization functions like a frame around a picture to isolate and surround all the pieces within, thereby diminishing whatever differences exist among the constituent parts. A wall, fence, row of vegetation, or any other design element that encloses an area around its perimeter can produce compartmentalization.

Referenced Resources

Bell, Simon. *Elements of Visual Design in the Landscape.* London: E & FN Spon, 1993.
Ching, Francis D. K. *Architecture: Form, Space, & Order.* Hoboken, NJ: John Wiley & Sons, 2007.
Reid, Grant W. *From Concept to Form in Landscape Design*, 2nd edition. Hoboken, NJ: John Wiley & Sons, 2007.
Simonds, John Ormsbee. *Landscape Architecture: A Manual of Site Planning and Design*, 3rd edition. New York: McGraw-Hill, 1997.

Further Resources

Dee, Catherine. *Form and Fabric in Landscape Architecture: A Visual Introduction.* London: Spon Press, 2001.
Motloch, John L. *Introduction to Landscape Design*, 2nd edition. New York: John Wiley & Sons, 2001.

Landscape Space 2

As discussed in the previous chapter, form is a primary means for molding space in landscape architectural site design and is the fundamental medium for creatively organizing design elements so that space is perceived. Space is the essence of the landscape and is the stage for people to relax, play, recreate, eat, socialize, celebrate, mourn, memorialize, entertain, and interact with the natural world (2.1). A landscape composed of well-conceived spaces goes beyond the mere arrangement of objects and functions to yield an enveloping environment that engages, nurtures, and inspires all senses. The creation of outdoor space is one of the distinguishing facets of landscape architecture and is what differentiates it from other disciplines that plan and manage the landscape.

This chapter presents elementary concepts of space, fundamental spatial types, the relationship between form and space, and considerations for molding space during the design process. The specific sections of the chapter are:

- Space
- Creating Space
- Spatial Types
- Spatial Sequence
- Form and Space
- Design Process

2.1   Examples of landscape space.

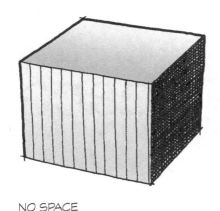

NO SPACE

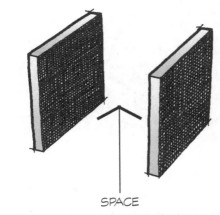

SPACE

2.2 Right: Space is the cavity between solid elements.

2.3 Below: Space is the void between objects we see.

SPACE DEFINING ELEMENTS

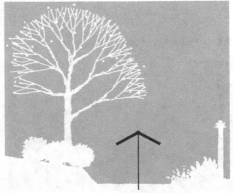

SPACE: VOID BETWEEN ELEMENTS

Space

The term *space* in design means a cavity or gap between solid elements (2.2). Similarly, space in the landscape is the invisible void filled with air that exists between the objects we see (2.3). Sometimes referred to as an "outdoor room," landscape space is the emptiness people live in and view through in the exterior environment. The concept of space is perhaps most readily appreciated when considering indoor rooms where finite floors, walls, and ceilings forge space (left 2.4). The sense of being in a cavity surrounded by solid or semi-solid planes on all sides is easily recognized. These same planes of enclosure also exist in the landscape (see next section) but are sometimes harder to perceive because of the indefinite shapes and casual distribution of many landscape elements (right 2.4). Nevertheless, landscape space exists and varies greatly depending on where we are and what is around us.

For the design neophyte who has learned throughout life to focus on objects, the notion of space may initially seem like an alien concept. Space is simply not what most people tend to see when they experience the exterior environment. Yet for landscape architects, architects, and other designers, the creation of space is at the core of design. Space is what landscape architects mold and shape when they organize "objects" like pavement surfaces, topography, plant materials, walls, fences, awnings, trellises, and so on. While a great deal of attention is given to where these objects are placed and what they look like, the real purpose is to use their location and physical qualities to define space and to impart a desired feeling to the landscape. The creation of space is the "architecture" in landscape architecture.

INTERIOR SPACE   EXTERIOR SPACE

2.4   Both interior and exterior space possess a floor, walls, and a ceiling.

Creating Space

Space is an invisible vapor that has no definition or shape by itself. It is an amorphous, indefinite entity that exists only when solid planes and objects are employed to define its edges and give it shape (left 2.5). Space is sometimes defined as being the "negative" between solid or "positive" elements, very much like the relationship between the air in an empty bottle and the glass that surrounds it. Space has an interdependent relationship with the elements that delineate it; space does exist without them and they do no exist without space around them. The reciprocal relationship between positive and negative space in a design is revealed in a figure/ground study (2.5).

In the landscape, three planes of spatial enclosure forge the mutual relationship between solid and void (Dee 2001, 34–5; Simonds 1997, 194):

- Base Plane
- Vertical Planes
- Overhead Plane

2.5   Figure/ground comparison of space.

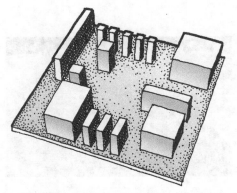

SPACE DEFINED by SOLID ELEMENTS

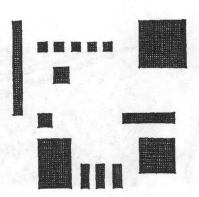

FIGURE: SOLID ELEMENTS

GROUND: SPACE BETWEEN

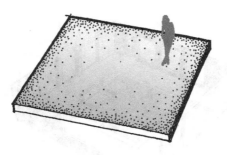
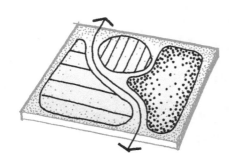

2.6 The base plane.

Base Plane

The base or ground plane is the floor of exterior space (left 2.6). It may be defined by bare earth, grasses/meadow, lawn, ground cover, pavement, or water (2.7). Furthermore, the ground may be level, sloped, rolling, or irregular in contour.

The base plane represents spiritual earth and is the symbolic source from which all plants grow and, by extension, all other life forms dependent on plants. The layout of the base plane defines the functional and spatial framework of the landscape, and so its organization is the foundation of design (Simonds 1997, 195) (right 2.6). Furthermore, the base plane is the anchor for all elements in the landscape; everything in the landscape must directly or indirectly connect to and be secured in place to the base plane. The ground plane therefore serves as a physical continuum that knits all landscape elements together into an endless fabric. The base plane is the subject of the most wear in the landscape, and so its material cover must be carefully selected to withstand use and surface runoff while protecting soil and all the living organisms contained within it (Simonds 1997, 196).

2.7 Sample base plane materials in the landscape.

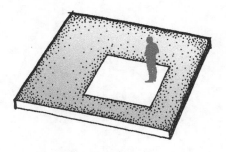

MATERIAL CHANGE

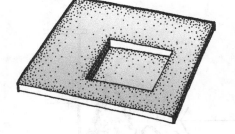

EXCAVATION INTO

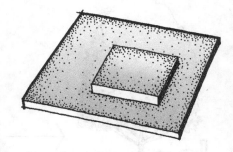

ELEVATION ABOVE

In the landscape, space is implied on the ground plane by a change of material (left 2.8). This is the weakest method of defining space, but nevertheless does so by suggestion just like a picnic blanket spread out on the grass in a park indicates a space. Space in this instance is created by the designation of a contrasting use on the floor, not by physical envelopment. Space can also be implied by abruptly elevating or depressing selected areas in relation to their surroundings (Ching 2007, 103) (middle and right 2.8). Even though it may be completely open to its surroundings, the raised area is perceived to be a space because it is bound by a distinct edge. By comparison, the lowered area does have a feeling of containment because of vertical planes around its edge.

2.8 Above: Alternative ways to imply space on the base plane.

2.9 Below: The vertical planes.

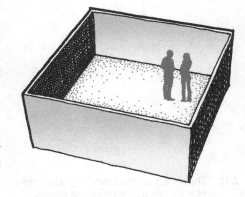

Vertical Planes

The vertical planes are the walls of outdoor space (2.9). They are the space dividers, baffles, screens, and backdrops that surround space (Simonds 1997, 200). Vertical planes may be generated in landscape by building walls, freestanding walls and fences, various plant materials, landform, or anything else that extends upward from the ground plane (2.10).

2.10 Examples of vertical planes in the landscape.

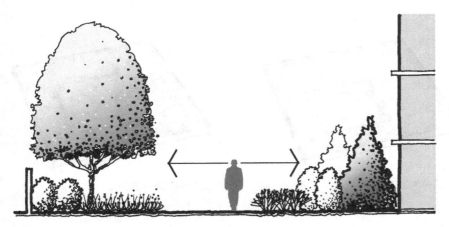

2.11 The vertical planes are the most readily seen and so have the greatest impact on the sense of enclosure.

The potential effect of the vertical planes on adjoining space is wide ranging because of their variability in height, solidity, texture, and color. Despite this diversity, the vertical planes have the most appreciable impact in defining space because people tend to look horizontally through the landscape (2.11). The vertical planes should be employed if there are few elements available for creating a sense of space. In addition, the vertical planes control views, affect a sense of privacy, filter and/or screen sun and wind, impact the quality of enclosure, provide backgrounds, serve as accents, and/or are the structural support for the overhead plane (Simonds 1997, 202–4).

Spatial enclosure by the vertical planes is affected by their position, height, and solidity. A single solid plane at or above head height establishes a minimum awareness of space while more enclosure is afforded when the plane turns one or more corners (2.12). Likewise, a low vertical plane implies partial confinement, a sensation that increases as height increases (left 2.13). And, enclosure is most pronounced by a solid vertical plane although many degrees of semitransparency can be created by partial openness in material (right 2.13). Even a glass wall can suggest space, although it may not limit views.

2.12 The vertical planes create a greater sense of enclosure as they surround an area.

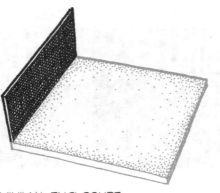

MINIMAL ENCLOSURE

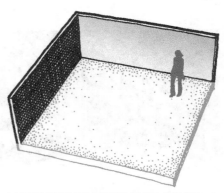

MORE PRONOUNCED ENCLOSURE

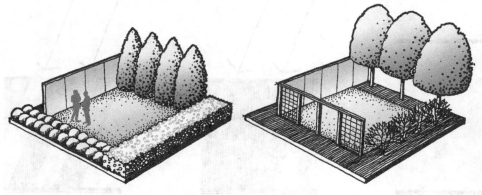

VARIATIONS in HEIGHT   VARIATIONS in SOLIDITY

2.13 Left: Potential variations in height and solidity of the vertical planes.

2.14 Below: The overhead plane.

Overhead Plane

The overhead or "sky" plane is the ceiling of outdoor space (2.14). It is that which is above and can be articulated by awnings, umbrellas, overhead trellises, pergolas, tree canopies, and so on (2.15). The sky, which seems infinite and undefined except by clouds, is also an ever-present overhead plane.

The overhead plane has a direct influence on a person's sense of comfort and refuge (Simonds 1997, 198–9). In addition to providing shelter from precipitation and sun, the overhead furnishes a sense of protection. People and animals alike seek to get under something above their heads in time of danger or to feel at ease. Similarly, the overhead plane influences the feeling of vertical scale or how large a space feels (left 2.16). A low overhead plane provides a personal, intimate atmosphere while a relatively high ceiling establishes a more communal setting. Because most light in the landscape emanates from the sky, the overhead plane affects the amount of light within a space and can cast appealing shadow patterns onto the other two planes (right 2.16).

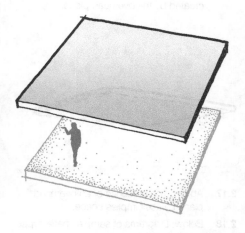

2.15 Examples of the overhead plane in the landscape.

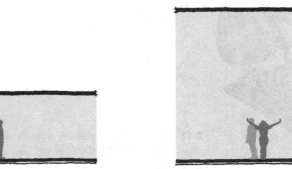
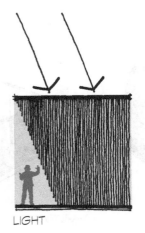
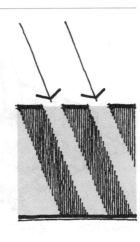

SCALE
LIGHT

2.16 Potential variations in scale and light created by the overhead plane.

The mere presence of an overhead plane suggests a spatial volume bound by it and the ground. Such a space needs no other articulation in the other two planes to be appreciated (2.17). Like the vertical plane, the overhead plane is highly variable in the potential degree of confinement. It may be rather diaphanous and allow filtered light to pass through or it can be opaque, thus creating a shady space. The overhead plane must be connected to ground at some point and often establishes vertical boundaries of a space in doing so.

Spatial Types

While it is useful to study the three planes of spatial enclosure by themselves, the reality is that they coexist in the landscape as an intertwined milieu of topography, vegetation, buildings, site structures, pavement, and water. All these elements are interdependent and affect one another in location, degree of enclosure, and ambience of space. Collectively, the design elements in the three planes of enclosure are capable of creating countless spatial types in the landscape that can be categorized in numerous ways. Among various spatial typologies, three are: physical envelope, landscape setting, and descriptive experience.

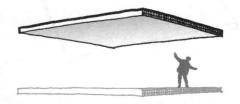

2.17 Above: The presence of an overhead plane by itself implies space.

2.18 Below: Diagrams of sample spatial types created by the physical envelope.

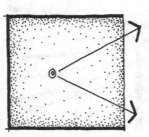
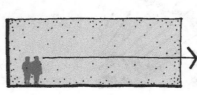
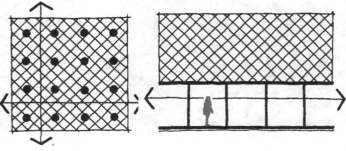

ALCOVE
GROVE/BOSCO

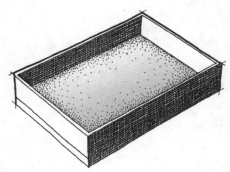

VOLUMETRIC SPACE

Physical Envelope

This method for classifying landscape space treats the elements that articulate space as abstract physical entities whose relative location, spacing, and solidity affects spatial typology. One such system identifies prototypical spaces as being the open box, pierced room, alcove, colonnade, allee, bosco, and amphitheater, among others (Booth and Zink 1994) (2.18). A similar methodology identifies two widely employed spatial types as being volumetric or cubist (Condon 1988) (2.19). Volumetric space is articulated by landscape elements that are located around the perimeter of the space, thus leaving the interior open. This is a simple space with clearly defined edges and is characteristic of many classical gardens. In cubist space, the delineating elements are positioned both around and within the space. The space is not only enveloped by the design elements, but also moves through and around them in a manner that blurs spatial boundaries. This spatial type is found in many modern-style and contemporary landscapes.

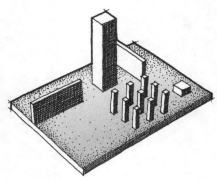

CUBIST SPACE

Landscape Setting

Another way to categorize exterior space is by the presence of a dominant landscape element. Potential spatial types include topographic space, vegetative space, built space, and water space (Dee 2001, 54–80) (2.20). Each typology in this framework is further subdivided into more specific spatial types; for example, built space includes public squares, courtyards, and walled gardens (Dee 2001, 69–75).

2.19 Above: Comparison between volumetric and cubist space.

2.20 Below: Sample spatial types based a dominant landscape element.

BUILT SPACE

VEGETATIVE SPACE

WATER SPACE

37

Descriptive Quality

Landscape space can also be typecast by a descriptive adjective or noun that portrays a prevailing geographic location, setting, scale, use, feeling, and so forth. A sampling of descriptive qualities for these various categories includes:

Urban	Rural
Human	Monumental
Wooded	Meadow
Relaxing	Compelling
Mysterious	Tiresome
Inspiring	Sober
Warm	Damp
Nebulous	Absolute
Level	Undulating
Bright	Gloomy

Each adjective or noun evokes a vivid mental image of a particular kind of space. Listing descriptive attributes is a useful technique for determining desired spatial qualities and is a recommended exercise in the early stages of the design process (see Design Process). In some instances, it is helpful to start with a list of descriptive qualities generated by others as a means of stimulating one's own thinking (see Simonds 1997, 241–245). These descriptive traits typically do not occur by themselves but rather occur in virtually any combination. For example, one can imagine a private, dramatic, sunlit desert space.

Clearly, the landscape architect has great latitude to create space that fulfills a desired quality and is appropriate for its landscape location. Form is a tool for achieving whatever spatial type and temperament is desired. Consider the implied personality forged by the forms in the thumbnail sketches of Figure 2.21. Consequently, form should be employed not as an end in itself but rather as a means to shape the intended traits of an environment.

2.21 Examples of varied personae created by different forms.

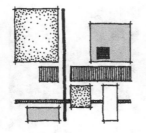   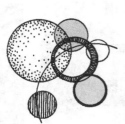 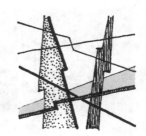

Spatial Sequence

Another fundamental aspect of landscape space is that no space exists as an isolated entity. Instead, every space is always preceded and followed by another. Sometimes, adjoining spaces are clearly separated, and other times they interlace so that one imperceptibly morphs into another. The intent of landscape architectural site design should be to choreograph the relationship among adjoining spaces so that each space is designed in the context of others. The experience of moving between and among spaces should consider the degree of enclosure, descriptive qualities, path traveled, connections and thresholds, and views for each space in association to adjacent spaces.

In addition, an attempt should be made to strike a balance between similarity and contrast (Dee 2001, 52–53), mystery and legibility, and comfort and inspiration among spaces. Neighboring spaces that are too much alike are apt to be monotonous to experience and are easily forgotten (left 2.22). By comparison, a sequence of spaces that have a distinct change in size, proportion, degree of enclosure including the overhead plane, amount and quality of light, ground plane elevation, materials, and so forth create an animated and often memorable experience (right 2.22). Some of the most exciting spatial sequences create deliberate contrasts between spaces. For example, consider moving from a tight, dark space to a bright large space or from a simple open space dominated by a lawn panel to an elaborate one filled with a profusion of perennials. The quality of each space is made more apparent by the association with its adjoining spaces.

The forms of a design are directly associated with the variety and similarity within a spatial sequence. It is often, though not always, advisable to employ a family of like forms as a means of unifying a sequence while other spatial qualities vary as previously suggested in Chapter 1. However, form itself can also vary as means of interjecting diversity. A change in form from one space to the next does not have to be dramatic to be noticeable as demonstrated on the right of 2.22.

2.22 A spatial sequence should usually include contrast between adjoining spaces.

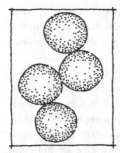
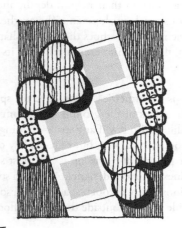

NO SPATIAL CONTRAST

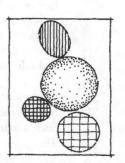
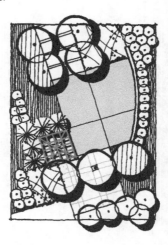

SPATIAL CONTRAST

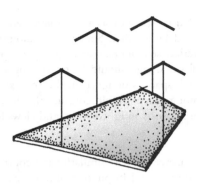
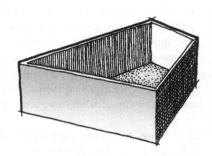
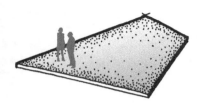
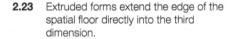

SPATIAL FLOOR

EXTRUDED VERTICAL PLANES

2.23 Extruded forms extend the edge of the spatial floor directly into the third dimension.

Form and Space

The individual planes of spatial enclosure and their assemblage into outdoor rooms rely on form for their organization. The evolution of space and its association with form in landscape architectural design often starts by defining the floor of a space based on the size and proportions appropriate for its use (also see Design Process) (left 2.23). From this initial gesture, the form of the space simultaneously evolves with the articulation and refinement of all planes of enclosure. There are three general ways that space and the form of these planes can potentially interact: extruded forms, multiple forms, and independent forms.

Extruded Forms

This method for creating space from a ground form is accomplished by extending its edges upward to enclose space (middle and right 2.23). The vertical planes tend to be wall-like and are located immediately on the edge of the ground form (2.24). Although structural in quality, the vertical planes can vary in their height, depth, and opaqueness to create a wide range of possible degrees of spatial envelopment. The overhead plane may be open to the sky or defined by a design element that echoes the ground shape and is anchored to the perimeter vertical planes. Again, there are numerous options in its height above the ground and solidity.

The result of simple extrusion is "volumetric" space," a plain spatial shell with an open interior that directly reflects the edges of the ground form from which it was generated. Such a space is the most "roomlike" with few if any space-dividing elements located inside. The ground plane may be elaborate in pattern, but remains low or two-dimensional, thus not subdividing the space. The process of extrusion is the most simplistic of all strategies and the easiest to realize by an inexperienced designer. Although somewhat facile, extrusion is appropriate for design situations where an open space with absolute edges is necessitated or where there is limited available site area outside the defined floor area.

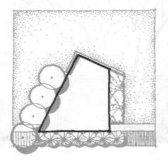

SPATIAL FLOOR

VERTICAL FORMS

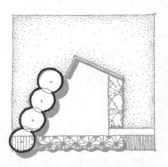

OVERHEAD FORMS

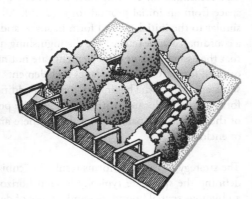

2.24 Above: Example of a design based on extruded forms.

2.25 Left & Below: Example of a design based on multiple forms.

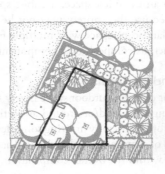

SPATIAL FLOOR

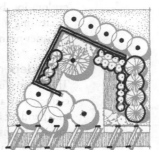

VERTICAL FORMS

OVERHEAD FORMS

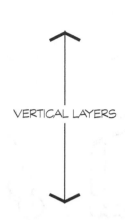

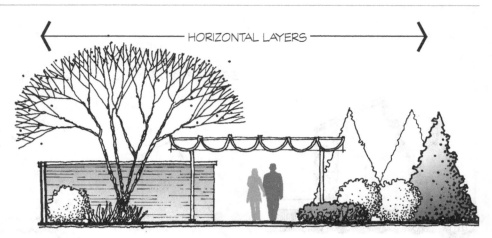

2.26 Multiple forms have the potential to create layered depth in a space.

Multiple Forms

This technique for creating outdoor space employs multiple planes and elements to create space from an initial ground form (2.25). All the design components are the same as or similar to the initial ground form in shape and orientation, giving the overall composition a coordinated appearance. The distinguishing quality of this tactic of spatial development is that the assorted planes and elements are not necessarily located directly on the edge of the original form. Rather, the planes and elements may be located anywhere, some next to and some apart from the beginning form. In addition, some elements may overlap the original form and/or be located within it. When the potential variability in the height and solidity of the constituent parts is considered, there are almost limitless possibilities in the extent of enclosure.

The strategy of multiple forms results in "cubist space." The multiple planes and elements defining the space are typically layered horizontally and vertically, consequently creating ambiguous spatial boundaries and a sense of depth when viewing through the space (2.26). Compared to an extruded space, a cubist space is frequently more engaging and invites exploration because the entirety may not be understood from one position. The process of creating a landscape space with multiple forms requires the designer to simultaneously consider numerous compositional components and to think three-dimensionally.

Independent Forms

This means for creating outdoor space is very similar to multiple forms by employing many elements arranged on and/or around an initial ground form. Nonetheless, the process of independent forms differs by utilizing some design components that do not echo the original form in terms of shape and/or alignment. That is, some design elements are autonomous in their location within the overall composition.

Like multiple forms, independent forms results in an elaborate, polyphonic space with numerous parts and indefinite spatial margins (2.27). This design construct requires the most design skill because it entails synchronization in all dimensions with elements that are

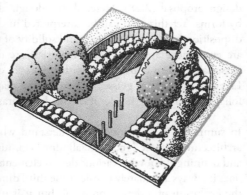

2.27 Example of a design based on independent forms.

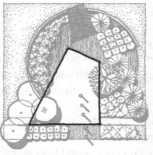

SPATIAL FLOOR

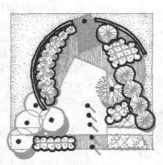

VERTICAL FORMS

OVERHEAD FORMS

often dissimilar. Again, the landscape architect must be able to see and create multifaceted space, often with the aid of sections, perspectives, isometrics, hand-built models, and/or computer-generated models.

Despite whatever approach is taken to coordinating forms and space, it is essential to realize that forms by themselves do not describe height or solidity of walls, fences, plant materials, planters, or water features, and so do not completely articulate spatial enclosure. The landscape architect must go beyond plan view and think three-dimensionally. If it is difficult to "see" space in plan as it sometimes is for fledgling designers, then it is imperative to use other means like perspectives and models to more fully comprehend what a design will look like. Furthermore, forms provide only the armature of a design and do not govern its appearance. Forms provide a structure that must be added onto with more definitive denotation of materials.

This notion is perhaps best illustrated by first creating what might appear to be a finished design proposal (2.28). Here, all the design elements are clearly shown and coordinated by forms. Yet this plan can be interpreted in dissimilar ways, each with its own look and disposition based on the height and solidity of the design elements (2.29). These variations are even more apparent when materials are defined. For example, the wall creates one personality when constructed with brick, yet quite a different one if made of glass block. Likewise, the area of grasses will establish a diaphanous edge if composed of thin, feathery foliage, but a jarring border if the blades of grass are wide and sharp in appearance.

In summary, it is essential to understand what forms can and cannot do in landscape architectural site design, especially for beginning designers. Molding a design with forms and defining them with various design elements does not constitute a complete design, nor does it always adequately consider the third dimension. Working with forms is integral with the evolution of a design proposal, but it is only one step that must be augmented with numerous supplementary design decisions.

Design Process

The purpose of this section is to discuss and demonstrate how forms are employed as an organizational tool in the landscape architectural design process. This examination is not meant to be a thorough presentation of the design process because that is better accomplished in other sources. The intent here is to focus on the role of forms in the evolution of a site design with the understanding that the design process is a multifaceted activity entailing numerous considerations beyond form.

While the outline of the design process varies somewhat depending on the source, many include steps similar to these: acceptance, analysis, definition, ideation, ideation selection, implementation, and evaluation (Koberg and Bagnall 1995, 41). In landscape architecture, these design stages often translate to project acceptance, analysis, problem definition, conceptual studies, preliminary/schematic design, master plan, construction documents,

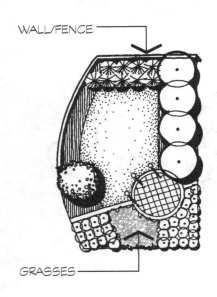

WALL/FENCE

GRASSES

2.28 Above: "Finished" site plan.

2.29 Right: Alternative interpretations of the above site plan.

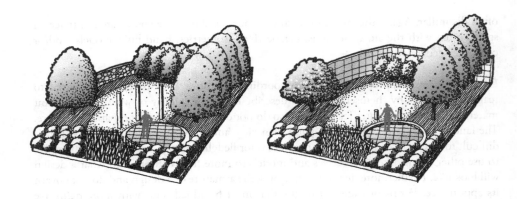

and postconstruction evaluation. Structural organization and form, the focus of this text, are integral to this design process in two ways: (1) during analysis and problem definition, the objective is to determine what forms are apropos to the particular project circumstances; and (2) in conceptual studies and subsequent design phases, the intent is to use structural organization and form as a means for shaping landscape space. The following paragraphs discuss the role of form in these design steps in more detail.

Analysis

This phase of design is intended to gain as much as knowledge as possible about a site and its context so that the eventual design solution can be sensitively and creatively calibrated to fit the unique circumstances of the site. The process of analysis normally involves gathering physical, environmental, social, cultural, historical, and regulatory information about a site and then evaluating it to determine how existing qualities and features of the site should shape the eventual design. A site analysis can be conducted and communicated in many ways, but it always attempts inform a design and give it direction.

In addition to the typical array of data collected and evaluated during site analysis, there are a number of physical factors that should be studied for their possible impact on the structure and forms of a site design. These include regional character, site context, and site macro patterns and features.

Regional Character. Every geographic region has a distinct visual and physical character that is forged by topography, geological forms and features, prevailing vegetation species, water bodies, climate, and so on. This natural persona of a region and that created by the human footprint on the landscape can frequently be drawn upon for suggesting forms on a particular site. One means for interpreting regional character is to identify broad natural and human patterns from large-scale maps and aerial photographs (2.30). Another technique is to abstract specific features or elements of the regional landscape (2.31).

2.30 Above: Examples of different regional topographic patterns.

2.31 Below: Examples of distinct regional characters.

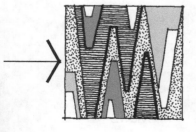

ABSTRACTION

45

2.32 Contextual patterns that can potentially inform the forms on a site.

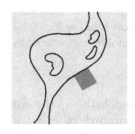  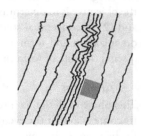

NATURAL FEATURES

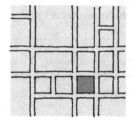  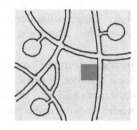

ROADS/STREETS

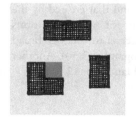 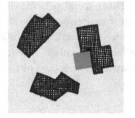 

BUILDINGS

 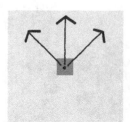 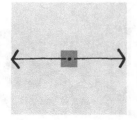

VIEWS

Site Context. Similar to the regional character, there are a number of natural and human factors in the immediate surroundings of a site that can be drawn upon to suggest site design form. Among these factors are distinguishing natural features like water bodies and topography, adjoining streets and roads, footprint and orientation of nearby buildings, direction and point(s) of arrival, notable views to and from site, and so on (2.32).

Macro Patterns and Features. Potential forms for a design project can also be discovered in the macro patterns and unique features within a site's boundaries. Macro patterns are the sweeping configurations established by the edges, distribution, and general shape of topography, geological formations, vegetation, water bodies, infrastructure, circulation routes, buildings, and so on. A good method for seeing comprehensive patterns is to represent them as simple lines and masses on a significantly reduced site map (2.33). This forces one to concentrate on the gross pattern, not the detail. These simple drawings can be abstracted even more to portray the very essence of a pattern. In Figure 2.34, a green space with scattered trees is dissected by diagonal paths. To establish a design for the setting, the trees and paths are abstracted into simple geometric shapes that serve as the inspiration for a design.

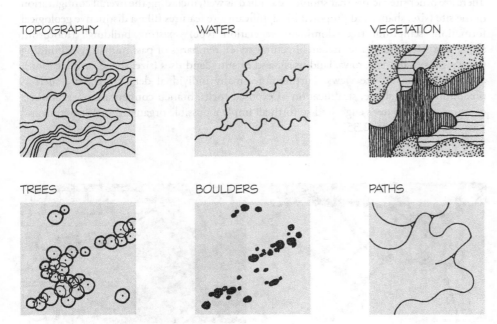

TOPOGRAPHY

WATER

VEGETATION

TREES

BOULDERS

PATHS

2.33 Sample macro site patterns that may affect design forms on site.

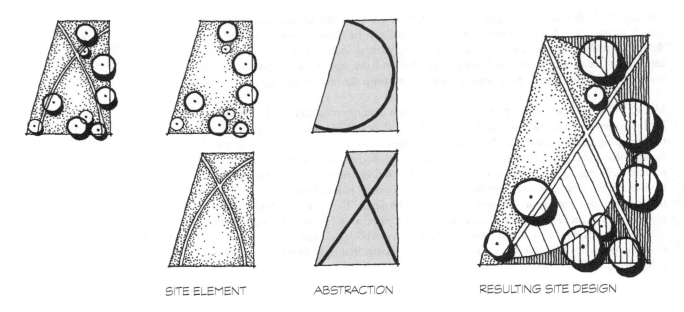

SITE ELEMENT   ABSTRACTION   RESULTING SITE DESIGN

2.34 Example of how site patterns can be abstracted to define forms.

2.35 Site details that could influence design forms.

There are other site factors that should be studied as well, including the overall configuration of the site (size, shape, and proportion), significant site features (like a distinctive geological formation, sculptural tree, dominant vegetation type), existing buildings (footprint, shape, organizational structure, architectural style), remnants of past human use (building foundations, walls, tree rows, land uses), and existing land uses (size, shape, and location), and on-site and off-site views. Furthermore, many individual details on a site such as predominant leaf shape, stratification of exposed rocks, branch configurations, groupings of stone along a water's edge, and so forth all imply a possible organizational structure and form for a site design (2.35).

Envisioning

The next step of the design process that aids in determining what organizational structure and forms are appropriate for a given project is to foresee what the design solution should be. This step may also be referred to as definition, problem definition, and ideation and can occur while undertaking the site analysis or as a subsequent outgrowth of its conclusions. The purpose of this design phase is to decide what uses/spaces, physical elements, and experiential qualities are required and/or aspired in the eventual design. There are numerous ways to create and communicate design intent. Among them is the recommendation that simple diagrams be employed to suggest concept and rudimentary structure as a technique for defining appropriate forms (2.44). It is important that the diagrams remain broad-brushed at this point in the design process and not be overly specific or committed to a particular genre of forms. Design intent should address the following: parti, required spaces and elements, desired spatial qualities, budget, and anticipated maintenance.

2.36 Examples of forms derived from a parti.

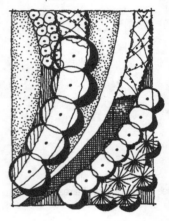

INSPIRATION

ABSTRACTION

RESULTING SITE PLAN

BASED ON
KANDINSKY"S
COMPOSITION VIIII

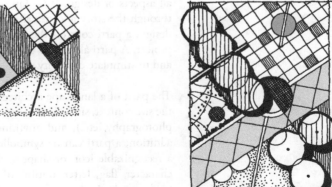

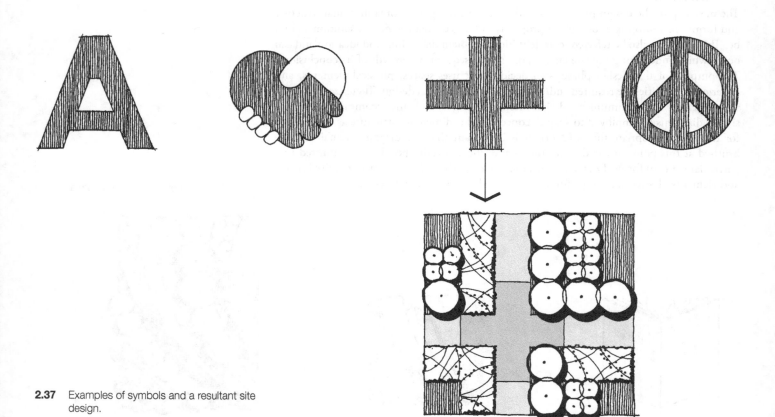

2.37 Examples of symbols and a resultant site design.

Parti. A parti, sometimes called a theme or "big idea," is the overriding concept that governs all aspects of design. It is akin to the plot in a novel, the underlying thread that weaves through the story and ties all characters and chapters together. In landscape architectural design, a parti controls the overall organization, character, appearance, and meaning of a project. A parti also helps to give a design a sense of place, to make solutions site specific, and to stimulate creativity.

The parti of a landscape architectural site design can be based on many things, including the site context, site, client, users, program, other creative expressions (art, music, literature, photography, etc.), and anything else that provides an organizing structure (2.36). In addition, a parti can be symbolic or metaphorical. A site design based on a symbol uses a recognizable icon or shape such as a company or organization logo, universal signage character, flag, letter, outline of a familiar object, and the like (2.37). A metaphorical landscape is similar and is evocative of a distinct environment, object, or feeling like a grove, prairie, winding river, fish, moon surface, secret garden, and so forth (2.38) (also

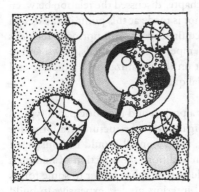

MOONSCAPE

WINDING RIVER

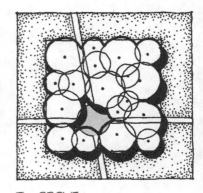

The GROVE

see Dee 2001, 39). One word of advice in using symbols and metaphors is that someone experiencing the landscape should recognize and understand them. Symbols and metaphors should not be appreciated only when viewing from above in plan view.

2.38 Examples of site designs based on metaphor.

Design Program. A typical activity during this phase of design is to identify and list all the spaces and elements that are required in the design. The process of preparing a design program should determine the use or function of each space along with the physical qualities such as size, form, and proportion that are necessary to support the function. The well-known statement of "form follows function" should be kept in mind so that the proper form supports the function of each space. Every form has an inherent use based on its shape and proportion that should be respected and worked with (2.39). The relation between form and function is also discussed in a section titled "Landscape Uses" in all the following chapters of this text.

2.39 Form and function are inextricably linked.

DIRECT

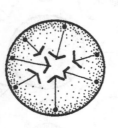

GATHER/
CONVERSE

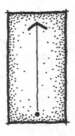

REVERANCE

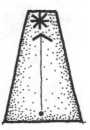

FOCUS

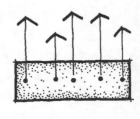

OBSERVE

MEANDER

51

Desired Spatial Qualities. A previous section of this chapter discussed the relation between form and experiential quality of space. An initial attempt is made at this point in the design process to define what the ideal qualities are for each required space. This normally includes articulating the degree of enclosure, the overall visual temperament, materials, views, and so on. Decisions about these factors have a direct impact on the organizational structure and forms that are suitable to achieve the anticipated spatial qualities.

Budget and Maintenance. The available budget for a project and the anticipated type of maintenance also have a bearing on what is the best organizational structure and forms for a design. The means for mowing, pruning, irrigation, and so on all should be considered when deciding what forms will be used in a design. In addition, the selection of materials will have a bearing on forms because many materials lend themselves better to some forms than others. Generally, simple forms with uncluttered interiors are less expensive to build and maintain than more complex ones.

Collectively, conclusions from the site analysis and envisioning should assist in determining what organizational structure and forms are appropriate for a given design. One objective of these two design phases should be to define a range of acceptable and unacceptable forms for a particular deign setting. The purpose is not to definitively decide on specific forms but to narrow the range of possibilities and to provide a beginning point for the next phase of the design process. Hopefully it is clear that there are innumerable factors to consider in determining what organizational structure and forms are fitting for any given design project (2.40). Whatever forms are decided upon, they should be a synthesis of multiple factors including proper fit to site, parti, program requirements, desired spatial qualities, and budget.

2.40 Factors that influence design form in the landscape.

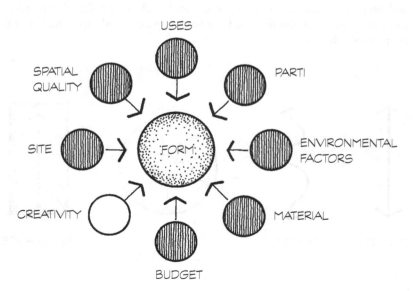

Diagrams

Until this point in the design process, the primary intent has been to determine what organizational structure and forms are appropriate for the given project circumstances. Now, attention shifts to employing form as a tool for organizing and shaping outdoor space. To demonstrate this, a case study of an actual site and program will be used to illustrate the subsequent steps of the process. The selected urban site is located in a major metropolitan area immediately adjacent to a vibrant indoor market containing numerous local vendors and regional farmers. The site is currently a parking lot and surrounded by the market to the west and streets to the north, east, and south (2.40). The surrounding urban neighborhood is a revitalized district of housing, restaurants, night clubs, hotels, parking garages, and various small businesses a short distance from the city's convention center and within eye-sight of multistory office buildings in the urban core (2.41). Key site issues include a lack of human scale, an impervious ground surface, an askew eastern site boundary, unsightly views to the east, a need for screening the service area, and significant pedestrian movement to the north door of the market (2.42–43).

The intent of the proposed design is to convert the parking lot to an outdoor extension of the market with spaces for:
- Vendors
- Outdoor eating
- Flexibly programmed activities, performances, and gatherings
- Buffering of the backsides of the buildings to the east
- Service access to the market
- Any other use or element that would creatively augment the market atmosphere

2.41 Above: Views of the market site.

2.42 Left: Location and context of the market site.

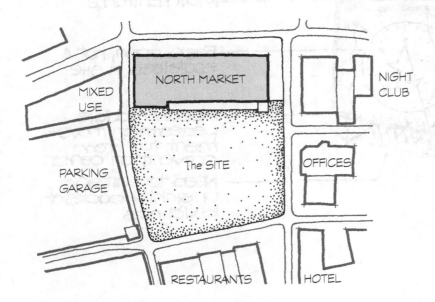

Following site analysis and envisioning, the first step of graphically organizing the design solution is to prepare a series of concept diagrams that delineate the principal program elements and spaces in a broad-brushed manner (2.44). Not all spaces or elements that will eventually comprise the design should be included at this point, only the largest and/ or most essential spaces and elements that affect the global layout of the site. The chief purpose of these initial diagrams is to explore the relative location, size, and proportion of the principal spaces and elements without reference to the specifics of the site. Concept diagrams permit the designer to seek the ideal arrangement among the spaces and so a number of alternatives are usually created as a means of testing ideas. These first diagrams are drawn in a bubble-like manner in a nonrealistic graphic language without a particular scale and often without being directly referenced to the site. The graphic symbols are rough and quick in quality and should make no attempt at representing the shape of the spaces. Nevertheless, concept diagrams can and should begin to study the overall organizational structure of the design by means of structuring elements like axes, spines, circulation routes, orientation of spaces, and so forth.

2.43 Summary site analysis of market site.

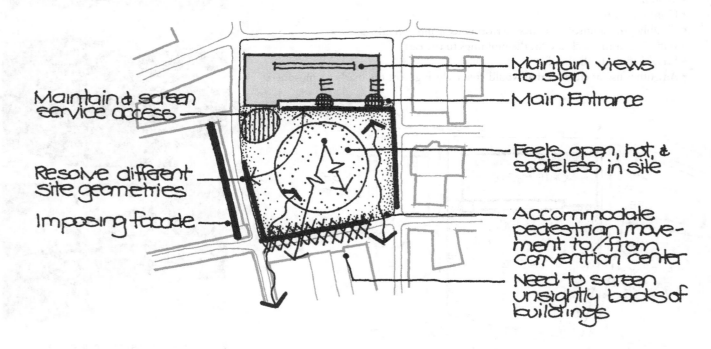

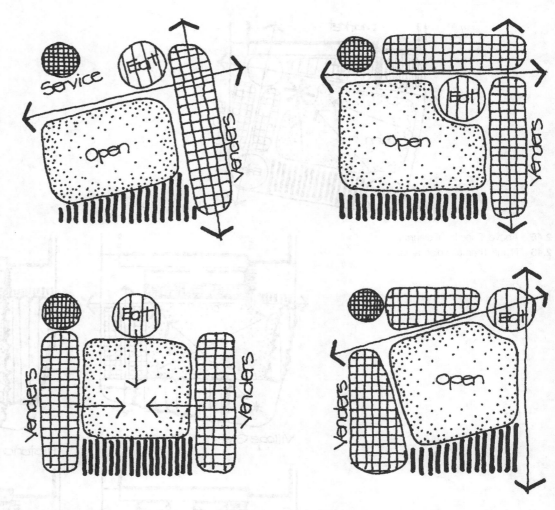

2.44 Concept diagrams.

The series of alternative concept diagrams should be reviewed for their relative merit and ability to meet the design objectives. Often one diagram, or sometimes a combination of diagrams, is selected for further exploration. The next series of diagrams, regularly referred to as functional diagrams, starts from the concept diagram and proceeds to add additional spaces, circulation connections, primary views and visual accents, beginning consideration of spatial edges, and so on (2.45). In addition, functional diagrams are drawn on a scaled base of the site, thus allowing the size and location of the spaces to be calibrated to the actual site conditions. As with concept diagrams, the intent of functional diagrams is to study the overall configuration of the design but with added detail and more thought about the quality of the proposed spaces. Functional diagrams should be drawn with the same or similar graphic language as conceptual diagrams and should be drawn quickly, again to facilitate the exploration of alternative ideas.

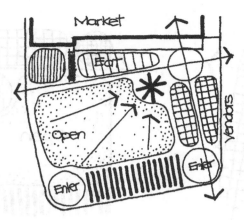

2.45 Above: Functional diagram.
2.46 Right: Thematic diagrams.

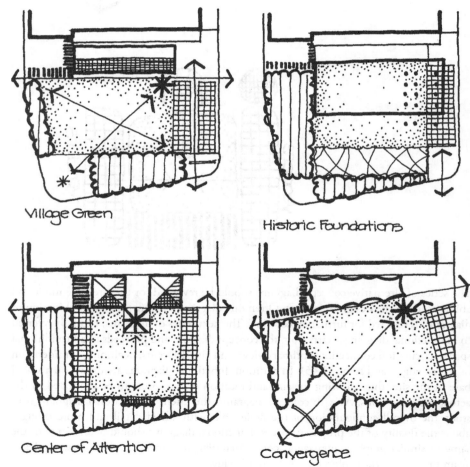

Village Green

Historic Foundations

Center of Attention

Convergence

The last set of diagrams, called thematic diagrams or sometimes schematics, begin to transition toward preliminary design by giving more specific structure to the design organization and by exploring the types and qualities of the constituent spaces (2.46). These diagrams start with a functional diagram and proceed to again prepare a series of alternatives, each based on a different theme. Consequently, it is often helpful to give each diagram a name that encapsulates the essence of the motif. It should be noted that all the alternatives shown in 2.46 have essentially the same location of spaces and elements based on the previous functional diagram. However, each diagram represents a different theme or parti. To accomplish this, the thematic diagrams incorporate one or more of the primary structuring organizations (i.e., line, grid, symmetry, or asymmetry) and bold, sweeping forms that encompass the entire site. Collectively, all these means of ordering the site are intended to examine the definition and quality of each space. Building edges, structures, walls, tree masses, topographic change, pavement areas, and so on are shown in a broad-brushed graphic manner to suggest approximate spatial edges. In summary, it is critical to see and understand that the creation of outdoor space and the use of form to structure it have their foundation in diagrams.

It is recommended that all diagrams be drawn at a significantly reduced scale in comparison to subsequent drawings. This permits diagrams to be created quickly and to focus on the overall layout of the design without getting prematurely caught up in the details. One is forced to think of the comprehensive organization when working in this manner. Furthermore, drawing diagrams as quick thumbnails facilitates the exploration of alternative ideas and so promotes creativity because thoughts can flow freely without being encumbered by their graphic representation or specificity. The intention is to brainstorm many ideas rather than attempting to perfect one solution. It is also strongly suggested that diagrams be drawn by hand or on graphics tablet connected to a computer. Both of these means of drawing encourage the spontaneous nature of diagrams. Drawing diagrams with a mouse interacting with a computer graphics program does not provide the same ability and is often more constraining than helpful.

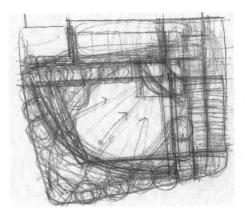 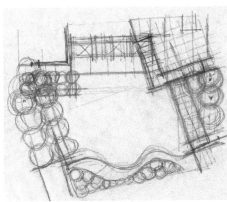

2.47 Sketches of preliminary design in progress.

Preliminary Design

The next step of the process begins with a selected thematic diagram, or a combination of diagrams, and proceeds to add specificity in both thinking and graphic representation. To begin with, the scale of the drawing becomes larger, often 1"=10', 1"=20', or 1"=30', depending on the size of the site and the amount of required detail. While it might seem like the selected thematic diagram could simply be enlarged and given more graphic detail, this is not the case. The thematic diagram serves as a point of departure with the understanding that the design is very apt to evolve and change, sometimes substantially, as one begins to incorporate realistic and scaled depiction of the design elements. Using pencils, pens, and/or markers, the designer begins to define the edges and makeup of all the spaces. As with the diagrams, this should start with global forms that encompass the entire site. The forms on the ground plane, vertical planes, and overhead planes are all studied simultaneously in a rough graphic manner. It is normal that the first steps of this process will be sketchy and somewhat imprecise. Further, it is common for the designer to explore alternative forms, each overlaid on another, thus creating a layer cake of optional ideas (2.47). This process often causes the specifics of the design to change in relation to where it started, usually a healthy indication that the designer is actively engaged in critical analysis and thinking while designing. A competent designer is constantly seeking a better design solution by testing new ideas, many of which are simply discovered through ongoing review and experimentation.

With time and effort, the process culminates in a preliminary design that represents all the spaces and design elements in a graphically realistic style (2.48). Building edges, site structures, wall, fences, steps, water features, trees, shrub masses, pavement, lawn, ground covers, and the like are all orchestrated with various forms to define the design's spaces. These elements collectively define a series of spaces with different purposes and temperaments to meet the program requirements and to offer a medley of spatial experiences (2.49).

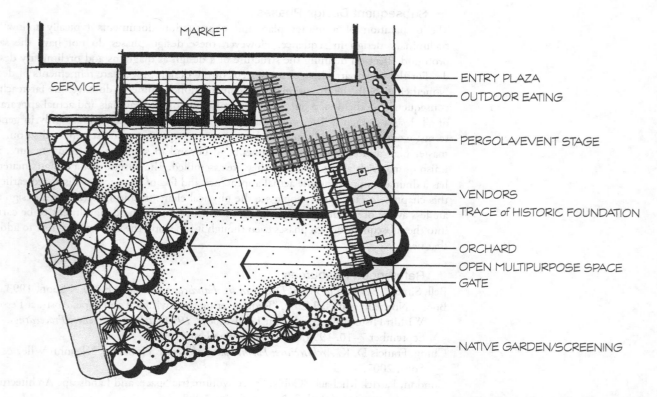

MARKET

SERVICE

ENTRY PLAZA

OUTDOOR EATING

PERGOLA/EVENT STAGE

VENDORS

TRACE *of* HISTORIC FOUNDATION

ORCHARD

OPEN MULTIPURPOSE SPACE

GATE

NATIVE GARDEN/SCREENING

2.48 Above: Market preliminary design.

2.49 Below: Varied spatial qualities found in the market preliminary design.

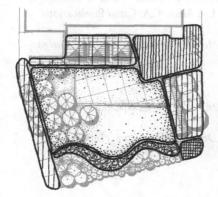

VARIED BASE PLANE QUALITIES

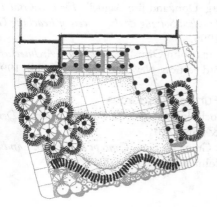

VARIED DEGREES *of* ENCLOSURE in the VERTICAL PLANE

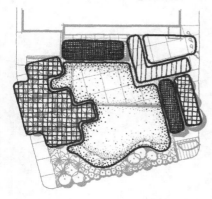

VARIED DEGREES *of* ENCLOSURE in the OVERHEAD PLANE

Subsequent Design Phases

The preparation of a master plan and construction documents typically follow the preliminary design in sequence. However, these design phases do not have the same profound effect on defining the structure of a design as diagrams and preliminary design do. For the most part, these ensuing steps of the design process are refinements of detail. Nonetheless, both the master plan and construction documents do have one far-reaching consequence on the design outcome: determination of the materials and actual appearance of all design elements. The preliminary design typically defines materials only in general terms: wood pergola, sculpture, shade tree, concrete pavers, metal screen, and so on. The master plan and construction documents go beyond to stipulate the color, texture, and finish of materials along with how they are assembled. The selection of a design's materials has a dramatic impact on the actual appearance and feel of its spaces as discussed earlier in this chapter. In fact, most people see the physical elements and materials of a design and are less aware of the design structure. So, it is essential for the design intent to be carried into the subsequent design phases even though it is beyond the scope of this text to address that need.

Referenced Resources

Bell, Simon. *Elements of Visual Design in the Landscape*. London: E & FN Spon, 1993.

Booth, Norman, and Gail Zink. "Rediscovering the Invisible Landscape; Abstract Lessons Within Historically Significant Landscapes." *1994 CELA Conference, Proceedings*. September 7–10, 1994, Mississippi State University.

Ching, Francis D. K. *Architecture: Form, Space, & Order*. Hoboken, NJ: John Wiley & Sons, 2007.

Condon, Patrick Michael. "Cubist Space, Volumetric Space, and Landscape Architecture," *Landscape Journal* (Vol. 7, No. 2), Spring 1988.

Dee, Catherine. *Form and Fabric in Landscape Architecture: A Visual Introduction*. London: Spon Press, 2001.

Koberg, Don, and Jim Bagnell. *The Universal Traveler: A Soft Systems Guide to Creativity, Problem Solving & the Process of Reaching Goals*. Los Altos, CA: Crisp Publications, 1995.

Simonds, John Ormsbee. *Landscape Architecture: A Manual of Site Planning and Design*, 3rd edition. New York: McGraw-Hill, 1997.

Further Resources

Motloch, John L. *Introduction to Landscape Design*, 2nd edition. New York: John Wiley & Sons, 2001.

Reid, Grant W. *From Concept to Form in Landscape Design*, 2nd edition. Hoboken, NJ: John Wiley & Sons, 2007.

The Straight Line 3

The discussion of orthogonal forms begins with the straight line or vector, the most fundamental component of all flat-sided forms. The straight line is the elementary component from which the square, rectangle, and other orthogonal forms are created. The sides, internal axes, and implied internal grid of the square and rectangle are all straight lines placed at right angles to one another. The straight line is also integral to the grid, symmetrical, and asymmetrical organizational structures composed of multiple squares and rectangles. In all its potential variations, the straight line is the basis for shaping a landscape that possesses clearly articulated edges and a human, architectonic design character.

While the straight line is integral to all orthogonal geometries, the focus of this chapter is on the straight line as a singular design element that has its own unique qualities and uses as an organizing element in landscape architectural site design. This chapter reviews inherent qualities, possible uses, and associated guidelines for employing the straight line as a principal design element in molding landscape space. The sections of this chapter include:

- Fundamental Characteristics
- Landscape Uses
- Design Guidelines

3.1 Examples of line in the landscape.

3.2 Line's directionality.

Fundamental Characteristics

A line is a design element whose length far exceeds its width, thus giving it the perception of being a one-dimensional element. While all physical objects must actually possess two dimensions, a line is nevertheless a proportionally narrow entity that occupies a relatively thin area over a protracted distance. The straight line is distinguished from other lines like the diagonal, arch, or curvilinear line by virtue of connecting two points in the shortest distance. The straight line is an expression of efficiency, decisiveness, and uninterrupted movement.

The straight line is primarily a human construct, although examples of direct lines are seen in redwood trunks and other similarly structured trees, stratification of rocks, the distant horizon of a large body of water, parts of flowers, and so on. In the human landscape, the straight line is created by any extended, narrow two-dimensional element such as a walk, road, channel of water, and band of a pavement material or by a thin three-dimensional object like a fence, wall, and hedge (3.1). In addition, a straight line is implied by a continuous row of individual elements like trees, columns, lights, and flagpoles.

DIRECTIONALITY MOST PERCEIVED

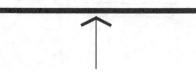

DIRECTIONALITY LEAST PERCEIVED

3.3 Above: The line's directionality is most evident when viewed along its length.

3.4 Right: A line's directionality is reinforced by vertical planes along its length.

NO. LINE LACKS TERMINUS

YES. LINE TERMINATES WITH EMPHASIS

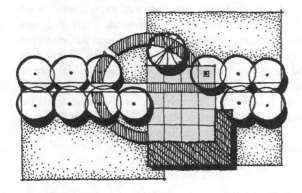
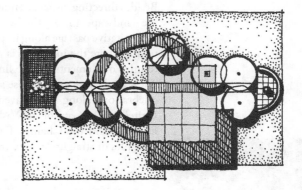

Landscape Uses

The straight line's one-dimensionality, directness, simplicity, and continuity serve as the basis for numerous uses in landscape architectural site design. While separated here for clarity of explanation, many of these functions are mutually reinforcing and occur simultaneously with each other giving the straight line the ability to accomplish a number of design objectives at once. Potential landscape uses of the straight line are: direct the eye, accommodate movement, establish a datum, establish a dividing edge, provide an architectural extension, imply human control, and create rhythm.

Direct the Eye

All lines in the landscape capture and direct the eye although the straight line does this most emphatically (3.1–2). The straight line's uninterrupted, extended length seizes the eye to lead it to an end point or notable interruption on the line. This is most obvious when one is located directly on the line or next to the line looking along its length (3.3). A straight line is less directional when viewed from the side. The straight line's directionality is most apparent when it is reinforced in the third dimension by parallel vertical planes of buildings, walls, or plants (3.4). The vertical planes function like blinders to constrain one's attention along the corridor space to the termini. This is one of the most forceful visual experiences in the landscape and should be employed only in situations where such unequivocal focus is warranted.

Similar to the rectangle, the line's termini should be appropriately accentuated because of the concentrated visual focus on them (3.5). This is especially so when the straight line is integral to a linear space. A sculpture, significant building, water feature, special plant, framed view, or any noteworthy element can potentially serve as the accent at the end points (3.6). The accumulated energy of the straight line is unnecessarily dissipated when the terminus lacks a focal point.

3.5 A line should be accented with a proper terminus.

3.6 Examples of potential termini.

Movement

Besides directing visual attention, paved lines can be arteries of physical movement through the landscape (3.7). The straight line supports efficient, unequivocal, controlled, and authoritative passage along its protracted length. A straight line is best used to accommodate transit where the intention is to move nonstop between two points, to focus attention on termini or elements on the line, and/or to fit an architectonic or symmetrical landscape. The straight line can likewise support ceremonial movement like parades and other public celebrations along grand avenues and boulevards. Pennsylvania Avenue leading to the United States Capitol in Washington, D.C.; the Mall leading to Buckingham Palace in London; and the Champs Elysées leading to the Arc de Triomphe in Paris are notable examples of straight, stately streets used for public parades and celebrations.

Datum

A datum is a point, line, or surface that is used as a reference or place of origin in surveying and mapping. Similarly, a datum in design is a line, plane, or volume that other elements in a composition relate to (Ching 2007, 366). A straight line is a datum when it extends through an entire assemblage of elements and unifies them by its presence (3.8). A straight line's unrelenting simplicity and continuity provides a shared commonality and a visual anchor that all the other elements are compared to. Furthermore, the straight line is a dominant feature that unifies by diminishing the dissimilarities among other components as previously discussed in Chapter 1. The more visual authority the line possesses, the more effective it is in melding the composition.

The straight line fulfills the role of a datum in two forms: axis and spine. An axis is the datum of a symmetrical composition with all elements and spaces being located on the axis or equally balanced along its sides (left 3.9). The axis's centrality prevails over all elements of a design composition, relegating them to secondary roles. Everything in a symmetrical design depends on the axis, yet is subjugated by it. The axis is discussed in more detail in Chapters 1 (Foundational Concepts) and 7 (Orthogonal Symmetry).

3.7   Above: Examples of the line's ability to provide a corridor for movement.

3.8   Right: The straight line as a datum.

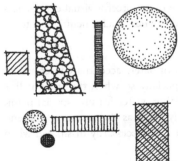

NO DATUM   DATUM

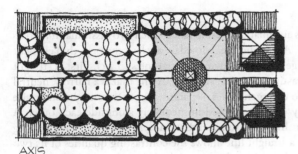

AXIS

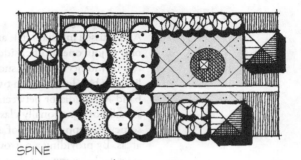

SPINE

A spine is a datum in an asymmetrical configuration (right 3.9). Like an axis, a spine extends through a design as a prevailing, harmonizing element. In the left of 3.10, the landscape lacks unity with unrelated spaces and elements. In the right of 3.10, the straight datum visually threads all the spaces and elements together into a cohesive design. Two contemporary examples of using a straight line as a spine and coordinating component include WaterColor, a park and demonstration gardens in Walton County, Florida, by Nelson Byrd Woltz and the IBM Japan Makuhari Building by Peter Walker Partners. In the latter, a spine is formed by a line of lights in the ground that traverses through separate garden spaces and the building.

3.9   Comparison between an axis and spine.

3.10   A spine can unify a landscape with its emphatic authority.

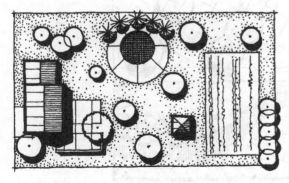

NO UNITY

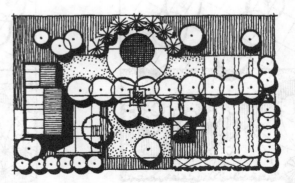

UNITY CREATED BY SPINE

Dividing Edge

As discussed in Chapter 1, an edge is automatically established when two dissimilar materials or uses join one another side by side. A straight line defined by a relatively long, thin element can be interjected along such an edge and serves two potential roles (3.11). First, a straight line can be a foil between two contrasting materials and uses. A line that is a narrow, neutral band is a mediator between the two divergent sides, separating areas that might otherwise visually or functionally clash if they were juxtaposed immediately alongside each other. A somewhat opposite use of a straight line to is to accentuate differences between adjoining areas. By providing a narrow space, a straight line allows the contrasting qualities of its two sides to be compared, but without direct interference of the other. A straight line serves this purpose better than an arc or curvilinear line because of its consistency and simplicity.

One applied example of this is Copia, the American Center for Wine, Food, and Arts in Napa, California, designed by Peter Walker Partners (3.12–13). Here an elongated, stepped pool of water and adjoining gravel promenade reinforced by flagpoles and rows of columnar poplars collectively create a bold line in the landscape that clearly divides two very distinct areas of the design. A grid of garden plots occupies the east side of the line while utilitarian tasks of arrival and parking take up the west side. The extended line through this design purposely celebrates the striking disparities between the east and west side of the site rather than trying to disguise them.

3.11   The use of a straight line to separate areas of divergent characters.

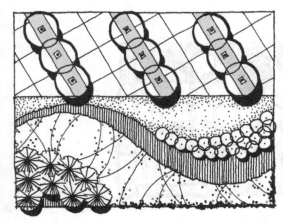

NO SEPARATING EDGE

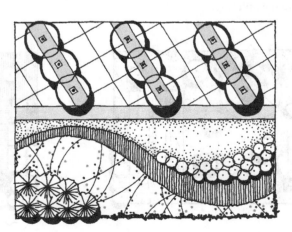

SEPARATING EDGE

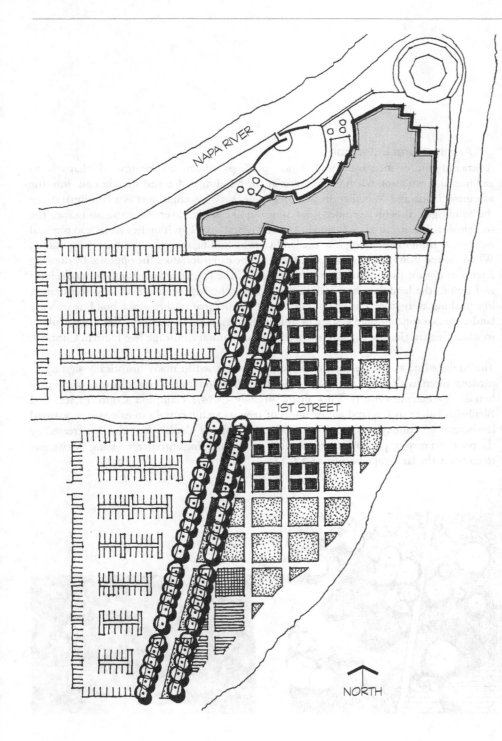

NAPA RIVER

1ST STREET

NORTH

3.12 Left: Site plan of Copia.

3.13 Below: The pool and allee of poplars form an architectural extension from the building at Copia.

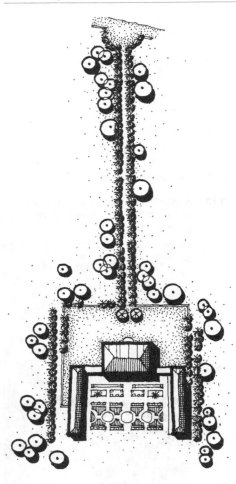

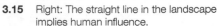

Architectural Extension

A straight line defined by a wall, fence, pool, pavement, and/or row of plants is an architectural extension when it originates at the building's edge and stretches out into the adjoining landscape. Whether an axis or a spine, such a straight line is a continuation of the building's orthogonal geometry, reaching out like an arm to embrace the landscape. The straight-line architectural extension has several functions. First, it invites visual and physical movement from the building into the landscape by leading the eye away from the building. When viewed from the landscape, the straight-line extension does the opposite by drawing attention toward the building. In both instances, the line as architectural extension joins and unifies the landscape and building into one cohesive statement. Finally, the straight line pushing away from a building transmits the structured quality of the building into the landscape as a concentrated gesture of human influence and fabrication. This is particularly so when the straight line extends into a pastoral or natural landscape (see Human Control).

The straight line as architectural extension has been used in many historically significant gardens, often as a central axis leading into the landscape from a villa, chateau, or country house. Seventeenth-century Villa Pietra in Italy (3.14), Hampton Court Palace, and Blenheim Palace in England all use allees of trees as architectural extensions into pastoral landscapes. A contemporary example is the landscape of Copia where the line created by the pool and rows of poplars extends south from the building entrance, crossing a city street to embrace the landscape beyond (3.12–13).

3.14 Above: Site plan of Villa Pietra, Italy, with an alle of trees creating an architectural extension.

3.15 Right: The straight line in the landscape implies human influence.

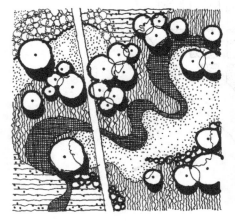

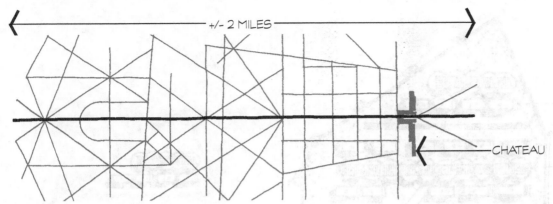

+/- 2 MILES

CHATEAU

Left: Axes and avenues at Versailles.

3.17 Below: Rows of plants represent the human ability to control nature.

Human Control

The efficient structural quality of the straight line can be utilized to suggest human control in the landscape. While it is possible to find straight lines in nature as previously outlined, they are not common occurrences. Noted landscape designer William Kent echoed this in the 1600s by stating: "Nature abhors a straight line." The human ability to organize, simplify, and control nature's complex patterns is epitomized in the straight line's purity. An undeviating road, railroad line, irrigation channel, and utility line each imply human jurisdiction as they cross the landscape. The straight line can also be a deliberate design element inserted into the landscape to contrast the natural and imply human regimentation (3.15).

While all straight lines imply human regulation of the landscape, the axis moreover symbolizes the ability to dominate because of its undeniable supremacy in the landscape. There are numerous examples of using the axis to suggest the power of a government, a deity, or important individual. The central axis or processional line at Queen Hatshepsut's temple in Egypt, the axis in Rome that passes through the heart of Saint Peter's Square to the doorway and papal window of Saint Peter's Church in the Vatican, and the middle axis of Vaux le Vicomte each represented sovereignty. The mall in Washington, D.C., is the principal fulcrum for the layout of Washington and suggests the influence of U.S. government to the country and the world. Perhaps the most notable example of the axis's potential symbolism is at Versailles, where the monumentally long primary axis extended through the King Louis XIV's bedroom and bed, symbolizing his dominion over all (3.16).

The straight line as a representation of human management is likewise evident in rows of plants in the cultivated field, orchard, vineyard, and allee (3.17). One of the first examples of using straight lines to regulate the landscape occurred in early agricultural practices of planting crops in straight lines to facilitate irrigation. Many ancient gardens in Egypt and Mesopotamia likewise placed plants in rows to accommodate irrigation. The practice of placing plants in straight lines was subsequently stylized and became a recurring component of many classical landscapes even when there was no need for irrigation. A number of

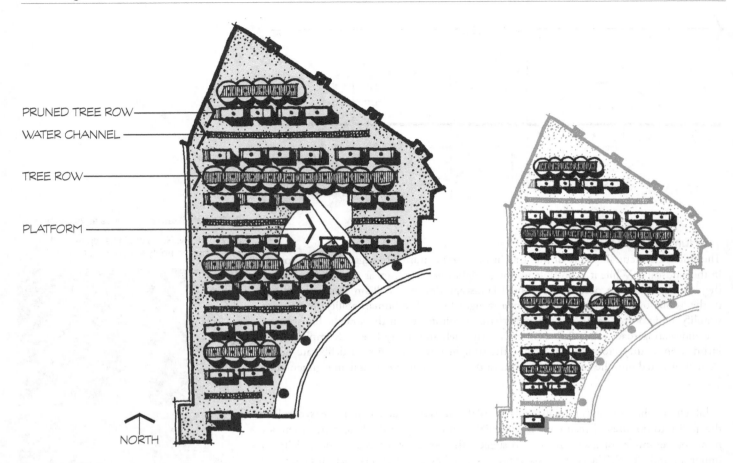

PRUNED TREE ROW

WATER CHANNEL

TREE ROW

PLATFORM

NORTH

3.18 50 Avenue Montaigne uses rows
of trees to instill a strict order reflective of
historic precedents and rows of crops.

contemporary landscape designs like the 50 Avenue Montaigne project in Paris, France, by Michael Van Valkenburgh Associates have similarly used plant rows as metaphors of the human agrarian landscape (3.18). Rows of trees alternating with gravel walks and channels of water imply the agricultural basis of a plant nursery and recall the historic precedent of Andre LeNotre's works. The rows of trees are also aligned with nearby streets, thus giving the courtyard an implied connection to its urban context (Madec 1994, 95).

Create Rhythm

The straight line's quality of movement lends itself to creating visual cadence in the landscape by locating regularly spaced variations directly on the line or its edge (3.19–20). The former approach can be created by an alteration in pavement material, spacing of elements in a fence/wall, or by repeating members of an overhead structure above a walk. The later concept can be implemented by the periodic placement of trees, shrubs, light poles, bollards, and benches along a walk or linear space. In all cases, the periodic punctuation along a line provides a meter to movement and reinforces the sense of advancement.

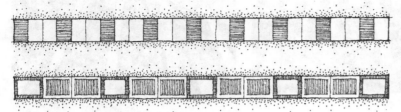

RHYTHM CREATED ON THE LINE

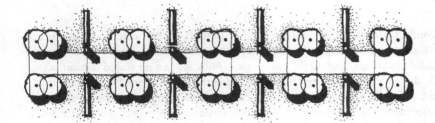

3.19 Left: Examples of rhythm created along the length of a line.

3.20 Below: Examples of rhythm created by vertical elements along a line.

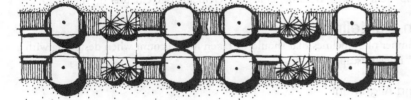

RHYTHM CREATED NEXT TO THE LINE

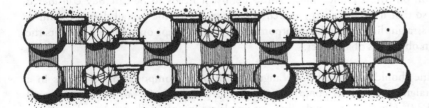

RHYTHM CREATED ON and NEXT TO THE LINE

3.21 Rhythm created with a pattern of lines on the ground in the garden of Visceral Serenity.

3.22 A line is most in harmony when it is 90° or parallel to other orthogonal forms.

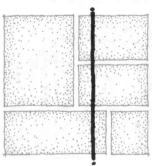

IN HARMONY WITH

IN CONTRAST TO

A separate concept is to use the straight line itself as the design component that is duplicated to form a visual tempo in the landscape. A series of straight lines placed in a repeating pattern establishes rhythm, leading the eye across a landscape in a measured fashion as they do in the Garden of Visceral Serenity by Yoji Sasaki at the Cornerstone Festival of Gardens in Sonoma, California (3.21). Here, bands of concrete pavement on a grass ground plane provide a strict pattern that invites disciplined progression through the small garden space. This technique potentially has similarities to a line grid, especially if the line is used as a structural component to organize other landscape elements (see Chapter 6, The Grid).

Design Guidelines

There are a number of guidelines that should be taken into account when designing with a straight line in the landscape.

Intent and Alignment

A straight line is a potentially potent element in the landscape that can readily capture the eye and invite movement. This is especially true when a straight line is relatively long, contrasts other elements, and/or is expressed in the third dimension (see proceeding text discussion on Third Dimension). Consequently, it needs to be carefully considered and located so that its visual energy is well coordinated with the overall design intent. A pronounced straight line should be incorporated in the landscape only when it benefits the overall design objectives of a project.

A straight line should be thoughtfully aligned with other compositional elements in a design. A straight line is most congruous when it is parallel or 90° to other orthogonal forms (left 3.22). However, a straight line can be placed intentionally at an angle to other compositional forms if the purpose is to contrast the line and to make a bold statement (right 3.22) (see Chapter 9, The Diagonal).

Third Dimension

The length of a line and its expression in the third dimension collectively influence the visual strength of a line in the landscape. As already suggested, a line is least apparent when it is a two-dimensional element on the ground plane defined by pavement, water, low plants, or the like (left 3.23). A line restricted to the ground is usually perceived only when one is in very close proximity to it and may easily become hidden as one moves away. A line is most evident in the landscape when defined by a wall, hedge, line of trees, or other elements of height (middle and right 3.23). A three-dimensional line can often be seen from a distance, especially if it is higher than nearby elements. Further, a line with height has the ability to enclose space and direct views. Thus, a line's height is critical and should be carefully studied to achieve the desired visual effect.

Topography

A straight line fulfills its uses best when it is situated on relatively level topography where its entire length can be seen as an uninterrupted gesture through the landscape (left 3.24). A straight line may also fulfill its potentialities when located on a uniform slope (middle 3.24). Rolling, hilly, or uneven topography does not provide a good location for a straight line because high points and ridges break the line's continuity and diminish its vitality (right 3.24). Nevertheless, there are instances where it is desirable to permit a straight line to disappear out of view over a ridge as a means of creating invitation and intrigue in the landscape. The viewer is encouraged to move along the line to the top of the ridge to seek out what is beyond.

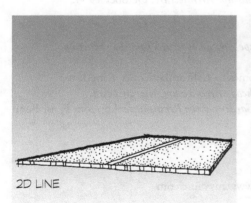

2D LINE

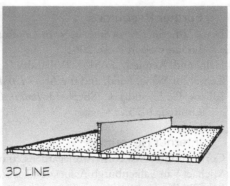

3D LINE

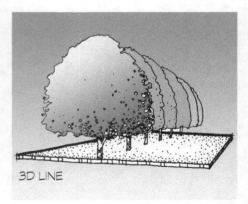

3D LINE

3.23 A line has the most visual strength when expressed in the third dimension.

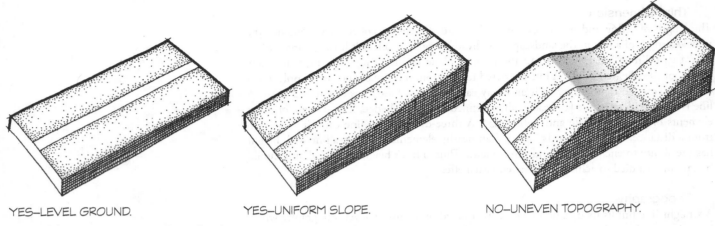

YES—LEVEL GROUND.   YES—UNIFORM SLOPE.   NO—UNEVEN TOPOGRAPHY.

3.24 A line functions best on level or uniformly
sloped ground.

Referenced Resources

Ching, Francis D. K. *Architecture: Form, Space, & Order.* Hoboken, NJ: John Wiley &
 Sons, 2007.
Madec, Philippe. "French Connection." *Landscape Architecture,* October 1994.

Further Resources

Dee, Catherine. *Form and Fabric in Landscape Architecture: A Visual Introduction.*
 London: Spon Press, 2001.
Helphand, Kenneth, FASLA. "Villandry Comes to California; Copia: American
Center for Wine, Food, and the Arts." *Landscape Architecture,* March 2005.
Jellicoe, G. A., and J. C. Shepherd. *Italian Gardens of the Renaissance.* London: Ernst Benn
 Limited, 1925.

Internet Resources

CornerStone: www.cornerstonegardens.com
Michael Van Valkenburgh Associates, Inc.: www.mvvainc.com
Peter Walker and Partners: www.pwpla.com

The Square

4

The straight line discussed in the previous chapter is the basic component used to create all orthogonal typologies including the square. It will be recalled from earlier discussions that the square is one of the three primary shapes and is the most elementary orthogonal form with its four straight sides. The square can be employed by itself as the underpinning of an individual landscape space or transformed by subtraction, addition, and so forth to serve as the foundation of more elaborate designs. However it is used, it is necessary to first understand the square's unique geometric qualities and potential applications in landscape architectural site design. The topics discussed in this chapter include:

- Geometric Qualities
- Landscape Uses
- Design Guidelines

Geometric Qualities

In addition to being composed of four straight and equal sides placed at right angles to each other, the square also possesses the following distinguishing geometric traits.

Symmetrical Axes and Diagonals

The square's equal sides, symmetrical axes, and diagonals collectively suggest a perfect form in which all the component parts are proportionally balanced and in harmony with each other. The square's absolute symmetry imbues it with special merit and virtue.

Like an animal skeleton or a leaf's veins, the square's axes and diagonals are a compositional armature that suggests edges for transforming the square into smaller areas (4.1). In turn, these primary lines and the resultant spaces can be divided in half, quarter, and so on to create a logical and mathematical organizational system of subdivision that has an infinite number of potential patterns and designs (4.2). These internal designs may use the axes, diagonals, and center point to forge symmetrical designs or they may use other lines of division for asymmetrical compositions. These same lines also suggest where and how the square is connected to other forms.

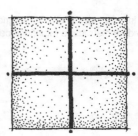
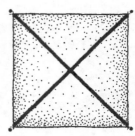
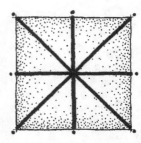

4.1 The square's primary internal axes and diagonals.

75

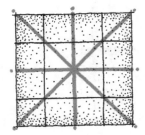

4.2 The internal axes and affiliated grid provide the structure for infinite patterns.

ETC.

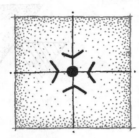 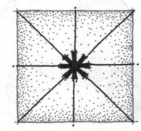

Center

The square's center is an inherent focal point and a critical component of its geometry. The center is always an authoritative point and visual anchor even when the inside of the square remains blank (left 4.3). However, the importance of the center becomes even more apparent when the square's axes and/or diagonals are expressed (right 4.3). The center draws energy and attention inward within the square to create a centroidal composition. A symmetrical organization within a square is often most successful when the center is rightfully acknowledged and reinforced (4.4).

4.4 The square's center is reinforced and celebrated as the inherent focal point of this design.

Corners

Another unique quality of the square is its explicit 90-degree corners that create a clear division between each of the four sides. When considered from an internal viewpoint, the square's corners are visual cavities that capture and retain the eye, especially when the sides of the square are extruded into the third dimension to establish an obvious seam between the adjoining planes (4.5). The corners of the square are critical for defining space because the enveloping quality of the vertical planes is most evident at the 90-degree corners, more so than along the individual sides of the square. The embracing enclosure at the corners is often sought as a refuge where one is protected on two sides while maintaining a vantage point overlooking the rest of the square.

4.5 The corners of a square capture and retain the eye.

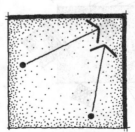

PLAN

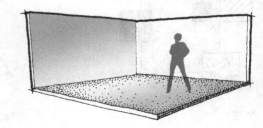

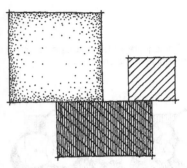

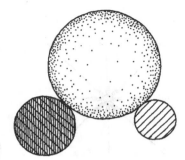

MOST MUTUAL SURFACE

LEAST MUTUAL SURFACE

4.6 The connection of orthogonal forms creates the greatest amount of mutual surface between adjoining forms.

Straight and Distinct Sides

One consequence of the square's self-evident flat and distinct sides is that they establish visually stable compositions with other flat-sided shapes. It will be recalled from Chapter 1 that the optimum connection in face-to-face additive transformation is between adjoining flat-sided shapes (1.24). A square placed directly next to another square, rectangle, or triangle establishes such an attachment with a continuously flush and extended union (4.6). By comparison, only a single mutual point is established when circles meet or when triangles are juxtaposed corner to edge. The square's straight sides ensure a visually sound composition with other orthogonal forms and thus are relatively easy to design with. The only time disjointed compositions are created with squares is when they are placed at non-90-degree angles to each other (4.7).

Another implication is that each side of the square, although equal in length, is indeed separate from the next by the clear demarcation at the corners. This severance gives each side of a square its own identity and distinction, a fact reinforced by being able to assign

4.7 Ninety-degree relationships among orthogonal forms generate visually stable compositions.

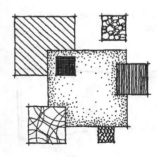

YES

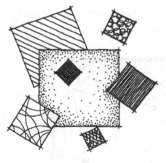

NO

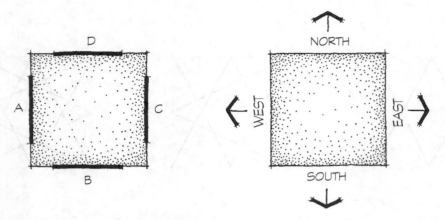

4.8 The square has separate and distinct sides.

it a sole identifying label like A, B, C, and D or front, right, back, and left side (4.8). The singularity among sides further implies identifiable territories and spheres of influence associated with each side. Consider four people sitting around a square table, each with his/her "own" side.

Similarly, the square's four sides can be equated to the cardinal directions of north, south, east, and west when so oriented (Shepherd and Shepherd 2002, 335). This orientation gives each side of a square space its own particular exposure to sun and prevailing wind throughout the year. Likewise, the different metaphorical associations attached to the four cardinal directions by many cultures, including Native Americans, is reinforced by a square aligned in a north/south/east/west orientation.

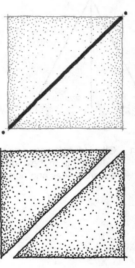

4.9 Above: The square's diagonal defines two right-angle isosceles triangles.

4.10 Left: Smaller right-angle isosceles triangles are defined with additional diagonals and cross-axes.

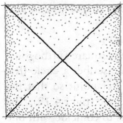

4 TRIANGLES

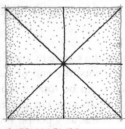

8 TRIANGLES

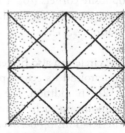

16 TRIANGLES

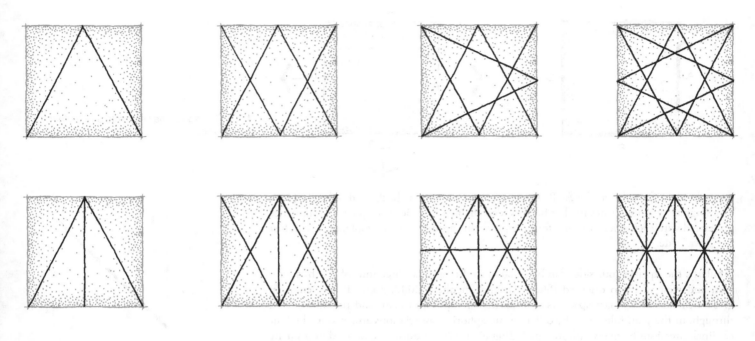

4.11 Other triangles are defined by diagonals extended from the midpoint of the square's sides and orthogonal axes.

Relation to Other Forms

The square has an inherent geometric relation with the other two primary shapes as discussed in Chapter 1 (1.12). For example, the delineation of one diagonal within the square defines two right-angle isosceles triangles, each one half the area of the square and sharing a common hypotenuse (4.9). These triangles are sometimes called 45–45–90 triangles, half square triangles, or triangle squares. These two triangles can be divided into progressively smaller triangles that each retains the same proportions (4.10). Other triangles can be generated with the diagonals extended from the midpoints of the square's sides to opposite corners (top 4.11). Again, these can be subdivided to create smaller triangles. Still more triangles can be discovered within the square by exploring other diagonals and axes (bottom 4.11).

The circle can also be generated from the square by rotating one of the square's orthogonal axes around its center point. As it pivots, the end of the axis circumscribes a circle (left 4.12). In addition, the entire square can be rotated around its center point so that the midpoint on each side of the square traces the circumference of a circle (right 4.12). The interrelationship between the circle and square permit the two forms to coincide with one another, a recurring compositional strategy in symmetrical design (4.13). This may be done to express the close association between these two fundamental geometric forms, to create contrast, or to suggest the symbolism affiliated with each as presented in the next section.

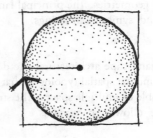

ROTATION of RADIUS

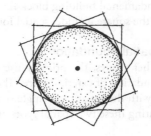

ROTATION of SQUARE

4.12 Left: Two methods for creating a circle inside the square.

4.13 Below: Design strategies that exploit the interrelationship between the square and the circle.

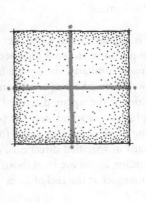
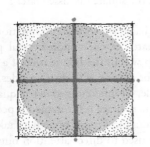
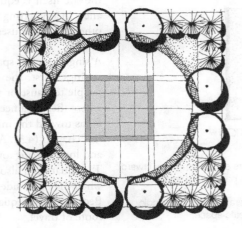

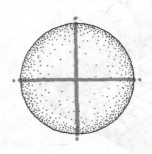
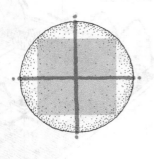
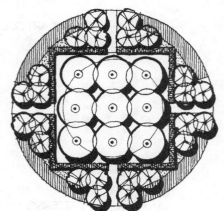

Landscape Uses

There are numerous roles the square can fulfill in the landscape, either as a singular form or as a fundamental building block for other orthogonal geometries. The principal landscape uses of the square include: spatial foundation, node, and symbolic meanings.

Spatial Foundation

Like other shapes, the primary use of the square in landscape architectural site design is the foundation of exterior space. There are two fundamental spatial typologies that can be forged with the square: (1) single space and (2) ensemble of multiple spaces. The strategies for creating these two spatial types are discussed in the following paragraphs.

Single Space. A single square space is a self-contained, undivided entity that is primarily defined by its four distinct sides. Such a space exists in the landscape as an enclosed courtyard, urban plaza, building forecourt, public green space, garden, and so on or where the site itself is equal in its plan proportions. The single square space can also be created anew in any setting to establish a simple, distinct space that exists among others or to fulfill other landscape uses of the square discussed later in this section.

A single exterior space based on a square foundation is appropriate in a number of design settings. First, the square's equal, nondirectional proportions are well-disposed to urge people to pause or stop within the boundaries of a space. Similarly, the square is apropos where there is a need for a space with distinct sides, well-defined corners, and an intrinsic focus toward the middle, all inherent geometric qualities of the square discussed earlier in this chapter (4.3). A square space is favorable for people to sit or stand along its perimeters and look inward toward a focal point or activity taking place within the space (top 4.14). The square can also be used to direct attention outward in specified directions, especially when the other sides of the space are solid planes extending above eye level (bottom 4.14). Because of these qualities, the square is a fitting terminus space at the end of an axis or other route of travel.

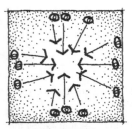

INWARD FOCUS

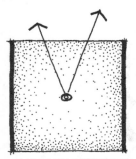

OUTWARD DIRECTION

4.14 Above: A square space can focus inward or outward in a particular direction.

4.15 Below: The characteristics of a single square volumetric space.

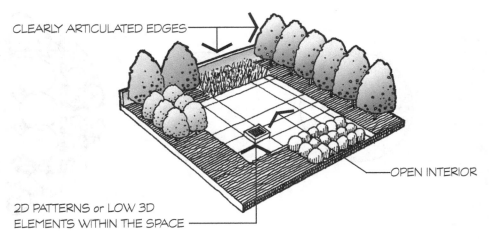

CLEARLY ARTICULATED EDGES

OPEN INTERIOR

2D PATTERNS or LOW 3D
ELEMENTS WITHIN THE SPACE

SIMPLE EXTRUDED EDGE

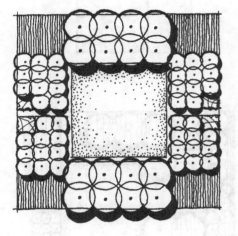

EDGE of VARIED FORMS & MATERIALS

EDGE of VARIED DEPTHS & HEIGHTS

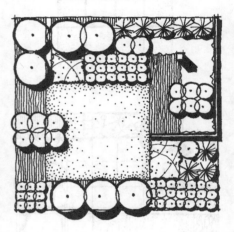

The interior of a single square space should be treated uniformly to assure that it is perceived as one space. This is most easily achieved with a volumetric space that is defined primarily on its edges with clearly articulated vertical planes, leaving the interior uninterrupted and open (4.15). In addition, the ground and overhead planes should be homogeneous in material and pattern, though this does not necessarily mean simple. Elements that are located within the interior of the space should remain low so that they are perceived more as two-dimensional patterns than three-dimensional objects.

While all these techniques to establish a single space may forge a simplistic and predictable space, they don't necessarily have to. As previously discussed in Chapter 2, the vertical edges around a single space can be elaborate and layered as long as the interior remains relatively open and undivided (2.27–28). Similarly, the perimeter of a square space can be composed of many different elements located at varied depths and orientations with respect to the square base (4.16). These elements do not necessarily have to be symmetrical to maintain the sense of an individual space. A single square space can also be cubist if the interior elements are distributed throughout the space and are relatively thin or low so they do not partition the space (4.17). A grove of trees on a square foundation is one example of a single cubist space.

4.16 Alternative treatments of the edge around a single square space.

4.17 A single square space can be cubist if uniformly treated throughout the space.

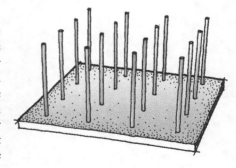

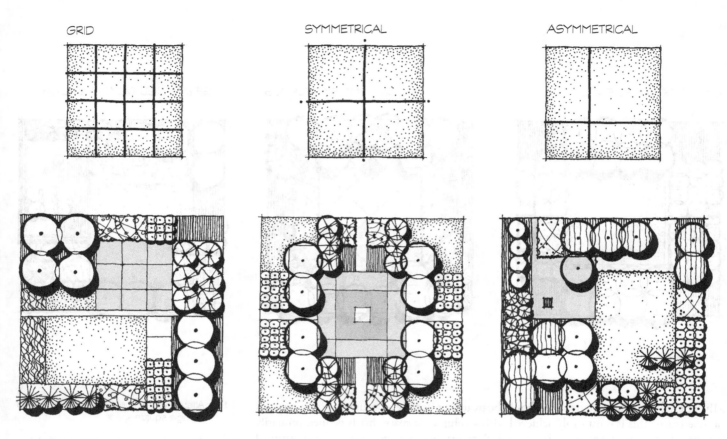

GRID   SYMMETRICAL   ASYMMETRICAL

4.18 Alternative organizational systems for subdividing the square.

Multiple Spaces. The square can be employed as the basis of multiple associated spaces in the landscape. The process for generating these spaces from a single square is primarily accomplished by two means of transformation: subtraction and addition (see Form Transformation, Chapter 1).

Subtraction. The transformation process of subtraction or subdivision is used to generate multiple spaces and/or material areas within the confines of a square. This is an appropriate strategy where the square's edges are fixed in place by site circumstances and/or when there is programmatic need to have more than one use or material area within a square's boundaries.

There are a number of alternative means for subdividing the square, including the principal organizational structures discussed in Chapter 1: grid, symmetry, and asymmetry (4.18). The grid typically is based on an equal division of the square along one or two dimensions. The size of the grid is a variable that depends on the actual dimensions of the square and

OTHER FORMS

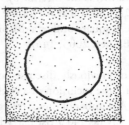

INDEPENDENT

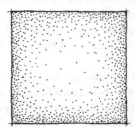

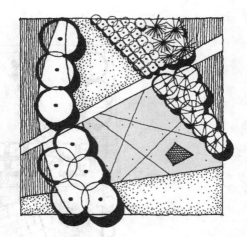

4.19 Left: Example of subdividing the square with other forms.

4.20 Right: The square treated as a frame around an independent structure.

the required program uses. Symmetrical subdivision is centered on one or more of the square's primary axes and may include, though not necessarily, the diagonals to forge a cross-axial design. This tactic of subdividing the square is common in orthogonal symmetrical designs as discussed more in Chapter 6. Finally, lines of division within the square can be determined asymmetrically while remaining in an orthogonal alignment with the square's sides. Each of these structural organizations forges a different design temperament and so should be chosen thoughtfully to properly correlate to a given site and design program.

The previous methods of subdivision within the square all work with the square's internal geometry so that the resulting composition is visually in sync with the square's orthogonal temperament and its internal geometry. In addition, there are two other strategies of subdivision that are less associated with the square's inner layout and so offer more freedom of expression and experimentation. The first is to introduce other forms into the square (4.19). As pointed out earlier in this chapter, both the circle and triangle exist within the square and can be utilized as the basis for subtracting areas from within it.

Another technique of subdivision is to organize the inside of the square without regard for its implied internal geometry (4.20). The interior composition is informed by any number of objectives unrelated to the square's structure, thus allowing the design to be organic, irregular, or even haphazard. With this approach to design, the square is like a frame around a picture and melds the interior by means of compartmentalization, one of the unifying principles discussed in Chapter 1. One example of this is the DIN A4 courtyard for the German Institute of Standards in Berlin designed by the Australian landscape architectural firm 4.3.1 (4.21). Here, a square unifies a discordant set of lines, trees, and an inclined plane that represents a piece of standard European A4 paper (Weller and Barnett 2005, 144).

One last means of subdividing a square into multiple spaces and use areas is to combine two or more of previously discussed means of subdivision. For example, a square's internal layout might be based on a fusion of the grid, asymmetry, and the inclusion of a circle. All of these design strategies can be further transformed by rotation and intervention as presented in Chapter 1. A number of these strategies were the basis for the design of a plaza in the Great West Life Headquarters in Denver, Colorado, designed by Civitas and artist Larry Kirkland (4.22). Here, the axial structure of the square was transformed into a seemingly random placement of other squares and fundamental geometric forms.

4.21   The DIN A4 courtyard.

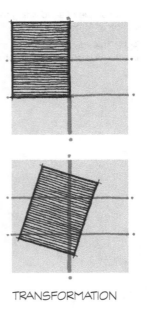

TRANSFORMATION

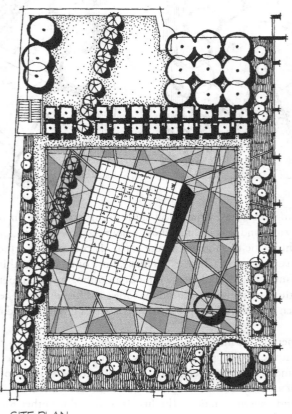

SITE PLAN

4.22 Great West Life Headquarters garden.

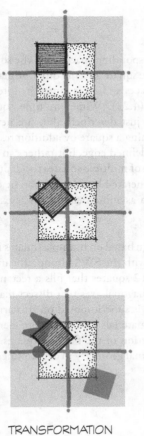

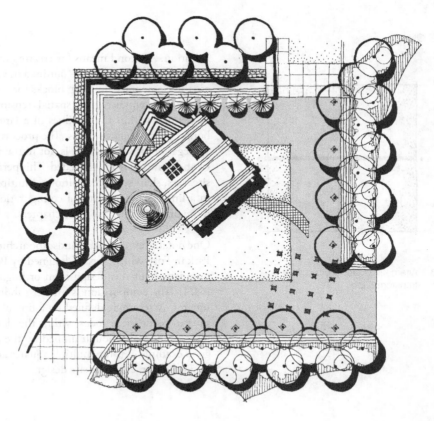

TRANSFORMATION

SITE PLAN

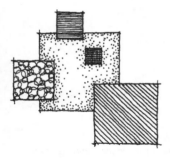

INTERLOCKING

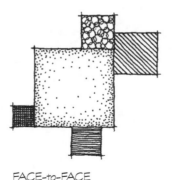

FACE-to-FACE

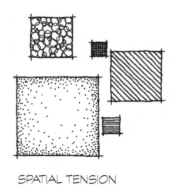

SPATIAL TENSION

FUSION

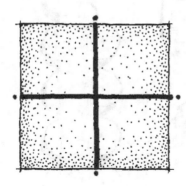

4.23 Alternative means for additive transformation.

Addition. A second means for creating multiple corresponding spaces with the square is by additive transformation. As outlined in Chapter 1, the square and the other primary shapes are the elementary building blocks for a cluster of spaces and areas forged by interlocking, face-to-face contact, and spatial tension addition (4.23). While multiple squares can be defined within the confines of a larger square as just described, they are nevertheless bound by the square's edges. The process of transforming a square by addition results in an aggregation of squares that is not restrained by a predefined edge, but rather can be added to or subtracted from as needed. This permits a design of multiple squares to adapt to varied site sizes, shapes, and conditions. Multiple squares generated by addition can be organized in a line, grid, symmetrical configuration, and/or an asymmetrical design as explored in more detail in the next three chapters.

One notable example of a landscape architectural design based on multiple squares is Burnett Park in Fort Worth, Texas, designed by Peter Walker with the SWA Group. The underlying foundation for this design is an orthogonal grid of 12 squares that fills a rectangular site (4.24). The composition is further subdivided with diagonal axes that dissect many of the squares. A rectangle defined by a line of water pools is superimposed on this armature of squares to define a focus within the design. Plant materials and other site elements are placed randomly though unified by the clear articulation of the field of squares. This is a good example of using multiple squares and their internal geometry in a disciplined manner to produce an eloquent site design.

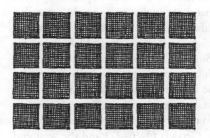

MULTIPLE SQUARES

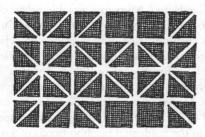

DIAGONALS

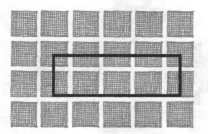

POOLS

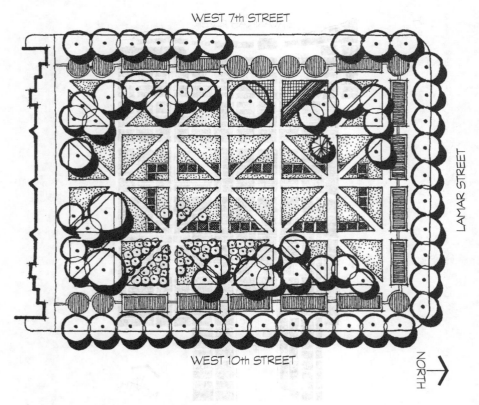

WEST 7th STREET

LAMAR STREET

WEST 10th STREET

NORTH

4.24 The use of multiple squares as the basis of Burnett Park.

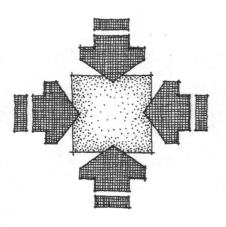

4.25 A square can serve as a node for gathering within the urban setting.

4.26 Right: Plan of Savannah showing the many squares that are voids in the urban fabric.

4.27 Below: Examples of Savannah's squares.

Node

The square's equal sides and proportions make it highly suitable as a node or gathering place in the landscape. Numerous notable urban open spaces throughout the world are called "squares," including Times Square (New York), Trafalgar Square (London), Tiananmen Square (Beijing), Red Square (Moscow), Harvard Square (Cambridge), Mellon Square (Pittsburgh), Pioneer Square (Seattle), Ghirardelli Square (San Francisco), and Fountain Square (Cincinnati). Many of these "squares," though not actually geometrically square, are centrally located in their urban settings, often at the convergence of major streets. These squares do share the commonality of being centripetal spaces that draw focus and energy inward (4.25). *Square* is similarly the term applied to numerous orthogonally shaped park spaces in the residential neighborhoods of Savannah, Georgia (4.26–27) and the west end of London. The origins of the term *square* for such urban spaces is not clear though the formation of outdoor urban space based on orthogonal geometry does have its roots in the Hellenistic Greek cities of Priene and Miletus (French 1978 11–12, 49–60).

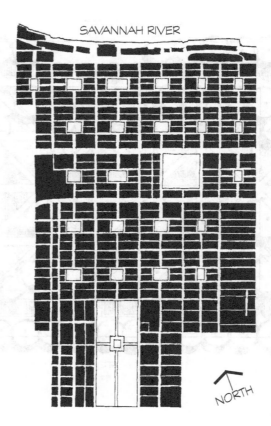

SAVANNAH RIVER

NORTH

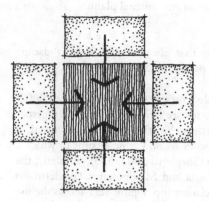

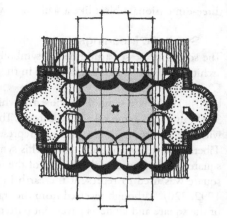

4.28 The use of the square as the middle of a centralized design.

A square is likewise a proper form to be the middle space of a centralized design organization comprised of a series of secondary spaces/functions located around the perimeter (Ching 2007, 196) (4.28). The square and the other primary geometric shapes are well suited as a central space because of their equal proportions, relatively few sides, and inherent symmetry.

The square can also be a node in an asymmetrical design organization. Because the square is nondirectional, it attracts attention when properly designed in terms of location, scale, and material (4.29). It should be noted that a square isn't automatically a node. A square that is intended to be an accent must be strategically placed and differentiated from its context. Additionally, a notable material such as water, mass of flowers, or special pavement must define the square. The square as node can also be a ground form that is the base for a special

4.29 The use of the square as a visual node.

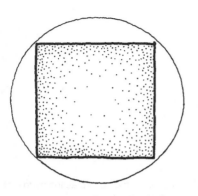

4.30 The square representing the earth inside heaven (circle).

4.31 A Cambridge, Massachusetts, garden designed by Morgan Wheelock uses the square to symbolize the earth.

three-dimensional object like a sculpture, water feature, or ornamental plant.

Symbolic Meanings

The square possesses a number of symbolic meanings that can be exploited in landscape architectural site design as examined in the following paragraphs.

Earth. The square symbolizes the earth while the circle represents heaven (Shepherd 2002, 335) (also see Chapter 13, The Circle). These two forms are frequently depicted together with the square inside the circle to represent the earth within the cosmos as occurred in Tibetan Buddhist imagery (4.30). This symbolism also exists on Chinese coins in which a square hole is placed in the middle of the round coin (Shepherd 2002, 335). Similarly, the square was used to represent the earth in ancient Persia and Mesopotamia (Biedermann 1992, 320). Although reversed from the traditional relationship, Figure 4.31 shows the use of the square and circle as pavement pattern in a garden setting intended to have meaning beyond its function as a sitting space.

Stability and Correctness. The concepts of stability and correctness are synonymous with the square. Much of this association is based on the square's straight, flat sides that join at right angles. The flat sides easily establish rigid, sturdy visual and structural connections when placed face to face or at right angles with other flat-sided forms (4.7). Non-90-degree associations are considered visually weak and precarious. To "square up" nearby forms or objects is to establish a stable, 90-degree connection. A "T-square" is the foundation for drafting equipment and is used to establish right-angle relationships on paper.

The affiliation of the square with sound visual connections among forms can also be extrapolated to broader applications. The phrase "to square away" a situation means to correct or make it right. Similarly, the phrases "square deal," "fair and square," and "square meal" all incorporate the word *square* to imply something that is fit and proper.

Familiar and Traditional. The square is one of the most prevalent forms in the built environment as evidenced in street patterns, buildings, building materials, common objects, and so on. In fact, the square is so known as to be potentially routine and tiresome. Consequently, many designers spend a great deal of time and thought attempting to "break out of the box" with more creative solutions.

The square's association with the commonplace also has negative social connotations. A person who is referred to as "square" is usually perceived as being stiff, awkward, conservative, and/or traditional. It is typically not flattering to be labeled "square," especially among young people or those who consider themselves to be artistic. The title to an article in *Dwell*, "It's Not Hip to Be Square," echoes this sentiment as it relates to architectural design (Gardiner 2003, 128).

ROWS

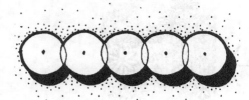

MASSES

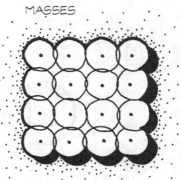

SINGLE PLANT

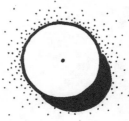

4.32 Vocabulary of plant material configurations for reinforcing the structure of a square.

4.33 Example of plant materials reinforcing the square's internal structure.

Design Guidelines

The square is a relatively easy form to work with in landscape architectural site design because of its equal proportions and orthogonal geometry. Still, there are some general recommendations for designing with it, as outlined in the following paragraphs.

Material Coordination

The orchestration of plant materials, pavement, walls, steps, and other elements in a square space should reinforce its inherent orthogonal geometry. To accomplish this, woody plant materials should be organized in a vocabulary of three fundamental forms: rows, orthogonal mass, and single plant (4.32). Rows or lines of plants are typically employed to function like walls and should be parallel to the sides of the square, along axes, along diagonals, and/or aligned with the square's implied internal grid (4.33). Plant masses should be orthogonal in shape and filled with rows of plants. Single plants are best used as accents strategically located to attract the eye. Herbaceous plant masses should also be orthogonal in shape although individual plants can be arranged in a loose manner within the mass (4.34).

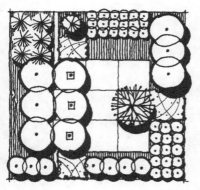

SITE PLAN

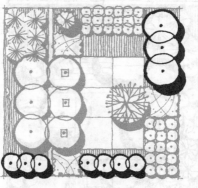

ROWS

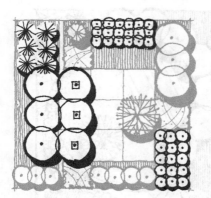

MASSES

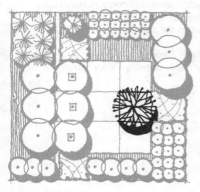

SINGLE PLANT

93

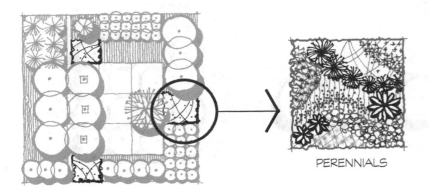

PERENNIALS

4.34 Example of herbaceous plants loosely arranged within an orthogonal area.

Having said this, it should be acknowledged that there are instances when it is preferable to organize plants in a nonorthogonal fashion when designing within and around a square space. One occasion is to reinforce the shapes of other forms and geometries that are incorporated into the square as discussed in the previous section (4.35). In other settings like casual gardens and pastoral sites, plants can be arranged in a much looser manner simply to counterbalance the potential rigidity of the prevailing orthogonal geometry (4.36). The advice with this approach is to still mass plants, particularly shrubs, perennials, and annuals, so that they provide a sense of order even if they do not bolster the orthogonal geometry.

Pavement patterns should likewise reinforce the overall structure of the square by being orthogonally aligned with the square. In some instances, however, it is advisable to orient pavement patterns in a different direction for emphasis or to provide visual relief to the prevailing geometry (4.37).

4.35 Left: Example of nonorthogonal plant masses to reinforce other geometries within the square.

4.36 Right: Example of a casual arrangement of plants within a square space.

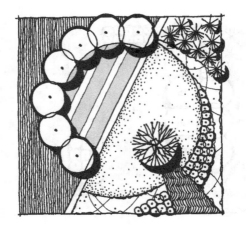

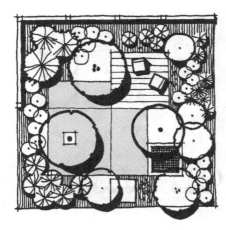

REINFORCE SQUARE

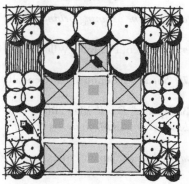

CONTRAST SQUARE

4.37 Alternative treatments of pavement within a square space.

Topography

An individual square space should have a visually level ground plane to support the underlying geometric simplicity of the form and to enhance the perception of being one space (left 4.38). If grade changes are necessary, they are best located at or near the perimeter of the space to maintain a uniform interior. A square that is subdivided into multiple spaces and areas is more accommodating of grade changes. If and when they occur, grade changes should be located between spaces in the form of retaining walls and steps that define the edges of level terraces (middle 4.38). These structural elements should be aligned with the square just as previously suggested for plant materials. Grade changes should be treated similarly for designs composed of multiple squares created in an additive process (right 4.38).

4.38 Alternative ways to treat the ground plane of single square space.

IDEAL for BASE of ONE SPACE

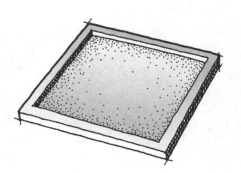

ACCOMMODATE GRADE at EDGE

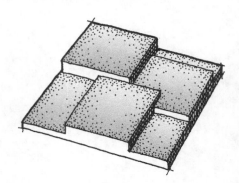

GRADE CHANGE BETWEEN SPACES

95

Referenced Resources

Biedermann, Hans. *Dictionary of Symbolism: Cultural Icons and the Meaning Behind Them.* New York: Facts on File, 1992.

Ching, Francis D. K. *Architecture: Form, Space, & Order.* Hoboken, NJ: John Wiley & Sons, 2007.

French, Jere S. *Urban Space: A Brief History of the City Square.* Dubuque, IA: Kendall/Hunt, 1978.

Gardiner, Virginia. "Houses We Love: It's Not Hip to Be Square." *Dwell*, May 2003.

Shepherd, Rowena, and Rupert Shepherd. *1000 Symbols: What Shapes Mean in Art & Myth.* New York: Thames & Hudson, 2002.

Peter Walker William Johnson and Partners. *Art and Nature.* Tokyo, Japan: Process Architecture Company, 1994.

"Great West Life Headquarters," *Land Forum 11.* Berkeley, CA: Spacemaker Press, 2001.

Weller, Richard, and Rod Barnett. *Room 4.1.3: Innovations in Landscape Architecture.* Philadelphia: University of Pennsylvania Press, 2005.

Further Resources

McCormick, Kathleen. "Escape into Art." *Landscape Architecture*, October 1994.

Internet Resources

Peter Walker and Partners Landscape Architecture: www.pwpla.com

The Rectangle

5

The rectangle is the second fundamental orthogonal form and is derived from the square by dimensional transformation (Ching 2007, 52). The rectangle's flat sides, right angle corners, organization around axes, and symmetry have the same design consequences as they do for the square. However, the rectangle's elongated length sets it apart and affords it with a number of discrete geometric qualities and landscape uses as discussed in this chapter. This chapter presents the following aspects of the rectangle:

- Geometric Qualities
- Landscape Uses
- Design Guidelines

Geometric Qualities

The rectangle's extended proportions give it a number of unique qualities as outlined in this chapter.

Directionality

The noticeable difference between the square and rectangle is the elongated dimension of the rectangle along one axis (5.1). Unlike the static quality of the square, the length of the rectangle gives it a dynamic gesture of energy, direction, and movement. The rectangle's directionality becomes more pronounced as the length is stretched in comparison to width. At an extreme, the rectangle can be transformed to a form possessing the qualities of a one-dimensional line.

One result of the rectangle's directional quality is an orientation and focus toward the narrower ends (5.2). Visual attention and physical movement are directed along the length of the rectangle, with more attention conveyed to the ends than the long sides. Therefore, the rectangle's ends are ideal locations for accents that capture and celebrate the energy that is directed toward them. This phenomenon is emphasized when the rectangle's long sides are enclosed in the vertical plane with tall shrubs, walls, and trees that function like blinders to restrict attention to the ends of the space.

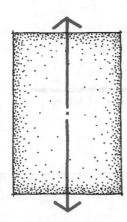

5.1 Above: The rectangle possesses inherent direction along its length.

5.2 Below: Perspective views illustrating the comparative direction along the length of rectangle.

SQUARE

GOLDEN RECTANGLE

5.3   Golden ratio.

A + B is to A as A is to B

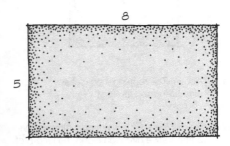

5.4   Golden rectangle with sides having a ratio of 5:8.

Proportions

Because the rectangle's long dimension is variable, the question arises as to what constitutes correct proportions. One answer is that it depends on the context and intended use of the rectangle. The best proportions of any given rectangle are those that visually fit with the rest of a design composition. What is appropriate in one setting may not be well suited in another.

Another answer is based on the proportions of the golden ratio, also called the "divine proportion." This proportion is established by dividing a line into two segments in manner that the ratio of the entire line to the large segment is the same as the ratio of the large segment to the small segment (5.3). This creates a mathematical ratio of 1:1.61803398874. This ratio is unique and creates a relationship that is both visually and mathematically harmonious between the whole and its corresponding components.

This golden ratio or golden section is also associated with the numbers in the Fibonacci sequence: 0, 1, 1, 2, 3, 5, 8, 13, 21, 34, 55, 89, 144, and so on. The sequence begins with 0, 1, 1, and progresses in a manner that when any two adjacent numbers are added together, they equal the next highest number. For example, 2 + 3 = 5, 8 + 13 = 21, 55 + 89 = 144, and so on. The ratio between two adjacent numbers in the Fibonacci sequence is also 1:1.61803398874, a phenomenon that becomes more mathematically accurate as the value of the numbers increases. A rectangle is called a "golden section rectangle" when it has a width-to-length ratio comprised of two adjacent numbers of the Fibonacci sequence such as 8:13 or 89:144 (5.4).

The golden rectangle can be created numerically by scaling the sides to establish a 1:1.6180339887 ratio, or it can be constructed geometrically with some of its components. To do this, first start with a square (5.5a). Next, define the midpoint on one of the sides of the square (b). Then extend a diagonal line from that midpoint to one of the opposite corners (c). The diagonal is then rotated around the midpoint to a position that coincides with the rectangle's side. The new length of this side in relation to original dimension of the square defines the exact proportions of a golden section rectangle.

There are other fixed proportional rectangles that can potentially serve as the foundation for orthogonal compositions. One such rectangle is referred to as the "root 2 rectangle," a rectangle that can be endlessly subdivided into smaller rectangles, each with the same proportions as the original rectangle (Elam 2001, 34).

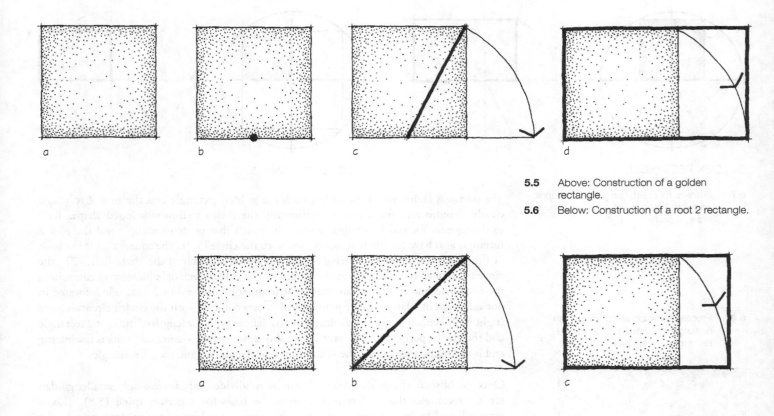

5.5 Above: Construction of a golden rectangle.

5.6 Below: Construction of a root 2 rectangle.

The width-to-length ratio of a root 2 rectangle is 1:1.41, rather similar to the ratio for golden section rectangle. Because of the root 2 rectangle's ability to be repeatedly divided into ever-smaller rectangles of the same proportions, it has been adopted as the basis for the European system of paper sizes.

The construction of a root 2 rectangle is similar to the process of creating a golden section rectangle and likewise starts with a square (5.6a). Next, extend a diagonal between two opposite sides of the square (b). With one end of the diagonal serving as a fixed center point, the diagonal is then rotated to a position that coincides with one of the sides of the rectangle (c). As with the golden rectangle, the new length of this side in relation to original dimension of the square defines the exact proportions of a root 2 rectangle. Again, the diagonals can be used to form smaller root 2 rectangles within the original one.

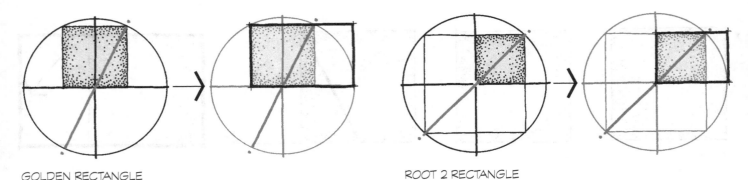

GOLDEN RECTANGLE   ROOT 2 RECTANGLE

5.7 Process for creating a golden rectangle and root 2 rectangle based on a square within a circle.

5.8 Process for subdividing the golden rectangle into smaller proportional rectangles as the basis of a spiral.

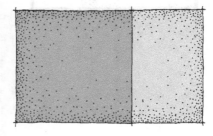

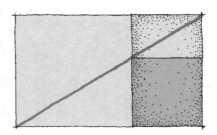

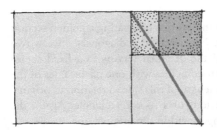

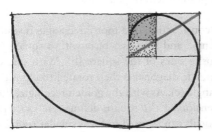

The previous techniques for creating both the golden rectangle and the root 2 rectangle clearly demonstrate the intrinsic relationship these two well-proportioned shapes have to the square. Viewed in a larger context, it is seen that golden rectangle and the root 2 rectangle also have an inherent association with the circle (5.7). The square that is the basis of the golden rectangle is centered on an axis inside one half of the circle (left 5.7). The circle's diagonal axis that defines the length of the golden rectangle likewise circumscribes the circle's perimeter. The square that is the foundation of the root 2 rectangle is located in one quadrant of a larger square whose four corners coincide with the circle's circumference (right 5.7). Here, too, the circle's diagonal axis defines both the length of the root 2 rectangle and the circle's periphery. The interrelationship among these elemental forms is fascinating and is no doubt a reason for the visual appeal of the golden and root 2 rectangles.

Once established, the golden rectangle can be subdivided into increasingly smaller golden section rectangles that collectively serve as the basis for a perfect spiral (5.8). This is accomplished by first defining a square at one end of a golden rectangle. Interestingly, the "leftover" area is itself a golden rectangle, thus revealing the fact that both a square and another golden rectangle exist inside this ideal shape. This same procedure of subdivision is next applied to the smaller golden rectangle and subsequently to the ever-smaller rectangles that are defined. An associated phenomenon is that a diagonal line drawn between two

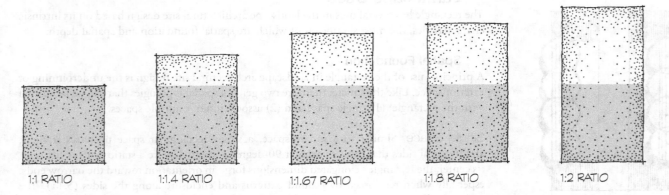

1:1 RATIO 1:1.4 RATIO 1:1.67 RATIO 1:1.8 RATIO 1:2 RATIO

opposite corners of each golden rectangle coincides with one of the common corners of the next smaller square and golden rectangle. All of this provides the basis for a spiral that arcs between the opposite corners of all the subsequently smaller squares within a golden rectangle. An almost mystical affiliation exists among the golden rectangle, square, and spiral.

5.9 Comparison of rectangles with different proportions.

People have an intuitive preference for the golden section rectangle, as indicated in various studies. When shown an array of rectangles with differing proportions, the majority of people chose the golden section rectangle as the most pleasing (Elam 2001, 6–7) (5.9). The proportions of the golden section are also the basis of many natural objects including the human body (Elam 2001, 8–19). Similarly, many renowned human designs in architecture, sculpture, painting, and graphic design, including the façade of the Parthenon in Athens, the Notre Dame Cathedral in Paris, and various furniture designs by Le Corbusier and Mies van der Rohe, are all based on the golden section (Elam 2001, 20–23). Even the design of the contemporary Volkswagen Beetle incorporates these proportions (Elam 2001, 98–99). Thus, the proportions of the golden section rectangle serve as a profound and almost occult foundation for both natural and human creations that are considered visually pleasing.

5.10 Sites and spaces that are golden rectangles have better proportions for design.

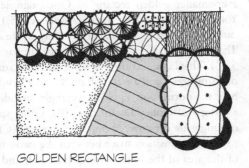

GOLDEN RECTANGLE

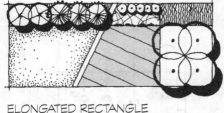

ELONGATED RECTANGLE

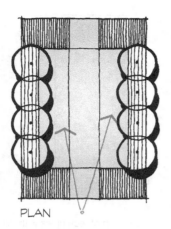

PLAN

5.11 The rectangle's elongated proportions forge an orientation toward its ends.

5.12 The rectangle can be employed as viewing area to look out into the adjoining landscape.

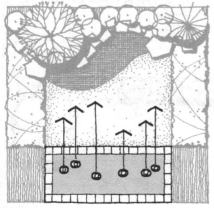

Landscape Uses

The rectangle has several uses in the landscape architectural site design based on its intrinsic characteristics, the most significant of which are spatial foundation and spatial depth.

Spatial Foundation

A principal use of the rectangle in landscape architectural site design is the underpinning of exterior space. Like the square, there are two general spatial typologies that can be fabricated with the rectangle: (1) single space and (2) association of multiple spaces.

Single Space. Similar to a square space, a single rectangular space possesses straight, architectural sides that meet at explicit 90-degree corners. Unlike a static square's focus on its center, the rectangle's elongated dimensions forge an orientation toward the narrow ends, especially when reinforced by ground patterns and enclosure along the sides (5.11). The ends actually garner more attention than the sides. So a single rectangle is appropriate to use as the foundation of architectural-like space where movement and/or visual orientation between the ends is desired.

Another potential use of the rectangle is to support viewing along its length (5.12). While this is opposite the inherent focus toward the ends of the rectangle, its sides nevertheless afford an extended area along which many people can watch activity within or outside the space. Rectangular spaces are well suited to direct attention toward a particular area of the landscape.

Multiple Spaces. The rectangle is also a principal orthogonal building block that can be transformed into an ensemble of many spaces. Like the square, the primary means of metamorphosis are subtraction and addition, although the other means of transformation examined in Chapter 1 can also be applied.

The rectangle is readily subdivided into multiple spaces based on the grid, symmetrical, or asymmetrical organizations. As with the square, the rectangle's internal axes, inherent grid lines of equal division, and diagonals all provide potential lines for partitioning. Another means of subdivision is to start with a golden section rectangle and to proceed to define ever-smaller golden rectangles. One example of this strategy is Greenacre Park in New York City designed by Sasaki Associates (5.13–14). This small vest pocket is a series of carefully crafted spaces that collectively create an urban oasis with plentiful shade and water. The overall shape of the park is very similar to a golden section rectangle ("A" on right 5.13). This large rectangle is sectioned into smaller rectangular spaces and areas for sitting, planting areas, and a waterfall on the north end of the site. Many of these rectangles likewise have the portions of a golden rectangle including the primary sitting area that is covered by a canopy of Honey Locust trees (B). Other spaces and areas with proportions of a golden rectangle are the covered upper sitting area (C) (actually the size of two gold rectangles end to end), a transition space between the two sitting spaces (D), the entrance steps (E), most of the area of the lower sitting space (F), and the center of the waterfall (G). All of these spaces are intuitively appealing because of their proportions.

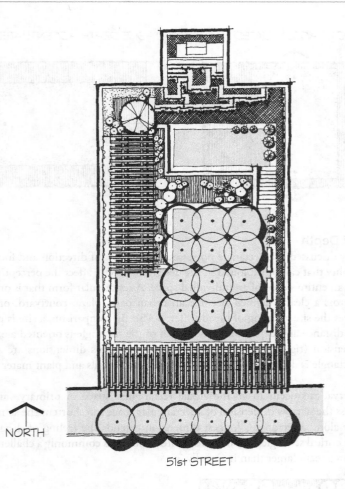

NORTH

51st STREET

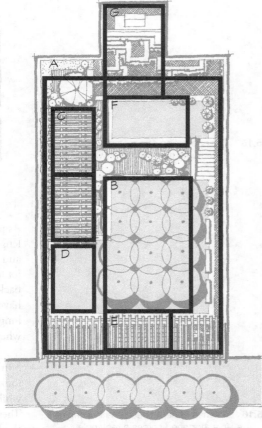

ALL OUTLINED RECTANGLES are GOLDEN
RECTANGLES

5.13   Above: The use of the golden rectangle
as the basis for Greenacre Park, New
York.

5.14   Left: Greenacre Park.

SITE WIDTH ACCENTUATED   SITE DEPTH ACCENTUATED

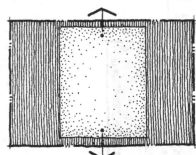
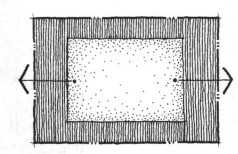

5.15 The orientation of a rectangle can accentuate the breadth or width of a site.

Spatial Depth

As previously discussed, the rectangle possesses a clear sense of direction and focus along its length, a quality that can be exploited in site design to directly affect the perception of depth and focus of an entire site or of an individual space. A rectangular form that is oriented with its length across a clearly defined site like an urban park, plaza, courtyard, or residential backyard gives the site a feeling of breadth (left 5.15). By comparison, a site is perceived to have greater distance and depth when the length of the rectangle is oriented along the site's longest dimension (right 5.15). These perceptions of a site's dimensions are accentuated when the rectangle is defined in the third dimension with walls and plant materials.

Similar observations occur in an individual rectangular space. A primary vantage point looking across the narrow dimension of a rectangular space foreshortens the sense of depth, while a view along a rectangle's longest dimension extends the feeling of distance (5.16). These can be critical strategies in small urban sites where it is commonly a challenge to make the limited area seem larger than it actually is.

5.16 A sense of depth can be enhanced or foreshortened across a rectangle.

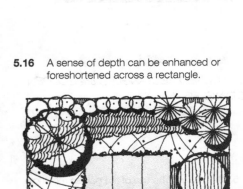
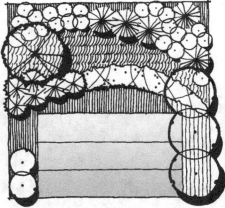

EXTENDS SENSE of DEPTH   FORESHORTENS SENSE of DEPTH

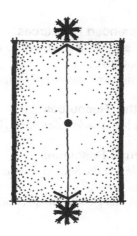

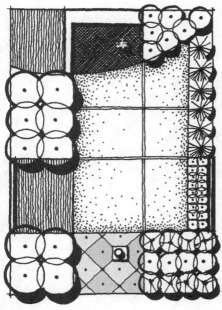

5.17 The ends of the rectangle are appropriately reinforced with visual accents.

Design Guidelines

There are several recommendations for designing with the rectangle as the basis of landscape space as outlined in this section.

Accent

It is vital to take advantage of the inherent concentration on the narrow ends of a rectangular space when viewing along the length. This can be accomplished by placing one or more accent elements on the narrow ends to reinforce the attention that is directed there (5.17). In some settings, the ends can be a framed opening to a view of the landscape beyond. To do otherwise is a missed opportunity that dilutes the rectangle's intrinsic qualities. While the scrutiny on the rectangle's ends is similar to what occurs along a line, a rectangle does not possess the constricted and unwavering focus that is trained on the end of a line, and so is sometimes overlooked.

Material Coordination

The same design guidelines that need to be considered for designing with various landscape elements and materials associated with the square also apply to the rectangle. Structural elements, plant materials, and pavement should all reinforce the inherent orthogonal geometry of the rectangle unless there is a deliberate objective to do otherwise. In the later case, any deviation from a right-angle system should be forceful and obvious so that is doesn't appear to be a mistake.

Topography

Like the square and other primary forms, the ground plane of a single rectangular space should a relatively flat plane to support the perception of its being one volume. If a grade change is necessary across the rectangle, it should be accommodated at its edges or between the rectangular space and an adjoining space.

5.18 The end of a rectangular pool is accented with a sculpture and architectural frame.

Referenced Resources

Ching, Francis D. K. *Architecture: Form, Space, & Order*. Hoboken, NJ: John Wiley & Sons, 2007.

Elam, Kimberly. *Geometry of Design*. New York: Princeton Architectural Press, 2001.

Further Resources

Johnson, Jory. *Modern Landscape Architecture*. New York: Abbeville Press, 2001.

Internet Resources

The Circle and the Square: www.numberharmonics.com/info_archive/golden_proportion.htm

Golden Rectangle and Golden Ratio: www.jimloy.com/geometry/golden.htm

The Grid 6

The line, square, and rectangle can be assembled in a number of ways to forge landscape space. Among these is the grid, one of the principal organizational structures previously discussed in Chapter 1. An orthogonal grid is defined as two or more sets of parallel lines overlaid at right angles to form a matrix of lines, squares and/or rectangles (6.1).

The orthogonal grid has been used as an organizational framework in art during many stylistic periods from the Renaissance through modern explorations of Piet Mondrian, Frank Stella, Sol LeWitt, and others. In architecture, the grid has been a structuring system in numerous buildings throughout history, including works by noted 20th-century architects Frank Lloyd Wright and LeCorbusier. During the 20th century, the grid was a key foundational structure in numerous modern landscape architectural projects by noted designers like James Rose, Thomas Church, Garrett Eckbo, and Dan Kiley. Many contemporary landscape architects like Peter Walker continue to use and explore the grid as an organizational framework for their designs.

6.1 A grid is formed by overlapping two sets of parallel lines perpendicular to each other.

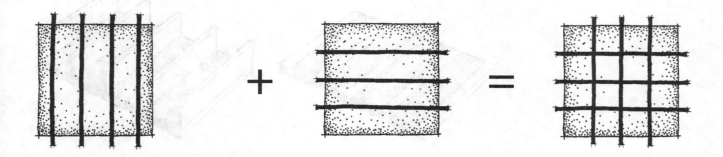

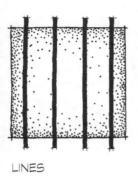  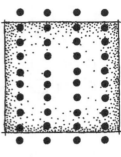

LINES   BANDS   ROWS of ELEMENTS

6.2 A line grid can be formed by parallel lines, bands, or rows of elements.

This chapter investigates the organizational qualities of the orthogonal grid in landscape architectural site design by means of the following chapter sections:

- Grid Typologies
- Grid Variables
- Landscape Uses
- Design Guidelines

Grid Typologies

To effectively design with grids in the landscape, it is first essential to understand the typology of grids including their characteristics and potential uses. As discussed in Chapter 1, there are four fundamental grid types, with a fifth created by a fusion of the others: line grid, mesh grid, modular grid, point grid, and fusion.

6.3 A line grid can be expressed two-dimensionally or three-dimensionally.

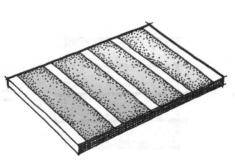 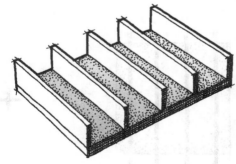

TWO-DIMENSIONAL LINE GRID   THREE-DIMENSIONAL LINE GRID

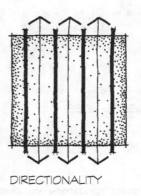

DIRECTIONALITY

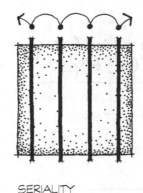

SERIALITY

6.4 A line grid posesses both directionality and seriality.

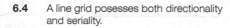

Line Grid

The line grid, or discontinuous line grid, uses the straight line discussed in Chapter 3 to create a field of parallel gestures composed of two- or three-dimensional lines, bands, or rows of independent elements (6.2–3) (Scherr 2001, 34). A succession of lateral pavement bands, ribbons of ground cover, walls, fences, hedges, and/or rows of trees can all establish a line grid. This is very similar to the use of the straight line to create visual rhythm in the landscape although subtly different because the line grid is principally an organizational structure for framing multiple materials and spaces in the landscape, not merely a visual artifice.

One of the distinguishing characteristics of the line grid in comparison to the other grid types is that it possesses both directionality and seriality. A discernible sense of direction

6.5 The regularity of a line grid can harmonize otherwise unrelated design elements.

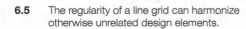

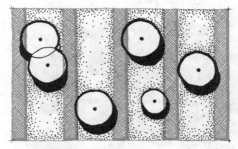

SCATTERED TREES

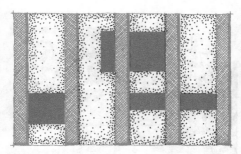

RANDOM PAVED AREAS

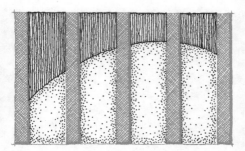

VARIED GROUND PATTERNS

LINE GRID ARMATURE

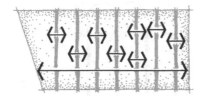

TRANSECT GAPS

PAVED SPACES

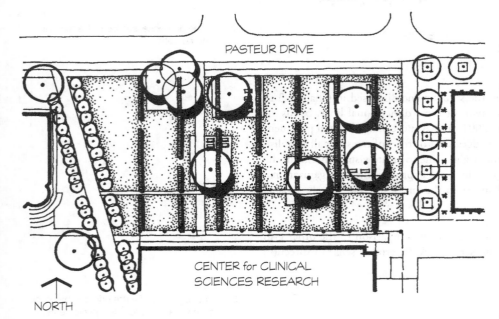

PASTEUR DRIVE

CENTER for CLINICAL
SCIENCES RESEARCH

NORTH

6.6 Above: Organizational components of the Center for Clinical Sciences Research sculpture garden.

6.7 Left: Site plan of the Center for Clinical Sciences Research sculpture garden.

6.8 Center for Clinical Sciences Research sculpture garden.

occurs parallel to the grid lines, establishing visual movement and orientation along their length, a quality that is most compelling when the lines are expressed in the third dimension (left 6.4). Simultaneously, there is serial progression that rhythmically moves from one line to the next across the composition (right 6.4). Seriality is most apparent when the grid lines are seen collectively on the ground or as low three-dimensional elements.

The line grid is an especially suitable system to emphasize a particular direction or orientation on a site and to create a metrical cadence. The line grid is also useful to create an obvious and uninterrupted structure that serves as a visual foil for otherwise disparate elements and their incidental locations within the design (6.5) (also see Site Coordination). One example is the design of the sculpture garden at the Center for Clinical Sciences Research at Stanford University designed by Peter Walker Partners (6.6–8). The garden is formed by series of hedges that extend north-south across a panel of lawn. The regularity of the pattern is interrupted by openings in the hedges, some which accommodate a walk that transects the garden and some that occur erratically throughout the garden. The supremacy of the grid lines fuses randomly placed paved areas, live oaks, and sculpture.

Mesh and Modular Grids

The next two grid typologies, the mesh and modular grids, are discussed together because one can be considered the inverse of the other. The mesh grid, also called a line continuous grid, is established by overlapping two sets of parallel lines perpendicular to each other (top 6.9) (Scherr 2001, 34). By comparison, the modular grid or shape grid is composed of the interstitial areas that are formed between the grid lines and is a matrix of spaces (6.10) (Scherr 2001, 34). A mesh grid invariably forms a modular grid though a modular grid does not necessarily establish a mesh grid. This dichotomy can be readily seen when the selected grid components are projected into the third dimension (6.11). The extrusion of the lines creates a three-dimensional mesh grid, while the extension of the spaces creates a modular grid.

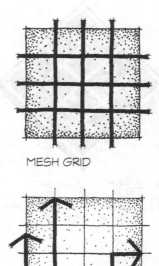

MESH GRID

DISTRIBUTION SYSTEM

6.9 Above: The mesh grid is a distribution network offering options of movement.

6.10 Below: The modular grid is a matrix of areas that hold selected content.

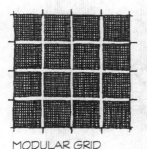

MODULAR GRID

CONTENT PATTERN

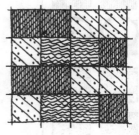

CONTENT PATTERN

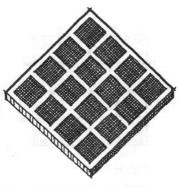

2D MESH/MODULAR GRID

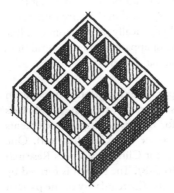

3D MESH GRID

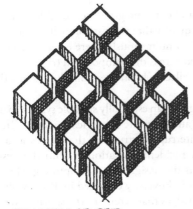

3D MODULAR GRID

6.11 Above: Comparison between the mesh grid and modular grids.

A mesh grid is a distribution system that allows movement from one point to all destinations in the network (bottom 6.9). In the landscape, a mesh grid is most typically employed for the dispersal of utilities, vehicles, pedestrians, and so on. As a circulation network, the mesh grid establishes controlled movement by limiting flow to two directions, repeatedly turning corners at ninety degrees, and never being allowed to wander diagonally or in an erratic pattern. However, a mesh grid does provide alternative routes of movement between two points. A mesh grid can be created in the landscape by streets, paths, or pavement patterns on the ground plane while hedges, walls, fences, and so on can form a mesh grid in the third dimension (left 6.12).

A modular grid is principally an organization of squares or rectangles (6.11). In essence, the modular areas are repositories that may be occupied by content that is two-dimensional or three-dimensional, uniform or dissimilar. Whatever occurs inside each module, the overall grid is unified by a rhythmic repetition of the modules across the field. Circulation through a modular grid proceeds directly from one module to the next and potentially permits

6.12 Designs based on the mesh grid and modular grid.

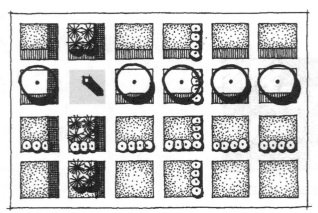

MESH GRID

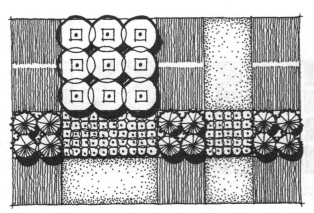

MODULAR GRID

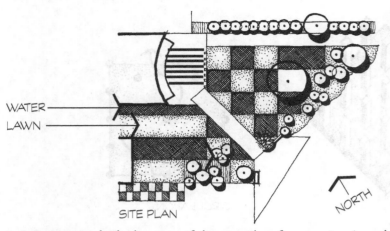

WATER
LAWN

SITE PLAN

NORTH

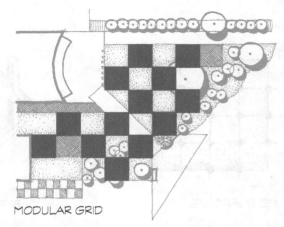

MODULAR GRID

movement in multiple directions if the ground surface permits. A modular grid can be formed in the landscape by blocks of tree masses, lawn, ground cover, pavement, or water that fill and define the underlying grid structure (right 6.12).

6.13 NTT Research and Development Center garden.

One example of a modular grid is the garden adjoining the NTT Research and Development Center designed by Yoji Sasaki in Musashino City, Tokyo, Japan (6.13). A modular grid defined by water and lawn creates a ground pattern that is a metaphor of the Japanese rice field (NTT Musashino Research and Development Center 2002, 63). Furthermore, the grid visually coordinates numerous cherry trees and an array of different paved areas. The rigidity of grid is deliberately permitted to vary to adjust to different site conditions and program needs. The result suggests an underlying continuous water surface upon which square panels of lawn visually hover. It should be noted that the appearance of a checkerboard modular grid like this varies for a person standing on the ground. Viewed straight on (left 6.14), the grid appears to be orthogonal as it does in plan view. However, the grid is seen to be more a pattern of diamonds arranged in rows when looked at from an angle (right 6.14).

6.14 Variations in the perception of a modular grid from different vantage points.

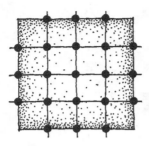

FIELD of POINTS

6.15 Characteristics of the point grid.

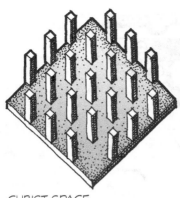

CUBIST SPACE

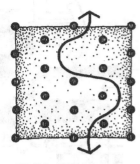

CIRCULATION

Point Grid

The fourth fundamental grid is formed by a pattern of separate points that coincide with the intersection of lines in the mesh grid (left 6.15). The points are conventionally expressed by placing an element at each junction, forming a uniform field of evenly spaced, independent members. Each element exclaims the intersection of the grid lines though its individual significance is tempered when it is seen among other corresponding elements. The repetitive spacing and alignment of elements as well as the straight voids between them infer grid lines without the lines being explicitly defined. When extruded into the third dimension, the points create cubist space with the space-defining elements being located within, not to the exterior edge of the composition (middle 6.15) (Condon 1988). Rather than being an open void, the space is rhythmically punctuated by the three-dimensional elements extending into the space. Physical and visual movement through a point grid can parallel the rows of elements or occur freely in any direction through the field (right 6.15). A point grid can be generated in the landscape by the repetitive placement of any element like sculpture, columns, water features, or trees as in a grove or bosque (6.16–17).

6.16 Above: Field of Corn in Dublin, Ohio, is an example of the point grid.

6.17 Right: Example of a design based on the point grid.

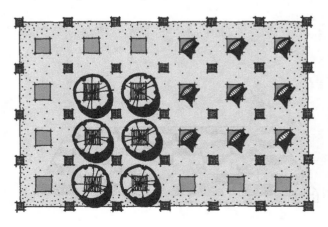

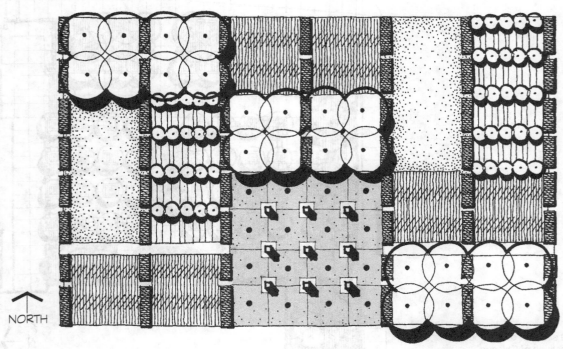

6.18 A design based on a fusion of the four basic grid types.

Fusion

In addition to being employed individually, the four basic grid types frequently are combined to form a more complex grid structure with each grid genre functioning in concert with the others. Typically, one grid type is used to establish the overall framework within which the other types are placed in a supporting role. In Figure 6.18, a line grid creates the overall organization with a serial arrangement of north-south hedges. An east-west line grid is implied by measured spaces in the hedges and the linear alignment of the trees and shrub masses. The placement of the trees, shrub masses, lawn, and different ground cover areas is based on a module grid while a point grid is used to structure the central paved area. Another example of a fused system of grids is Dan Kiley's original design of the South Garden at the Art Institute of Chicago (6.19). Here a point grid defined by symmetrical placed bosques of Hawthorns forms the primary structure of the composition (left 6.20). The point grid in turn delineates both mesh and modular grids that are the organizational basis for the remainder of the garden (middle and right 6.20).

SOUTH MICHIGAN AVENUE

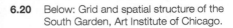

MORTON WING

NORTH →

6.19 Right: Original site plan of the South Garden, Art Institute of Chicago.

6.20 Below: Grid and spatial structure of the South Garden, Art Institute of Chicago.

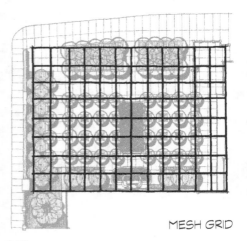

MESH GRID

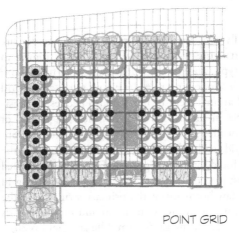

POINT GRID

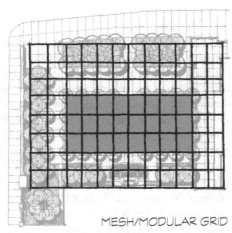

MESH/MODULAR GRID

Grid Variables

Each of the four fundamental orthogonal grid types provides the designer with a distinct structure in the landscape. As defined, these elemental typologies are uniform grids with consistent spacing and a homogeneous treatment of the lines, intersection points, and interior modules. This is appropriate where a uniform treatment of the landscape is desired but not in circumstances where variation is sought. To deviate from the basic grids' homogeneity, a series of variables can be modified. These are spacing, compositional makeup, orientation, and complexity.

Spacing

The spacing of the lines in the four primary orthogonal grid types is predictability the same. To provide visual interest and greater design flexibility, the spacing of grid lines can be altered along one or both dimensions to create a multiform grid with squares and/or rectangles of varying sizes (6.21). This modification is most suitable for the line, mesh, and modular grids where the grid lines and/or modules are most evident. A multiform grid provides the foundation for a more varied spatial organization giving opportunity for a more heterogeneous landscape and a more flexible adaptation to site conditions.

Compositional Makeup

Another variable is the size, shape, material, color, and so on of the grid lines, modules, and/or intersection points. For example, the width and/or content of the grid lines can fluctuate on a repeating pattern or simply be accomplished randomly to suggest hierarchy, rhythm, or visual intrigue (left 6.22). The internal composition of the spaces in a modular grid and the elements used to define the intersection points in a point grid can likewise be varied (middle and right 6.22). Collectively, these variables yield a wide range of design possibilities (6.23).

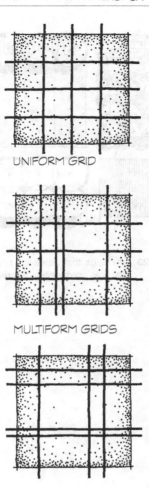

UNIFORM GRID

MULTIFORM GRIDS

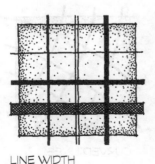

LINE WIDTH

MODULE CONTENT

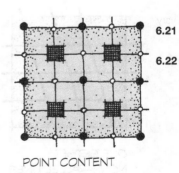

POINT CONTENT

6.21 Above: Variation in the spacing of the grid lines.

6.22 Left: Variation in the compositional makeup.

117

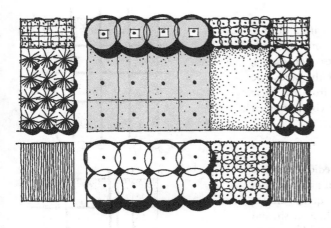

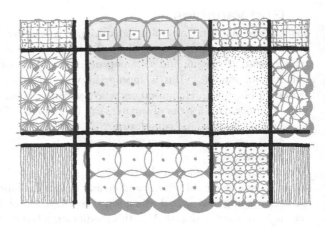

6.23 A design that varies line spacing and module composition to create interest.

Orientation

A third variable is the orientation of the grid lines in relation to each other. The typical parallel and perpendicular affiliation among the grid lines can be changed to establish non-orthogonal lines and internal parallelograms (left and middle 6.24). This configuration is appropriate in a design setting where the objective is to change the orientation of a composition or to deviate from the strict geometry of right angles. A nonorthogonal grid is likewise suitable where some existing site elements are not parallel or at right angles to other components. Though right angle relationships are absent, the nonorthogonal grid should nevertheless retain the essence of a typical grid with its overall character, allocation of spaces and uses, plant massing, circulation, and so on (6.25). One other prospect for the nonorthogonal grid is to have one or both sets of grid lines defined with curved lines to forge a warped grid (right 6.24). This grid typology is plastic and fluid with a sense of movement. It is suitable in pastoral settings, to acclimate the grid to undulating topography, or to provide a transition from a typical orthogonal grid to a less defined landscape pattern.

6.24 The orientation of the grid lines may vary to create nonorthogonal grids.

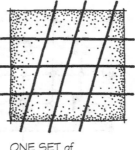

ONE SET of
NONPARALLEL LINES

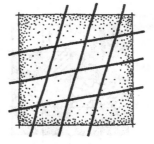

TWO SETS of
NONPARALLEL LINES

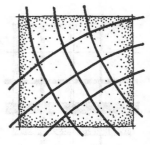

CURVED LINES

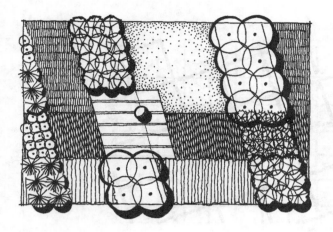

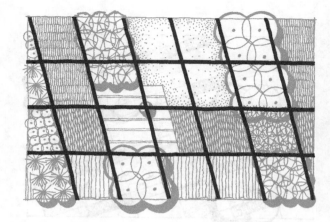

6.25 A design based on grid lines with different orientations.

Complexity

The number of sets of grid lines in a composition is another variable. The four elemental grid types are typically composed of two sets of parallel lines placed 90 degrees to each other. Overlaying additional sets of grids on top of the original ones creates a composite of multiple grids. One technique for doing this is to offset different grids from each other (left 6.26). This configuration retains the fundamental qualities of a conventional grid, yet provides more complexity and depth in the patterning. It can be executed in the landscape by having one set of grid lines expressed by a selected material while the second set of grid lines is defined by a different material. Still another variation is to rotate one set of grid lines while overlaying it on top of a second set of grid lines (middle and right 6.26). The composite tapestry formed by this grid provides the underpinning for an intricate and highly elaborate landscape of different spaces and materials (6.27). A case in point is the parterre garden adjoining the Kempinski Hotel at the Munich Airport, Germany, designed by Peter Walker and Partners (6.28).

6.26 Composite grids composed of one or more sets of grid lines provide a more complex design structure.

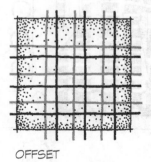

OFFSET

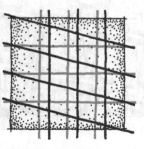

PARTIAL ROTATION

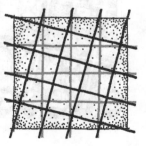

FULL ROTATION

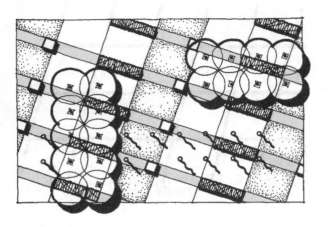
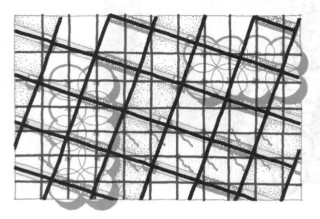

6.27 Above: A design based on composite grid lines.

6.28 Right: Site plan for parterre garden at Kempinski Hotel.

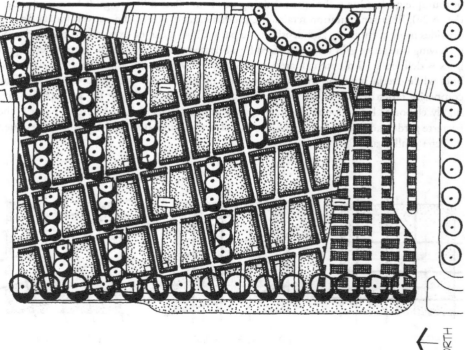

NORTH

Landscape Uses

The grid is an extremely versatile structuring system in site design and can be engaged to inform many design decisions from overall site configuration to the detail selection and composition of materials. Specific uses of the grid in site design include: spatial foundation, site coordination, detail patterning, and urban fit.

Spatial Foundation

The grid, one of the principal organizational structures discussed in Chapter 1, can be used as an underlying armature to shape a single space or multiple spaces in the landscape. While retaining many of the characteristics of other orthogonal spaces, the grid provides the foundation for an array of spatial types with many diverse dispositions and qualities.

Single Space. The orthogonal grid can be employed as the underlying armature for a single, discrete space that is situated by itself or among other spaces in the landscape. A single space based on the grid shares many spatial qualities with the square and rectangle discussed in the previous two chapters (Figures 4.15–17). That is, an individual space can be volumetric or cubist, enclosed or open, simple or complex, or have vertical edges located at varying distances from the floor of the space. In many instances, a lone space based on an orthogonal grid may appear no different from one based on the square or rectangle.

However, there is one notable quality that differentiates an orthogonal grid space from a square or rectangular space: the potential for flexibility. This trait is especially evident along the edge of a space where transformation can add and/or subtract grid modules to create a spatial perimeter with protrusions and indentations (6.29). This gives the grid space the possibility of being more complex and engaging than can be achieved with a simple square or rectangle. The grid's pliable edge also permits it to adjust to varied site conditions. It should be noted a grid space does not have to possess this quality, but it can if needed.

6.29 A grid-based space has the potential for a flexible edge.

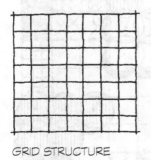

GRID STRUCTURE

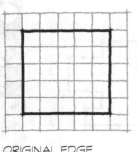

ORIGINAL EDGE

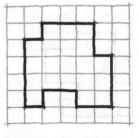

SUBTRACTED EDGE

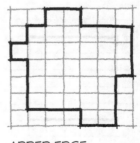

ADDED EDGE

Another distinguishing aspect of a single space based on an underlying grid is that all the design elements on the ground plane, vertical planes, and overhead plane are placed on or aligned with the grid structure (see Site Coordination). The design elements are connected to the grid so that an inherent compositional order is established even when the grid is not explicitly expressed.

Finally, an orthogonal grid permits divergent spatial persona to be forged. On one hand, a grid-based space can be a restrained, disciplined composition in which the location of the design elements is highly regulated and often repeated via seriality (6.7, 6.28, top 6.30). This method in employing the grid is left-brained with logical reasoning prevailing. On the other hand, the grid can be used to create outdoor space that expresses spontaneity (bottom 6.30). Design elements are freely intermixed, overlapped, and located without any regularity while still being guided by the grid. This second approach is a right-brained process using impromptu decisions and creativity.

6.30   A grid is the foundation for many types of spaces.

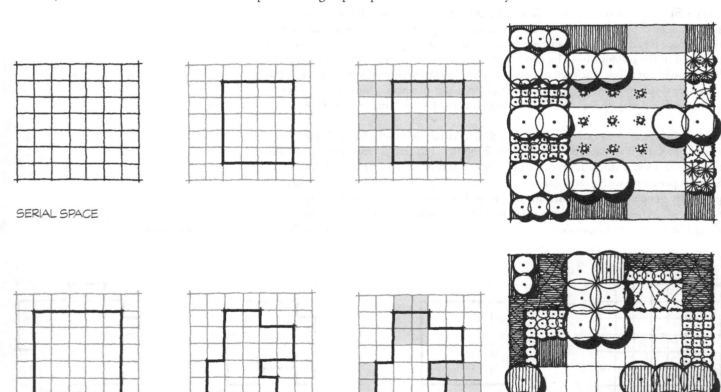

SERIAL SPACE

ASYMMETRICAL SPACE

122

Multiple Spaces. The orthogonal grid is likewise a flexible structure for coordinating multiple associated spaces in the landscape. In addition to being an armature, the underlying grid provides a systemized approach to design so that different spaces and elements are all coordinated to fit with one another. Despite potential variations of spatial size, enclosure, material makeup, and so forth, multiple spaces are fused by the presence of a consistent module throughout a site.

One example of using the grid as an integrating system for an ensemble of spaces and uses is a residential garden in South Orange, New Jersey, designed by James Rose in the 1940s (6.31). Rose advocated the concept of "modular gardens" as a means of organizing residential gardens and as a method to create an efficient system of standardized design components that could be used in any garden setting" (Rose 1958, 17). The basis of Rose's modular gardens was a three-foot square that defined all pavement areas, lawn panels, planting beds, tree locations, and site structures (Rose 1958, 17).

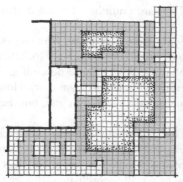

PAVEMENT & LAWN

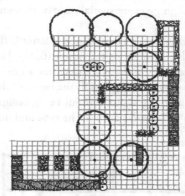

PLANT MATERIALS

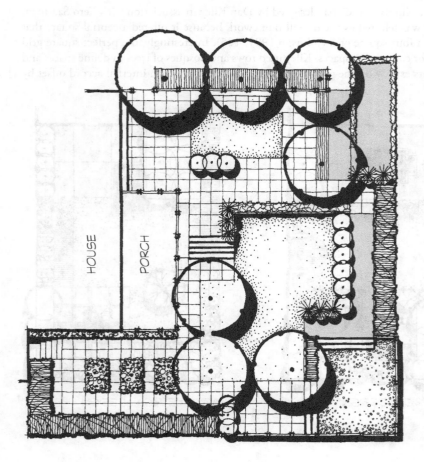

HOUSE

PORCH

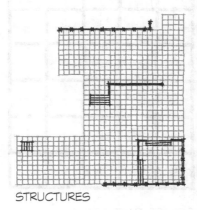

STRUCTURES

6.31 South Orange garden based on a three-foot grid.

There are a number of variables that affect how the grid structures multiple spaces as outlined in the following paragraphs.

Symmetry/Asymmetry. While providing a framework for assembling multiple spaces in the landscape, the orthogonal grid is augmented by by symmetry or asymmetry (6.32). Spaces placed within a grid can be symmetrically organized around axes or they can be located by means of an intuitive balance depending on the circumstances of the site and design intent. Thus, a grid of connected spaces always possesses either symmetry or asymmetry. However, the reverse is not always so. Both the orthogonal symmetrical and asymmetrical organizations can and often do employ a grid, but they do not need to in order to orchestrate multiple landscape spaces (see Chapters 7 and 8).

Grid Expression. Another variable in designing multiple spaces within an orthogonal grid is the degree to which the structuring grid is expressed. One option is for the underlying grid to be explicitly manifested by articulating its presence with spatial and material edges, pavement patterns, and so on. This creates a clear sense of unity within the design and permits contrasting spatial qualities and materials to be visually coordinated (also see Site Coordination). By contrast, the grid can be implicitly expressed by being partially or totally hidden within the design layout. This is appropriate where the intent is to use the grid as a unifying foundation but without the necessity of aligning every spatial edge or element precisely with it.

One iconic example of the latter is the Miller Residence in Columbus, Indiana, designed by Dan Kiley in association with Eero Saarinen, the architect of the house (6.33). Here, a nine-square grid was selected as the overall framework because it offered a central square that could be used as a space, not an object, as is the case with a four-square grid (Johnson 1991, 125). Interestingly, the perfect square grid was transformed to fit the needs of the program and desire for contrasting spaces. Kiley used rows and bosques of trees to define spaces and their edges, but without being obligated to align all elements exactly on the grid lines. Consequently, there is an internal accord offset by a notable variance in the type and quality of spaces.

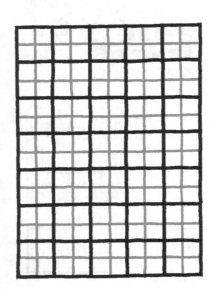

STRUCTURING GRID

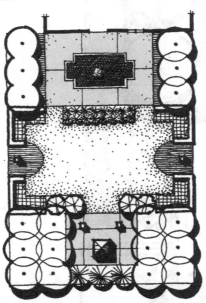

SYMMETRICAL DESIGN

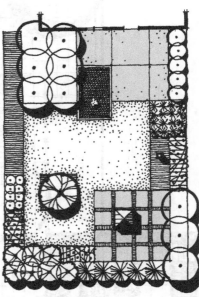

ASYMMETRICAL DESIGN

6.32 A grid may result in either a symmetrical or asymmetrical structure.

6.33 The Miller Residence.

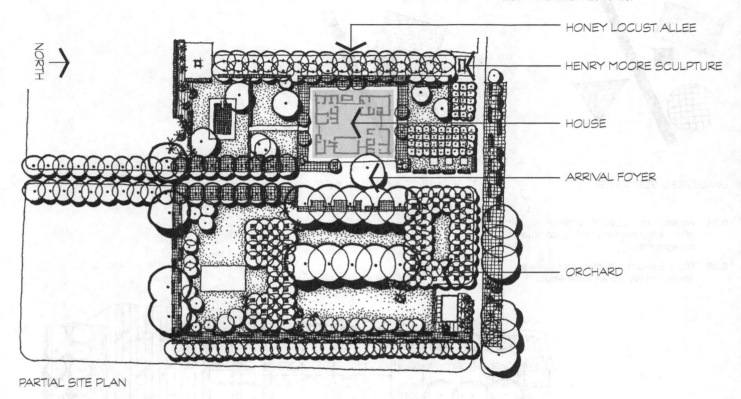

NORTH →

HONEY LOCUST ALLEE

HENRY MOORE SCULPTURE

HOUSE

ARRIVAL FOYER

ORCHARD

PARTIAL SITE PLAN

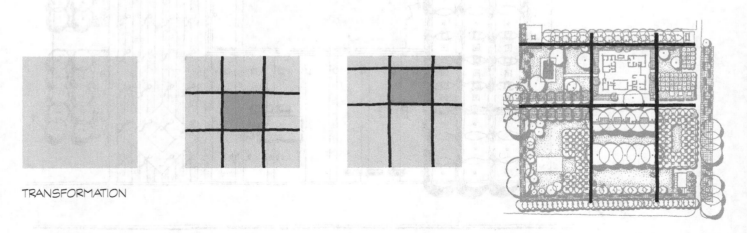

TRANSFORMATION

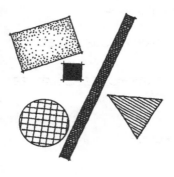

UNRELATED ELEMENTS

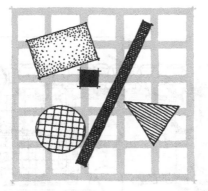

ELEMENTS UNIFIED BY GRID

6.34 Above: A grid can unify a group
of unrelated elements with its common
background.

6.35 Right: Site plan completed for Conway
Street and Welcome Center Plaza.

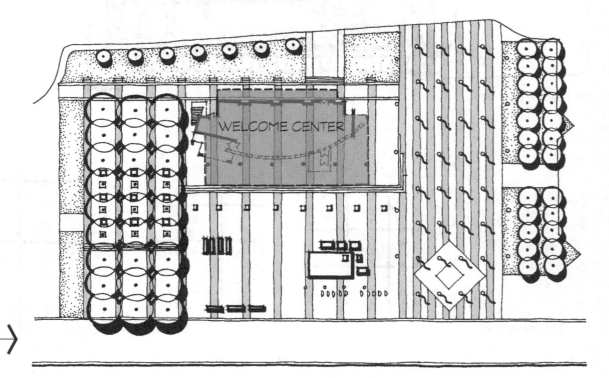

WELCOME CENTER

NORTH →

Site Coordination

The grid can be employed in a number of ways to coordinate and unify assorted spaces and elements on a site. The grid's measured and repetitive structure provides a mutual pattern for visually integrating all elements placed within its field. Site coordination with a grid can be accomplished by means of common ground, prevalent framework, or visual linkage.

Common Ground. The four fundamental grid types can be utilized individually or in combination with each other to establish a distinct ground plane pattern to unify a site design. A clearly articulated grid provides a dominant order that diminishes potential differences of shape, size, and orientation among individual objects in its field (6.34). The more idiosyncratic a grid is on the ground plane, the more effectively it furnishes a unifying field. A grid typically functions as a common ground when expressed in a pavement pattern although other ground materials also work. A grid pavement pattern can be applied to coordinate disparate existing elements or to create a unifying organizational structure for proposed trees, walls, lampposts, flagpoles, drainage basins, and so on within a site plan.

One example is the proposed site plan completed by Martha Schwartz, Inc. in a design competition for the Conway Street and Welcome Center Plaza in Baltimore's Inner Harbor (6.35). Here, the east/west line grid in the pavement pattern integrates numerous spaces and elements across the site. It even extends into the Welcome Center's interior as a means of visually merging it with the surrounding urban plaza. A similar instance also designed by Martha Schwartz, Inc. is the pavement pattern in the Federal Courthouse Plaza in Minneapolis, Minnesota (6.36). Here too, a line grid is employed to visually integrate a series of separate mounds and assorted site furniture. The grid as a common ground is similarly effective for synchronizing oddly shaped (left 6.37) or fragmented sites by overlaying a pavement pattern across the entire site (right 6.37).

6.36 Above: Federal Court House Plaza.

6.37 Common pavement pattern based on a grid unifies oddly shaped or fragmented sites.

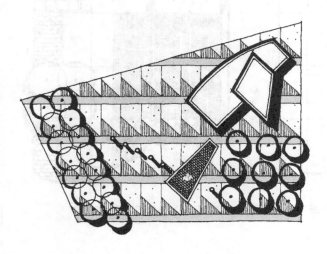

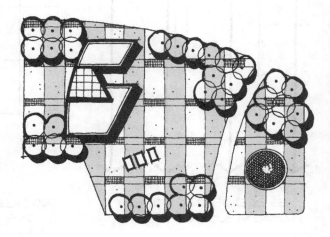

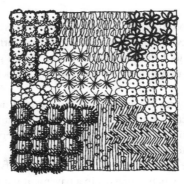

UNRELATED PLANTS

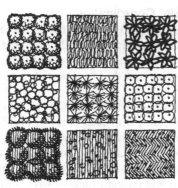

PLANTS UNIFIED BY GRID

6.38 Right: A prevalent grid framework unifies otherwise unrelated plant materials.

6.39 Below: The use of the grid to visually coordinate a site and adjoining building.

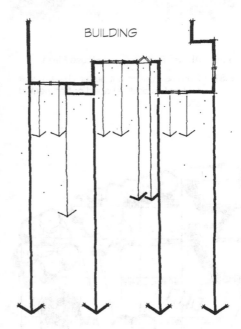

LINES EXTENDED INTO SITE *from* PROMINENT BUILDING FEATURES

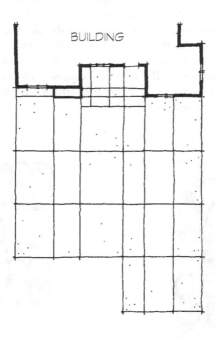

GRID BASED ON ADJOINING BUILDING

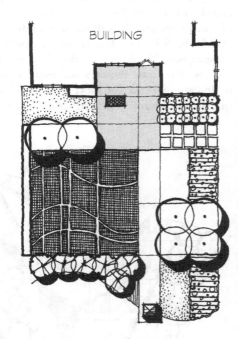

SITE PLAN BASED ON GRID

Prevalent Framework. Another strategy for integrating dissimilar compositional elements is to place them within a grid framework. Again, the absolute consistent size and shape of the grid's modules diminishes disparities that exist in size, shape, color, and texture of the material within the modular boundaries. The regularity of the modules functions like a uniform worn by diverse individuals within the military, law enforcement, or company. This technique is useful for unifying a broad range of plant materials within a garden, especially where the desire is to display the plants as in a botanical garden. The diversity of the plant materials is minimized by the prevalent framework of the structuring grid (6.38).

Visual Linkage. The grid can be applied to visually link a building to an adjoining landscape. The grid is a means for creating a site design that directly relates to and is aligned with key building features so that the building and resulting landscape appear to be one interdependent statement. To realize this, the first step is to extend lines out away from the building into the site (left 6.39). The most crucial lines are related to building corners or other edges where the building massing projects or recedes. The next most important lines are those that relate to door edges or material changes on the building façade that extend to the ground. Finally, the least critical lines are those aligned with window edges or other elements on the building façade that do not touch the ground. Collectively, these lines form a series of parallel lines that extend across the site (middle 6.39). The second set of lines that complete the grid are those parallel to the building facade. These are more arbitrary in their determination and can be based on any logical dimension or one defined by the projection or recession from the building façade. In 6.39, the spacing of the grid lines parallel to the building is based on the depth of the building projection on the east side of the façade. Once the grid is created, the site design can be structured in numerous ways as previously discussed. It should be kept in mind that the grid is most significant as a coordinating device near the building and becomes progressively less meaningful farther away from the building. Consequently, one might expect to see the grid most revealed next to the building and least acknowledged as distance increases away from the building (right 6.39).

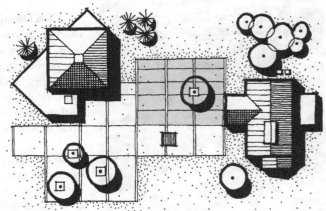

6.40 A grid used to integrate otherwise separate site elements.

UNRELATED SITE ELEMENTS

SITE ELEMENTS INTEGRATED by GRID

129

LEFT: UNRELATED GROUND AREAS

RIGHT: GROUND AREAS RELATED by GRID

6.41 Above: The use of a grid to coordinate adjoining areas of varied ground materials.

6.42 Below: Examples of site details conforming to a site grid.

A similar method is to use a grid to compositionally unite detached buildings or other elements in the landscape by extending lines outward from each building to form an interconnected mesh of coordinating lines (6.40). Again, the grid lines function best when they project into the adjoining landscape from prominent features of each building like corners or center lines. Consequently, a grid employed for visual linkage will frequently be a random one that plainly coincides with the buildings or site elements being connected.

A third technique for employing the grid for site coordination is to integrate adjoining materials on the ground plane. Different ground materials juxtapose one another throughout the landscape but frequently with no attempt to synchronize them other than by corresponding color and/or texture (left 6.41). A grid that extends among two or more ground materials unifies them by providing a common structure and alignment of the extended lines (right 6.41).

Site Detail

In addition to being a means for fashioning the overall layout of a landscape design, the grid is additionally a useful mechanism for locating and coordinating a range of site elements like planters, pools, walls, overhead structures, benches, flag poles, bollards, catch basins, and so on. Similarly, the grid can also be used to compose material patterns in pavement, walls, fences, benches, and overhead structures. The use of a grid in this manner is most easily applied and seen with a grid pavement pattern which serves as a background surface upon or next to which various site elements are aligned (6.42–43).

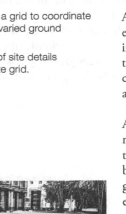

Decisions about shape, size, and location of detail elements are all made within the context of the site grid, a task that takes a great deal of forethought and planning throughout the entire design process from conceptual design to construction documents. It also requires close coordination with a design's infrastructure including grading, placement of catch basins, location of pipes and wires, location of lights, and so on. This typically involves communication among numerous people and trades. When successful, the application of the grid at all scales of design creates a landscape with an unmistakable sense of congruity.

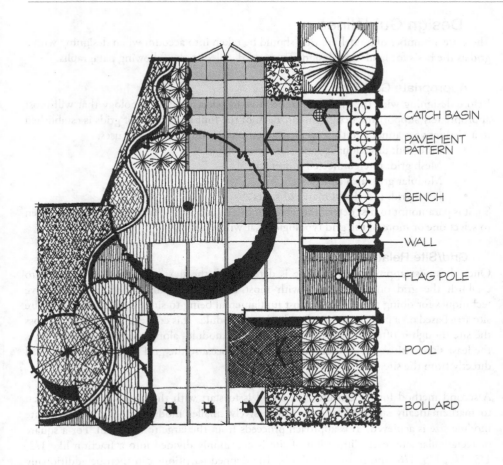

CATCH BASIN

PAVEMENT PATTERN

BENCH

WALL

FLAG POLE

POOL

BOLLARD

6.43 Left: The grid should affect location and size of site details and elements.

6.44 Below: The grid is in accord with the urban landscape and in contrast to a naturalistic one.

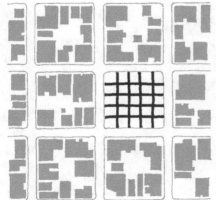

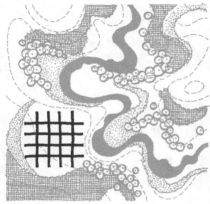

Urban Fit

The grid is one of the most compatible organizational systems for site design in urban areas given the prevalence of grid street patterns and property configurations in most American cities and villages (top 6.44). Plazas, vest-pocket parks, corporate forecourts, enclosed courtyards, confined residential spaces, and so on in urban settings can all be designed with a grid framework to compatibly fit within their context (6.7, 6.20, and 6.35). A grid-based site design settles into the urban fabric and is a continuation of the surrounding two- and three-dimensional forms.

By contrast, a site design with a grid configuration contrasts the undeveloped rural landscape (bottom 6.44). Here, the grid provides a noticeable divergence that clearly distinguishes a design from its surroundings. Like most orthogonal designs, the grid represents human regimentation that contradicts nature's perceived randomness. This is not necessarily a detriment particularly if the character of the design is clearly understood and purposely intended to be a singular statement in its setting.

Design Guidelines

There are a number of guidelines that should be taken into account when designing with a grid as the basis for landscape design. These are detailed in the following paragraphs.

Appropriate Grid Type

Before designing with the grid, it is imperative to select the grid typology that will most appropriately support the design intent. Each of the four basic types of grids is established in a distinctive manner and thus is suited to emphasize different design uses:

- Line grid: directionality and serial progression
- Mesh grid: interconnected movement
- Modular grid: area and content
- Point grid: individual marks or spots

So, it is paramount to first determine which of these qualities is desired in a design and then to select one or more of the grid typologies that will attain it.

Grid/Site Relationship

Once the most appropriate grid type is determined, the next step is to explore how to establish the grid on the site. As with most design procedures, there are alternative techniques for doing this with the most fundamental being to simply subdivide the entire site area based on a predetermined and fixed grid module. This creates a uniform grid across the site though it often results in only partial grid modules along some site edges. This is the least site-sensitive method among the options because the grid module is not derived directly from the site.

A second method for establishing a site grid is to start with the total site area and then to mathematically subdivide it into progressively smaller modules until an appropriate module size is achieved. This approach proceeds from the large to the small. For a square or rectangular site, each dimension of site is commonly divided into a fraction like 1/2, 1/3, 1/4, 1/5, 1/6, and so on (left 6.45). The defined partitions can then be additionally subdivided as desired. The advantage of establishing the grid in this manner is that the grid always fits the site with no leftover area though the grid modules may not be square.

A third method for establishing a site grid modules performs in an opposite manner. Rather than starting with the overall site area, this method is based on the size of a relatively small design element like a paving unit, bench, tree grate, and so on. This module size is then multiplied and expanded outward until the entire site is filled (middle 6.45). The advantage of this approach is that individual design elements are assured to fit the grid structure. Further, this technique tends to create a grid module that has a comfortable human scale because it begins with an element that is already proportioned to the human body.

The last technique for devising the site grid is to base it on the edges of a structure that adjoins the site (6.39, right 6.45). As previously discussed, this process is intended to create a visual continuum between the site and associated building. In doing so, this technique is likely to result in a flexible grid module that varies to correlate to the nearby structure.

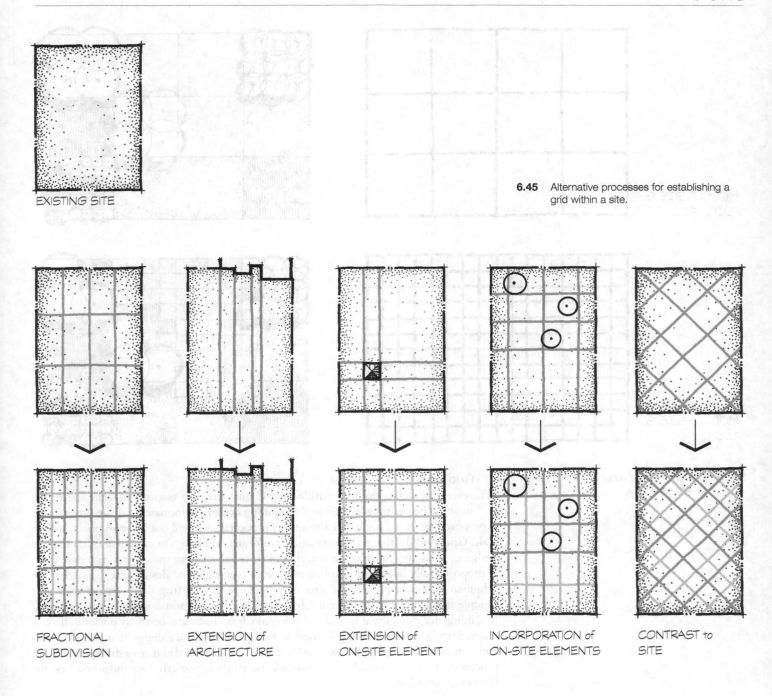

EXISTING SITE

6.45 Alternative processes for establishing a grid within a site.

FRACTIONAL
SUBDIVISION

EXTENSION of
ARCHITECTURE

EXTENSION of
ON-SITE ELEMENT

INCORPORATION of
ON-SITE ELEMENTS

CONTRAST to
SITE

133

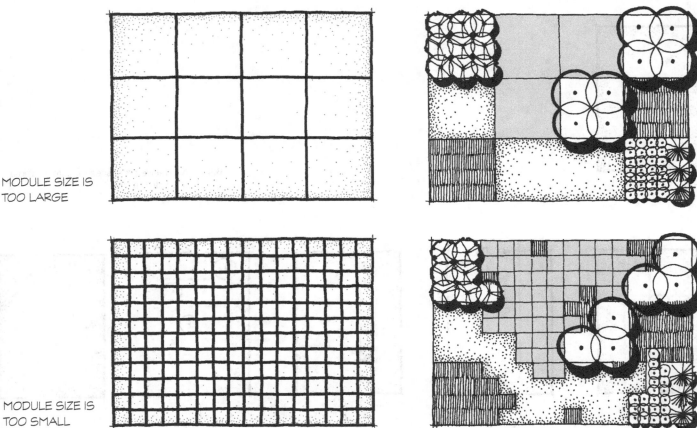

MODULE SIZE IS
TOO LARGE

MODULE SIZE IS
TOO SMALL

6.46 The grid module should not be too large or too small.

Grid Size

Whatever approach is taken to position a grid on a site, it is essential that the size of the grid modules be carefully studied so the resulting design appropriately fits the site context, is proportional to the size of the site and its proposed uses, and has an appropriate human scale. Grid modules that are too expansive create an underlying structure that offers too few design options and provides inadequate guidance for locating spatial and material edges. A proportionally large grid is apt to result in a coarse-grained design and spaces that are inhuman in scale especially for sites over one acre in area (top 6.46). However, a grid module that is notably undersized offers too many options and is likely to be perplexing in guiding decisions about spatial and material edges. There are too many possible choices. Consequently, an undersized grid module is likely to produce a design that is fragmented and unnecessary complex (bottom 6.46). It may take some trial and error during the design process to determine a module size that is between these two extremes and works best for the design situation.

SPATIAL DIAGRAM

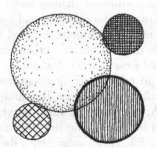

GRID FITS SPATIAL AREAS

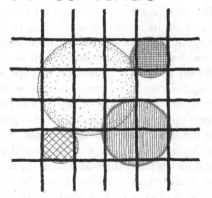

SUBDIVISION of SMALL SPACES

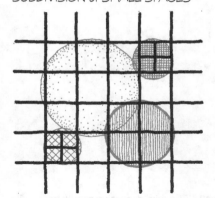

A grid's module size should also relate to the desired dimensions of a design's constituent spaces and elements. Ideally, the module size should be gauged to fit the area of each space and element without forcing it to unnecessarily expand or contract. When done correctly, there is an interdependent affiliation between program elements and grid modules where each corresponds to the other (6.47). It should be kept in mind that one of the benefits of working with a grid is that its module size can easily be added to or subdivided, thus making it potentially adaptable to varied area needs (right 6.47).

6.47 The grid module size and area of program spaces should be compatible.

Grid Orientation

A grid's orientation on a site is another consideration. On orthogonal sites, the default inclination is parallel to the sides of the site though it may be desirable in some instances to orient the grid otherwise to emphasize a direction toward a significant off-site point or trajectory (left 6.48). For non-orthogonal sites, a grid's orientation is less apparent and should be aligned to correspond to a noteworthy on-site or off-site feature such as a building, adjoining road, significant point of entry, and so on (middle and right 6.48).

6.48 The grid may be oriented to align with selected on and off-site elements.

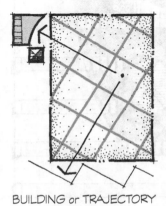

BUILDING or TRAJECTORY

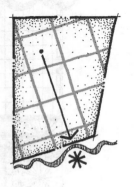

NOTABLE VIEW

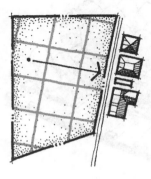

SIGNIFICANT EDGE

Third Dimension

The use of the grid to structure the landscape is often accomplished on a level base plane, especially in contemporary design, to emphasize compositional flatness and repetitive patterns. The preeminence of two-dimensional pattern over three-dimensional expression provides visual restraint and accord as evidenced in numerous projects designed by Peter Walker and others. While this concept works well in many public and urban settings, it frequently creates an open landscape without a marked sense of space. It should be kept in mind that the grid can be exploited as effectively as any other structuring system to create space and engaging landscapes that engender exploration and discovery. The consideration of the third dimension should begin by exploring the ground plane. Like everything else with the grid, variations in the ground plane should be done within the grid framework and are typically expressed as relatively level terraces of different elevation giving the ground an architectonic character. Steps and retaining walls are integral elements of the third dimension within a grid system (6.49). Plant materials, freestanding walls, structures, and so on should complement the ground plane and add to the spatial variety.

6.49 The third dimesnion should be coordinated with the grid.

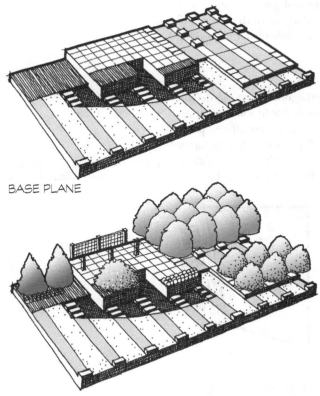

BASE PLANE

PLANTING & STRUCTURES

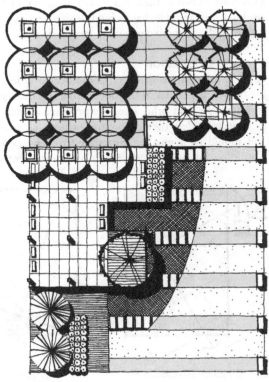

SITE PLAN

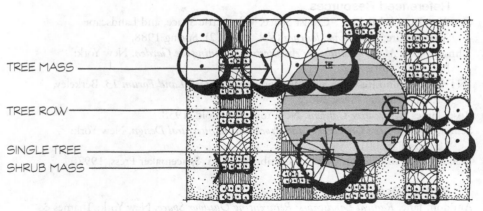

TREE MASS
TREE ROW
SINGLE TREE
SHRUB MASS

6.50 Left: Planting within in a grid should be in masses and rows.

6.51 Below: Trees may be in continuous grid masses or fragmented masses.

6.52 Below Left: Herbaceous plant materials may be in drifts if contained within a grid module.

Material Coordination

Woody plant materials, like all other elements, should conform to and reinforce the grid structure by being organized in rows and orthogonal blocks that are aligned with the underlying grid (6.50). Woody plants in sweeping drifts or "naturalistic" groupings are inappropriate though this does not mean sound environmental practices should be ignored. To the contrary, a carefully planned arrangement of mixed species can provide necessary diversity while maintaining the desired grid structure. In addition to being in solid masses or groves, trees may also be organized in a slightly more fragmented manner by editing out selected trees from a solid mass (6.51). This establishes an open structure allowing increased light from the sky into a space. Single trees can likewise be used in a grid layout as long as they are not overused and compositionally spotty. Unlike woody plants, herbaceous plant material can be arranged with more freedom in drifts and random mixtures as long as they collectively define blocks within a grid (6.52).

CONTINUOUS GRID MASS

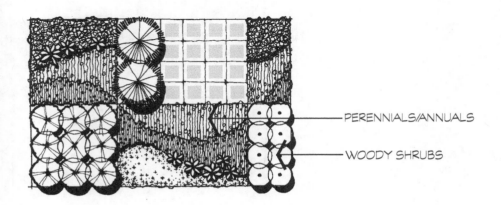

PERENNIALS/ANNUALS

WOODY SHRUBS

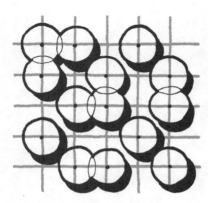

FRAGMENTED GRID MASS

137

Referenced Resources

Condon, Patrick Michael. "Cubist Space, Volumetric Space, and Landscape Architecture." *Landscape Journal* (Vol. 7, No. 2), Spring 1988.

Johnson, Jory. *Modern Landscape Architecture: Refining the Garden*. New York: Abbeville, 1991.

"NTT Musashino Research and Development Center," *Land Forum 13*. Berkeley, CA: Spacemaker Press, 2002.

Rose, James C. *Creative Gardens*. New York: Reinhold, 1958.

Scherr, Richard. *The Grid: Form and Process in Architectural Design*. New York: Universalia, 2001.

Walker, Peter. *Minimalist Gardens*. Cambridge, MA: Spacemaker Press, 1997.

Further Resources

Amidon, Jane. *Radical Landscapes: Reinventing Outdoor Space*. New York: Thames & Hudson, 2001.

Baker, Geoffrey H. *Design Strategies in Architecture: An Approach to Analysis of Form*, 2nd ed. New York: Van Nostrand Reinhold, 1996.

Ching, Francis D. K. *Architecture: Form, Space, & Order*. Hoboken, NJ: John Wiley & Sons, 2007.

Margolin, Victor. *Design Discourse: History, Theory, Criticism*. Chicago: University of Chicago Press, 1989.

Schwartz, Martha. *Transfiguration of the Commonplace*. Cambridge, MA: Spacemaker Press, 1997.

Thompson, J. William. "A Passion for Restraint." *Landscape Architecture* (Vol. 81, No. 12) December 1991, pp. 61–67.

Internet Resources

Yoji Sasaki: www.ohtori-c.com/information.html

Peter Walker and Partners: www.pwpla.com

Symmetry

7

Orthogonal symmetry, like all symmetrical organizations previously discussed in Chapter 1, is distinguished by the placement of spaces and elements along one or more axes. What is unique about orthogonal symmetry is that the domineering axes are perpendicular and/or parallel to one another, thus forming a network of right-angle centerlines (7.1). Individual spaces and elements based on the square and rectangle are centered on the axes or in reflective pairs on either side of it. Other forms are occasionally incorporated for contrast, accent, or as secondary elements.

Orthogonal symmetry's rational, calculated, and authoritative qualities have made it one of the most enduring organizational systems through history. This geometric genre is particularly emblematic of western gardens from the earliest of civilized times through the 20th century, including early Roman, Italian Renaissance, French Renaissance, Dutch, English Formal, U.S. colonial, and 19th- and 20th-century U.S. estate gardens. It is a design style that continues to be explored in some contemporary landscape architectural design as well with innovative spatial qualities and materials.

This chapter explores the unique attributes and noteworthy uses of orthogonal symmetry in landscape architectural site design. Specific sections of the chapter are:
   • Symmetrical Typologies
   • Landscape Uses
   • Design Guidelines

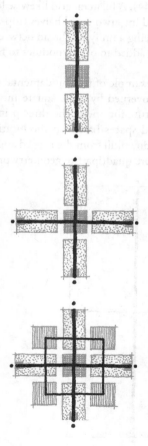

7.1   A network of right-angle axes distinguish orthogonal symmetry.

Symmetrical Typologies

Symmetrical orthogonal geometry can be classified into three typologies based on the presence or absence of a grid and the extent of adherence to strict symmetrical balance: grid orthogonal symmetry, multiform orthogonal symmetry, and implied orthogonal symmetry. In general, these organizational typologies progress from the most stringent to the least with each having its own organizational framework and characteristics as discussed in the following paragraphs.

Grid Orthogonal Symmetry

As the name indicates, this type of symmetry utilizes a grid of squares or rectangles as the foundation for its organization and shares many of the grid's traits discussed in the previous chapter. However, a symmetrical grid is notable for the presence of an axis that establishes an explicit compositional centerline. The symmetrical grid can be formulated in four fundamental ways in coordination with the axis: bilateral grid, cross-axial grid, aggregate grid, and subdivision.

Bilateral Grid. As discussed in Chapter 1, a bilateral symmetrical design organization positions all spaces and elements along one dominant axis (left 1.44). A bilateral grid likewise locates individual grid modules on a single axis by centering each module directly on the axis so that it is bisected into two equal halves (top 7.1, left 7.2). By being internal to the modules, the axis is an integral component of each module as well as being a unifying thread between adjoining grid modules. Depending on size, each grid module may be treated as its own distinct space or be added to other modules to fabricate the foundation of a larger space (right 7.2).

An iconic example of this fundamental method for creating a bilateral grid is the design of Villa Lante in Bagnaia, Italy, where the overall design is governed by three square modules organized bisymmetrically along a central axis (7.3–4). Each square module serves as the understructure for one of the three primary terraces of the design. The northern two square modules are further subdivided into smaller terraces and spaces based on the location of secondary cross-axes. The three square modules are the basis for a spatial sequence that progresses downhill from the rugged and enclosed quality of the upper natural grotto to the open and refined character of the lower parterre garden where quadripartite geometry prevails.

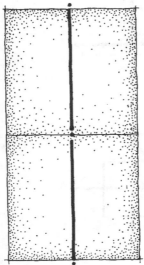

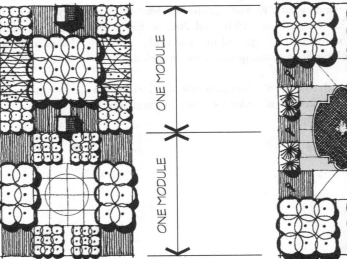

7.2 Grid modules can be the basis for one space or separate spaces.

SITE PLAN   GRID MODULES

NATURAL GROTTO

UPPER TERRACE

WATER LATTER

CARDINAL'S TABLE

VILLA

LOWER PARTERRE GARDEN

NORTH

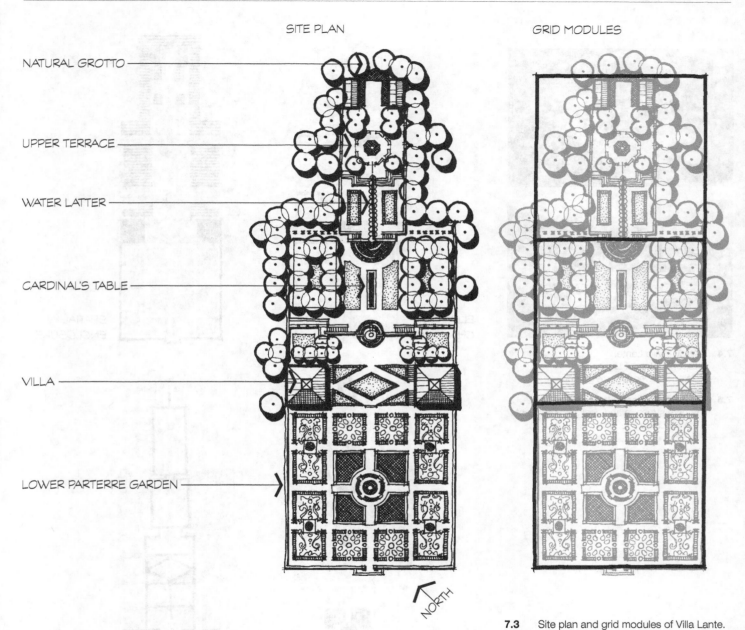

7.3   Site plan and grid modules of Villa Lante.

7.4 Above: Villa Lante.
Top: Fountain of Lights.
Below: Lower parterre garden.

7.5 Right: Relationship between the three-square structure and design components of Villa Lante.

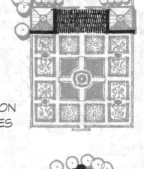

ELEVATION
CHANGES

SPATIAL
ENCLOSURE

WATER
FEATURES

PRIMARY
CIRCULATION

While not all the design elements are exactly aligned with the edges of the square modules, it is clear they nevertheless have deference to them and the axes. Virtually all design components including elevation changes, spatial enclosure, water features, and primary circulation have been located in relation to square grid modules (7.5). It is particularly interesting to note how the elevation changes between the terraces are coordinated with the minor cross-axes and the edges between the modules, thus permitting the garden to fit into the site's slope from north to south.

A variation to the system of grid modules centered on the axis is to arrange pairs of modules that symmetrically flank it (7.6). These matching sets of modules can comprise the entire composition or be integrated with centered modules to create a varied spatial sequence that occasionally extends away from the axis (7.7). The axis typically serves as a common edge and hinge between the duplicate grid modules rather than an inner fulcrum as it does for modules centered on the axis.

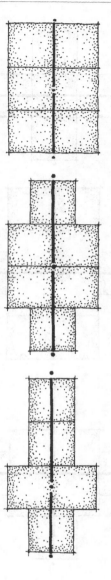

7.6 Above: Grid modules used in pairs along the axis of a bilateral organization.

7.7 Left: Bilateral design incorporating modular pairs along the axis.

143

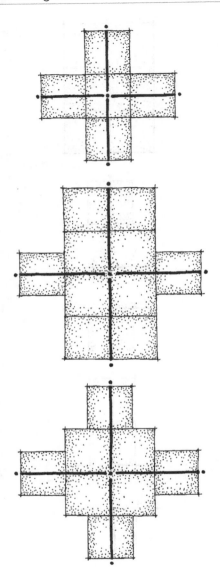

Cross-Axial Grid. A cross-axial grid structure arranges the grid modules along two or more axes (middle 1.44). Similar to a bilateral composition, grid modules can be directly centered on the axis as single entities or in pairs that are symmetrically placed next to the axis (7.8–9). The first approach provides a simplified method for establishing the grid while the second technique offers more complexity and options to design within. Note the circulation options and varied spatial experiences that exist in Figure 7.9. A cross-axial design works best on sites that are level and or permit terracing (see Design Guidelins).

Aggregate Grid. A third concept for establishing a symmetrical orthogonal grid as the basis of landscape design is to expand the grid outward from the axes (7.10). This scheme multiplies the grid modules beyond a direct affiliation with the axes to forge an extended field. The grid modules can be added on to without limit as long as they remain symmetrically balanced around the axes. Additionally, the grid modules are often smaller in relative size than those used in either the bilateral or cross-axial grids, thus providing

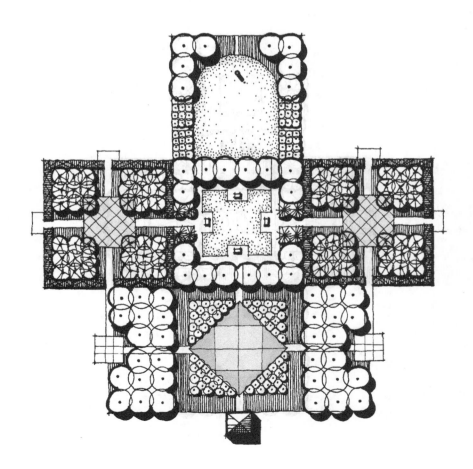

7.8   Above: Pairs of grid modules organized along two axes.

7.9   Right: Cross-axial design incorporating modular pairs.

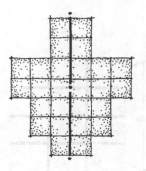
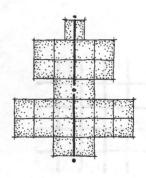
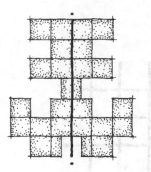

7.10 Left: Aggregate grid modules.

7.11 Below: Example of a symmetrical design based on an aggregate grid.

SITE PLAN

AGGREGATE GRID

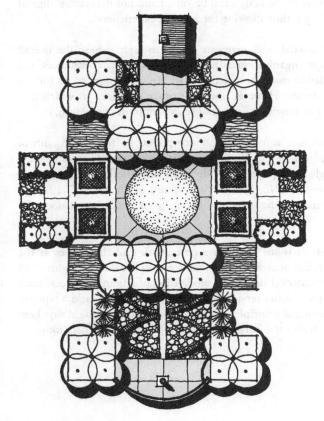

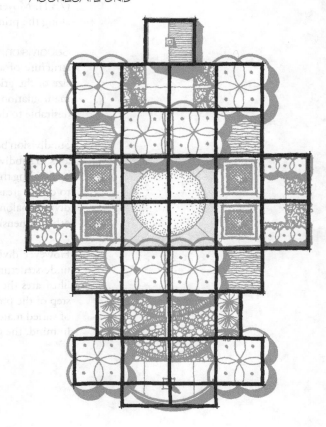

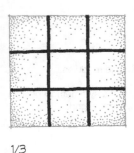

1/3

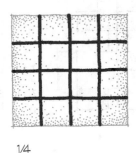

1/4

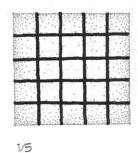

1/5

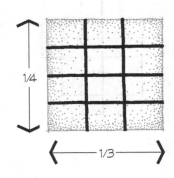

1/4

1/3

7.12 Subdivision of a square module.

for a finer scale framework to design within. Consequently, an aggregate symmetrical grid supports a potentially complex and diverse design that has multiple spaces and elements (7.11). Movement and views through the design can be varied and not necessarily aligned along the primary axes of the design, thus allowing for assorted experiences.

Subdivision. The bilateral, cross-axial, and aggregate grids can each fashion the overall structure of a symmetrical design organization as just described. In many instances, the size of the grid is adequate to define spaces and elements within the design, so no further manipulation of the grid is necessary. However, there are other situations in which it is desirable to define a smaller grid to provide a finer grained system to design within.

Subdivision begins with a single square or rectangle and incorporates its internal structure of axes to subdivide the area into a smaller grid. The segmentation is commonly accomplished by dividing the square or rectangle into equally spaced divisions across both of its dimensions to create areas that are a fraction (1/2, 1/3, 1/4, 1/5, and so on) of the whole (7.12). The divisions along one dimension may be the same or different from the divisions along the other dimension.

However divided, the fractional divisions establish a framework grid that serves as the understructure for delineating different areas and materials within the design. Figure 7.13 illustrates the evolution of a symmetrical design via subdivision of adjoining spaces. Each step of the process divides the spaces into ever-smaller areas that ultimately yield a tapestry of varied materials. While fundamental principles of composition and space are always kept in mind, the grid nevertheless remains the foremost controlling factor for all decisions.

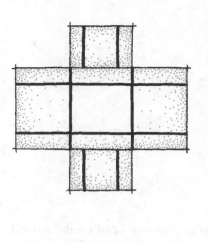

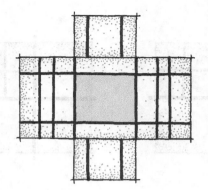

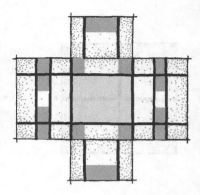

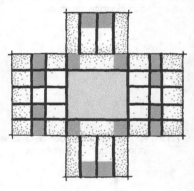

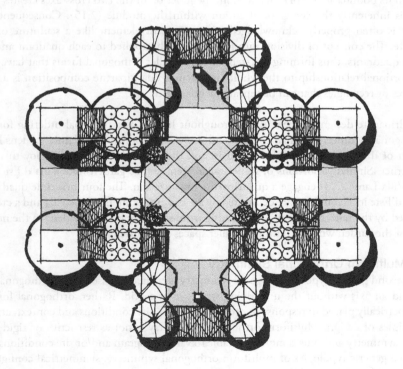

7.13 Process of subdividing joining spaces into a smaller grid as the basis of a symmetrical design.

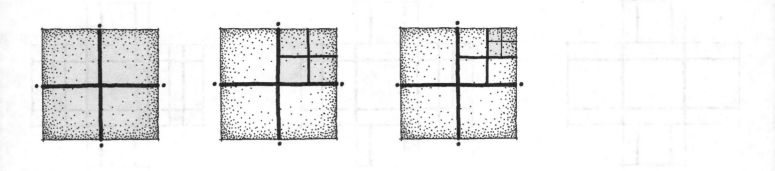

7.14 The subdivision of a square into a quadripartite structure.

7.15 A quadripartite structure creates an inherent point of emphasis.

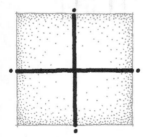

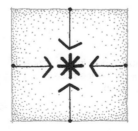

Quadripartite Design. One specialized type of design structure based on the internal subdivision of an orthogonal module is quadripartite design, a symmetrical organization that uses the two primary axes of a square or rectangle to define four equal quadrants within its boundaries (7.14). In addition, the junction of the two cross-axes creates a point that is inherently the center of attention within the module (7.15). Consequently, this point is often properly acknowledged with an accent element like a sculpture or water feature. The concept of division into four can also be applied to each quadrant and again to its quadrants, thus forming a system of ever-smaller orthogonal forms that have a fixed proportional relationship to the whole. In essence, quadripartite composition is a grid of squares or rectangles that can be repeatedly quartered.

Quadripartite design has been used throughout history as a principal ordering format of orthogonal symmetry. Persian gardens and numerous noteworthy Islamic gardens like the Court of the Lions at Alhambra in Spain and the Taj Majal in India employ this design construct. Similarly, portions of some Italian Renaissance gardens like Villa d'Este (7.16) and Villa Lante (7.3) engage a quadripartite organization. The four principle quadrants at Villa d'Este in Tivoli, Italy are delineated by an axis extending from the villa and a cross-axis formed by the reflecting pools. The quadripartite structure is most evident in the northern half of the garden where it outlines smaller spaces and garden areas.

Multiform Orthogonal Symmetry

The second general type of orthogonal symmetry is created by assembling orthogonal forms around an axis without the underlying structure of a grid. Rather, orthogonal forms are symmetrically placed in response to program, existing site conditions and context, and basic principles of design. Multiform orthogonal symmetry is not as restrictive or rigid as grid based symmetry and thus is more adaptable to varied program and/or site conditions. There are two generic typologies of multiform orthogonal symmetry: symmetrical configuration and nonsymmetrical configuration.

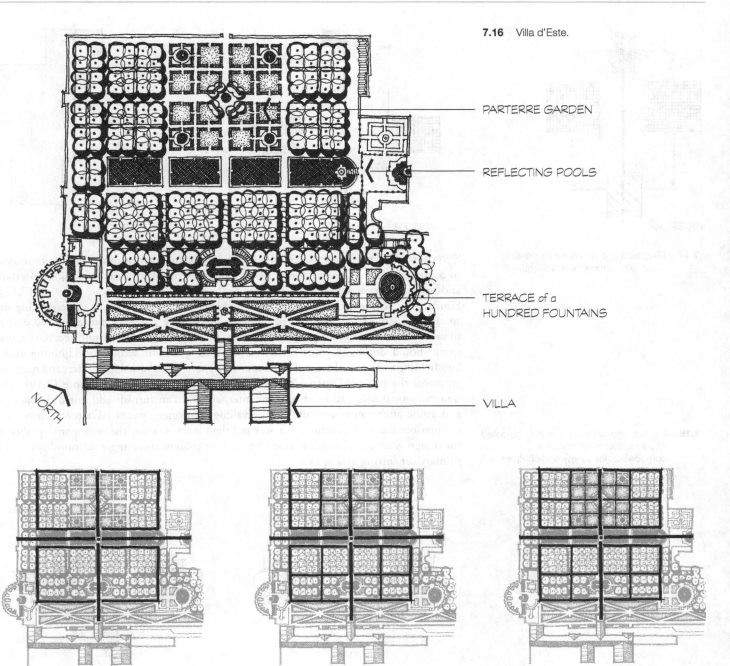

7.16 Villa d'Este.

PARTERRE GARDEN

REFLECTING POOLS

TERRACE of a
HUNDRED FOUNTAINS

VILLA

NORTH

SUBDIVISION into a QUADRIPARTITE STRUCTURE

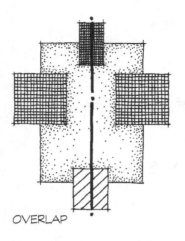

OVERLAP

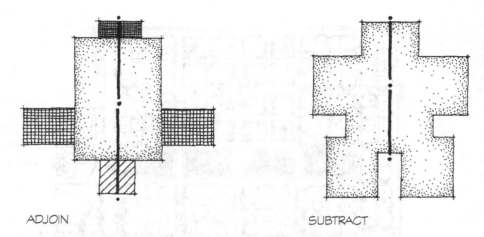

ADJOIN   SUBTRACT

7.17 Diagrammatic variations for creating multi-form symmetrical designs.

Symmetrical Configuration. The simplest technique for creating multi-form symmetry is to compile varied orthogonal forms around a central axis. The forms may adjoin, overlap, and/or be subtracted from one another to create the foundation of a design (7.17). Similarly, nonorthogonal forms may be interjected for accent or as the underpinning for spatial diversity (7.18). The size of different spaces may also vary and allow the design to easily adapt to different program requirements. Typically, though not necessarily, one space should dominate while others serve as subspaces or secondary adjoining areas. Subdividing the internal areas of the framework spaces with varied form, size, and material enhances the potential spatial diversity of this design strategy even more (7.19). The nonorthogonal orientation of selected internal areas can furnish additional distinction and guide attention away from the prevailing 90-degree system. Whatever forms and orientations are used to delineate spaces and their internal areas, the orthogonal quality of the design is nevertheless maintained by the ever-present right-angle relationships of the primary organizing axis or axes.

7.18 Nonorthogonal forms may be interjected into a multiform symmetrical composition for variety and contrast.

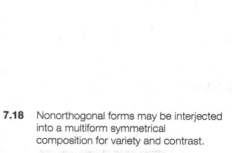

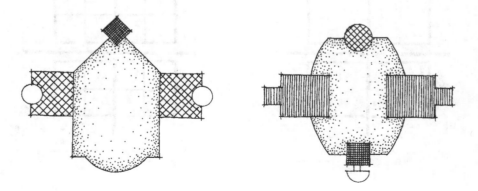

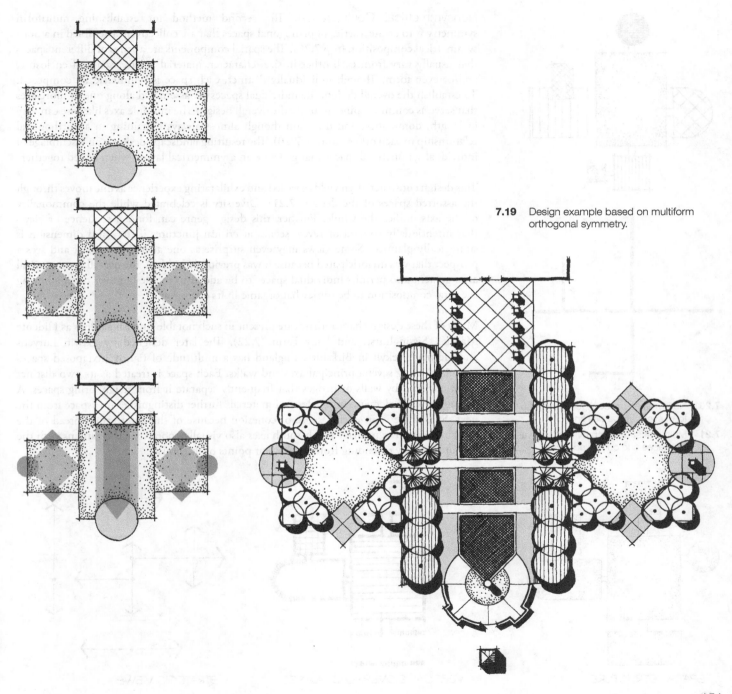

7.19 Design example based on multiform orthogonal symmetry.

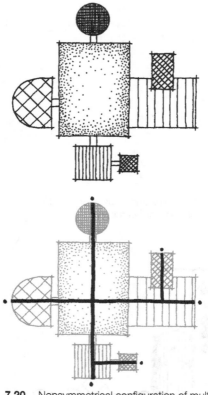

Nonsymmetrical Configuration. The second method for establishing multiform symmetry is to create a series of orthogonal spaces that are collectively assembled in a nonsymmetrical composition (top 7.20). The spatial components are a series of different spaces that usually vary from each other in size, character, material palette, sense of enclosure, and/or even form. Though individually distinct, each space is symmetrically composed. To establish the overall design, the individual spaces are assembled along one or more axes that serve as common spines to unify the overall design. The multiple axes likewise can vary in length, dominance, and direction though almost always remaining in an orthogonal relationship to each other (bottom 7.20). The resulting landscape design is an assemblage of individual symmetrical spaces that generate an asymmetrical layout when added together.

This design construct often yields a varied and exhilarating experience as one moves through the assorted spaces of the design (7.21). Diversity is celebrated while the commonality of the axis unifies the whole. Further, this design genre can forge a sequence of views that intentionally conceal or reveal scenes at critical junctures if the third dimension is strategically planned. Some views may even surprise as one arrives at a point and sees a prospect that was unanticipated because it was previously hidden. The overall asymmetrical arrangement also permits individual spaces to be added to the design over time, allowing the total composition to be somewhat organic in its evolution.

Many of these design characteristics are present in such notable English gardens as Hidcote Manner, Sissinghurst, and Folly Farm (7.22). The later designed by Edwin Lutyens and Gertrude Jekyll in Birkshire, England has a multitude of tightly juxtaposed spaces organized along several principal axes and walks. Each space is treated as its own distinct room enclosed by walls or hedges that frequently separate it from neighboring spaces. A prevailing set of elements and palette of materials further distinguishes one space from the next. Still, there is an overall sense of cohesion because of the connecting thread of the principle axes. The primary north/south axes also visually coordinate the gardens with the manor house by extending from prominent points of the house.

7.20 Nonsymmetrical configuration of multiform symmetrical design.

7.21 Multiform structure provides for a variety of spaces and controlled views.

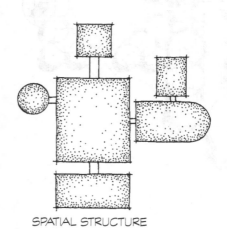

SPATIAL STRUCTURE

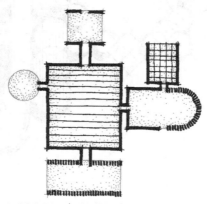

VERTICAL & OVERHEAD PLANES

STRATEGIC VIEWS

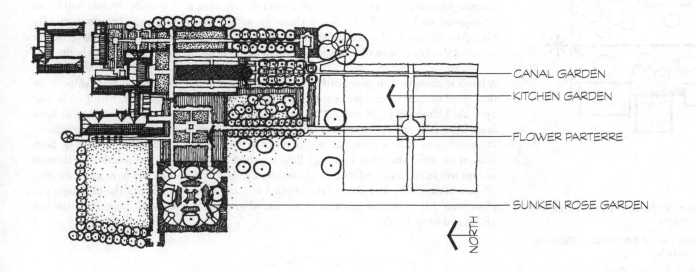

CANAL GARDEN

KITCHEN GARDEN

FLOWER PARTERRE

SUNKEN ROSE GARDEN

NORTH

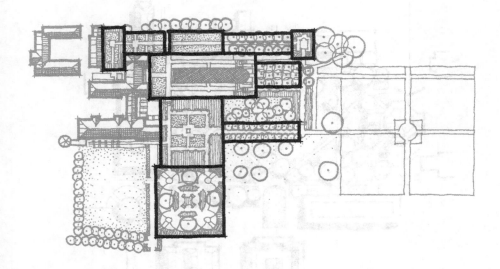

7.22 Varied modules of Folly Farm.

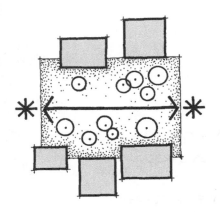

Implied Orthogonal Symmetry

The third classification of orthogonal symmetry is the illusion of equal balance within a square or rectangle framework, but without the strict adherence to it. Implied orthogonal symmetry is the least regimented and autocratic type of orthogonal symmetry. It is commonly comprised of an axis with a notable terminus at one or both ends within an orthogonal enclosure (7.23). Some elements within this setting may be symmetrically placed in relation to the axis while others are not. The dominance of the axis nevertheless provides the impression of balance even when parity of components is not entirely present.

A familiar example of implied orthogonal symmetry is found on many college campuses in the layout of their central green space. The "quad" at UC Davis, University of Illinois, and Syracuse University (7.24 and 7.25) along with Harvard Yard and the central lawn at Iowa State University are all examples of implied orthogonal symmetry. Most of these prominent campus spaces have a principal axis terminated by a celebrated building at one or both ends of the axis. The other buildings flanking these spaces are not symmetrical to the axis or uniform in architectural design. Consequently, these spaces typically have a comfortable alliance between the formality of the implied axis and the informality of the buildings and plant materials. A similar situation is also found in many public parks designed in the late 1800s and early 1900s.

7.23 Above: Concept of implied orthogonal symmetry.

7.24 Right: Plan of the "quad" at Syracuse University.

7.25 Below: Views of the "quad" at Syracuse University.

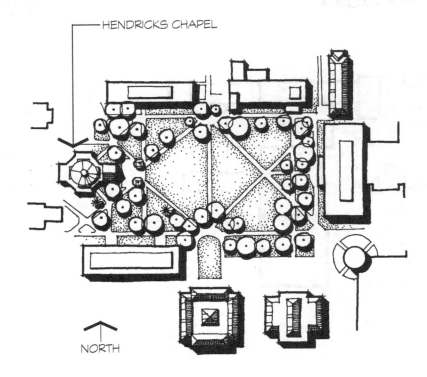

HENDRICKS CHAPEL

NORTH

154

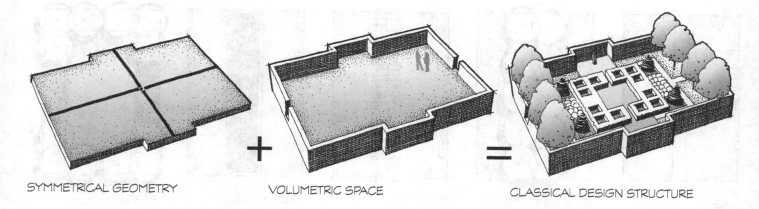

SYMMETRICAL GEOMETRY   +   VOLUMETRIC SPACE   =   CLASSICAL DESIGN STRUCTURE

Landscape Uses

Orthogonal symmetry has a number of potential uses in the landscape. As with other fundamental organizational systems, many of these applications are mutually inclusive allowing orthogonal symmetry to simultaneously realize a number of functions. The principal roles of orthogonal symmetry are: spatial foundation, emphasize frontal views, architectural extension, and imply human control.

Spatial Foundation

The primary landscape use of orthogonal symmetry is to serve as the basis of outdoor space. This genre of landscape space is commonly referred to as being classical or "formal," the most enduring design genre in the Western world from ancient times to the present moment. The following paragraphs outline the distinctive qualities and uses of single and multiple classic spaces.

Single Space. The square and rectangle are the basis for every individual orthogonal symmetrical space. Consequently, most spatial characteristics like right-angle corners, methods of subdivision, potential edge configurations, and points of emphasis previously discussed for these two geometric forms in Chapters 4 and 5 also apply to a single symmetrical space, but with several notable differences. First, most symmetrical orthogonal spaces are volumetric in character (7.26). In classical design, buildings, walls, tree masses, hedges, and so on are commonly located around the perimeter of the space to define an explicit, wall-like edge. Consequently, there is a marked separation between the interior and exterior of the space with a further feeling of isolation and inward focus if the outer edge is at or above eye level. By contrast, the interior of a classic volumetric space is typically open and symmetrically patterned with low elements that permit unobstructed views from edge to edge. A symmetrical walled garden with ornate parterres is the prototypical classical design (7.27).

7.26 Above: Symmetrical geometry underlies the classical design structure.

7.27 Below: Examples of classic design structure.

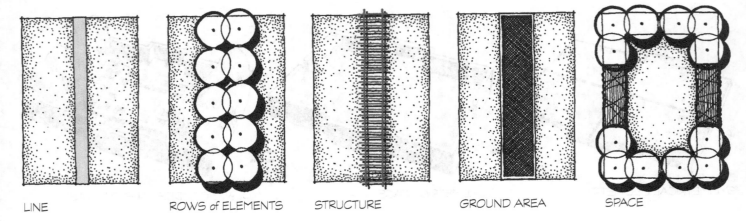

LINE   ROWS of ELEMENTS   STRUCTURE   GROUND AREA   SPACE

7.28 Above: Alternative means for expressing the axis in a symmetrical space.

7.29 Below: Standard components of an symmetrical orthogonal space.

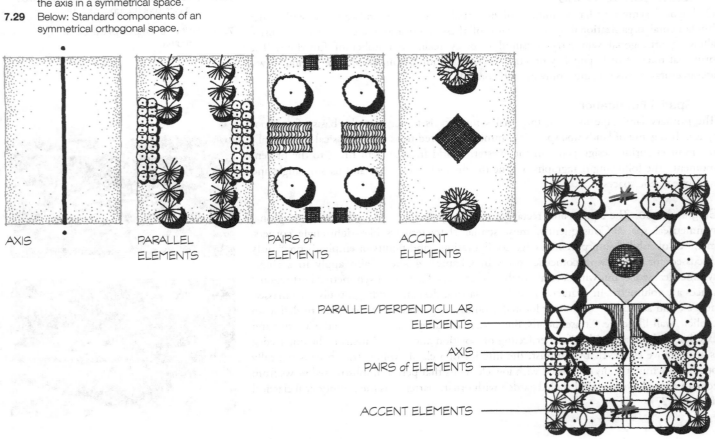

AXIS   PARALLEL ELEMENTS   PAIRS of ELEMENTS   ACCENT ELEMENTS

PARALLEL/PERPENDICULAR ELEMENTS

AXIS

PAIRS of ELEMENTS

ACCENT ELEMENTS

The other notable feature of a single symmetrical space is an axis, an element that is ever-present physically and in its influence on other components in the space. An axis is a linear fulcrum that can be expressed in a number of ways (7.28). Perhaps the most obvious and explicit means of demarcating the axis is with a line like a walk that extends through the space. This line can be a two dimensional element on the ground plane or be reinforced in the third dimension with parallel elements like a row of trees. The axis can also be defined with a linear structure like a pergola or pool. The former can be walked through while the later extends the eye but must be walked around to progress through the site. Finally, the axis can be designated as a linear space. This is an implicit means of defining the axis and demonstrates the concept that the axis can be a void, not necessarily a physical element.

However it is portrayed, the axis impacts all aspects of a symmetric orthogonal space. First, an axis establishes a predetermined organizational system for locating all other elements and material areas within a space (7.29). This structure compels some design elements to be positioned parallel or perpendicular to the axis to reinforce it presence. The exact nature and location of these elements depends on how apparent the axis is intended to be. Design elements and materials areas that are not directly associated with the axis must be configured in pairs so that whatever is done on one side of the axis is reflected on the other side. Finally, single design elements serve as accents and so are placed directly on the axis at intersections with other axes, at its termini, or to its side, usually at an intersection of secondary axes.

An axis also regulates movement through a space by limiting passage along a fixed path that is always straight ahead and provides the same experience for all who traverse it (middle 7.30). This restraint is occasionally employed to create a deferential progression toward a symbolic terminus like a cultural monument or spiritual icon. In other instances, movement through a symmetrical space may temporarily shift from the axis to secondary paths or an unrestricted open area (right 7.30). Such alternative routes usually return to a primary axis, especially before exiting a space.

7.30 The axis governs movement through a symmetrical space.

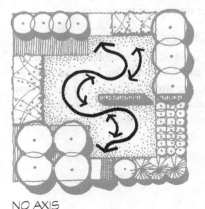

NO AXIS

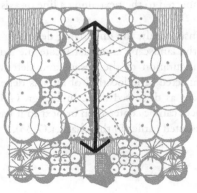

AXIS

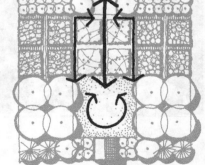

SECONDARY ROUTES

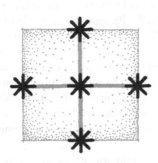

7.31 Inherent accent points within a symmetric orthognal space.

7.32 Examples of termini at the edge of a space.

Similarly, an axis in a symmetrical design governs views. Frequently a person can experience the surrounding space only from an axis or secondary axes as just described for circulation, thus restricting exploration and the ability to see the space from other vantage points (also see Frontal Views in this section). Simultaneously, an axis concentrates attention along its length to the intersection with other axes or termini at the edge of the space (7.31). While the eye is free to wander about a symmetrical space, it is continually enticed back to these prominent points. Hence, these notable junctions are rightfully acknowledged by a dominant space or accent feature like an obelisk, sculpture, water element, and so forth. Similarly, the terminus at the perimeter of a space is regularly celebrated as a niche, gateway, and/or framed opening of a distance view (7.32).

Multiple Spaces. The symmetrical orthogonal design structure likewise lends itself to assembling multiple spaces in the landscape as seen and demonstrated in the numerous graphic examples throughout this chapter. Despite the many variations in the number of axes, symmetrical typologies, and resulting complexity, almost all designs of composite symmetrical spaces are essentially linear organizations. That is, each space is sequentially connected to the next along a line or axis. This is so for one axis or many axes.

Consequently, the underlying design strategy for assembling multiple symmetrical spaces in the landscape is to first locate the axis or axes on the site. This establishes the overall configuration of the design and determines where and how individual spaces will be connected. The location of an axis depends on particular site conditions and the design intent as discussed more in Design Guidelines. Once an axis is placed, then individual spaces can be centered on or next to it based on one or more of the symmetrical typologies presented earlier in this chapter (7.33).

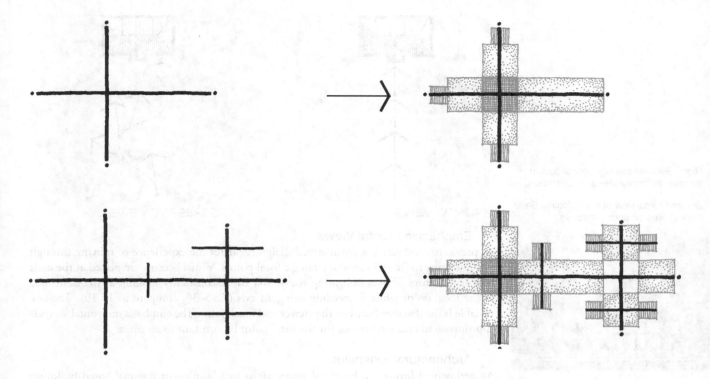

7.33 Above: Multiple symmetrical spaces are connected via an axis.

7.34 Below: Example of abrupt transitions between adjoining symmetrical spaces.

There are several other typical traits of an assemblage of symmetrical orthogonal spaces. First, each individual space possesses well-defined edges as previously indicated. Therefore, there is often an obvious and sometimes abrupt transition from one space to the next (7.34). While potentially jarring, such a passage can be rather dramatic when the adjoining spaces are notably different in character. Imagine walking immediately from a shaded, canopied space to one that is sunlight and filled with colorful perennials. Similarly the quick change between spaces can sometimes create surprise when the third dimension is properly employed as discussed in Design Guidelines.

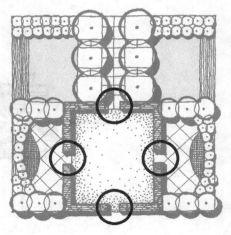

The transition between adjoining spaces is also noted for almost always being on the axis. As with the internal circulation in an individual space, the circulation between symmetrical spaces is highly controlled and limited to specific points of entry and exit. Again, this strictly choreographs the overall experience of the design and assures that it is similar for everyone.

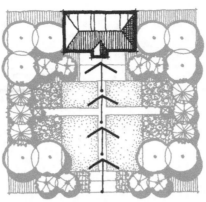

FRONTAL VIEWS

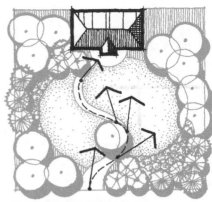

PROGRESSIVE VIEWS

7.35 Right: Symmetrical orthogonal design establishes frontal views of a terminus.

7.36 Below: Frontal view of the California State Capital, Sacramento, California.

Emphasize Frontal Views

As previously indicated, a symmetrical design regulates the experience of moving through the landscape to frontal views of strategic focal points. Visual accents are placed at the ends and/or junctures of axes obligating the viewer to be constantly looking at the same side of the focal point while proceeding along an axis (7.35–36; compare to 15.19). The one variable is the distance between the viewer and focal point. The emphasis on frontal views is appropriate to create reverence for the focal point by constant focus on it.

Architectural Extension

All orthogonal forms can be visual protractions to adjoining orthogonal based buildings as discussed in previous chapters. Orthogonal symmetry is suited to permit a landscape and an adjoining symmetrical building to have a reciprocal relationship by centering outdoor spaces on the building's axes or on other axes that parallel the building (7.37). This establishes one integral composition of corresponding components, a concept that has been employed throughout history from Italian Renaissance villas to contemporary settings.

7.37 A symmetrical orthogonal design can unify a symmetrical building with the adjoining landscape.

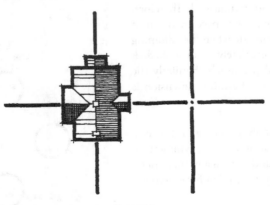

EXTENDED BUILDING AXES

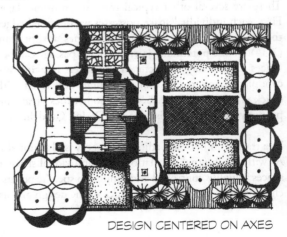

DESIGN CENTERED ON AXES

Imply Human Control

A final potential landscape use of orthogonal symmetry is to suggest human regimentation in the landscape, a function that is imbedded in all of the previous uses discussed in this section. It will be recalled from Chapter 3 that the straight line also fulfills this same landscape use. However, orthogonal symmetry implies human authority over a much broader area of land beyond a linear corridor. The entire composition is indicative of the human capacity and inclination to regulate the landscape. The discipline of its two-dimensional structure is many times extended into the third dimension so the resultant landscape is entirely contrived including the shape of plant materials (7.38). Ian McHarg reiterates this observation in *Design with Nature* when speaking of the Western garden style: "In this tradition, decorative and tractable plants are arranged in a simple geometry as a comprehensible metaphysical symbol of a submissive and orderly world, created by man" (McHarg 1971, 71). The symmetrical environment exists due to human intervention and long-term management, the antithesis of a sustainable landscape.

In many instances, symmetrical orthogonal forms moreover suggest a disregard for nature especially when this geometry is imposed on the landscape without regard to natural patterns of topography, hydrology, soil, vegetation, microclimate, and so on. Even when considered, existing site features like water bodies are reshaped and sometimes relocated to comply with the axes, squares, and rectangles of orthogonal geometry. D. W. Meinig echoes this attitude in "The Beholding Eye"; "A rigid linear geometry has been set discordantly but relentlessly upon the varied curves of nature" (Meinig 1979, 37).

In summary, a single symmetrical orthogonal space is routinely a disciplined environment that tightly controls the experience of a person looking into or walking through it. This is appropriate in settings that require a cerebral atmosphere with calculated placement of interior subspaces and elements. However, this doesn't necessarily equate to bland because the manipulation of the third dimension (see Design Guidelines) and the selection of materials can all contribute to a vibrant space.

7.38 Examples of symmetrical orthogonal geometry's ability to imply human control.
Top: Levens Hall, England.
Bottom: Het Loo, Netherlands.

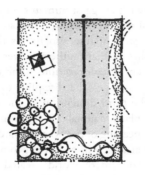

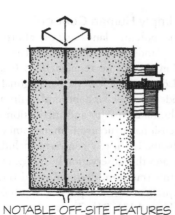

7.39 The location of an axis should respond to given site conditions.

ON-SITE RESTRICTIONS   NOTABLE OFF-SITE FEATURES

Design Guidelines

The following guidelines are recommended for composing orthogonal symmetrical landscape designs.

Axis Location and Orientation

The axis needs to be prudently located within a site because of its import. For a simple orthogonal site, the presumed position is directly on the site's center line(s) where it reinforces the inherent focus of the site. This location is appropriate for a uniform site that lacks notable on and off-site features. However, the tacit location is not suitable when the site has varied topography, random geologic features, scattered trees, incidental placement of structures, and so forth The axis should be placed elsewhere so that the overall design avoids difficult or sensitive site areas (left 7.39). Significant buildings or building entrances, walks, views, and so on around the site's periphery also suggest the axis be oriented to acknowledge these unique features (right 7.39). Both of these strategies may result in the orthogonal design not filling the entire site and not being symmetrical to the site (7.40).

7.40 The orientation of the axis on a nonorthogonally shaped site can be based on significant on-site or off-site elements.

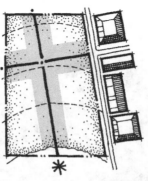
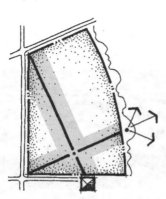

PROMINENT EDGE &   INTERSECTION &
FOCAL POINT   SIGNIFICANT BUILDING

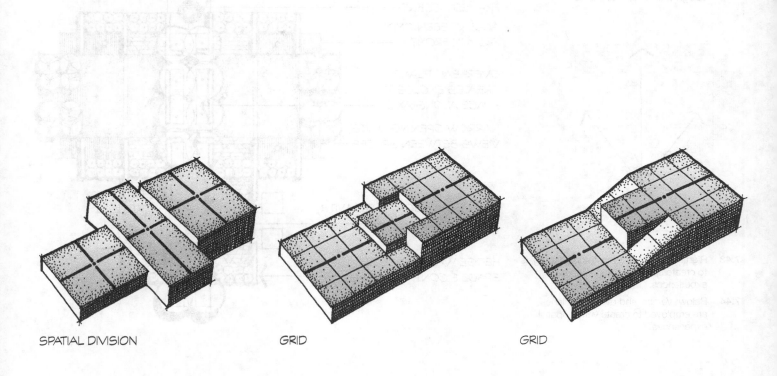

SPATIAL DIVISION   GRID   GRID

Relation to Topography

As with the straight line, orthogonal symmetry appears and functions most effectively when situated on relatively level ground or a uniform slope where the internal geometric relationships are most unified. This is especially necessary for single symmetrical spaces to preserve the visual continuity of the axes and the associated elements. Orthogonal symmetry should not be located where a high point or ridge extends through the composition, thus visually separating the design into disjointed segments.

If orthogonal symmetrical design must be placed on sloped topography, the ground should be terraced to create a series of level ground planes divided by retaining walls or slopes. Such elevation changes should be located between spaces or directly aligned with the axes and fractional modules within a space (7.41). Numerous Italian Renaissance gardens like Villa Lante were skillfully acclimated to sloped topography in this manner (7.3–5).

7.41 Elevation changes should be coordinated with divisions between spaces or a grid.

163

7.42 Absence of third dimension creates a design with no spatial interest.

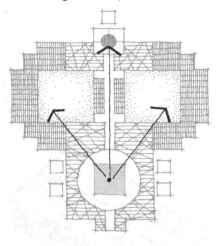

FRAMED ACCENT

ACCENT SEEN ONLY FROM IN FRONT

OVERHEAD PLANE CREATES ENCLOSED SPACE ALONG AXIS

NARROW OPENING LIMITS VIEWS BETWEEN SPACES

OPEN SPACE CONTRASTS WITH TREE ALLEE

HEDGE WALLS ENCLOSE SPACE & CONTROL VIEWS

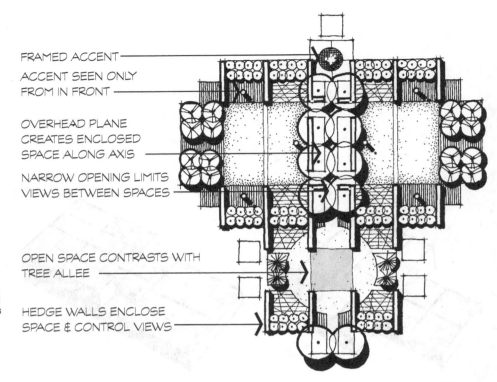

7.43 Right: Site plan demonstrating strategies to create space and varied spatial experiences.

7.44 Below: Vertical and overhead planes are employed to create varied spatial experiences.

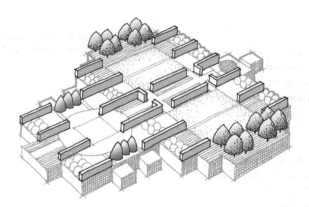

VERTICAL PLANE

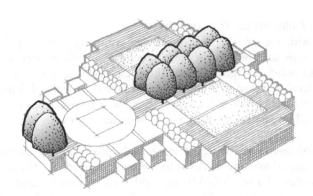

OVERHEAD PLANE

7.45 Examples of narrow openings in walls at Sissinghurst that focus and limit views between spaces.

Third Dimension

The manipulation of the third dimension in orthogonal symmetry is wide ranging. At one extreme, this design paradigm may be treated as a two-dimensional pattern unfolded across the landscape as is typical in many French Renaissance gardens. Here, spaces are open yet unified because of the ability to see and visually associate all parts. However, such a landscape may lack a sense of human scale and often discourages movement and exploration because the entire composition can be seen from one vantage point (7.42).

An alternative approach is to use the third dimension to emphatically enclose and spatially subdivide a symmetrical design. Some of the most engaging symmetrical landscapes are ones that include a pronounced third dimension in the form of trees, walls, hedges, and so on to create distinct spaces that are varied in character and degree of enclosure from one to the next (7.43–44). Such designs typically employ carefully choreographed changes in the ground, vertical, and overhead planes to create a diverse spatial sequence. Visual connections among spaces are limited to restricted openings often placed on the axes, making it difficult to comprehend much beyond the space one is presently in (7.45). Consequently, one is enticed to physically move from one space to the next, exploring and discovering in the process. Visual surprises are common as previously hidden views and objects are revealed from selected vantage points. Note how this is accomplished in Figure 7.44 with carefully located walls. When the third dimension is properly expressed, orthogonal symmetry defies the common perception of being a predictable and monotonous experience. In fact, it can be quite the opposite and every bit as engaging as other design paradigms.

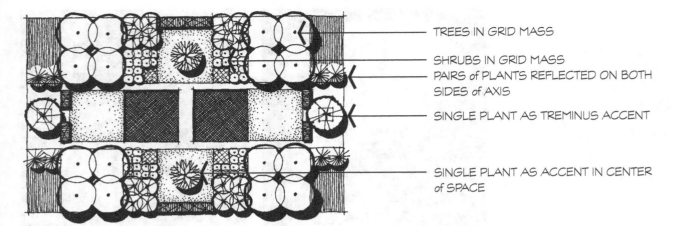

TREES IN GRID MASS

SHRUBS IN GRID MASS

PAIRS of PLANTS REFLECTED ON BOTH SIDES of AXIS

SINGLE PLANT AS TREMINUS ACCENT

SINGLE PLANT AS ACCENT IN CENTER of SPACE

7.46 Alternative techniques for using plant materials in an orthogonal symmetrical design.

Material Coordination

Woody or structural plant materials should generally be organized in straight rows and grid masses just as recommended for the grid (see Design Guidelines, Chapter 6). Of course, plant materials must also be equitably placed around an axis for balance, thus forming corresponding pairs flanking both sides of an axis (7.46). Single plants are best used as accents placed at the end of an axis, at the intersection of multiple axes, or in the center of a space. Such strategically located plants should be special specimens with sculptural form and appealing foliage, flowers, and/or fruit. As in a grid, drifts or naturalistic plantings are not recommended in a symmetrical landscape unless they occur within the bounds of an orthogonal area (7.47). Such a concept is best applied to annuals and perennials. Finally, it should be noted that symmetrical planting schemes are sometimes criticized for their lack of sustainability and plant diversity. However, this often depends more on the choice of plants used, not their arrangement. In fact, a symmetrical design can indeed have a wide variety of

7.47 Plant materials should be in rows, grid masses, or contained within an orthogonal planting area.

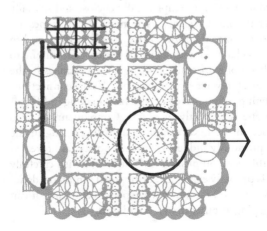

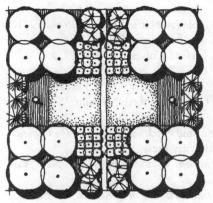
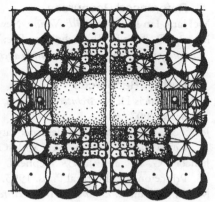

LESS PLANT DIVERSITY   MORE PLANT DIVERSITY

plants that foster ecological diversity and habitat health (7.48).

7.48 Symmetrical design incorporating plant diversity for ecological health.

Challenge the Guidelines

Following the previous guidelines generates a sound compositional structure in a symmetrical design. This is fitting in a context that requires an orthodox response but may not be suitable where a more contemporary or advant-garde solution is sought. It is advantageous in some instances to challenge the adherence to the axes to instill a design with creative energy. This can be done by first establishing the underlying symmetrical structure with the position of the primary spaces and elements. On the left of 7.49, the pavement, tree masses, and other planting areas are located within a quadripartite structure to create the anatomy of orthogonal symmetry. Then, selected components are interjected to provide contrast and some degree of noncompliance with the inherent structure. Placing the primary axis off center and locating various focal points and planting masses nonsymmetrically to the axis on the right of 7.49 circumvent absolute symmetry. Additionally, a trapezoidal pool transects the quadripartite configuration to provide spontaneity and a visual foil.

7.49 Example of designs that challenge conventional notions of orthogonal symmetry.

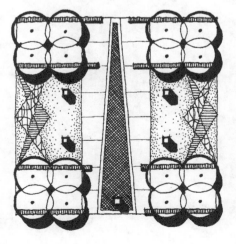
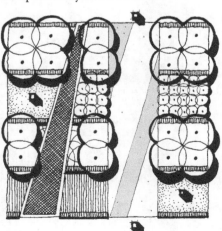

167

Referenced Resources

McHarg, Ian L. *Design with Nature*. New York: Doubleday/Natural History Press, 1971.

Meinig, D. W., ed. "The Beholding Eye; Ten Versions of the Same Scene." *The Interpretation of Ordinary Landscapes*. Oxford: Oxford University Press, 1979.

Further Resources

Ching, Francis D. K. *Architecture: Form, Space, & Order*. Hoboken, NJ: John Wiley & Sons, 2007.

Jellicoe, Geoffrey, and Susan Jellicoe, Patrick Goode, and Michael Lancaster. *The Oxford Companion to Gardens*. New York: Oxford University Press, 1986.

Jellicoe, G. A., and J. C. Shepherd. *Italian Gardens of the Renaissance*. New York: Princeton Architectural Press, 1993.

Mann, William A. *Landscape Architecture: An Illustrated History in Timelines, Site Plans, and Biography*. New York: John Wiley & Sons, 1993.

Newton, Norman. *Design on the Land*. Cambridge, MA: Belknap Press of the Harvard University Press, 1971.

Steenbergen, Clemens M., Wouter Reh, and Gerrit Smienk. *Architecture and Landscape: The Design Experiment of Great European Gardens and Landscapes*. New York: Prestel, 1996.

Tankard, Judith B. *Gardens of the Arts and Crafts Movement: Reality and Imagination*. New York: Harry N. Abram, 2004.

Internet Resources

Sissinghurst Castle and Gardens: www.nationaltrust.org.uk/main/w-vh/w-visits/w-findaplace/w-sissinghurst-castle/

Villa d'este: www.villadestetivoli.info/storiae.htm

Villa Lante: www.gardenvisit.com/garden/villa_lante

Asymmetry 8

The last orthogonal design structure is asymmetry, a framework that organizes the straight line, square, and/or rectangle into an informal and tacitly balanced composition. Compared to the grid and symmetry discussed in the previous chapters, asymmetry provides the designer with relative freedom in assembling spaces and their constituent components. Asymmetry is the least constrained orthogonal organization and is very suitable to present day aesthetic preferences.

Asymmetric orthogonal design came into prominence in the early 1900s as one of the principal design structures of the modern design movement. Pablo Picasso, George Braque, and others explored paintings with multiple points of view and abstract geometric forms in what was labeled "Cubism." Piet Mondrian epitomized the abstraction in art by simplifying the vocabulary to orthogonal shapes and primary colors (8.1). In architecture, Le Corbusier, Walter Gropius, Mies van der Rohe, and Frank Lloyd Wright incorporated an asymmetric orthogonal structure in their work during the 1930s and 1940s. An emblematic example is the Barcelona Pavilion designed by Mies van der Rohe for the 1929 Barcelona International Exhibition (8.2). The planar walls, flat roof, open floor plan, and interplay between the interior and exterior characterize core concepts of the modern design era.

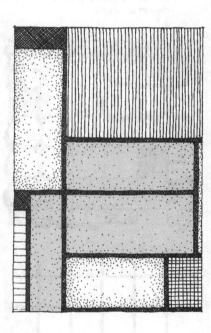

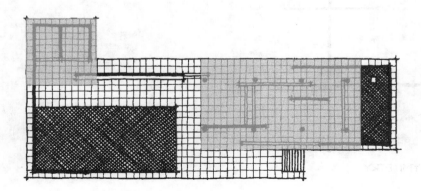

8.1   Above: Illustration of Tableau I by Piet Mondrian.

8.2   Left: Plan of the Barcelona Pavilion.

The initial use of asymmetrical design in landscape architecture is credited to James Rose, Garrett Eckbo, Dan Kiley, and Thomas Church, who incorporated it into their projects beginning in the 1940s. These early pioneers of modern landscape architectural design utilized the asymmetric orthogonal organization as one of the means of disassociating landscape design from the historical precedents of symmetry. Asymmetric orthogonal design continues to be applied in contemporary landscape architecture and has developed a new appreciation with the "rediscovery" of mid-20th-century modern design with its affinity to simple, bold forms lacking extraneous decoration.

This chapter explores the many facets of asymmetric orthogonal design by focusing on these topics:
- General Characteristics
- Landscape Uses
- Design Guidelines

8.3 Comparison between the grid, symmetric, and asymmetric orthogonal design structures.

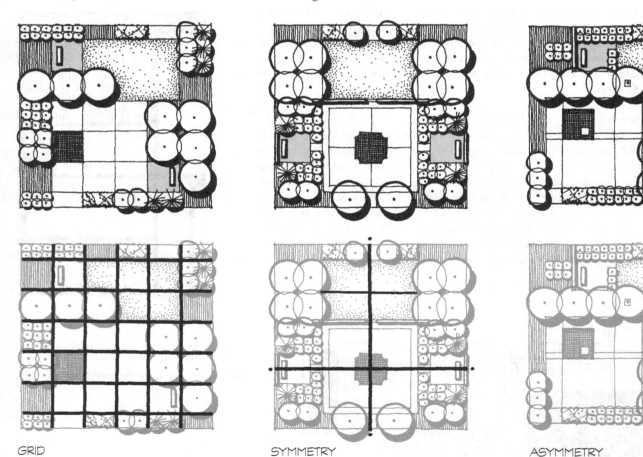

GRID

SYMMETRY

ASYMMETRY

General Characteristics

Many of the fundamental qualities of asymmetry and comparisons to other organizing structures were presented in Chapter 1 (1.46–48). It should be recalled that the components of an asymmetrical composition are organized to forge a design that is subjectively balanced without the restraints of an underlying grid or commanding axis (8.3). An asymmetrical design is composed as much by feel and intuition as it is by practical and functional considerations. Consequently, the size, location, and material composition of the constituent elements in an asymmetrical design are potentially more wide ranging while being unified by the prevalence of orthogonal forms in right-angle relationships.

Another unique aspect of asymmetrical design is the relation of the individual parts of the design to the whole. In a symmetrical design, the constituent elements are all subservient to the overall arrangement. That is, their primary function is to be one of many components that collectively contribute to the overall composition. By comparison, the individual elements in an asymmetrical design are each significant for their own merit. Their relation to the whole is less important, although they need to remain in accord with it. Consequently, individual spaces and design elements can be experienced independently from one another and can be appreciated for their singularity. Again, this allows for and even encourages greater variation in both the totality and detail of a landscape design.

The intrinsic qualities of the straight line, square, and rectangle are ever present in an asymmetric orthogonal design, instilling it with a human imprint like the other orthogonal typologies. However, asymmetrical orthogonal geometry also exhibits spontaneity that derives from the perceived random placement of elements and spaces. This design construct provides the designer relative freedom to create a landscape based on subjective impulses rather than methodical rationale. The asymmetric orthogonal structure is in the approximate middle of the continuum between highly controlled designs and completely indiscriminate ones and thus is a fitting design organization to integrate the qualities of each.

Landscape Uses

The asymmetric orthogonal design organization has a number of potential uses in landscape architectural site design. While some of these applications are similar to those previously presented for the other orthogonal typologies, a number of other uses are uniquely based on asymmetry's inherent qualities of implied balance in affiliation with architectonic forms. The principal uses of asymmetric orthogonal forms in landscape architectural design include: spatial foundation, exploratory experience, architectural extension, urban fit, and site adaptability.

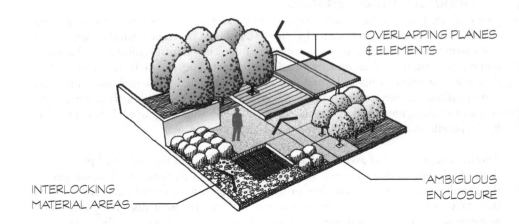

OVERLAPPING PLANES
& ELEMENTS

AMBIGUOUS
ENCLOSURE

INTERLOCKING
MATERIAL AREAS

8.4   Typical spatial qualities of an asymmetric
orthogonal space.

8.5   Example of overlapping ground
materials in a modern style design.

Spatial Foundation

A principal use of asymmetry in site design is to serve as the underpinning of individual and multiple outdoor spaces. As discussed in the following paragraphs, asymmetric orthogonal design is the cornerstone for a number of idiosyncratic spatial qualities.

Single Space. The asymmetrical design organization can be employed to forge either volumetric or cubist space in the landscape although the latter best capitalizes on asymmetry's relative latitude in locating elements within a space. As discussed in Chapter 2, cubist space is delineated by design elements located along the perimeter and within the space itself, resulting in a spatial volume that exists around as well as between enclosing elements (2.19) (Condon 1988). Additionally, a single asymmetrical space characteristically employs multiple forms and elements at varied distances and heights in relation to the spatial floor, a more elaborate configuration than a simple, extruded volume (2.24–25).

Cubist space based on asymmetric orthogonal forms is sometimes fabricated by overlapping ground materials, vertical planes that extend across different material areas and into the space, and overhead planes that do not necessarily coincide with the ground or vertical planes (also see additive transformation of Multiple Spaces) (8.4–5). Consequently, a typical asymmetrical space has vague, ambiguous boundaries that are often partially open to its context. Enclosure of an asymmetric orthogonal space is regularly implied rather than being plainly defined by clear and simple planes. A similar quality of an asymmetric orthogonal space is that it may not be completely seen from every vantage point (see Exploratory Experience). Some areas of the space may be partially or completely hidden by a protruding plane or elements within the space. Finally, an asymmetric orthogonal space often possesses a number of accent points that are strategically, but not symmetrically or uniformly located throughout the space (see Design Guidelines). These provide sequential points of interest that can entice a person to move about the space to seek new vantage points and notice areas that were previously obscured.

Multiple Spaces. In addition to shaping an individual space, an asymmetric orthogonal organization can also be employed to create an associated group of spaces in the landscape. The foremost means for doing so are subtraction and addition, two means of transformation presented in Chapter 1 (1.12, 1.16, 1.17, and 1.21). The result of both processes is a sequence of orthogonal spaces that collectively have spatial characteristics like an individual asymmetrical space.

Subtraction. Subtraction is the process of taking away and is a suitable transformation technique for subdividing an entire site into smaller spaces and areas (1.14–16.). Such a process is very similar to the technique of working with a grid. That is, the overall site area is progressively subdivided into ever-smaller areas until the desired size of each area is achieved. The outcome is a series of adjoining or face-to-face spaces that have an overall quiltlike quality that is akin to a grid but without its repetitive and sometimes limiting module (8.6). Each adjoining space has its own identity while retaining the spatial qualities previously discussed for an individual asymmetrical space.

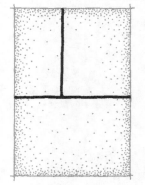
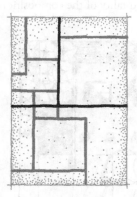
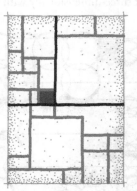

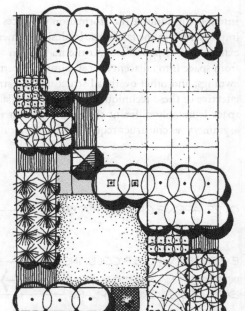

8.6 Example of a site design based on subdivision.

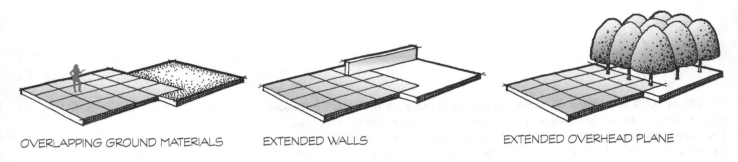

OVERLAPPING GROUND MATERIALS   EXTENDED WALLS   EXTENDED OVERHEAD PLANE

8.7 Alternative strategies for overlapping design elements.

Addition. The second general tactic for producing multiple asymmetrical spaces in the landscape is by means of addition. Addition is the transformation process of progressively building onto an existing space or area, resulting in a design configuration that expands outward into the adjoining landscape (1.17, 1.21). Three techniques of additive transformation that lend themselves to creating multiple, asymmetrical spaces are: interlocking, face-to-face, and spatial tension.

Interlocking additive transformation produces a composition of orthogonal forms that touch and overlap each other a strategy that can be implemented in the landscape by design elements in three separate planes of space (8.7). On the ground plane, the material of one area can extend into or partially cover the material in a neighboring area. Walls, fences, hedges, lines of trees, light poles, and the like can extend from space into adjacent spaces. Similarly, vertical planes can intersect and pass through each other. In the overhead plane, tree canopies, awnings, and other overhead structures can stretch between contiguous spaces in a manner that fractionally covers each. The cumulative effective of these techniques is to blur material and spatial edges so that one area gradually transitions into the next (8.8). This quality of space is notably different than that inherent in symmetrical design and the other types of asymmetrical organization. The interlocking asymmetrical construct requires the designer to think three-dimensionally with the totality of the composition in mind.

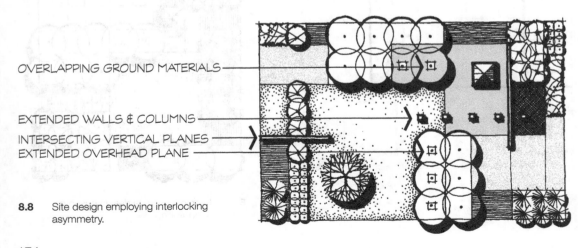

OVERLAPPING GROUND MATERIALS

EXTENDED WALLS & COLUMNS
INTERSECTING VERTICAL PLANES
EXTENDED OVERHEAD PLANE

8.8 Site design employing interlocking asymmetry.

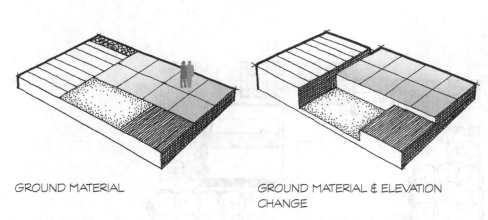

GROUND MATERIAL

GROUND MATERIAL & ELEVATION
CHANGE

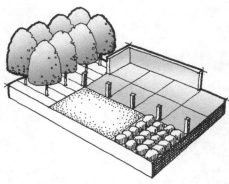

GROUND MATERIAL & 3D ELEMENTS

8.9 Above: Alternative means for defining
face-to-face spaces and areas.

A second tactic for adding asymmetrical spaces to each other is adjoining or face to face transformation. In the landscape, this tactic locates different spaces and uses immediately adjacent to one another. Each space can be distinguished from adjacent areas with different materials on the base plane, by ground elevation changes, or by creating spatial definition with three-dimensional elements like shrubs, walls, and trees (8.9). Consequently, adjoining spaces can vary in the interplay between them from complete partition to outright openness. Such an approach was the underpinning for many modern style designs like the proposal for a backyard designed by Garrett Eckbo when he was a student at Harvard (8.10).

The third technique for the additive transformation of asymmetrical spaces is spatial tension. This approach separates individual areas and design components from one another with distance and space, creating a dispersed composition. The space between the orthogonal components is a supplementary ingredient in this organization and is as important to the

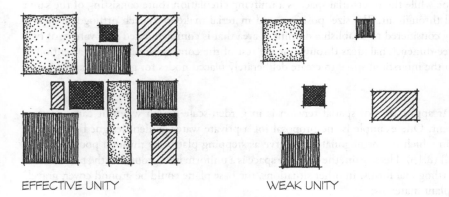

EFFECTIVE UNITY

WEAK UNITY

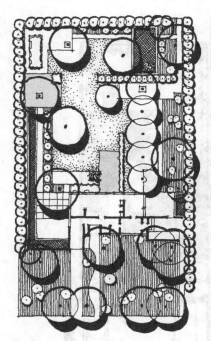

8.10 Above: Eckbo design based on face-to-
face and interlocking asymmetry.

8.11 Left: The effect of spacing on unity.

175

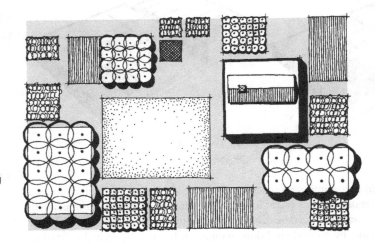

8.12 Right: Example of a site plan employing spatial tension.

8.13 Below: Eckbo water garden design demonstrating use of spatial tension.

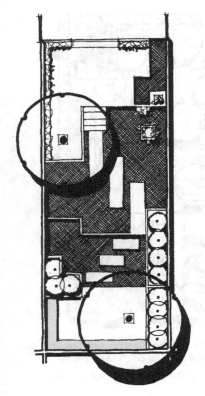

composition as the orthogonal forms themselves. When the orthogonal areas are placed in close proximity, the space functions as unifying commonality within the composition (left 8.11). As the space between the orthogonal areas increases, the sense of cohesion diminishes and can reach a point where the arrangement is a fragmented assembly of individual elements with little visual association among them (right 8.11).

Spatial tension can be used in several ways in the landscape. One is to serve as a framework for a cluster of individual orthogonal use areas (figure) separated by relatively narrow walks and nodes (ground) (8.12). Here, each orthogonal area is a unique element or space in the landscape while the interstitial space is a unifying circulation route consisting of the same material throughout. The size, position, and material makeup of each orthogonal area is carefully considered to establish a dominant area that is complemented by a variety of two and three-dimensional areas throughout the rest of the composition. Further, attention is given to the interstitial space to create deliberately placed nodes for gathering and activity centers.

A similar application of spatial tension is in garden-scale design where it can structure movement. One example is the proposal for a private water garden designed by Garrett Eckbo in which the orthogonal areas serve as stepping platforms through pools of water (ground) (8.13). Here again, the negative space is a uniform background to the prominence of the orthogonal forms. In other situations, the base plane could be ground cover, gravel, or low plant materials.

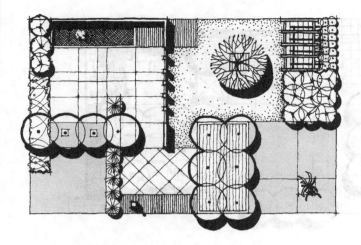

8.14 Asymmetrical design promotes an exploratory experience.

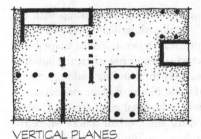

VERTICAL PLANES

CIRCULATION

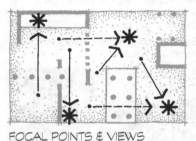

FOCAL POINTS & VIEWS

Exploratory Experience

An asymmetric orthogonal design structure can generate an exploratory experience in the landscape as previously suggested. Rather than moving predictably straight ahead as occurs in many symmetrical and grid based designs, one progresses along routes that periodically change direction in asymmetrical landscapes (8.8, 8.14; compare to 11.25, 15.19). Movement tends to be wandering and ambulatory in nature with constantly changing scenes that sequentially unfold as one proceeds (middle 8.14). However, this experience is not as casual or fluid as occurs along walks and spaces that are more curvilinear in form. A closely associated quality of the asymmetric orthogonal organization is the inclusion of multiple focal points that are strategically located to capture the eye and invite one toward it (right 8.14 and 8.32). Skillful use of the third dimension can hide or partially screen accents and views around corners so that one must move forward to points where a previously hidden scene is revealed. Collectively, the experiences in an asymmetrical landscape promote exploration and discovery to seek out new views. A person tends to be an active participant in such a landscape, not a passive observer who is content to only look.

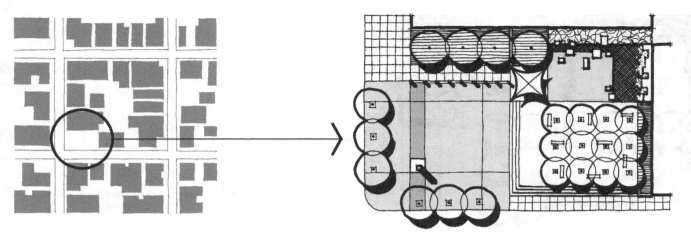

8.15 Above: Asymmetrical geometry is a suitable for a reciprocal relationship with the urban fabric.

8.16 Below: Examples of architectonic fit within urban spaces.

8.17 Right: Example of asymmetrical geometry used in a small condominium garden.

Urban Fit

Asymmetric orthogonal spaces are appropriate to forge a reciprocal relationship with the urban fabric and its ubiquitous rectangular shapes. While all orthogonal typologies fit the urban setting, asymmetric orthogonal design does so more readily because of its adaptability and informality. Asymmetric orthogonal geometry is particularly apropos where flat building walls, window patterns, and structural systems of immediately surrounding buildings can be echoed in a site with straight lines of steps, architectural walls, blocks of plant materials, and rectangular pavement patterns inherent in asymmetrical orthogonal geometry (8.15–16). Similarly, the asymmetric orthogonal structure is good for small urban spaces where the site area is notably confined like vest-pocket parks, building forecourts, condominium and rooftop gardens, and so on (8.17). Iconic examples of asymmetrical geometry in limited urban area include Greenacre Park in New York City (5.13–14). Asymmetrical geometry is able to make the most efficient use of the ground plane and avoids wasted areas and potentially awkward form relationships.

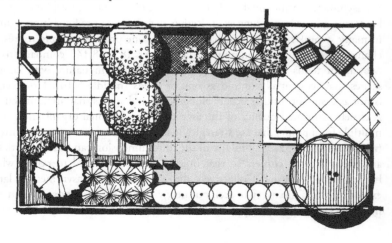

Architectural Extension

A corresponding use of asymmetric orthogonal design is to extend the organization of a nonsymmetrical building into the adjoining site so that building and landscape are perceived as one statement. This can be done by echoing the building footprint and internal organization of rooms in the landscape. Second, notable building lines and edges can be drawn into the landscape as can be done with the grid and symmetrical organizations (left 8.18). Then, pavement edges, walls, structures, and planting areas are strategically aligned with significant walls and features on the building's facade. This is particularly important immediately adjacent to the building where the connection between building and site is most apparent. The asymmetrical framework can extend across the entire site for the most discernible unity of building and site (middle 8.18). The asymmetrical configuration can also be employed immediately adjacent to a building as a transitional hinge that allows the site beyond to mutate into a different geometric structure (right 8.18).

8.18 The use of asymmetrical geometry as an architectural extension and transitional hinge.

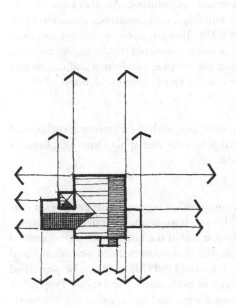

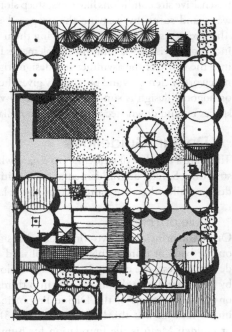

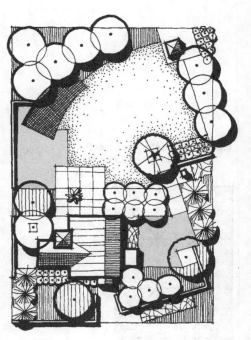

EXTENSION HINGE

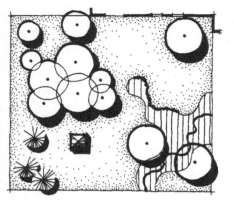

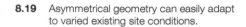
EXISTING SITE

CIRCUMVENTION

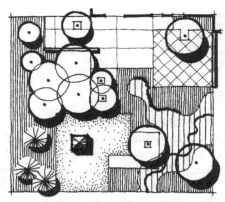
INCLUSION

8.19 Asymmetrical geometry can easily adapt to varied existing site conditions.

8.20 Ideal location for accents in photography and two-dimensional design.

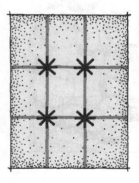

Site Adaptability

Asymmetry is the most flexible and accommodating of all the orthogonal typologies and is therefore an appropriate organizational framework for sites with varied existing conditions. As will be recalled, assorted site conditions are typically problematic for the grid and symmetry that are better suited to uniform sites where repetition and strict adherence to mirrored balance are more easily achieved. Asymmetric orthogonal design can readily adapt to sensitive site conditions like trees, steep slopes, unsuitable subsurface conditions, drainage ways, and so on by weaving the proposed uses and spaces around them (middle 8.19). This preserves fragile areas by allowing them to remain undisturbed. Another concept is to incorporate visually significant site elements like buildings, walls, specimen trees, and so on into the fabric of the asymmetrical design (right 8.19). This integrative technique embraces noteworthy elements and potentially gives them prominence within the design. Asymmetric orthogonal design is similarly adaptable to varied topographic conditions and can terrace spaces up and down steep slopes in a compliant manner (see Design Guidelines).

Design Guidelines

There are a number of guidelines to regard when designing with the asymmetric orthogonal structure. Several are fundamental compositional principles that apply to many spheres of design while others are more specific to the landscape.

Rule of Thirds

One basic principle of two-dimensional design composition is to organize design elements on the basis of thirds. This well-established "rule" in photography, painting, and graphic design suggests the compositional focus be located at one of the intersection points created by lines that divide the image area into thirds (8.20). This recommended practice is based on the proportions of the Divine Proportion (1:1.61803398874) that can be simplified into a ratio of one-third to two-thirds (2.3). As will be recalled, the Devine Proportion or Golden Mean is the foundation for numerous designs and objects that are inherently appealing to the human eye (see Chapter 5).

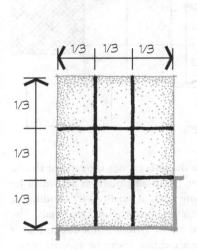

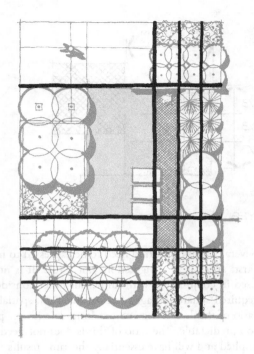

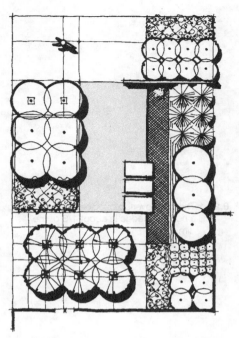

8.21 Use of the proportion of thirds as the basis for locating spaces and elements within a design.

The ratio of thirds can be applied in several ways to asymmetric orthogonal landscape design. First, it can be used to locate spaces and elements within a site by initially extending lines across the site at intervals that are approximately one-third the length and width. These delineations serve as guidelines for aligning edges of selected spaces and elements in a manner that is very much like a random grid (6.21, 8.21). Spaces within the design can also be divided into thirds as a means of locating elements within them or connecting to immediately adjoining elements. Thus, the concept of thirds can be applied in ever-smaller areas as a means of determining both size and location within a design.

A similar way to apply the ratio of thirds is to influence how individual orthogonal forms connect to each other. Face-to-face orthogonal forms with common edges should extend beside each other by almost one-third the distance along one of their sides (8.22). A mutual edge that is about one-half should be avoided because this tends to visually divide areas in two and is more in sync with symmetrical compositions than asymmetrical ones. Likewise, interlocking orthogonal forms should extend into each other by approximately one-third the area of one or both forms. Too little overlap creates a visually tenuous connection while too much overlap virtually obscures one of the forms (left and right 8.23). Also note how the orthogonal forms overlap one another in other graphic examples throughout this chapter.

181

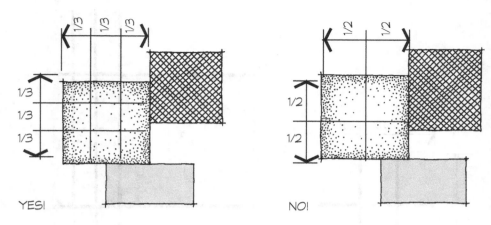

8.22 The ideal overlap of adjoining forms along a common edge is about 1/3 of the dimension.

YES!

NO!

Several words of caution need to be expressed to novice designers about the ratio of thirds. First, apply it as a suggestion, not a rule. It is not suitable in all situations and must be used in conjunction with numerous other considerations such as existing site conditions, required square footage of areas, function, spatial character, and proposed materials. The ratio of thirds can become too formulaic if over played and may result in a design that is too predictable. The ratio of thirds does not need to exact either. It can be approximately applied and will have essentially the same results. Ultimately, it is most critical that overall tone of asymmetry be kept in mind and that the design components be composed in a manner that reinforces this. Experienced designers apply the ratio of thirds intuitively based on a sense of good proportion and composition.

8.23 Use of the proportion of thirds as the basis for overlapping elements within a design.

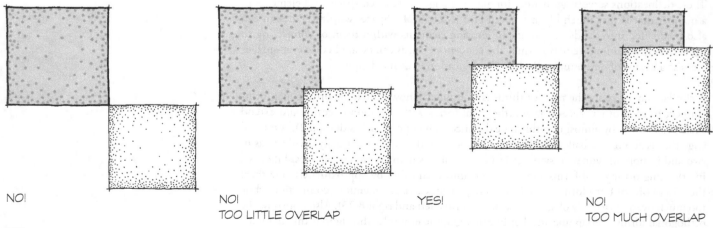

NO!

NO!
TOO LITTLE OVERLAP

YES!

NO!
TOO MUCH OVERLAP

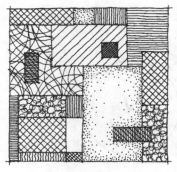

LESS DESIRABLE

MORE DESIRABLE

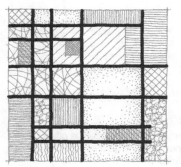
ALIGNMENT of EDGES

8.24 Above: Edges of selected orthogonal forms are aligned with each other.

Alignment

Another guideline related to the ratio of thirds advocates that edges of selected orthogonal forms within an asymmetrical design be aligned with each other (8.24). This strategy reduces the amount of randomness and provides visual reciprocity between separate design elements (8.9, 8.25). The result is visual accord among various edges and elements that are seen in relation to each other, like that which inherently occurs in a grid-based design.

A corollary is to this guideline is to prevent lines created by adjoining orthogonal forms from extending uninterrupted from one side of the design to the other (left 8.26). Lines that traverse completely through an asymmetrical design can visually divide it and fracture its singularity. A line with the potential of extending through an asymmetrical structure should be terminated with an orthogonal area that crosses its path before it reaches an opposite side or by a three-dimensional element like a wall, hedge, plant mass, and so forth that prevents the continuation of the line to other side (8.25, right 8.26).

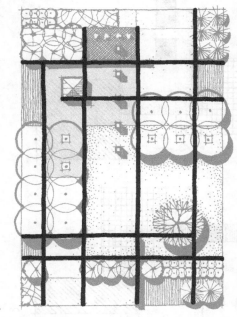

8.25 Above: Lines are intercepted before extending from side to side of site.

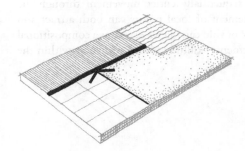

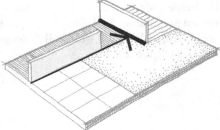

8.26 Left: Two-dimensional orthogonal areas and vertical planes intercept lines before they extend through the design.

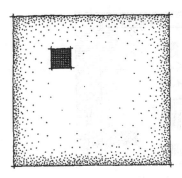

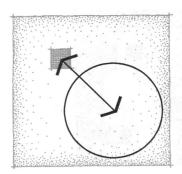

8.27 Right: Location of accent is offset by proportionally large area to bottom right of design.

8.28 Below: Position of other forms around the accent establishes overall compositional balance.

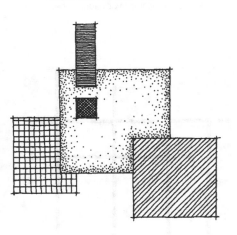

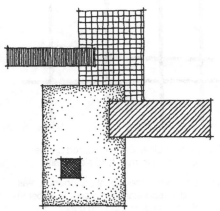

Accent Location

The location of visual accents is blatantly obvious in a symmetrical design, but not so in an asymmetrical organization. There is no unequivocal placement of a center of attention in asymmetrical orthogonal designs though several elemental principles need to be kept in mind. From a simple compositional standpoint, an accent in asymmetrical design is ideally located off-center while being visually counterbalanced by a notable area elsewhere in the composition that equalizes its visual energy. A relatively large area in an abstract design can offset a small, yet potent focal point (8.27). Similarly, the strategic massing of orthogonal forms on different sides of an accent can also neutralize its visual dominance (8.28). The placement of a compositional focus in all these situations is determined by intuitive judgment, not rational measurement.

Similar considerations should be made in asymmetric orthogonal landscape designs. An intentionally placed focal point like a sculpture, water feature, significant plant, singular structure, and so on can be located off-center within the overall site area and be counterbalanced with other elements (left 8.29). Another strategy is to employ multiple visual accents located at critical locations to sequentially entice movement through the landscape (middle 8.29 and 8.14). Such placement of focal points can both attract and reward progression. A relatively large open space or void can likewise serve as a compositional accent and be balanced with "solid" design elements skillfully placed elsewhere within the site area (right 8.29).

8.29 Alternative strategies for establishing an accent in an asymmetric orthogonal design.

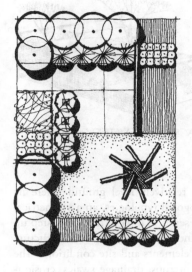

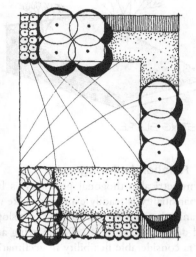

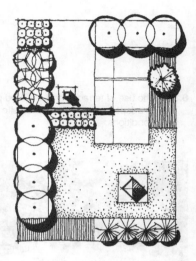

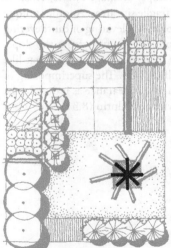

SINGLE ACCENT

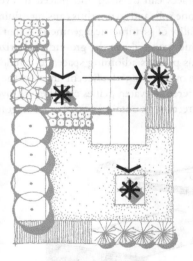

SEQUENTIAL ACCENTS

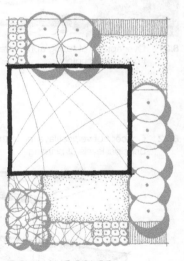

DOMINANT SPACE

185

8.30 The use of terraces and elevated planes to adapt to slopes and varied site conditions.

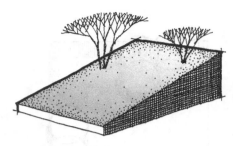

EXISTING SLOPE

TERRACES & ELEVATED PLANES

8.31 Overlapping of topographic levels in Forecourt Fountain.

Relation to Topography

Asymmetrical orthogonal geometry is best placed on relatively level ground where its planar quality is readily expressed. Like the other orthogonal typologies, an asymmetrical organization can also be adapted to a sloped site with a series of level terraces that step up and down a slope (8.30). While being adjusted to an incline, the asymmetrical structure offers considerable flexibility in acclimating to existing elements and site conditions. The terraces can be sized and placed to avoid trees, rock outcrops, drainage swales, erosion-prone soil, and so on, thus causing minimal disturbance to fragile site areas. Another unique quality of asymmetrical geometry is that it fosters the possibility of elevating or cantilevering some spaces above the ground on horizontal planes that project out away from the slope. This permits adjoining spaces to extend over one another in vertical layers somewhat like the overlapping of adjacent areas on the ground plane itself (8.7–9). The superimposing of different elevated planes can likewise give a layered topographic appearance as it does in the Forecourt Fountain in Portland, Oregon, designed by Lawrence Halprin (8.31).

8.32 Concept of vertical layering in the three principal levels of planting.

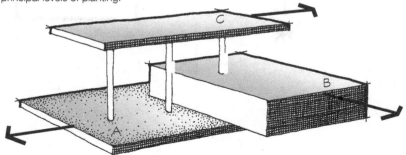

A: GROUND COVER/LOW PLANTS
B: SHRUB MASS
C: OVERHEAD CANOPY

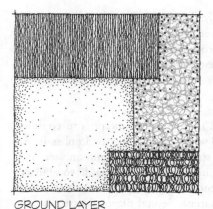

GROUND LAYER

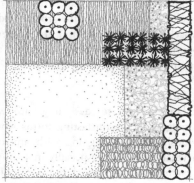
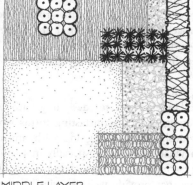

MIDDLE LAYER

OVERHEAD LAYER

8.33 Process of planting in layers in an asymmetric orthogonal design.

Material Coordination

Structural woody plants in an asymmetrical orthogonal design should be arranged in accordance with the design guidelines previous presented for the square and rectangle. What makes planting unique in an asymmetric orthogonal scheme is the opportunity to treat each of the three primary layers of plant materials as an independent though coordinated level that can extend underneath or above the others (8.32). It is typical to think of ground covers/low plants on the lowest layer, shrubs in the middle layer, and the canopy of trees in the overhead layer of a planting design. In an asymmetrical orthogonal scheme, these three layers can be woven together in a vertical mosaic so that each layer has a different relationship to other layers throughout the design. The process for this approach typically starts with organizing the ground plane into different material areas based on color, texture, season, and functional relationships (left 8.33). Then, the middle layer of shrubs is added with some masses of shrubs coinciding with the ground layer while others extend into

8.34 Introduction of other forms to complement an asymmetrical orthogonal design.

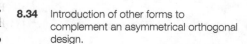

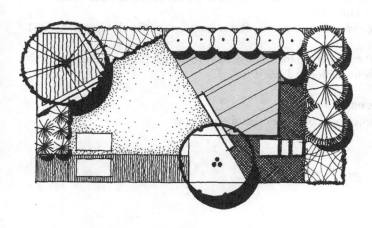

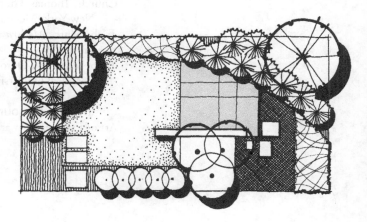

adjoining ground material areas (middle 8.33). Finally, the overhead layer of trees is added over selected areas of both the ground and middle layers (right 8.33). While this is an ideal approach, the reality is that all three layers must be considered simultaneously, so a back-and-forth coordination must take place to assure that all the layers form a synchronized three-dimensional quilt of vegetation.

Variations

One last guideline for designing with asymmetrical orthogonal geometry is to consider the integration of contrasting forms when the design context permits or implies it. As previously stated, designing with any orthogonal structure can be commonplace and somewhat predictable especially in settings that require a fresh or avant garde vocabulary. The asymmetric orthogonal framework can be augmented in such circumstances with other forms that provide well-conceived variation and contrast. Several diagonal gestures or a simple, elegant curve may be all that is necessary to create a counterpoint to the prevailing orthogonal structure (8.34). In fact, it is often best to carefully consider complementary forms and limit their placement so that they make the most impact with the least effort. Further, it is necessary to make sure that other forms properly meet the prevailing orthogonal geometry so that no awkward angles are created. When integrated properly, contrasting forms appear at ease with an orthogonal structure while providing compositional energy.

Referenced Resources

Condon, Patrick Michael. "Cubist Space, Volumetric Space, and Landscape Architecture." *Landscape Journal* (Vol. 7, No. 2), Spring 1988.

Further Resources

Brown, Jane. *The Modern Garden*. Princeton, NJ: Princeton Architectural Press, 2000.

Burton, Pamela, and Marie Botnick. *Private Landscapes: Modernist Gardens in Southern California*. New York: Princeton Architectural Press, 2002.

Church, Thomas, Grace Hall, and Michael Laurie. *Gardens Are for People*, 2nd edition. New York: McGraw-Hill, 1983.

Treib, Marc. *Modern Landscape Architecture: A Critical Review*. Cambridge, MA: MIT Press, 1993.

Treib, Marc, and Dorothee Imbert. *Garrett Eckbo: Modern Landscapes for Living*. Berkeley: University of California Press, 1997.

Internet Resources

Art of Europe: www.artofeurope.com/mondrian/thumbs.htm

The Diagonal 9

Like the straight line's association with orthogonal forms, the study of angular geometry appropriately begins with its most rudimentary element: the diagonal. This elementary component comprises the sides, axes, and internal connections between opposite corners of the triangle and other non-orthogonal polygons. The diagonal is also a design element that can be employed on its own in the landscape to exploit its unique qualities. While the diagonal is a straight line, it is seldom aligned parallel or perpendicular to other design elements in a composition. Consequently, the diagonal represents a transition between the similarity of orthogonal forms and the irregularity of organic forms.

Though somewhat unconventional in nature, the diagonal is nevertheless a distinctive element that fulfills assorted special uses. In historic classic gardens, the diagonal was occasionally incorporated as a subcomponent of the square and circle where it normally served as a conduit for views and movement across the grain of the design. The diagonal has continued to be employed in contemporary landscape architectural design as its own discrete element, routinely as an intervention in other geometric constructs or as an unorthodox foil to embolden an otherwise conventional composition.

This chapter examines various aspects of the diagonal in landscape architectural site design with attention given to these topics:
- Definition
- Typologies
- Landscape Uses
- Design Guidelines

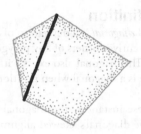
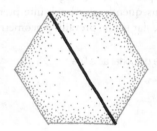
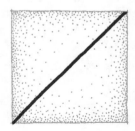

9.1 A diagonal is a line that connects two nonconsecutive points in any polygon.

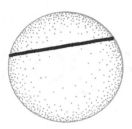 

9.2   The diagonal within a circle and triangle.

Definition

The word *diagonal* is a derivation of the Latin word "diagonus" meaning slanted line and is technically defined as a line that connects two nonconsecutive corners of any polygon (9.1). A diagonal is easily seen in the square and rectangle as a bisecting line that joins two opposite corners. The diagonal also exists within a circle as a diameter or a chord that is askew to the cardinal directions (left 9.2). Even the side of a triangle is a diagonal when positioned at an angle in relation neighboring lines or forms (right 9.2).

In all these instances, the diagonal is a derivative of the other geometric systems and possesses an oblique or slanted relationship to them. The diagonal's skewed alignment is not a quality of the line or form itself but rather its association with adjacent lines and forms. So, the aspect of being diagonal is a relative one and is not necessarily being at an angle to the cardinal directions of north/south, east/west. Consequently, this book interprets the term *diagonal* more broadly and defines it as being any line or shape that is not parallel or perpendicular to the prevailing geometry.

9.3   The diagonal as a line.

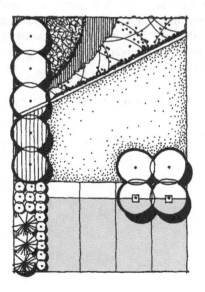 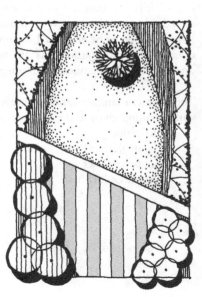

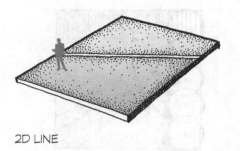

2D LINE

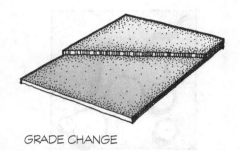

GRADE CHANGE

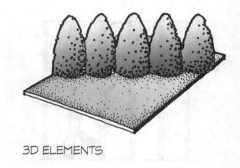

3D ELEMENTS

Typologies

There are three fundamental types of diagonals in the landscape. Though distinct from each other, they all fulfill the previous definition of being askew to the prevalent geometry within a given setting.

Line

A straight line tilted with respect to its surroundings is the most recognizable genre of the diagonal in the landscape (9.3). The diagonal line is typically an individual element that possesses most of the qualities of an orthogonal straight line except the diagonal line's alignment is askew (see Chapter 3, The Straight Line). The diagonal line may be expressed as a two-dimensional element on the ground, a distinct grade change, or with any number of elements that extend upward from the base plane (9.4). In the third dimension, the diagonal may be uniform in height or vary as a dynamic gesture through the landscape (9.5).

9.4 Alternative means for expressing a diagonal line.

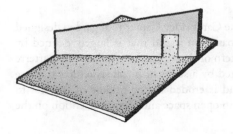

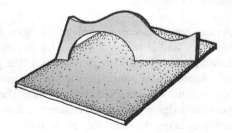

9.5 A diagonal plane may be uniform or varied in height.

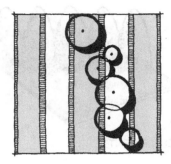
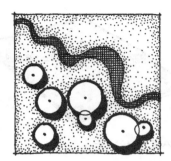
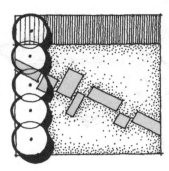

9.6   Different techniques for creating an implied diagonal.

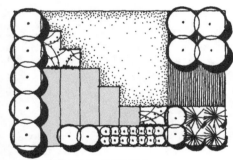

ORTHOGONAL DESIGN

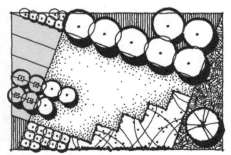

ROTATED DESIGN

9.7   The implied diagonal of the zigzag is relative to its design context.

Implied Diagonal

The implied diagonal is an assemblage of lines, and/or elements that collectively convey a diagonal in the landscape (9.6). Unto themselves, these lines and elements are arranged in their own geometric system that may or may not be the same as the overall organizational structure of the site. The implied diagonal may be expressed as a material edge, bench, wall, hedge, tree mass, and so on.

A common example of the implied diagonal is the zigzag, a series of continuous right angle corners placed at an angle to their context. The zigzag is clearly an orthogonal structure yet conveys an implied diagonal by being tilted in relation to the site borders of a conventional orthogonal site (top 9.7) or being at an angle in relation to the general inclination of a rotated alignment (see Rotation) (bottom 9.7). The zigzag, considered to be an imitation of the cubist aesthetic, was first experimented with in European gardens that were early precedents of the modern movement (Treib 1993, 96–99). These first experimentations with the zigzag were subsequently emulated in numerous modernistic gardens designed by Garrett Eckbo, Thomas Church, and others. One example is the Martin Garden, a beach side retreat designed by Thomas Church in 1948 in Aptos, California (9.8). Here, a low wood bench is designed as a saw-toothed element at the edge of a diagonally aligned checkerboard deck to suggest pockets for people to sit. The bench is an orthogonal design unto itself, but is placed to imply a diagonal edge to the sand play area and to echo the pattern of the deck.

A more contemporary example of the zigzag is the Cambridge Center roof garden designed by Peter Walker in 1979 (9.9). This design is based on a grid that is largely defined by raised planters filled with ground cover. The pattern of these planters emulates the parterre of a French Renaissance garden and is punctuated by a series of metal structures that are abstractions of trees (Sasaki 1989, 82). The grid is eroded in the middle of the site to generate a zigzag pattern of planters that frames an open space and focuses attention on the entrance along the south side of the roof.

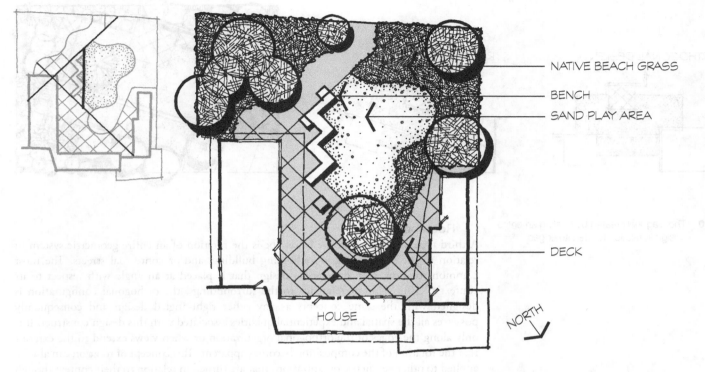

NATIVE BEACH GRASS

BENCH

SAND PLAY AREA

DECK

HOUSE

NORTH

9.8 Above: The Martin Garden.

9.9 Below: Cambridge Center roof garden.

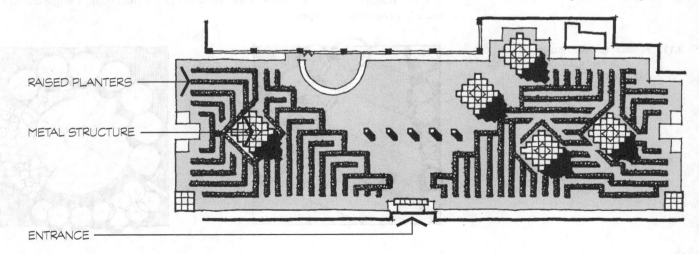

RAISED PLANTERS

METAL STRUCTURE

ENTRANCE

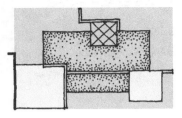

ORTHOGONAL DESIGN

ROTATED DIAGONAL

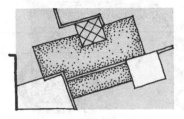

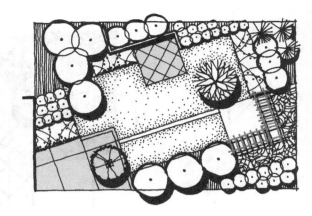

9.10 The diagonal created by rotating an entire design in relation to the site edges.

Rotation

A third type of diagonal in the landscape is the rotation of an entire geometric system in relation to the site boundaries, adjoining building, and/or contextual streets. The most common rotation is an orthogonal design that is placed at an angle with respect to its context (9.10). Without reference to the surroundings, the orthogonal configuration is designed with the same concepts as any other right-angled design and consequently possesses all the spatial and experiential qualities associated with this design construct. It is only along the edges of the orthogonal organization or when views extend to the exterior that the rotation of the composition becomes apparent. This concept of rotation can also be applied to other geometric organizations that are turned in relation to their context though their apparent divergence from it is sometimes subtle (9.11). Rotation is the most profound type of a diagonal because it embraces the entire site rather than being a single element like the other two diagonal types.

9.11 Rotation to create a diagonal can be accomplished in different geometric organizations.

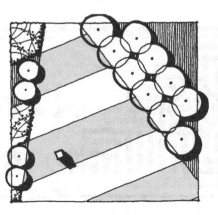

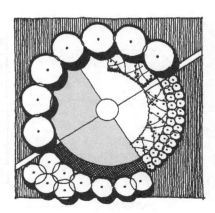

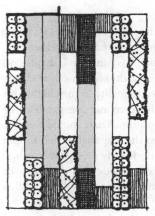

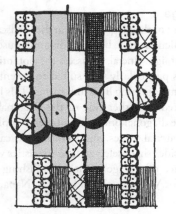

ORIGINAL DESIGN   DIAGONAL INTERVENTION

9.12 Left: Example of the diagonal used for intervention.

9.13 Below: The intervention of a diagonal is most apparent when it is in contrast to its context.

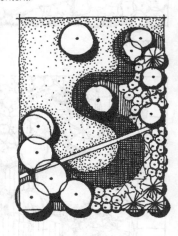

Landscape Uses

The diagonal is used in the landscape to fulfill specialized functions that are inherent to its canted orientation. Some of the applications are best fulfilled by one of the diagonal typologies while others are achieved equally well by all three. It has already been noted that the diagonal line and rotation design constructs share fundamental qualities with the straight line and orthogonal geometry. The same is true for their landscape uses. For instance, the diagonal line can direct the eye, accommodate movement, provide an architectural extension, and create rhythm in same manner as a straight line (Chapter 3). However, the diagonal is idiosyncratic it its ability to achieve these landscape uses: intervention, dividing edge, transform orientation, illusion of distance, and accommodate circulation.

Intervention

The diagonal's incongruous quality in relation to its context makes it an ideal element for intervention in a landscape. A diagonal line that is placed in an orthogonal organization is an incision that interrupts the continuity of the design and establishes a visual contradiction to the norm (9.12). Such a disruption often stimulates the composition with its inconsistency and inhibits potential monotony of an entirely homogeneous structure. Similarly, the skewed orientation and hard-edged temperament of a diagonal line contrast the graceful sweeping arcs of circular and curvilinear designs (9.13). In doing so, the diagonal emphasizes the undulation of the other geometries by its polarity of character. An implied diagonal is an intervention in the landscape when it is notably different in character to nearby forms and edges as is the case in the Martin Garden (9.8). And a rotated diagonal design construct is an interjection with respect to its surrounding context and is frequently a striking landscape because of its divergence (9.14).

9.14 A rotated diagonal design may be an intervention in its site context.

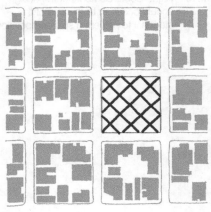

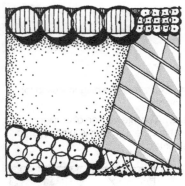

MATERIAL

STYLE

9.15 The diagonal can be used to divide different qualities of a design.

9.16 Right: Some elements of the design should occur on both sides of the diagonal to prevent a split composition.

Dividing Edge

A similar application of the diagonal line in the landscape is to impart an intentional fracture that creates a conspicuous edge between dissimilar uses, design styles, and/or materials (9.3, 9.15). While the straight line also possess the potential to fulfill this function (Chapter 3), the diagonal line is particularly well suited to accentuate a separation because it is clearly distinguishable from adjoining lines and forms. This idiosyncratic quality in turn highlights that which is located on either side of the diagonal line. However, caution needs to be exercised so that the diagonal line does not create a split composition. There should be some commonality of material, edges, and so forth that carry across the diagonal breach so that the two adjoining sides share selected characteristics while be noticeably divergent in others (9.16). One instance of a diagonal line establishing a deliberate divide in a design is the American Center for Wine, Food, and Arts in Napa, California, designed by Peter Walker Partners (3.12–13).

Transform Orientation

One of the primary qualities of the diagonal is its ability to capture and lead the eye in a direction that varies from its context. A diagonal establishes new reference points and planes that transform one's sense of orientation, a useful strategy when the site edges are too obvious or confining (9.17). Although a single diagonal can influence orientation in the landscape, a rotated diagonal design organization has the most profound ability to do so because it encompasses an entire space or site (9.10). The spatial edges and forms of the rotated diagonal collectively guide views to offer a divergent cognitive relationship to the surrounding landscape, sometimes to the point of disorientation. This can be disquieting in some circumstances but stimulating in others because of the unexpected aspect afforded.

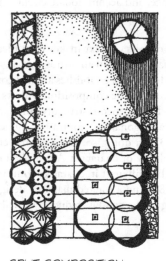

SPLIT COMPOSITION

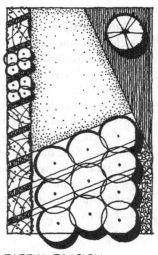

PARTIAL DIVISION

ORTHOGONAL
ORIENTATION

DIAGONAL
OVERLAY

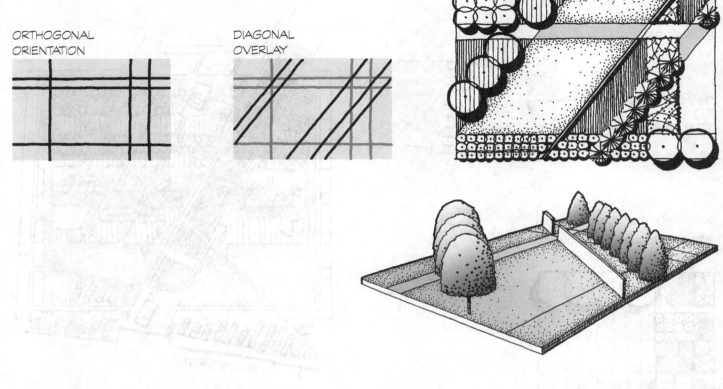

9.17 Above: The diagonal can alter the sense of orientation within a site.

9.18 Left: The diagonal can can direct the eye to points on or off the site.

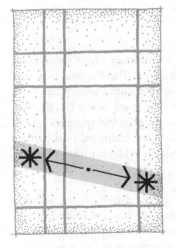

ON-SITE

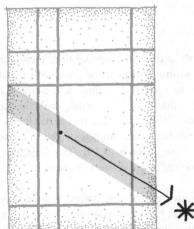

OFF-SITE

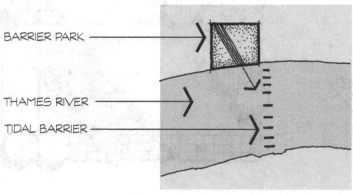

BARRIER PARK

THAMES RIVER

TIDAL BARRIER

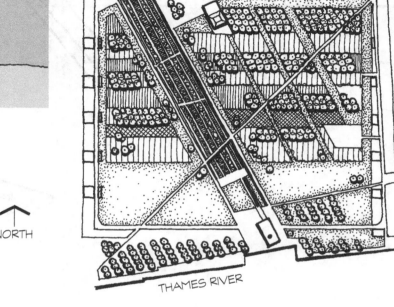

NORTH

THAMES RIVER

9.19 Right: Thames Barrier Park.

9.20 Below: An example of rotated pavement pattern.

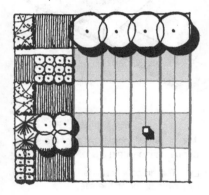

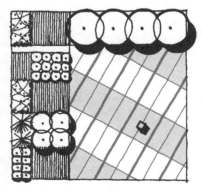

Similarly, a distinct diagonal line, plane, or corridor can intentionally direct observation along a route that is not aligned with the surrounding landscape. The diagonal may lead the eye to a specific location at the end of the line or focus observation toward an offsite prospect that is in a nonorthogonal direction in relation to the space or site (9.18). One example of this is the Thames Barrier Park in London where the principal space composed of a series linear plantings is canted to orchestrate attention to the sculptural tidal barriers in the Thames River (9.19). The diagonals also accommodate circulation from principal entry points at the corners of the site.

The rotated diagonal structure may be used more subtly as a pavement pattern within a single space (9.20). This strategy steers the eye only on the ground plane and communicates an alternative direction within an area without altering the alignment of the overall space or site. It is also a technique that can suggest larger spatial dimensions (see next section).

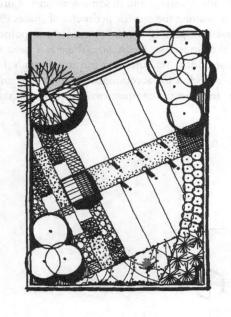

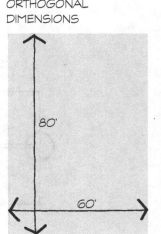

ORTHOGONAL DIMENSIONS

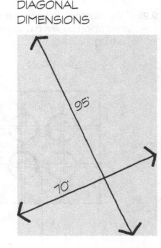

DIAGONAL DIMENSIONS

9.21 The diagonal can create the illusion of distance in a confined site.

Illusion of Distance

The diagonal is a superb device to employ in the landscape to give the impression of prolonged distance. Because the diagonal is oriented at an angle on an orthogonal site, it extends across greater distances than lines or forms that are parallel to the site boundaries (9.21). This circumstance can be taken advantage of to increase the apparent size of a site and make it feel larger than a design organization that is aligned with site edges. This technique is particularly applicable on small or confined urban sites that are enclosed by buildings, walls, or fences. A rotated diagonal configuration can give an entire site the illusion of being larger than its actual dimensions would otherwise convey.

Accommodate Circulation

The diagonal is a useful component to accommodate movement between opposite corners of spaces or sites, along random "desire lines," and on steep slopes as a means of providing a comfortable incline. In most urban settings and in some symmetrical orthogonal designs, the primary path of movement is along the outside perimeter of spaces (9.25). This makes the intersections of streets and axes primary gathering nodes and points from which to depart to other locations in the landscape. Frequently, there is a need to provide direct circulation routes between these critical junctures that traverse through the site rather than around it. Diagonal corridors are ideal for accommodating this need and readily fit into many situations because they are inherent components of squares, rectangles, and circles (4.1, 9.22).

9.22 The diagonal can accommodate circulation between opposite points in an orthogonal layout.

URBAN GRID

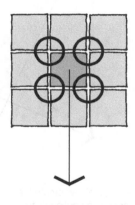

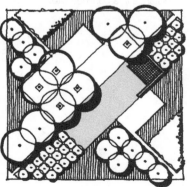

SYMMETRY

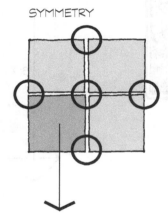

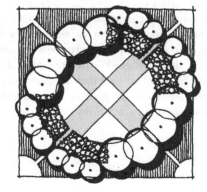

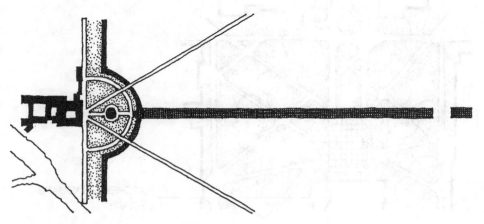

9.23 Left: Hampton Court with a goose-foot layout of principal avenues.

9.24 Below: The goose foot.

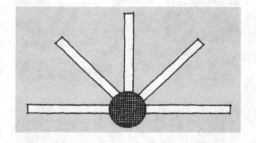

A specialized use of the diagonal for circulation in a symmetrical organization is the "goose foot," a series of walks or avenues that diverge from a central point (9.24). This design device evolved in French Renaissance gardens as a means of affording extended views through the landscape and as a way to provide circulation to and from a pivotal location. The goose foot was used at Versailles in France, Hampton Court in England (9.23), and in the plan for Washington, D.C., among others.

A second general use of the diagonal for accommodating movement is to provide paths along "desire lines" These routes of travel are actual paths of movement that pedestrians create between destinations in the landscape and usually do not fit a predetermined line that is compositionally synchronized. Rather, desire lines are random and located where needed as witnessed in campuses, parks, and urban plazas (left 9.25). Diagonal walks readily provide for such movement through the landscape with a design challenge to simplify and coordinate the placement of multiple paths (right 9.25).

9.25 Diagonal paths can accommodate desire lines through the landscape.

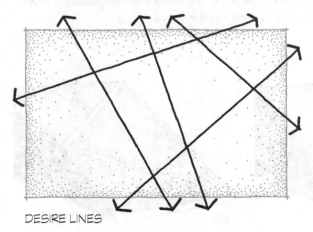

DESIRE LINES

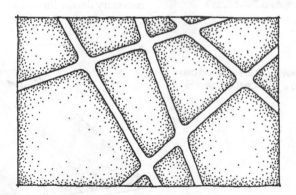

PATHS BASED on DESIRE LINES

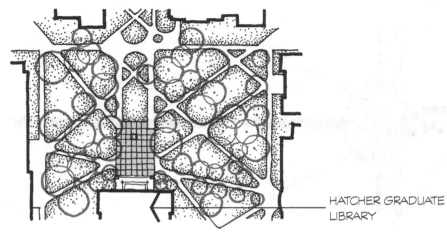

9.26 Right: Site plan of the "Diag" on the University of Michigan campus.

9.27 Below: The "Diag."

HATCHER GRADUATE LIBRARY

Two examples of the diagonal serving as a conduit for pedestrian movement on a college campus are the Diag on the University of Michigan campus in Ann Arbor and the Oval at The Ohio State University campus in Columbus (9.26–27, 14.21). The Diag, sometimes called the Diagonal Green, is a central open space that is crossed by numerous diagonal paths that intersect in a rectangular paved space. The Diag is the symbolic heart of the campus and the location for numerous planned and spontaneous events.

A third application of the diagonal in supporting passage through the landscape is by means of a gradually inclined path on a steep slope. A walk that is located perpendicular to the contours on a steep slope frequently exceeds the maximum allowable slope of 5 percent (left 9.28). A steeper walk gradient is considered to be a ramp and must adhere to its design guidelines, including a maximum slope of 8.33 percent. Consequently, a diagonal route across a slope will often provide a gradient that is less than 5 percent and permits the slope to be traversed in a zigzag manner (right 9.28). Retaining walls and handrails may be necessary details for this design strategy in some circumstances.

9.28 A diagonal walk on a steep slope can often provide a 5 percent gradient or less.

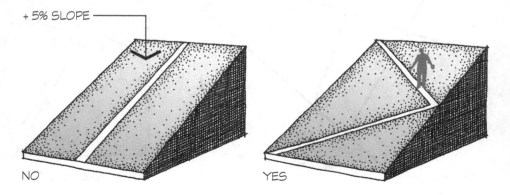

+ 5% SLOPE

NO   YES

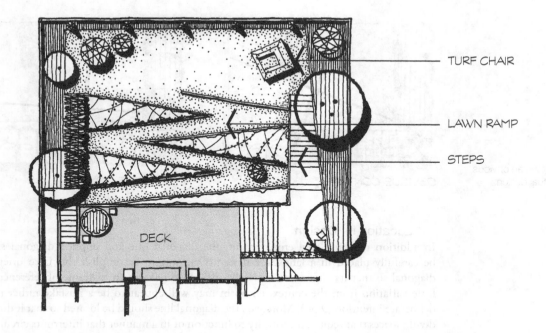

TURF CHAIR

LAWN RAMP

STEPS

DECK

An applied example of using a diagonal walk system is in a San Francisco hill-side garden designed by Andrea Cochran Landscape Architecture (9.29). Here, a 10-foot grade change between the back of the house and the lower level of the yard was connected by a broad set of stairs and a zigzag lawn ramp. Corten steel is used as retaining wall to hold the ramp in place and create crisp edges (Carlock 2005, 115–116).

9.29 A Pacific Heights, California, garden uses a diagonal lawn ramp to provide access across a steep slope.

Design Guidelines

The following guidelines are offered to facilitate the use of the diagonal in landscape architectural design. As always, these recommendations should be considered in the context of the overall design intent and the circumstances of any given site.

Use Intentionally

The diagonal is a potent design element and readily garners attention in the landscape because it is typically in contrast to its context. Therefore, the diagonal should be deliberately used to accomplish one or more of the landscape uses discussed in the previous section and should not be casually or impetuously employed. The diagonal is an idiosyncratic element and should be utilized as such. To do otherwise may cause the diagonal to be a disruptive factor in a design structure that fractures compositional cohesiveness. Further, an ill-conceived diagonal may unnecessarily draw attention to inappropriate on-site and off-site areas. So use the diagonal judiciously, doing so with all the imagination and boldness it deserves when it is incorporated into the landscape.

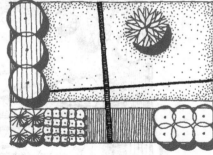

OBVIOUS CONTRAST   TOO LITTLE CONTRAST

9.30 The diagonal should have an obvious contrast to its contextual design.

Location in Design

In addition to considered employment, the diagonal line and implied diagonal should be carefully placed in a landscape design. One way to accomplish this is to orient the diagonal so that its alignment is clearly distinct in relation to its frame of reference. Too little variation from the contextual norm may well appear to be a mistake rather than a deliberate intention (9.30). Moreover, the diagonal line should be located so that it does not divide spaces that require uniformity to function or in a manner that interrupts circulation. Not all areas of a design can accept a diagonal line and still perform as intended. Similarly, a diagonal should not create unusable remnant spaces that are too small and compositionally meaningless (9.31). All these recommendations require the diagonal to be considered as an integral element that is incorporated into the design from the outset. The diagonal typically will be less successful if it is an element appended to a completed design.

9.31 The diagonal should not create remnant spaces that have little use.

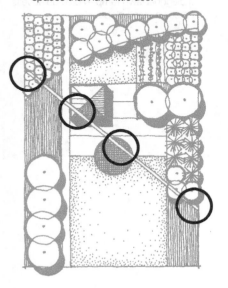

Connection to Context

The diagonal is always at odds with its context and so is automatically problematic in how it connects to adjoining forms and lines. Consequently, many of the design guidelines offered for the triangle also apply to the diagonal (see Design Guidelines, Chapter 10). The foremost recommendation is to position the diagonal in a design so that it does not create acute angles with nearby forms (9.32). As discussed in Chapter 10, acute angles create numerous functional and compositional problems that should be avoided.

Similar thoughts also apply to the rotated diagonal design construct. With this genre, the connections to site edges and contiguous buildings need to be carefully studied to avoid potential problems. Sometimes an abrupt disconnect with context is sought and so the visual discordance of forms is tolerable (left 9.33). In other circumstances, it is best to create a transition between the diagonal system and its surroundings to ease the connection between dissimilar design configurations (right 9.33).

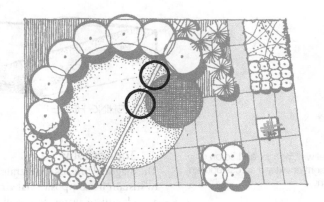

9.32 The diagonal should not create acute angles with other site elements.

Material Coordination

Materials along a diagonal line should be treated like they are along a straight line. Plant materials, especially trees and other woody structural vegetation, are effectively used along the length of the diagonal to reinforce its directionality and its effectiveness as a spatial edge (9.4 and right 9.18). Materials in a rotated diagonal structure should adhere to the guidelines of the orthogonal design organizations while accommodating sound connections to the site and its context (see Design Guidelines, Chapters 4–8).

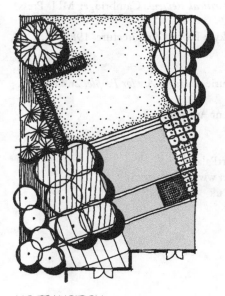

NO TRANSITION

TRANSITION

9.33 The transition of a diagonal design with the site edges should be carefully studied.

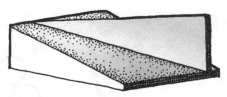

DIMINISHING HEIGHT

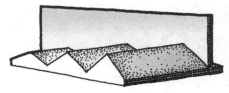

CONTRASTING HEIGHT

9.34 A diagonal wall, hedge, and so on may vary in height or extend across uneven topography.

Topography

The diagonal line, like the straight line, requires some aspect of three-dimensional consistency to sustain its compositional virtue through the landscape. A relatively flat diagonal line like a walk, rill of water, low wall, hedge, and so forth should be sited on level ground or a uniform slope just like the straight line (3.24). A three-dimensional diagonal line delineated by a wall or row trees is more flexible. Such a line can be sited on varied topography as long as it is visible throughout its extent. In some instances, this requires the line to maintain a constant top elevation while in other situations the height can change (9.5 and 9.34). The topographic base for rotated diagonal layout should be treated like the grid or asymmetrical orthogonal design structures (see Design Guidelines, Chapters 6 and 8).

Referenced Resources

Carlock, Marty. "The Short, Glamorous Life of a Show Garden." *Landscape Architecture*, April 2005.

Treib, Marc. *Modern Landscape Architecture: A Critical Review.* Cambridge: MIT Press, 1993.

Sasaki, Yoji, ed. *Peter Walker: Landscape as Art.* Tokyo: Process Architecture, 1989.

Futher Resources

Church, Thomas D., Grace Hall, and Michael Laurie. *Gardens Are for People*, 2nd edition. New York: McGraw-Hill, 1983.

Discover Thames Barrier Park. London Development Agency.

Internet Resources

Hampton Court: www.hrp.org.uk/HamptonCourtPalace

Peter Walker and Partners Landscape Architecture: www.pwpla.com

Thames Barrier Park: www.thamesbarrierpark.org.uk

The Triangle 10

The triangle is one of the primary forms identified in Chapter 1 and can be employed in landscape architectural design as a pure geometric form, combined with other triangles, or transformed to establish more complex geometric configurations. The use of the triangle is essentially a phenomenon of the modern design movement that evolved from abstract and cubist art during the first quarter of the 1900s. Garrett Eckbo was one of the first landscape architects to explore the use of triangles in some of his early residential designs (10.22). While they have never been a prevalent design genre, triangles in site design have been and remain a viable design motif to express creativity, animate a landscape, and resolve idiosyncratic site conditions. This chapter examines various aspects of triangles in landscape architectural design including:

- Geometric Qualities
- Landscape Uses
- Design Guidelines

Geometric Qualities

The triangle is the first and most fundamental polygon to be derived when attempting to enclose a space with multiple lines. The sides of a triangle connect three points that are nonlinear in their spatial relationship and are joined by three interior angles that total 180 degrees or half that of the square (10.1). Interestingly, the triangle's sides proportionally enclose the largest area in relation to the length of perimeter when compared to all other polygons. The triangle has other unique geometric qualities that differentiate it from the square and circle as described in the following paragraphs.

Angles

Perhaps the most distinguishing characteristic of the triangle is the conspicuous angles formed by the intersection of its sides. The very essence of the triangle implies sharp corners jutting into space and is the basis for much of the symbolism that is associated with the triangle (see Landscape Uses). Unlike the square, the triangle's interior angles can vary in size and fall into three general categories, each with its own distinction and design implications:

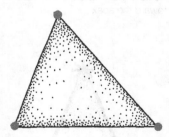

10.1 A triangle is formed by connecting three nonlinear points.

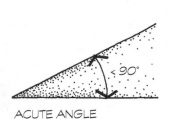

ACUTE ANGLE

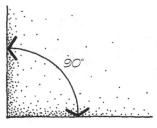

RIGHT ANGLE

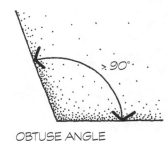

OBTUSE ANGLE

10.2 Types of interior angles.

acute angle, right angle, and obtuse angle. Acute angles are less than ninety degrees and are the most pronounced of all angles (left 10.2). The merging sides forcefully direct attention toward its apex, a consequence that becomes more noticeable as the angle narrows (10.3). When the acute angle is a two-dimensional form on the ground, this assertive orientation leads the eye outside the confines of the triangle to what lies beyond (middle 10.3) (see Landscape Uses). When the sides of the triangle are vertical planes, acute angle corners capture the eye and hold it captive, a phenomenon more pronounced than in the corners of a square (1.5 and right 10.3). This not only creates a sense of enclosure, but also causes a disquieting feeling of entrapment especially as the enveloping planes increase in height and/or as a person moves further into the corner. Consequently, acute angles are spatially and psychologically problematic in landscape architectural design (see Design Guidelines).

10.3 Acute angles capture the eye and direct it toward the apex.

Ninety-degree interior angles of a triangle share all the qualities of the square's corners (middle 10.2). An obtuse interior angle of a triangle is greater than 90 degrees and is a comparatively weak angle (right 10.2). That is, it is the most ambiguous angle to perceive

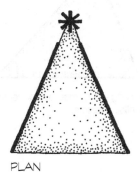

PLAN

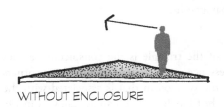

WITHOUT ENCLOSURE

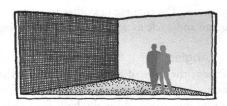

WITH ENCLOSURE

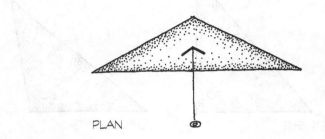

PLAN

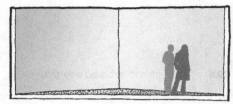

because the two adjoining sides tend to visually coalesce unless they are noticeably different in material composition (10.4). The two sides of an obtuse angle can readily be seen as one continuous edge when viewed straight on. Similarly, an obtuse angle lacks the enveloping quality of acute and right angles, relying almost entirely on height for a sense of enclosure.

Because each interior angle of a triangle directly affects the length of the opposite side, the dimensions of the triangle's sides are likewise potentially different from one another. Consequently, the triangle is a less consistent entity than either the square or circle making its design use more challenging. In some circumstances, the variability of the triangle can be celebrated to produce design compositions of intentional diversity (left 10.5). The assorted sizes and proportions create a random and mixed composition with an irregular silhouette. By comparison, triangles with the same size and/or proportion are needed to fashion a uniform pattern. In addition, these triangles must be placed so that identical sides and corners coincide with each other (right 10.5).

10.4 An obtuse angle produces a weak corner with little distinction between the two sides.

10.5 The uniformity of triangles affects how they can be assembled in a design.

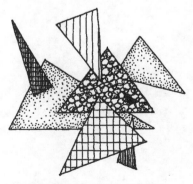

VARIED SIZE & PROPORTION

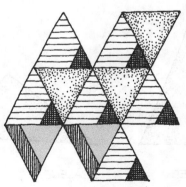

UNIFORM SIZE & PROPORTION

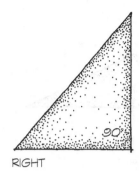
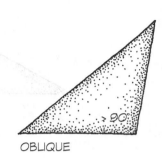
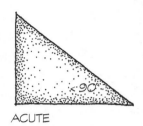

10.6 Types of triangles based on interior angles.

RIGHT   OBLIQUE   ACUTE

Types of Triangles

The triangle's variable interior angles create many kinds of triangles. One way to classify triangles is by the size of the interior angles relative to 90 degrees. A triangle with a 90-degree interior angle is referred to as a "right triangle" (left 10.6). A triangle that has one angle greater than ninety degrees is called an "oblique triangle" (middle 10.6) and a triangle with all three interior angles less than 90 degrees is termed an *acute triangle* (right 10.6).

The other method for categorizing triangles is by the relative proportions of the three sides and angles. An *equilateral triangle* possesses three interior angles that are each sixty degrees and accordingly three equal sides (left 10.7). The equilateral triangle is symmetrical and shares some qualities of the square and circle including interior axes which bisect each angle. An *isosceles triangle* has two interior angles that are the same and consequently two sides that are equal in length (middle 10.7). The angles and opposite sides in a *scalene triangle* are each different making it the most irregular triangle (right 10.7).

10.7 Types of triangles based on relative proportions of the sides.

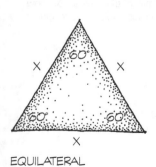
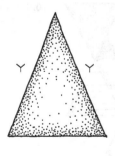
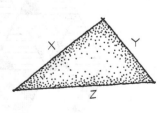

EQUILATERAL   ISOSCELES   SCALENE

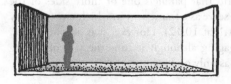

SQUARE

CIRCLE

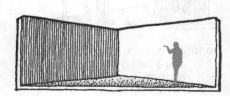

TRIANGLE

Landscape Uses

The triangle, either as a single entity or an assemble of multiple triangles, has a number of possible uses in the landscape architectural site design including the following: spatial foundation, alter orientation, direct views, guide movement, intervention, fit interstitial sites, sculptural accent, and suggest symbolic meanings.

Spatial Foundation

Like the square and circle, the triangle can be used in landscape architectural design as the foundation of outdoor space although the triangle is more limited in this capacity because of its inherent geometric qualities. As with the square, there are two fundamental spatial typologies that can be generated with the triangle: (1) single space and (2) an association of multiple spaces.

Single Space. A single triangular space is most appropriately used to direct views, guide movement, provide an intervention, and/or fit an irregularly shaped site (see other Landscape Uses in this section). Unlike the square or circle, a triangular space is not as well suited for congregation or other general functions because of its converging sides (10.8). As indicated before, the progressively narrow dimensions at the triangle's apex make this area too small for most landscape uses.

A single triangular space can be a volumetric space or cubist space, the two fundamental spatial typologies initially discussed in Chapter 2. An open volumetric space is established by extruding the triangle's sides with walls, planar masses of plant materials, rows of tress, and so forth (top 10.10). Such a space has a clear sense of enclosure but tends to focus attention towards its corners as previously discussed. A cubist space is forged by interlocking forms in the three planes of enclosure and/or interjecting elements within the space. A cubist space has a more complex interplay among design elements that negates the ever-present lure towards the corners (bottom 10.9 and 10.10). Both types of triangular spaces can be disorienting because of the lack of orthogonal sides and the inability to be aligned with the cardinal directions of north, south, east, and west.

10.8 Above: Comparison of the spatial enclosure created by the three primary shapes.

10.9 Below: Volumetric and cubist spaces based on the triangle.

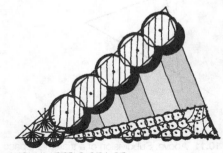

VOLUMETRIC SPACE

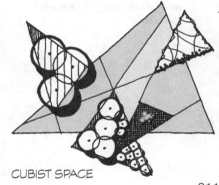

CUBIST SPACE

211

10.10 The confining nature of a triangular space can be minimized by interior elements and planes.

Volumetric and cubist triangular spaces can be subdivided into various material areas although not as clearly as in the square or circle where axes, inherent grid structure, or radii imply edges of smaller areas within. A relative easy way to partition the triangle is to create smaller triangular areas within the perimeter of the larger one (10.11). The location, size, and proportion of the smaller areas should be based on program and an eye for good composition. Another strategy is to create a grid that parallels one or more sides of the triangle (left 10.12). Or, the triangle can simply serve as a frame within which any typology of forms is inserted as a means of subdivision (right 10.12). However it is accomplished, a more elaborate triangular space is more engaging although it runs the risk of feeling partitioned and thus no longer being perceived as only one volume.

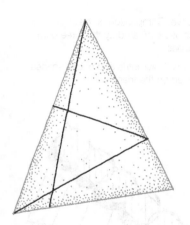

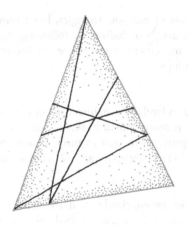

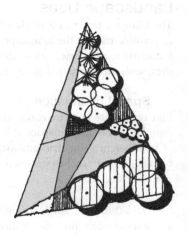

10.11 Above: Subdivision of a triangular space via smaller triangles.

10.12 Right: Subdivision of a triangular space via a grid or divergent geometric structure.

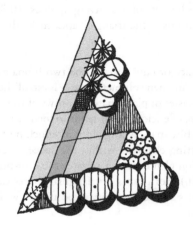

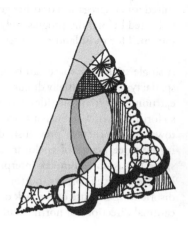

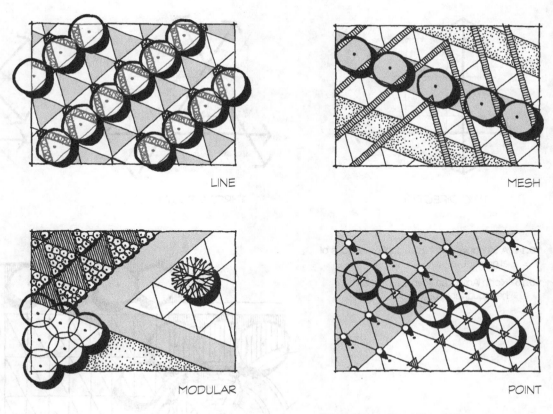

LINE

MESH

MODULAR

POINT

10.13 Triangular grid typologies.

Multiple Spaces. The triangle can also be used as a building block for an ensemble of associated uses that collectively have a more complex interplay of spatial volumes and the potential for fulfilling a range of landscape uses not possible with an individual triangle. The three principal organizational structures for assembling multiple triangles are the grid, symmetry, and asymmetry discussed in Chapter 1.

Grid. The simplest tactic for arranging multiple triangles as the basis of a landscape design is the grid, a configuration that is normally associated with the orthogonal geometry previously discussed in Chapter 6. However, if a grid is simply thought of as being a repetitive pattern based on the same shape, then any form including the triangle can forge a continuous, nonhierarchical field. A triangular grid can be established by equilateral, isosceles, or right triangles to create line, mesh, modular, or point grids (10.13). Scalene triangles do not lend themselves to a grid because of the dissimilar length of their sides. Like an orthogonal grid, a triangular grid is a disciplined, systematic approach to coordinating spaces and elements in the landscape.

213

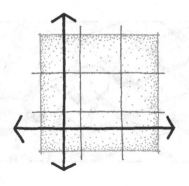

TWO DIRECTIONS

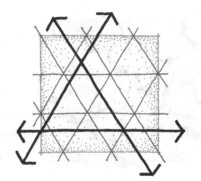

THREE DIRECTIONS

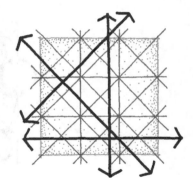

FOUR DIRECTIONS

10.14 A triangular grid has multiple directions of alignment.

10.15 North American Toyota Motor Sales headquarters courtyard.

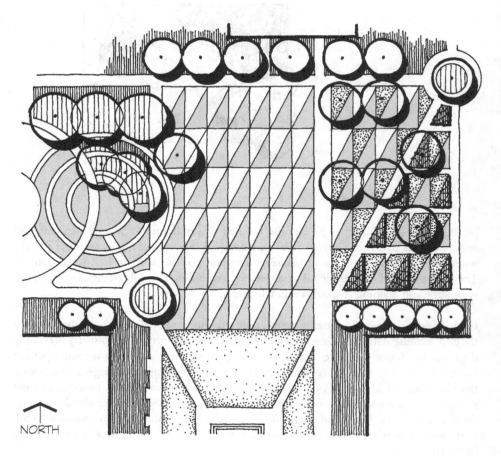

NORTH

214

A triangular grid has several unique qualities in comparison to the orthogonal grid. First, it has three or four directions of alignment instead of two (10.14). Isosceles and equilateral triangles create a structure that has three orientations and right triangles create a grid with four. These additional inclinations provide more options for movement through the grid. A second distinct quality of the triangular grid is that the angles between sides are not fixed as in an orthogonal grid. Consequently, a triangular grid can be acclimated to fit the shape of a site, existing site conditions, anticipated circulation routes, compositional objectives, and so on.

An illustration of a triangular grid is found in the design of the main courtyard of the North American Toyota Motor Sales headquarters in suburban Los Angeles (10.15). This award-winning project designed by LPA, Inc. uses a right triangle as the basis of a grid in the courtyard. Recalling Moorish tile patterns, the striking pattern is defined both within the pavement and in a garden area composed of trees, boxwood, lawn, and benches (Newman 2006, 118–125). The grid also accommodates a diagonal path of circulation between the entrance court to the south and another green space to the northeast.

Symmetry. Triangles, like orthogonal forms, can be assembled along one or more axes although these structures have limited application in landscape architectural design because of the challenge of connecting triangles. While symmetrical compositions of individual triangles can be easily depicted on paper, in reality it is difficult to accomplish this because the triangles must eventually join one another at a single point regardless of how they are assembled (10.16). One technique that does have merit for a symmetrical organization of triangles is the grid. By massing triangles together in a regular pattern, some of the issues of joining triangles can be minimized though not completely eliminated (10.17). Another potential symmetrical organization of triangles in the landscape is the subdivision of one triangle into smaller component areas.

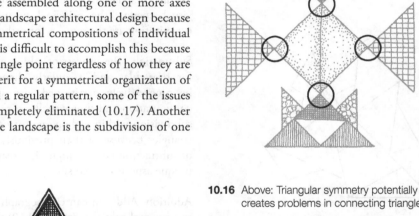

UNDESIRABLE CONNECTION

10.16 Above: Triangular symmetry potentially creates problems in connecting triangles.

10.17 Left: An example of a grid used as the basis of triangular symmetry.

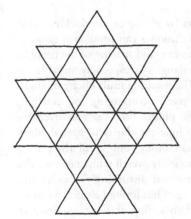

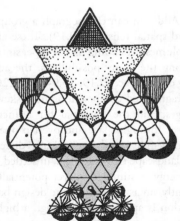

215

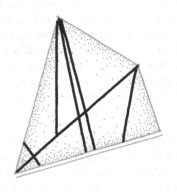

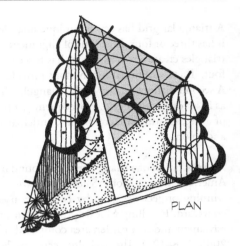

PLAN

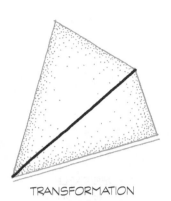

TRANSFORMATION

10.18 Use of subtraction to create a design that is in sync with an oddly shaped site.

10.19 Below: Example of face-to-face addition.

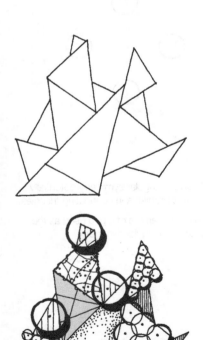

Asymmetry. An asymmetrical assemblage of triangles is befitting as the basis landscape architectural design because it capitalizes on the triangle's inherent variability and potential visual energy. The principal means of transforming triangles into an asymmetrical organization are the same as for orthogonal forms: subtraction and addition.

Subtraction. The process of taking away from or subdividing an area is most applicable for triangular and irregularly shaped sites because it permits these unusual sites to be progressively partitioned into smaller areas that are reflective of the overall site configuration and thus visually in sync with it (10.18) (also see Landscape Uses). Unlike subdivision within orthogonal forms, there is no common method for subdividing with triangles because of their previously discussed inconsistency. Consequently, the process of subtraction with triangles is a reactionary one that extemporaneously responds to the unique aspects of each site.

Addition. Addition can choreograph a group of triangles by means of interlocking, face-to-face, and spatial tension (10.19). These alternative techniques can produce a range of outdoor volumes depending on the type, similarity, alignment, and spacing of the triangles used. Among the many possibilities, the addition of triangles is especially suitable for fabricating cubist space (2.19, 10.9–10, 10.20, 10.21). The resulting multiplicity of angles creates a fragmented composition with askew lines and planes, converging and diverging spatial edges, and the potential for numerous vantage points. Vertical and overhead planes pierce through space and overlap one another to hide the clarity of spatial edges. Circulation wanders and is erratically directed along circuitous routes. All these traits result in a landscape that is restless, unsettled, and nervous in its overall temperament. This agitated energy is stimulating, yet potentially disquieting and disturbingly disorienting. Consequently, an asymmetrical site design based on triangles has limited situations where its disposition is appropriate although a high-energy urban setting or a site requiring an idiosyncratic statement is fitting.

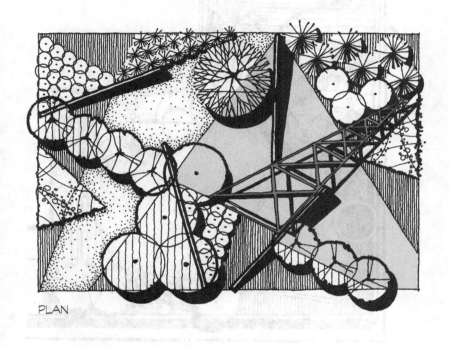

PLAN

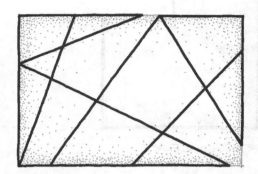

TRIANGULAR STRUCTURE

10.20 Left: The use of triangles to provide the foundation for cubist spaces.

10.21 Below: The three planes of enclosure as they relate to the triangular structure.

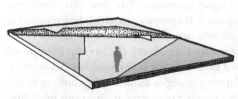

GROUND AREAS

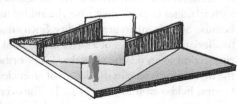

WALLS

WALLS & TREES

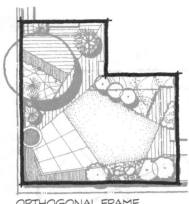

ORTHOGONAL FRAME

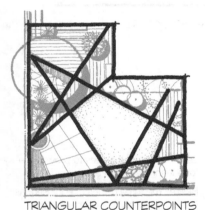

TRIANGULAR COUNTERPOINTS

10.22 Jones residence.

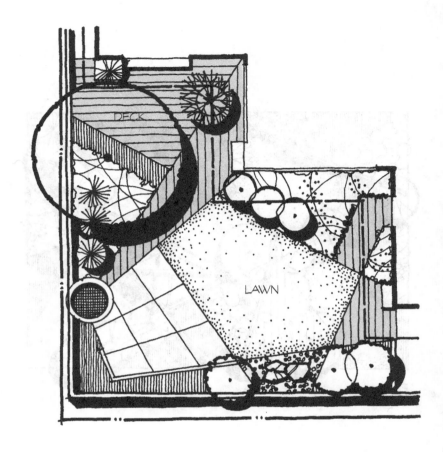

Alter Orientation

Similar to the diagonal discussed in the previous chapter, the triangle can alter one's sense of direction and orientation in the landscape. However, the affect is often more profound with triangles because they have the ability to suggest numerous directions within one site because of their inherent variability. Such an approach is apropos where the design intent is to alleviate the confines of a small orthogonal site or where the objective is to make a visual connection to an off-site view that is not orthogonally aligned with the site. An example of the first intent is seen in the design of an enclosed garden on the Jones residence designed by Garrett Eckbo around 1940 (10.22). The overlapping triangles diminish the confines of the surrounding orthogonal box and lead the eye in a number of divergent directions including toward a circular water feature. The site edges become merely a background frame for an engaging internal design.

Direct Views

The triangle's converging sides direct views in the landscape especially when they are expressed in the third dimension by buildings, walls, topography, and vegetation (10.3). The merging vertical planes function like blinders to screen exterior elements and to focus attention on the point where the enclosing planes meet. The phenomenon can be intentionally exploited to guide views to key locations and elements (10.23). This is a powerful action and should be used only where the focal point is worthy of concentrated attention.

A concurrent use of the triangle is to create a forced perspective in the landscape. When one looks through a space with parallel sides, it appears as if the sides visually move closer together the farther they extend into the distance (left 10.24). This is a normal occurrence and gives a sense of the depth to the view. This phenomenon is accentuated when the two sides of the space actually converge as they do in a triangle, thereby fooling the eye into believing the end point is farther away (middle 10.24). This same phenomenon can be used in the landscape to give the illusion of greater depth when looking through a space where it is expected the sides are parallel.

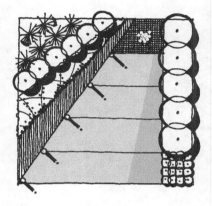

10.23 Above: A triangular space can concentrate views towards an accent.

10.24 Below: The effect of converging sides on the sense of depth.

VIEW ALONG RECTANGLE

VIEW ALONG TRUNCATED TRIANGLE

VIEW ALONG TRUNCATED TRIANGLE from OPPOSITE END

NOTE: THE DEPTH IS THE SAME IN ALL VIEWS

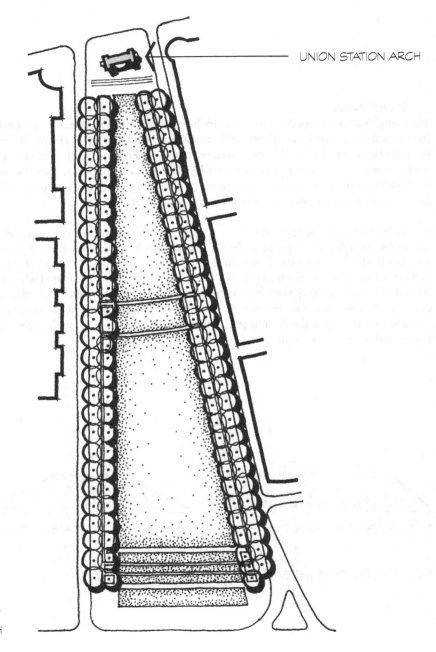

UNION STATION ARCH

10.25 Right: Site plan of McFerson Commons.

10.26 Below: McFerson Commons.

NORTH

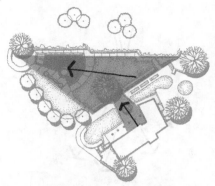

PERCEIVED DISTANCE EXTENDED

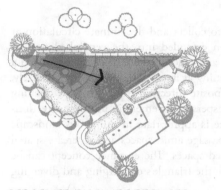

PERCEIVED DISTANCE REDUCED

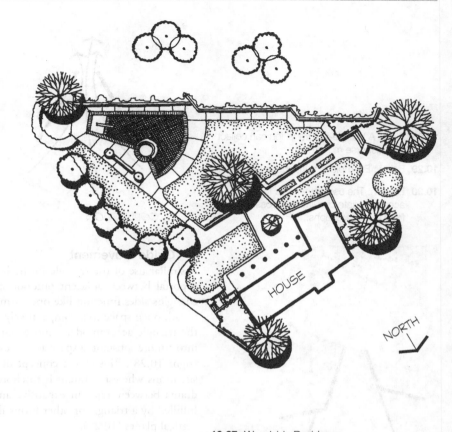

10.27 Woodside Residence.

One example using the triangle to focus vews and amplify distance in the landscape is McFerson Commons in Columbus, OH designed by the landscape architectural firm MSI (10.25–26). This open space is in the core of the Arena District, a large urban development project incorporating office, retail, residential space, and the Nationwide Arena. Adjoining buildings, streets, and rows of trees extend the length of the Commons to define the triangular form of the park. Collectively, these elements direct attention to the Union Station Arch, an architectural remnant of a historically significant train station that once stood several blocks away. The Arch is symbolically the heart of the Arena District and so is appropriately emphasized. From the southern end of the space, the triangular form of the Commons also exaggerates the north-south distance, making it appear longer than it actually is.

The triangle can likewise be used in the landscape for a completely opposite effect. That is, when one looks from the confined end of the triangle to its opposite side, the diverging sides of the triangle decrease the sense of depth and create the perception that the end of the space is closer to ones' vantage point (right 10.24). So, the triangle can furnish two completely opposite sensations of size and depth in the landscape depending on one's position relative to the triangle. A good illustration of this sensation is a residential landscape in Woodside, California, designed by Thomas Church in 1953 (10.27) (Church 1983, 200). Here, the backyard with a prominent tree, lawn, and pool seems larger when viewed from the house and porch because of the accentuated sense of depth. By comparison, the view from the diving board end of the pool toward the house is foreshortened, giving the feeling that the house and tree are closer to the pool.

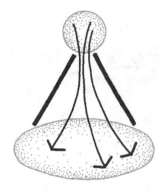

COLLECTION

DISPERSAL

10.28 Right: A triangle-like transition can collect and disperse movement.

10.29 Below: Example of a triangular transition.

10.30 Bottom: The use of triangles to accommodate circulation across a site from many directions.

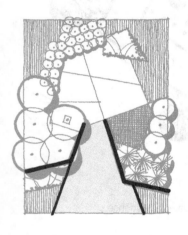

Guide Movement

A similar use of the triangle in the landscape is to collect and disseminate circulation at a portal between adjacent outdoor spaces. When extended into the vertical plane, the triangle's sides function like open arms to collect and guide pedestrian circulation from a broad, open space to a comparatively narrow opening at its apex (left 10.28). Conversely, the triangle accommodates movement in the opposite direction from a narrow opening into a more substantial space as a threshold that disperses movement in multiple directions (right 10.28). This classic concept of an entrance is appropriate in numerous landscape situations where the intent is to choreograph a passage amid spaces and to create spatial drama between adjacent expansive and constricted spaces. The entrance concept can be fulfilled by a triangle or other forms that replicate the triangle's converging and diverging vertical planes (10.29).

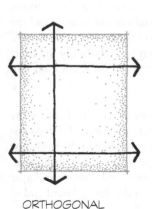

ORTHOGONAL

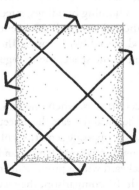

DIAGONAL

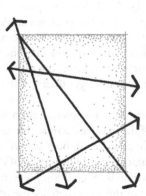

TRIANGULAR

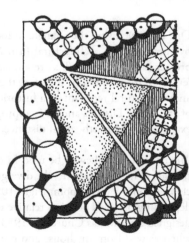

RESULTING PLAN

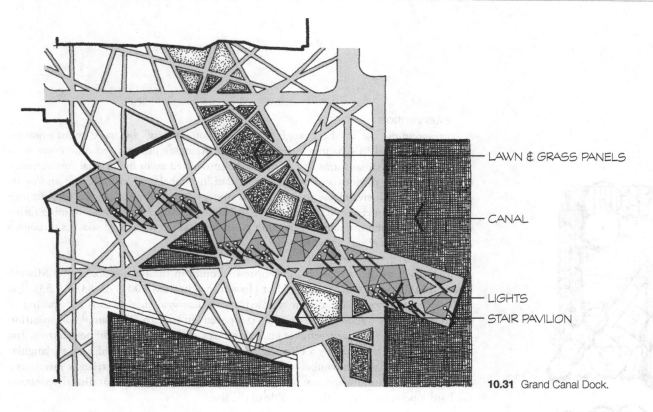

LAWN & GRASS PANELS

CANAL

LIGHTS

STAIR PAVILION

10.31 Grand Canal Dock.

Triangles can likewise be employed to embrace multiple circulation routes that are askew to site boundaries. Though this landscape use is similar to the diagonal line's ability to provide nonorthogonal routes of movement, it differs because the triangular design structure accommodates numerous independently aligned directions of movement, each with its own bearing (10.30). Even a triangular grid has the ability to provide for more directions of movement than either an orthogonal or diagonal grid as previously indicated. In addition, the triangular structure can forge a complete spatial experience that underpins and reinforces the circulation through a site.

An illustration of utilizing triangles to accommodate diverse circulation routes is the proposed design for the Grand Canal Dock in Dublin, Ireland, designed by Martha Schwartz, Inc. (10.31). As the centerpiece for redevelopment of the Docklands area, this public square is intended to be a principal gathering space and setting for a hotel, theater, and commercial building. The triangular composition is based on circulation desire lines that are woven into an intricate pattern of adjoining and overlapping triangles (Kelley 2006, 40–46.) All program elements, including areas of different pavement material, planters, a water feature, and a pavilion are skillfully integrated into the triangular structure to engender a dramatic setting.

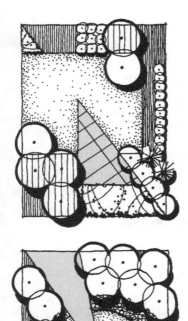

Intervention

A corresponding use of the triangle is intervention, one of the basic transformation processes discussed in Chapter 1. Because of the triangle's pronounced differences with orthogonal and circular forms, it can readily be interjected as an intentional counterpoint that generates an obvious and perhaps even clashing imbalance within a site and/or its context (10.32). There is little attempt in this strategy to make the triangular form fit into the prevailing geometry other than seeking to eliminate connections with adjoining forms that can cause functional and construction problems. Rather, the triangle slashes through a design and directs energy in a divergent orientation.

An illustration of the triangle as intervention is found in the open space at 560 Mission Street in San Francisco designed by Hart Howerton (Hinshaw 2004, 76–83) (10.33). The underlying structure of the design is based on a linear grid that extends the spacing of the adjacent office building into the site via a pavement pattern. This simple organization delineates the edge of a pool, series of grassed terraces, and a small grove of potted trees. The prevailing grid is fractured by a diagonal gravel walk that defines the edge of a triangular area densely planted with bamboo trees on the east side of the site. The triangle interjects a thicket of trunks and foliage, resulting in a verdant, intimate setting that directly contrasts the hard, open character of the west side of the site.

Fit Interstitial Sites

Another potential use of the triangular organization is to provide a design structure that deftly fits angular or atypically shaped remnant sites defined by askew streets, intersections, obliquely aligned buildings, and so on. Oddly configured sites also result from many contemporary buildings that have been deliberately designed to contravene conventional alignment with nearby streets and structures. Whatever the genesis, it is best to accept the underlying geometry of such sites rather than force a system that is at odds with it. A triangular design system often complements these sites and makes more efficient use of the available area than other design structures. One example of this use of the triangle is South Boston Maritime Park designed by Halvorson Design Partnership (10.34). This urban park sits on a site truncated by four streets near the waterfront in South Boston and includes a lawn area, café, pergolas, seating, and various elements suggestive of its location (Carlock 2004, 78–89). While ultimately comprised of numerous triangular areas, the underlying design concept for the park is two adjoining triangles created by bisecting the site on a diagonal between two opposite corners.

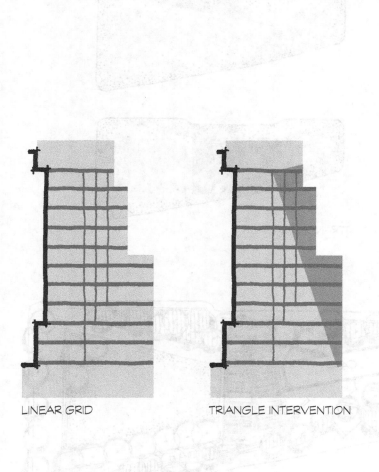

LINEAR GRID   TRIANGLE INTERVENTION

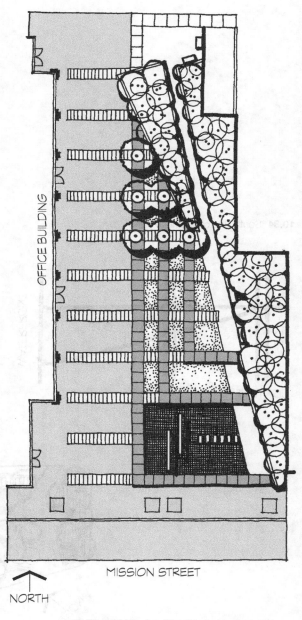

OFFICE BUILDING

MISSION STREET

NORTH

10.33 560 Mission Street open space.

225

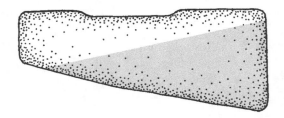

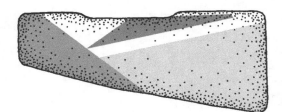

10.34 South Boston Maritime Park.

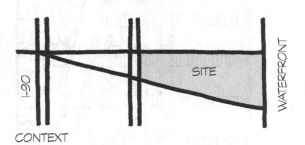

CONTEXT

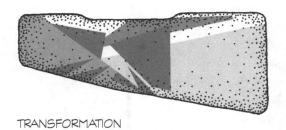

TRANSFORMATION

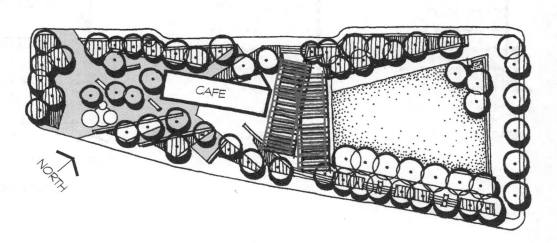

Sculptural Accent

The idiosyncrasies of a triangular based design discussed throughout this chapter can be taken advantage of to create a landscape that is intended to be a singular statement and create an enduring impression. This ability is most apparent when a triangular composition is placed in the context of a circular, curvilinear, or natural landscape where the angles are indisputably manifested (10.35). The angular forms convey discordant energy and imply tension, apprehension, and so on. One example of a design that utilizes the latent sculptural quality of a grouping of triangles is the Holocaust Memorial in Montevideo, Uruguay (10.36). This memorial designed by architects Fernando Fabiano, Gaston Boero, and Sylvia Perossio along with landscape designer Carlos Pellegrino pays tribute to the Jewish victims and families of the Holocost (Martignoni 2006, 117–120). The long wall represents the pilgrimage of Jewish people over time that is broken in the middle by a precarious massing of slanted walls symbolizing the Holocaust itself. A triangular design is uniquely suited to convey this message and serve as a landscape symbol.

Symbolic Meanings

There are many emblematic associations with the triangle that can be exploited in the landscape including its subconscious correlation with danger. As previously indicated, acute angles create harsh, abrupt, and lance-like corners that are intuitively unpleasant and imply a perilous situation. Consequently, the innate response to the triangle is one of avoidance. The traffic yield sign, the hazard warning signal on a car's dashboard, the international symbol for radiation warning, and the civil defense symbol for fallout shelter all incorporate the triangle. The unfavorable quality of the triangle is further reinforced by fundamental concepts of Feng Shui that suggest the triangle possesses evil energy in its apexes where it is trapped and cannot escape (Wong 1996, 152).

10.35 Above: Triangles can create a sculptural accent when contrasted to the site context.

10.36 Left: Holocaust Memorial.

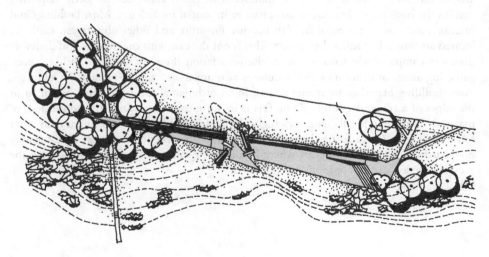

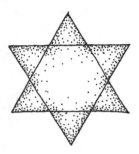

10.37 Star of David.

TWO POINTS = DIVISION

THREE POINTS = UNITY

10.38 The triangle creates a triad of unity among three points.

The triangle also represents action, movement, power, aspiration, growth, sun, and fire when its vertex is pointed up (Tresidder 2005, 487). This is sometimes considered to be a male symbol and is an extension of the triangle's ability to capture and direct attention as previously discussed. A triangle with the opposite orientation is a female symbol and suggests the moon, water, and rain (Tresidder 2005, 487). These two opposing triangles form a hexagram or six-pointed star when they are combined with a shared center (10.37). This is the Seal of Solomon and is widely recognized as the Star of David associated with the Jewish faith. The symbol stands for balance and devine union.

The triangle has special meaning in other religions as well. In Christianity, the triangle is emblematic of the Holy Trinity that unites the Father, Son, and Holy Spirit into one embracing God. In a larger sense, the notion of equality among three is a widely held concept. Two points are seen as possessing tension and division (top 10.38). The presence of the third point forms a balanced relationship with harmony fashioned between the initial two points (bottom 10.38). This principle is sometimes applied to design where elements are assembled in quantities of three because of the implied visual accord.

Design Guidelines

As previously alluded to, the triangle is a potentially awkward shape to design with in the landscape and can cause both functional and aesthetic complications if not employed properly. There are a number of recommendations that should be kept in mind to avoid possible mishaps and to exploit the triangle's innate qualities in landscape architectural design.

Appropriate Use

The triangle is a compelling shape to work with as an organizational element in the landscape because of its angled sides and its implicit energy. However a historic review of landscape architecture and architecture projects indicates that the triangle has not been frequently used as the basis for design due in large part to its spatial inefficiency. Most buildings and interior rooms are orthogonal in plan because furniture and other objects can easily be located anywhere including the corners. This is not the case with the triangle and therefore makes it comparatively hard to use as the foundation for most outdoor sitting spaces, gathering areas, or other uses that require maximum use of square footage. In addition, many building materials are manufactured in an orthogonal form and must be cut to fit the edges of a triangular form. While this is by no means impossible, the adjustment of materials to angles typically requires a higher level of skilled labor to implement than other form typologies. Considering these limitations, it is advisable to use the triangle for only noteworthy design circumstances where its distinct qualities like those discussed in the previous section can be appropriately exploited.

Acute Angles

One of the biggest challenges in designing with triangles in the landscape is working with their inherent acute angles. How and where acute angles are used in a design should be carefully studied because they have a direct affect on the disposition and practicality of a design. As general principle, acute angles less than 45 degrees should be minimized if not eliminated with the need to do so being more necessary the narrower the acute angle is. There are two primary reasons for this suggestion. First, many of the unpleasant associations with the triangle like apprehension and fear are accentuated in tight acute angles that imply entrapment from within or a piercing edge from the outside. Second, it is challenging to define a tight acute angle with many materials in a manner that is compositionally appealing and structurally durable.

While restricted acute angles can be easily drawn in plan, they are nevertheless difficult to create in actuality because few materials can be readily molded or cut to fit the progressively diminishing dimensions at an angle's apex on the ground plane or in the third dimension. The space in the apex of an acute angle literally contracts to inches, then fractions of inches, and finally nothing (10.39). This relatively small area is difficult to install and structurally support with rigid materials like pavement especially when the acute angle is surrounded only by soil or gravel. It often requires extra time and highly skilled craftspeople to exactingly cut pavement pieces to fit a tight acute angle. But even when pavement can be put in place in such a confined area, it still remains hard to support such pavement laterally and from below with adequate base material (left 10.40). There simply is not enough area in either direction to provide substantial support. Consequently, pavement in narrow acute angles is typically fragile and easily cracks or separates due to wear or freeze/thaw cycles (right 10.40 and 10.41). Paved acute angles are more practical if they are held within a larger pavement field where the surrounding pavement material can hold the acute angle in place.

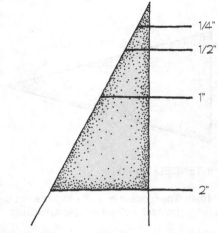

10.39 Actual size of a triangle at an apex.

10.40 Left: An acute angle of pavement is difficult to support and is thus likely to separate.

10.41 Below: Example of a cracked pavement within an acute angle.

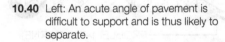

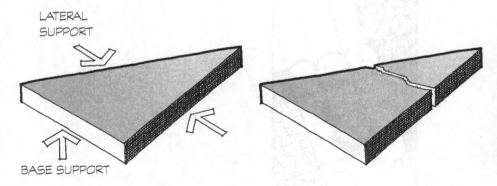

LATERAL SUPPORT

BASE SUPPORT

229

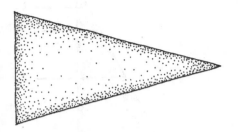

INTENDED FORM

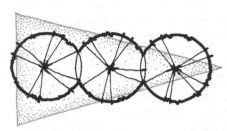

ACTUAL FORM: PLANTS

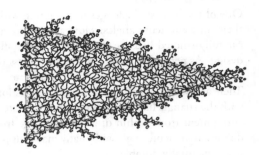

ACTUAL FORM: GROUND COVER

10.42 The space in an acute angle cannot be precisely defined with plant materials.

The same problems occur when trying to define acute angles with plant materials because there is no plant that can define the last inches of an acute angle. If plants are located in a triangle's apex, they frequently outgrow the area and thus no longer reinforce the form that was originally created on paper or during the initial installation (10.42). Similarly, lawn cannot be mowed in a small acute angle that is confined on its sides and must be cut by hand or with a weed trimmer, both of which require extra maintenance labor.

There are several strategies to reduce acute angles in a landscape design. One is to maximize the use of right triangles, equilateral triangles, or triangles with corners greater than 45 degrees. Finally, the apex of an acute angle might be truncated in some circumstances so the most awkward area of the triangle is eliminated (10.43–44). The one disadvantage of this last suggestion is that cutting off the tip of an acute angle may ruin the purity of a triangular design and diminish some of the triangle's inherent dynamic qualities.

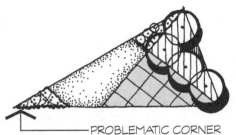

PROBLEMATIC CORNER

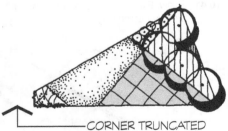

CORNER TRUNCATED

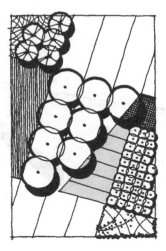

10.43 Above: A triangle can be truncated to eliminate a problematic apex.

10.44 Right Design incorporating truncated triangles.

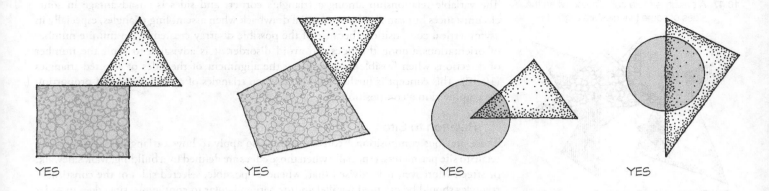

YES   YES   YES   YES

Compositional Connections

The triangle is renowned as a structurally sturdy figure and has been used throughout history as an integral component of buildings, bridges, towers, and other structures to insure their stability. This quality, however, does not directly translate to its use as a two-dimensional compositional form in landscape design. A triangle is most visually stable when its sides are parallel or perpendicular to adjacent straight lines, squares, rectangles, and other polygons (left and middle 10.45). This creates juxtapositions that have a maximum amount of concurrent surface between bordering forms or right-angle connections inherent to orthogonal geometry. Similarly a triangle has a strong association with a circle when one of the triangle's sides coincides with the circle's radius thus establishing a perpendicular angle between the two forms at the circle's perimeter (right 10.45). The least stable associations occur when the triangle's sides meet other forms at a haphazard angle or when the one of the triangle's corners merely touch a contiguous form (10.46). The latter creates a point of uncertainty and compositional tension.

10.45 Desirable ways to connect a triangle to other forms.

10.46 Unstable connections with a triangle.

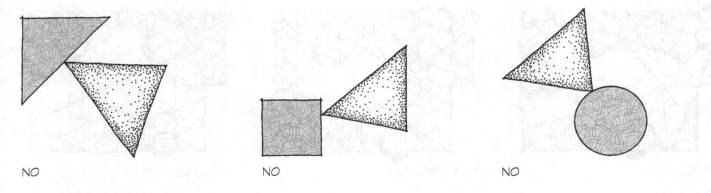

NO   NO   NO

10.47 A design is more coordinated when the sides of some triangles are aligned.

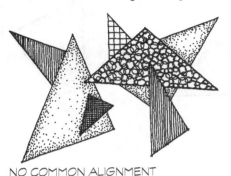

NO COMMON ALIGNMENT

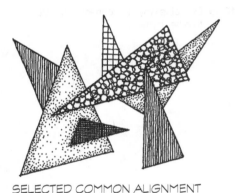

SELECTED COMMON ALIGNMENT

10.48 Triangles should ideally have some shared alignment with site edges.

The variable relationship among a triangle's corners and sides is an advantage in some circumstances but can also be a potential drawback when assembling triangles, especially in asymmetrical compositions because of the possible disarray created by an infinite number of orientations among the sides. To avoid disorder, it is advisable to limit the number of directions when feasible by paralleling the alignment of the sides of selected triangles (10.47). This concept is further reinforced when triangles of a similar size and proportion are employed in a composition.

Relation to Site

These previous compositional considerations also apply to how a triangular design should relate to site perimeters, especially when those edges are defined by a building, wall, sidewalk, or street. Moreover, it is advised that, whenever possible, selected sides of the constituent triangles should be oriented parallel and/or perpendicular to contiguous site edges in order to visually anchor the interior composition to its context (10.48). This recommendation is most important for asymmetrical designs where there is relative freedom in their organization, but is good advice for grid and symmetrical layouts as well (right 10.48). It should be kept in mind that an advantage of triangles is the flexible angle of their sides that allows them to forge common alignments even on oddly shaped sites.

In addition to alignment, it is also necessary to examine how the triangles connect to the straight edges of a site. There are two principal ways for this to occur, just as with landscape designs based on multiple circles (see Design Guidelines, Chapter 12). The first approach is to separate the triangles from the site edges with a negative or buffer space (left 10.49). Selected points of connection are made with walks that echo the overall character of the design. The second approach is to connect the perimeter triangles to the site edge in a way that avoids acute angles (middle 10.49). In either case, the point of a triangle should not merely touch the site edge because of the tenuous relationship that is created and the impracticality of circulation between site interior and exterior (right 10.49).

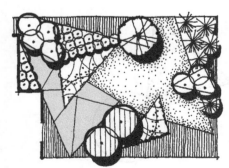

NOT RELATED

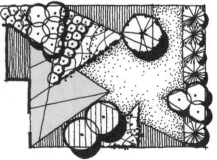

MORE RELATED

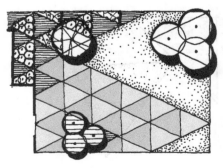

MORE RELATED

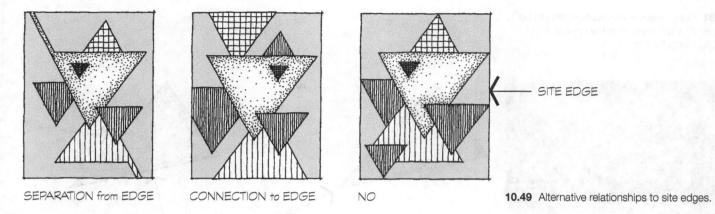

SEPARATION from EDGE   CONNECTION to EDGE   NO

SITE EDGE

10.49 Alternative relationships to site edges.

Process

The recommended process for designing with all geometric systems in the landscape is to start with the overall concept and progress to the details. Given the potential for discordance and multiplicity of direction, this counsel is even more salient when designing with a group of triangles. Thus, the largest triangular areas and/or the most significant directional lines through a site should be determined first. This issue of size is most important when the design process is additive and expands outward from its core as it does in many symmetrical and asymmetrical compositions (10.50). The location and orientation of the largest spaces should of course be determined by program needs and existing site conditions. The factor of direction is critical when the design process is one of subdividing a site into increasingly smaller areas. In this instance, the primary lines and related orientations of the triangles should be informed by the primary circulation routes into and through the site in addition to program and site factors (10.18).

10.50 The design should start with the largest spaces and proceed to add detail.

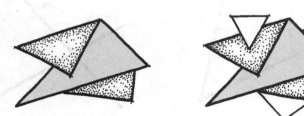

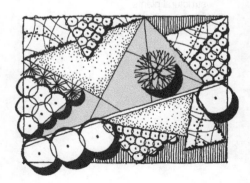

233

10.51 Right: Views and movement should be directed away from the apex of a triangular form.

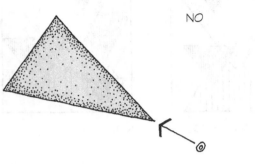

NO

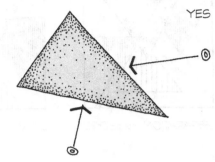

YES

Pointed Arrows

When used in the landscape, a triangle's acute angle should be placed and oriented so it does not forge a pointed arrow, an effect created when the apex is pointed directly toward someone. This association with a sharp point or blade is emphasized as the angle becomes narrower and is most readily perceived when the triangle is expressed in the third dimension. In particular, acute corners should not be pointed toward oncoming movement or views because a triangle's sharp edge is like a ship's bow that repels and divides that which lies in front of it (left 10.51–52). It is an uneasy sensation to be forced to look at or walk toward the end of triangle. It is preferable to approach a triangle at an oblique or perpendicular direction to one of its sides (right 10.51) or by truncating the end of triangle as suggested before to alleviate the ill affects of a pointed arrow.

10.52 Above: Example of a triangular area projecting into a walk.

10.53 Right: Fundamental vocabulary for structural plants.

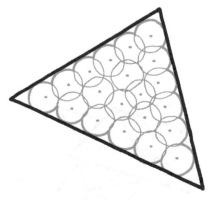

PLANT MASSES

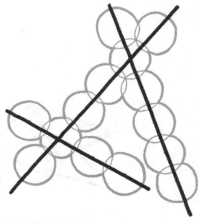

PLANT ROWS

Material Coordination

Similar to other fundamental geometric forms, materials should be organized within a triangle to reinforce its underlying structure. This typically means that woody plant materials, walls, structures, water bodies, pavement, and so forth all enhance the straight edges and implied internal triangles of a triangular shape. Plant materials should therefore be arranged in straight rows or triangular masses although this is not always easily accomplished as already indicated (10.53). Again, care must be taken in coordinating the proportion of a triangular planting area with the vegetation that is intended to define it. Masses of perennials, ground cover, or loosely defined shrubs that can readily fill any area are the easiest to use while large trees are the most difficult. Pavement patterns within a triangle can be uniform or be subdivided into other triangular areas as indicated before (10.54).

PLAN

UNDERLYING STRUCTURE

10.54 Elements and materials should reinforce the underlying structure of a triangular design.

PAVEMENT & POOL

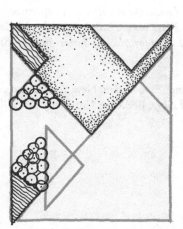

LAWN & SHRUB MASSES

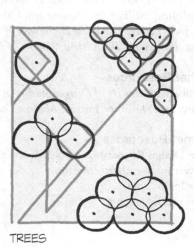

TREES

235

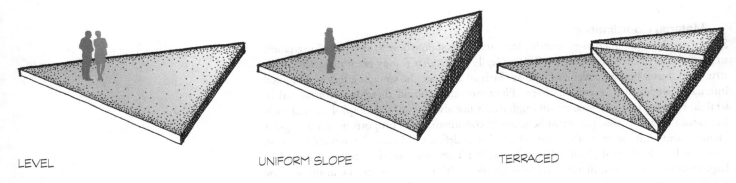

LEVEL   UNIFORM SLOPE   TERRACED

10.55 Alternative ways of accommodating grade changes within a triangular space.

Topography

Like the square, the triangle is typically treated as an architectural element in the landscape with a simple, flat ground plane, particularly when it is intended to be one space with a uniform use throughout (left 10.55). In a similar vein, the triangle can be tilted so that it has a consistent slope in one direction (middle 10.55). To create more pronounced grade changes within a triangle, terraced level changes can be delineated by walls and steps based on the previous guidelines for subdivision (right 10.55). These guidelines collectively suggest that the triangle is not well suited as an organizational form in notably varied topography unless it is purposefully inserted as a paradoxical element.

Referenced Resources

Carlock, Marty. "User Friendly in Boston." *Landscape Architecture*, October 2004.

Church, Thomas D., Grace Hall, and Michael Laurie. *Gardens Are for People*, 2nd edition. New York: McGraw-Hill, 1983.

Hinshaw, Mark. "Mission Statement." *Landscape Architecture*, January 2004.

Kelley, Stephen. "Dublin's Docklands: A Spectacle in Red, Green and Blue." *Landscape Architect and Specifier News*, August 2006.

Martignoni, Jimena. "For the Missing and Other Victims," *Landscape Architecture*, September 2006.

Tresidder, Jack, ed. *The Complete Dictionary of Symbols*. San Francisco, Chronicle Books, LLC, 2005.

Wong, Eva. *Feng-Shui: The Ancient Wisdom of Harmonious Living for Modern Times*. Boston: Shambhala, 1996.

Further Resources

Elam, Kimberly. *Geometry of Design: Studies in Proportion and Composition*. New York: Princeton Architectural Press, 2001.

Treib, Marc, and Dorothee Imbert. *Modern Landscapes for Living*. Berkeley: University of California Press, 1997.

Internet Resources

Halvorson Design Partnership: www.halvorsondesign.com

Hart Howerton: www.harthowerton.com

LPA: www.lpainc.com

MSI: www.msidesign.com

The Polygon

The diagonal and triangle are the foundation for an array of landscape design strategies as discussed in previous chapters. While each is idiosyncratic in character, the diagonal and triangular typologies share the common trait of creating straight edged, nonorthogonal spaces. One other genre of angular geometry that possesses these qualities is the multifaceted polygon. Polygons broaden the organizational possibilities of angular geometry in landscape architectural design and give the designer more options for devising a hard-edged, non-orthogonal landscape. The aspects of the polygon examined in this chapter are:

- Polygon Typologies
- Landscape Uses
- Design Guidelines

Polygon Typologies

By definition, a polygon is any two-dimensional shape that is enclosed by straight edges (11.1). The square, rectangle, and triangle are all polygons with the triangle being the most elementary. The polygons that are subject of this chapter are those composed of four or more sides joined by nonorthogonal interior angles. As with all the fundamental geometric forms, polygons can be categorized into different typologies based on the number of sides, the proportional relationship among the sides and angles, and presence or lack of symmetry as presented in this chapter.

11.1 Examples of polygons.

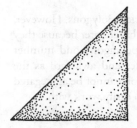 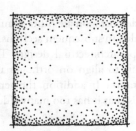 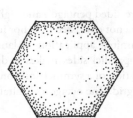 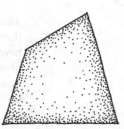 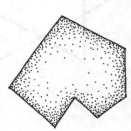

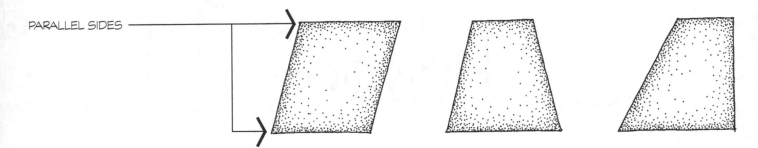

PARALLEL SIDES

11.2 Examples of trapezoids.

11.3 Below: The hexagon, a symmetrical polygon.

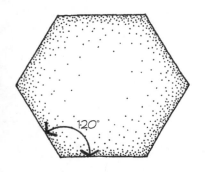

120°

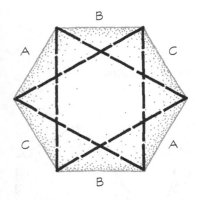

Trapezoid

A trapezoid is a quadrilateral or four-sided figure with one pair of parallel sides (11.2). Squares and rectangles are trapezoids by definition though they are excluded here because they are orthogonal. The potential variability of the trapezoid's two nonparallel sides creates a range of possible shapes including an isosceles trapezoid that has nonparallel sides equal in dimension. In designing with trapezoids, it is advisable to preclude interior angles less than 45 degrees to avoid problematic acute angles. Regardless of specific shape, all trapezoids are an amalgamation of rectangles and triangles; the parallel sides evoke the qualities of orthogonal shapes while the interior angles mimic the properties of triangles (11.9).

Symmetrical Polygons

Symmetrical polygons are composed of multiple straight sides that are equal in length and joined by identical interior angles. Among these, the six-sided hexagon is the most applicable in landscape architectural design (11.3). A distinguishing quality of the hexagon is that it has three pairs of parallel opposite sides thus sharing a trait with squares, rectangles, and trapezoids. The interior of the hexagon is noted by its 120-degree angles and the fact that it can be subdivided into two overlapping equilateral triangles. The hexagon is a naturally occurring form as exhibited by snowflakes, geologic formations like basalt columns, and bees' honeycombs (11.16).

The five-sided pentagon and eight-sided octagon are other symmetrical polygons. However, they are not discussed here nor included in subsequent sections of this chapter because they have limited application in landscape architectural design. The pentagon's odd number of nonparallel sides makes it difficult to align on orthogonal sites and awkward as the foundation of a symmetrical configuration. In addition, the pentagon cannot be aggregated into a grid. The octagon's limitation is that it has too many sides to easily work with.

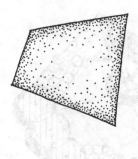
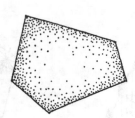
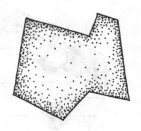

11.4 Examples of asymmetrical polygons.

11.5 Below: Example of an asymmetrical polygon with rounded corners.

Asymmetrical Polygons

Asymmetrical polygons, sometimes referred to as irregular polygons, are defined by multiple straight sides that vary in length and direction (11.4) (Reid 2007, 66). This organic genre of polygons is variable in proportion and orientation. The form can be compact and comparatively equal in balance or stretched along a particular dimension to emphasize a selected direction. Furthermore, an asymmetrical polygon can include sides that reverse the direction of enclosure before returning on itself to complete the shape (right 11.4). Consequently an irregular polygon is a highly adaptable form that can be used in numerous design circumstances (see Landscape Uses).

A subtle variation of the asymmetrical polygon is to round the intersection between sides. This technique gradually merges adjoining sides and gives the overall shape a softer appearance (11.5, 11.31). Rounded polygons exist in the natural world as cells within leaves and patterns of islands in wetlands. This genre of polygons is likewise emblematic of "modern" patterns and furniture design popular during the 1950s.

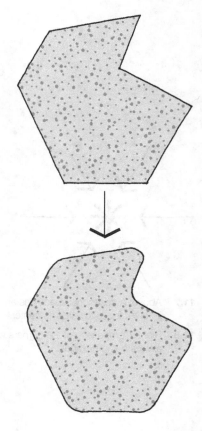

Landscape Uses

Polygons are a heterogeneous collection of forms that lend themselves to a range of possible uses in the landscape. Some of these like accommodating multiple directions of circulation, altering the sense of spatial orientation, and acclimating to irregularly shaped sites are shared with the diagonal and triangles. Other uses are more unique to polygons including spatial foundation, exploratory circulation, resolution of varied alignments, rugged landscape, and fragmented landscape. The common trait among all these uses is multiple straight sides and angles that are not 90 degrees.

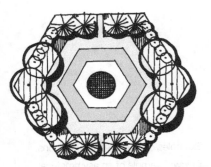

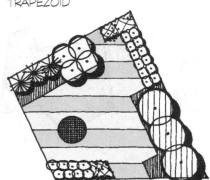

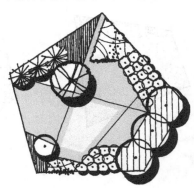

11.6 Volumetric spaces based on the different types of polygons.

Spatial Foundation

A primary function of polygons, like the square and triangle, is to serve as the underpinning of landscape space. Given the range of fundamental polygonal shapes identified in the previous section, there is a range of spatial typologies that can be generated including the single space and an aggregate of several spaces.

Single Space. The single landscape space is typically a simple volume intended to accommodate one principal use. Such a space may be a solitary entity in the landscape or one discrete space situated amongst others. However it is located, such a space may be volumetric or cubist as discussed in previous chapters. It will be recalled that a volumetric space is an open volume although its qualities vary depending on whether a hexagon, trapezoid, or irregular polygon is used as its foundation (11.6).

The hexagon creates the simplest volumetric space, resulting in a symmetrical space that has a circle-like enclosure and an innate focus towards its center (left 11.6 and 11.7). The hexagon's obtuse angled corners create relatively weak intersections between adjoining sides, a quality previously identified for obtuse angles in triangles (10.4). The sides of a hexagonal space tend to visually coalesce unless they are defined by different elements (11.8). Consequently, one's sense of enclosure is created more by the height of the perimeter vertical planes than by enveloping corners as occurs in orthogonal spaces. A single volumetric hexagonal space is appropriate as central node and collection point because of is symmetrical form.

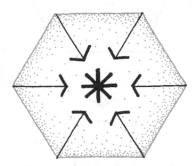

11.7 Above: A hexagonal space has an inherent focus towards its center.

11.8 Right: Comparison of the corners within a square and hexagon.

SQUARE

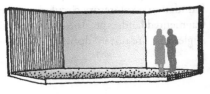

HEXAGON

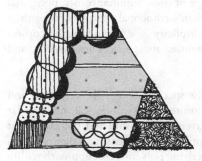 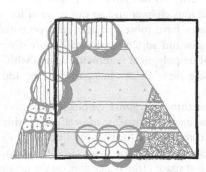 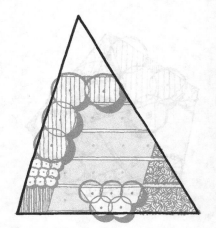

11.9 The trapezoid forms a space with qualities of the square and triangle.

A trapezoid can also be the foundation of a single space although the resulting volume is potentially more diverse because of the trapezoid's variability (middle 11.6) Most trapezoid spaces tend to be a blend between the spatial qualities of the rectangle and those of the triangle (11.9). That is, the trapezoid's parallel sides suggest the uniformity of square and rectangular spaces while the nonorthogonal corners imbue traits of the triangle. The trapezoid's four sides and distinct corners create spaces with clear sense of enclosure and corners that one can retreat into (11.10). Trapezoid spaces make good transitions between orthogonal and triangular spaces.

The asymmetrical polygon generates the most complex and organic volumetric space (right 11.6). The edges of this polygonal space are completely variable in length, orientation, and angle between adjoining sides. Furthermore, some corners may protrude out into the space and so limit the clarity of the surrounding vertical enclosure. This prominent point establishes a possible edge accent and provides intrigue because it may prevent the entire spatial perimeter from being easily seen from every vantage point within the space (11.11). A volumetric space based on an irregular polygon is apropos when there is a need for a simple, angular volume that is both engaging and somewhat jagged in temperament (also see Rugged Landscape).

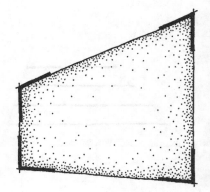

11.10 Above: A trapazoidal space possesses distinct and enveloping corners.

11.11 Left: The asymmetrical polygonal space can include a projection into the space.

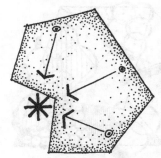

POTENTIAL FOCAL POINT

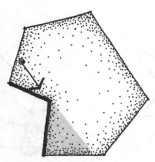

MAY HIDE SPACE

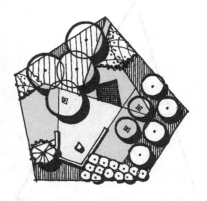

While dissimilar, all these volumetric spaces based polygons have many sides and corners that vary from wide obtuse angles to those less than ninety degrees. Polygonal volumes typically do not have the problems with corners that were discussed for triangles in the previous chapter and so can be used for a wider range of uses. Simultaneously, polygonal spaces have more variation and potential interest than orthogonal spaces because their angles and adjoining sides are more diverse. The multiplicity of sides and angled corners imbue polygonal volumetric spaces with dual personalities: these spaces are dynamic and energetic while also being disquieting and unsettled.

The three polygonal typologies can also frame cubist space although the trapezoid and irregular polygonal are most suited for this type of enclosure. The asymmetrical and irregular nature of these forms is well disposed to multiple layers of enclosure and the placement elements within the space (11.12). The method for integrating elements and planes within cubist space varies depending on the geometry of underlying polygon. One approach within the trapezoid is to use inner lines that parallel the sides, especially the set of parallel edges (top 11.13). An overlapping system of lines establishes a gridlike framework of smaller trapezoids that can be used to delineate spatial edges. A second method for subdividing the trapezoid is to extend lines between corners (bottom 11.13). Other lines can be integrated to create a network of overlapping triangles as discussed before in Chapter 10.

11.12 Above: Example of a cubist space (compare to right 11.6).

11.13 Below: Alternative ways for subdividing a trapezoid.

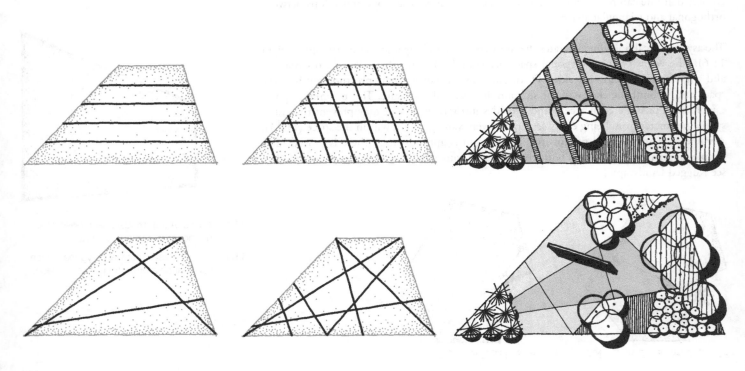

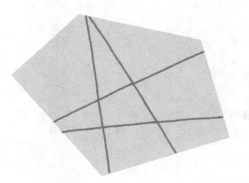
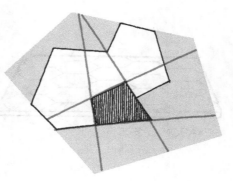
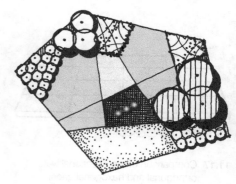

The structuring of material areas is less methodical within an asymmetrical polygon and is a process orchestrated more by intuition than by studied calculation inasmuch as there are no obvious internal components to work with. One tactic is to extend askew lines across the polygon to fabricate a network of smaller triangles and polygons that can be used to delineate material edges (11.14). Rather than being arbitrarily placed, these lines should be located by trial and error while trying to compose space and accommodate function. The overall objective should be to simulate the feeling and temperament of the asymmetrical polygon in addition to creating a well-composed and engaging spatial volume.

Multiple Spaces. Polygons, like other fundamental forms, can be assembled to forge a cluster of spaces that collectively create spatial diversity and accommodate an array of uses. As with orthogonal forms and triangles, the grid, symmetry, and asymmetry are the fundamental organizational structures for assembling multiple polygons. Nevertheless, there are a number of idiosyncratic characteristics that polygonal compositions hold when compared to other form typologies as outlined in the following paragraphs.

Grid. The hexagon is the most apt polygon to generate a grid because of its uniformity. The number of sides and the 120-degree interior angles allows one hexagon to be easily joined to another to produce an uninterrupted tiling of hexagons across an area (11.15). Interestingly, the most efficient and energy-effective connection of three lines in nature occurs at 120 degrees as seen in honeycombs, bubbles, and basalt columns. The honeycomb's hexagonal grid structure requires the least material to construct and is the most structurally stable (11.16) (Murphy 1993, 74–81). Unlike the orthogonal and triangular grids discussed in earlier chapters, a hexagonal grid has no lines that extend through the field in an uninterrupted manner. Consequently, a hexagonal grid is a static structure that readily holds the eye within its modules (11.17).

11.14 One method for partitioning an asymmetrical polygonal space.

11.15 Below: Example of a hexagonal grid.

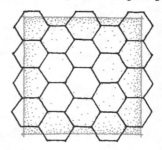

11.16 The honeycomb is an example of a hexagonal grid in nature.

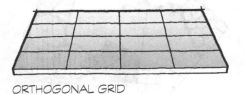

ORTHOGONAL GRID

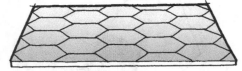

HEXAGONAL GRID

11.17 Comparison of the directionality in orthogonal and hexogonal grids.

An example of a hexagonal grid used as the foundation of a landscape is Tower Park in Peoria Heights, Illinois, designed by the landscape architectural firm Shive-Hattery (11.18). The hexagon grid was inspired by the vertical profile of the Village Hall that is located in the southeast sector of the site (Kelly 2006, 77). Different sizes of octagons were used in the grid. The largest hexagons appropriately define the primary public gathering space, while smaller hexagons designate a tot lot, sitting spaces, and circulation routes.

11.18 Tower Park.

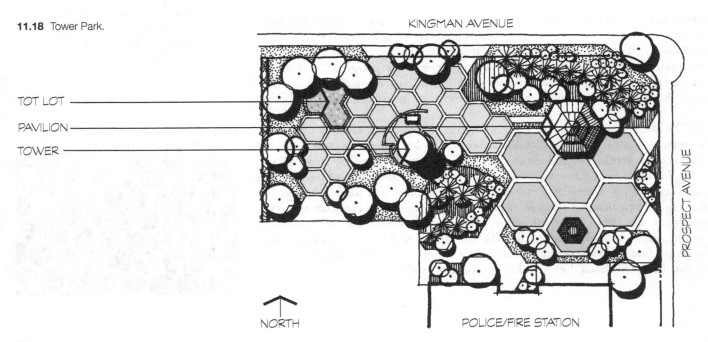

KINGMAN AVENUE

TOT LOT

PAVILION

TOWER

PROSPECT AVENUE

NORTH

POLICE/FIRE STATION

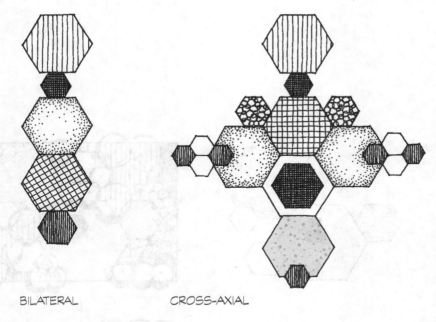

BILATERAL   CROSS-AXIAL

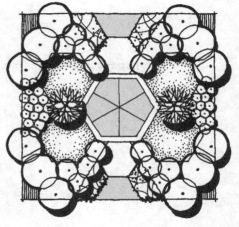

11.19 Left: The use of the hexagon to forge symmetrical configurations.

11.20 Below: The hexagon possess three non-orthogonal axes.

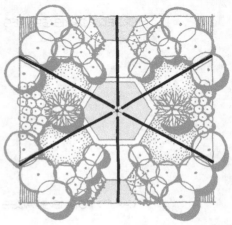

Symmetry. The hexagon is the only polygon that readily lends itself to a symmetrical configuration of landscape spaces although not as easily as orthogonal forms. Multiple hexagons can be fused along a single axis or several cross-axes by joining parallel sides together (11.19). Both of these basic layouts produce a rich tapestry of experiences when spaces of different size and character are integrated. The distinguishing quality of a symmetrical organization of hexagons is the existence of three nonorthogonal cross-axes that are the basis for an intertwined web of overlapping views and movement (11.20). While this system has the capacity to forge a diverse medley of choices and spatial episodes, it remains a challenge to design with because of the numerous sides of a space and the many potential points of entry into and exit from each space. In addition, the edges of a hexagon structure can only be lined up with an orthogonal site along one axis, thus limiting the accord between an orthogonal site's interior and perimeter.

245

11.21 Example of multiple polygons assembled via additive transformation.

11.22 Right: Alternative methods for treating the spatial makeup of multiple polygons.

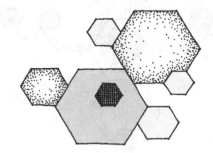

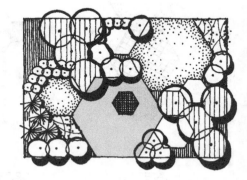

SEPARATE FORMS/SPACES

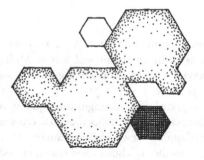

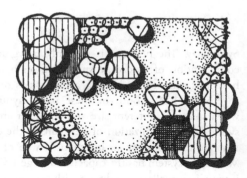

MERGED FORMS/SPACES

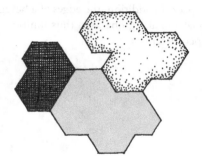

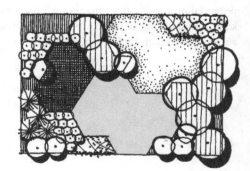

VARIED FORMS/SPACES

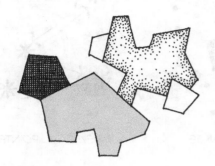
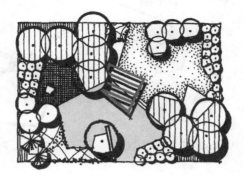

Asymmetry. The asymmetrical organizational design structure offers the most possibilities for assembling multiple polygons into a sequence of spaces because it accommodates the multifaceted nature of polygons more easily than either the grid or symmetry. Additive transformation provides the most versitility among the options for assembling polygons in an irregular arrangment.

Trapezoids and hexagons can fashion the underpinnings of outdoor space by connecting to, rotating, and overlapping one another in a range of sizes (11.21). The advantage of using these forms is that the fixed angles between sides lend consistency and cohesion to a landscape design. There are two alternative strategies for designing with trapezoids and hexagons in an asymmetrical organization. The first is to treat each individual polygon within the design as a distinct space or area unto itself (top 11.22). Altering the material palette, scale, and so on among the individual spaces, produces diversity and experiential appeal. The second tactic is to aggregate the individual polygons into one all-inclusive area (middle 11.22). This creates a space that is more dynamic with edges that push into, out from, and around corners. A similar design strategy is to create asymmetrical designs that use the angles of trapezoids or hexagons without incorporating the forms directly into the design (bottom 11.22). Such an approach gives the designer more liberty to mold the design in an intuitive manner because the length of each side of a space is an independent variable. However, the angles of the sides remain constant and foster homogeneity throughout the composition.

The use of asymmetrical polygons is the most pliable of all because it permits the design to be spontaneously shaped to fit site conditions, program needs, and compositional judgments of the designer (11.23). Furthermore, resulting polygonal spaces may have fluctuating edges that alternately project into and retract from the spatial volume. These spaces are not easily perceived from any one position and so invite movement to discover what is hidden around an angled bend in a space (see Exploratory Experience) (11.24). The freedom of this strategy is more challenging to work with although following a series of guidelines can minimize the potential problems (see Design Guidelines).

11.23 Example of using irregular polygons as the basis of an asymmetrical spatial configuration.

11.24 Selected areas of a polygonal space may be hidden to create intrigue.

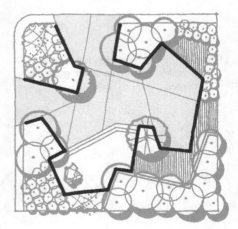

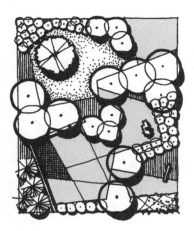

11.25 A sequence of polygonal spaces can create an exploratory experience.

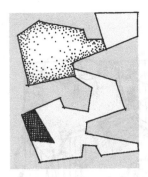

WALKING SURFACE

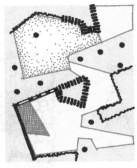

VERTICAL PLANES

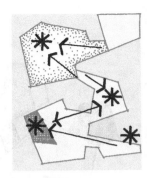

VIEWS/FOCAL POINTS

Exploratory Experience

The segmented outline of an asymmetrical polygon can delineate a constantly evolving route through the landscape with numerous changes in direction around angled corners (11.25). This is very similar to the movement that is possible through an asymmetrical orthogonal-based landscape (6.20). Both typologies possess an altering progression of spaces and areas of focus. Once arriving at the end of the space and turning a corner, another scene is revealed with the hint of still another beyond. Such a sequence of experiences promotes exploration by suggesting there is always something more to encounter just around the bend.

The polygonal circulation differs from its orthogonal counterpart by the fact that the sides of the circulation route in the polygon configuration are always converging or diverging in relation to one another. They are never parallel. This accentuates the perception of movement through space because the enclosing edges moves in or way as one progresses forward. These nonparallel sides also accentuate and foreshorten distance as previously discussed for the triangle. Furthermore, exploratory circulation through a polygon-based landscape is a contorted and somewhat fitful progression.

11.26 Polygons can be used to create a transition between different geometric genres.

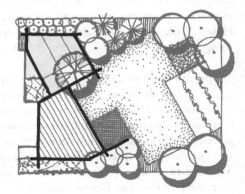

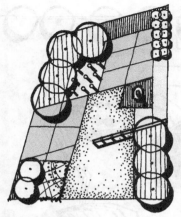
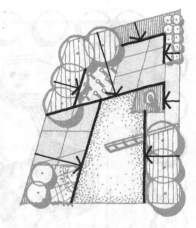

Alignment Mediator

Another use of polygons is to serve as a mediator between dissimilar geometric configurations. One application of this use is along the edges of site where a diagonal scheme within the site must connect to an orthogonal site boundary or building (left 11.26). Trapezoids and asymmetrical polygons can bridge the alignment of the two systems in an amiable transition. Similarly, polygons can reconcile the relationship between straight-edged forms and those that are curved, angular, or organic within a site (right 11.26). Finally, polygons can provide a design structure that acclimates to an oddly shaped site perimeter by restating the alignment of selected property lines in the internal composition of the site (11.27).

Rugged Landscape

One of the most idiosyncratic uses of polygons is to emulate uneven, rough-hewn landscapes. The outline of an asymmetrical polygon is a broken line whose fragmentation is suggestive of a craggy rock outcrop (top 11.28) (also see Chapter 16). This chiseled outline is masculine, robust, and sturdy in temperament, a quality that is most apparent when the polygon's perimeter sequentially projects into and recedes from its interior. Several landscape uses can exploit these attributes. The first is to use the irregular polygon as the basis of design in rough and stony settings as a means of blending human interventions into the landscape (bottom 11.28). Allowing boulders or rock outcrops to extend into the polygonal spaces further merges the human and natural realms. An opposite landscape use is to place a polygonal design in a soft pastoral landscape of undulating topography and drifts of vegetation as a stark contrast.

11.27 The use of polygons to relate to site edges.

11.28 An irregular polygonal line suggests a rugged landscape character.

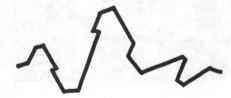

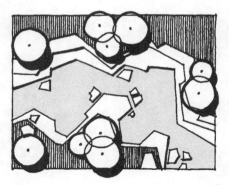

11.29 Right: Site plan of Lovejoy Plaza and Fountain.

11.30 Below: Images of Lovejoy Plaza.

NORTH

A second use of the irregular polygon's implication of a rugged landscape is in urban settings where it is a counterpoint to the prevalent orthogonal structure of the human environment. A paragon of this application is Lovejoy Plaza in Portland, Oregon, designed by Lawrence Halprin in 1966 (11.29–30). The concrete plaza is dominated by steps that look like exposed strata of stone, abstracted and pinwheeling across the site. In some areas, these steps extend upward to define subtle promontories. In other areas, the steps progress to lower elevations and a large pool. A waterfall erupts from a high point and falls turbulently into a placid pool that punctuates the entire plaza. The concept for the plaza's abstracted rock formations was based on extensive studies and sketches that Halprin undertook during numerous field observations in the Sierra Nevada Mountains (*Process: Architecture No.4*. 1978, 157–163).

Fragmented Landscape

Another use of the asymmetrical polygon's irregular outline is to create a splintered landscape with as a series of separate spaces that suggest remnant pieces broken from a previously whole entity. The initial site area is subdivided into progressively smaller polygons that are set apart by a negative space (left 11.31). The polygonal spaces may be similar or different in use depending on the program requirements.

The interstitial space may also vary depending on the scale of the design and needs. For a small garden space, the negative space can be filled with plants and other elements as a means of defining and separating the individual spaces. For larger sites like parks, campuses, and arboretums, the negative space is often used for circulation that weaves erratically through the site. The polygonal forms in Figure 11.31 are rounded to soften their appearance and to more easily accommodate movement around corners (compare to 13.19 and 15.14). The segregation of individual areas is counterbalanced by their uniform treatment and a simple, bold pavement pattern throughout.

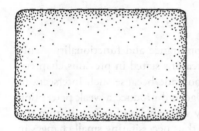

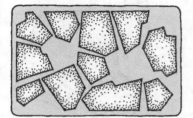

TRANSFORMATION

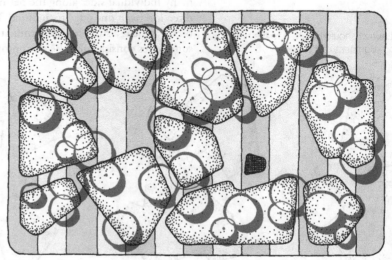

PLAN

11.31 The use of polygons to create a fragmented design.

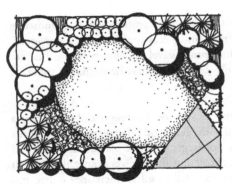

WEAK INTERIOR ANGLES

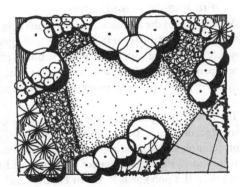

DECISIVE INTERIOR ANGLES

11.32 Overly wide internal angles produce little distinction between individual edges.

Design Guidelines

The following design guidelines should be contemplated when designing with polygons in landscape architectural site design. As always, these suggestions should be adapted to the particular circumstances of the design setting.

Internal Angles

The size of a polygon's internal angles is critical for appearance and functionality. Acute angles less than 45 degrees should be avoided for the reasons stated in previous chapters. At the other extreme, internal angles should not be too wide because such intersections create an insignificant change in direction along the edge and produce a weak perception of enveloping vertical planes (left 11.32). Unacceptably wide angles often result from too many individual sides along the perimeter of the space, thus necessitating small changes in direction from one edge to another. The exact determination of what constitutes an overly broad angle is a subjective determination although angles between 120 and 135 degrees are sometimes considered to be an appropriate limit (Reid 2007, 21–29).

11.33 Attention should be given to the angle and alignment of the sides.

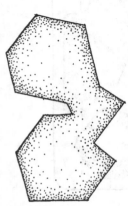

SIMILAR LENGTHS

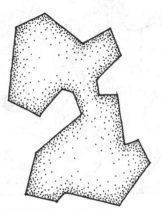

VARIED LENGTHS

NO PARALLEL SIDES

SELECTED PARALLEL SIDES

Sides

There are two suggestions regarding a polygon's edges. The first is that the length of an asymmetrical polygon's sides should vary for visual intrigue and to reinforce the perception of irregularity (left11.33). In addition, the dissimilarity in line length should be obvious. An insignificant contrast in the extent of nearby lines may give the impression of being a mistake rather than an intentional gesture.

A second recommendation is that some edges within a polygonal design structure should be parallel to one another to provide visual accord (right 11.33). The number of lines that should have a shared alignment is intuitive and entirely contingent on the designer's judgment. In general, a relatively simple polygon may not benefit from this guideline. However, a much more complex configuration is more unified if there are some edges that are parallel to one another. A well-composed polygonal configuration strikes a delicate balance between too little and too much variation in relative length and/or alignment.

Relation to Site

Thought should be given to how a polygon based landscape design relates to site edges and context given the polygons' inherent nonorthogonal quality. As with triangular designs discussed in the previous chapter, it is normally advisable to align selected sides of a polygonal design parallel and/or perpendicular to pronounced site edges like buildings facades, walls, rows of trees, street curbs, and so on (11.34). This forges a visual alliance between the site's internal layout and its perimeter where the two are seen in direct relation to one another. In addition, 90-degree connections between a polygon space and a straight site boundary successfully anchor the two geometries together.

11.34 There should be some alignment of a polygonal design with site edges.

NOT ALIGNED with SIDES

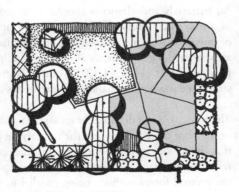

ALIGNED with SIDES

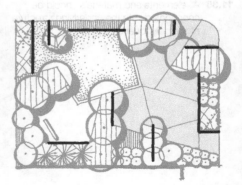

253

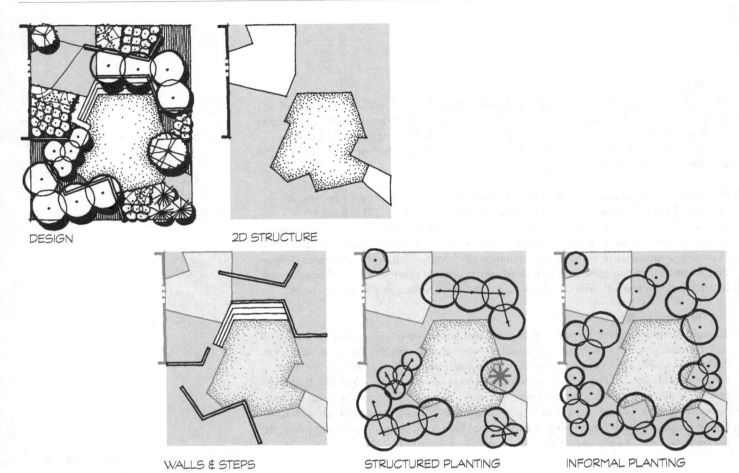

DESIGN

2D STRUCTURE

WALLS & STEPS

STRUCTURED PLANTING

INFORMAL PLANTING

11.35 All elements and materials should be coordinated with the underlying structure of the polygonal design.

Material Coordination

All materials and elements should be coordinated to reinforce the underlying structure of a polygonal landscape design. Exactly how this is accomplished depends on the type of polygons used and the desired spatial quality. For symmetrical and trapezoidal spaces, associated design elements should generally align with and reinforce the edges of the polygon forms (11.6, 11.13). Woody plant materials typically are organized in rows and structured masses that parallel selected sides of the space.

The strategy is less decided for an asymmetrical polygon where elements and materials may or may not directly augment the underlying polygonal form (11.35). What is important is that design elements echo the general character of the polygon without necessarily directly reflecting its shape. For example, selected walls in Figure 11.35 repeat the general shape of the ground forms without being parallel to them (bottom left). The same is also true for woody plant materials. For public and more structured landscapes, plants may be located

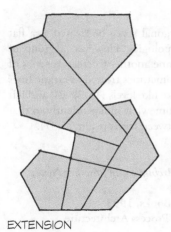

EXTENSION

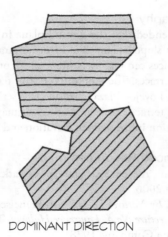

DOMINANT DIRECTION

11.36 Alternative techniques for designing the pavement pattern in a polygonal design.

parallel to the sides of the ground forms, thus extruding their shape into the third dimension (bottom middle). By contrast, the arrangement of plant materials can be more random in small garden settings or where the polygonal genre is used in a chiseled abstraction of natural geologic formations. A casual planting scheme is especially suitable for a design that has numerous projections and recesses in its edges where pockets of plants can be easily nestled (bottom right).

Pavement patterns also depend directly on the type of polygon that is employed as the underlying structure of a space. For asymmetrical polygons, two alternative strategies are to carry significant lines through the ground surface by extending adjoining edges into the pavement area or by paralleling modular or linear materials with a dominant side (11.36).

11.37 Polygon spaces can be terraced in a series of contour layers.

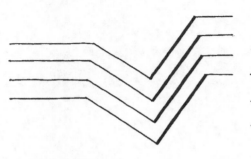

PLAN CONTOURS

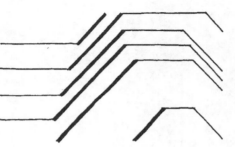

PLAN CONTOURS

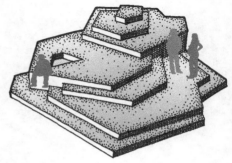

TERRACED LAYERS

255

Topography

It is recommended that the ground plane in a single polygonal space be treated as a flat or uniformly sloped plane like in other straight-sided typologies. However, a group of polygonal spaces can readily be stepped up or down from one another to create a series of interwoven terraces. The "contours" of this technique are sometimes treated as erratic lines as they are in Lovejoy Plaza, resulting in a series of layer cake like levels (11.29–30 and left 11.37). Each terrace can mimic others or may be treated somewhat independently so that there is variation in the vertical elevation and alignment between levels (right 11.37).

Referenced Resources

Kelly, Stephen. "A New Spark for Tower Park." *Landscape Architect and Specifier News*, February 2006.

Murphy, Pat. *By Nature's Design*. San Francisco: Chronicle Books, 1993.

Process: Architecture No.4: Lawrence Halprin. Tokyo, Japan: Process Architecture Publishing Company, 1978.

Reid, Grant. *From Concept to Form in Landscape Design*, 2nd edition. Hoboken, NJ: John Wiley & Sons, 2007.

Internet Resources

Lovejoy Plaza: www.greatbuildings.com/buildings/Lovejoy_Fountain_Plaza.html
www.altportland.com/consume/splash/play/lovejoy_plaza_f.shtml

Shive-Hattery: www.shive-hattery.com

The Arc 12

Orthogonal and angular forms discussed in the previous eight chapters are two broad categories of shapes employed to structure space in landscape architectural design. A third set is circular forms that include the arc, circle, oval, and curvilinear shapes. The arc is the most rudimentary among these and is an elemental component of the other circular typologies. The arc is also a linear element that shares many qualities with both the straight line (Chapter 3) and the diagonal (Chapter 9) although it is more graceful and poetic in tone than these other lines. While the arc has been occasionally used in the landscape throughout history, it has been embraced the most as a trendy structuring element in contemporary landscape architectural design as seen in projects created by Martha Schwartz, Kathryn Gustafson, and others. This chapter examines various aspects of the arc including its:

- Definition and Typologies
- Landscape Uses
- Design Guidelines

Definition and Typologies

The arc is a curved line that originates as a segment of a circle's circumference (12.1). The arc may have any degree of curvature determined by setting and design objectives as long as it is less than a half of a circle (12.2). An arc that extends beyond this acquires the qualities of the circle.

An arc should not be confused with or interchanged with the crescent. A crescent is a different geometric form created by two arcs that intersect each other to create a half-moon shape (left 12.3). Removing a smaller circle from a larger circle at its perimeter also creates a crescent (right 12.3). However conceived, the crescent is not a line segment like the arc and should be considered to be its own distinct geometric form.

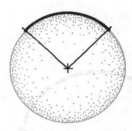

12.1 Above: The arc is a segment of a circle.

12.2 Below: The arc should extend less than one-half of a circle's circumference.

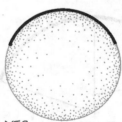

YES

NO

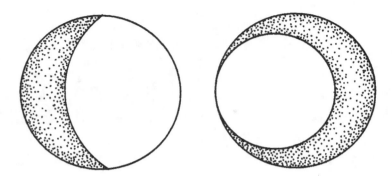

12.3 Examples of the crescent.

There are two basic types of arcs that are used in the landscape.

Uniform Arc

The uniform arc is the most fundamental and commonly used curved line. It is defined as an arcing line that has the same radius extending from a single center point throughout its length (top 12.4). The relative simplicity of the uniform arc makes it the easiest of the two types to construct and use in a landscape design.

Compound Arc

A compound arc is a line that has a changing degree of curvature as it extends from one end to the other (bottom 12.4) As the name suggests, the compound arc is composed of multiple curves, each with its own radius and center point. Despite the inclusion of multiple curves, the compound arc remains a continuous line with each segment seamlessly fusing into the next.

A *spiral curve* is a special type of compound arc that is usually associated with road alignment. A spiral curve is a transition between a uniform curve and a straight section of road (12.5). It was commonly used in railroads and early parkways as a means of visually linking the other two types of alignment together in a manner that permitted a vehicle to gradually and safely enter and exit a curve in the road.

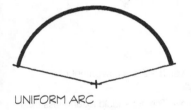

UNIFORM ARC

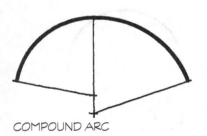

COMPOUND ARC

12.4 Above: Comparison between a uniform and compound arc.

12.5 Right: An example of a spiral curve.

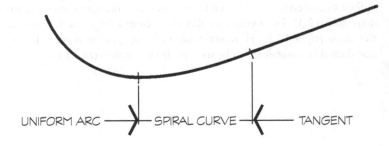

UNIFORM ARC ——⟩—— SPIRAL CURVE ——⟨—— TANGENT

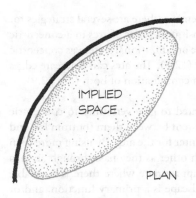

IMPLIED
SPACE

PLAN

12.6 The arch partially encloses a space when extended into the third dimension.

Landscape Uses

Collectively, the two fundamental arcs types can fulfill a number of uses in landscape architectural site design. Some of these are similar to the straight line and the diagonal although the arc's ever-present curvature instills qualities that are idiosyncratic. The arc's primary uses in the landscape include spatial foundation, direct the eye, accommodate movement, visual counterpoint, mask corners, and view receptacle.

Spatial Foundation

The arc is the most effective single line in enveloping space because of its curvature. While a single arc does not completely surround a space like a circle, it does imply enclosure and refuge by functioning as an embracing gesture that partially encompasses an area (12.6). This subtle suggestion of space is emphasized when the arc is expressed in the third dimension by plants, walls, or topography. The vertical articulation of an arc also gives the sheltered space an outward orientation away from the arc (12.7). This alcove-like space is an ideal location to sense protection at one's back while observing the landscape beyond.

12.7 The arch can create a sheltered alcove with an outward orientation.

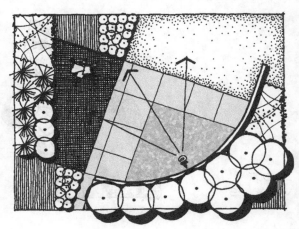

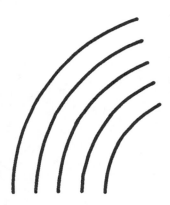

In addition to employing the arc as single encircling element, there are several strategies for using multiple arcs to structure space. The first is to position a series of arcs in a concentric relation to each other (12.8). This is essentially the same organizational system as concentric circles without complete enclosure around a midpoint (12.8). The arcs can delineate edges between material areas, lines of different elements, or a combination of both (top 12.9).

There are a number of variables that can be manipulated to give versatility to concentric arcs including spacing of the arcs and the landscape content between them (bottom left and middle 12.9). Another variable is the location of the center for the arcs. By using more than one center, the arcs can converge or diverge from each other as they pass through an area (bottom right 12.9). The concentric arc structure is appropriate where there is a notable center for the arcs, where movement through the landscape is a primary function, and/or where the design intent is to create a sweeping gesture of multiple layers (12.10).

12.8   Above: The concept of concentric arcs.
12.9   Below: Variables of concentric arcs.

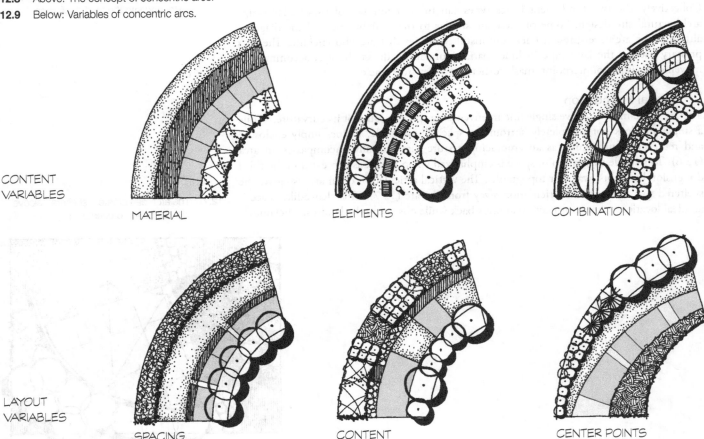

CONTENT
VARIABLES

MATERIAL   ELEMENTS   COMBINATION

LAYOUT
VARIABLES

SPACING   CONTENT   CENTER POINTS

An illustration of the concentric arc structure is the Mesa Entertainment and Arts Center in Mesa, Arizona, where a layered series of arcs establishes a central pedestrian spine for the complex (12.11). Designed by the landscape architectural firm Martha Schwartz Partners in collaboration with Boora Architects, this curved landscape core is conceived as being a "shadow walk" of varied light conditions created by a collage tree canopies, canvas sails, and open space (Dollin 2007, 96). An abstract arroya of water and stone impart visual continuity through the spine and a symbolic association to the regional landscape. Collectively, the layered arcs provide an effective organizing device that accommodates movement and a means for consolidating a complex series of spaces, elements, and associated experiences.

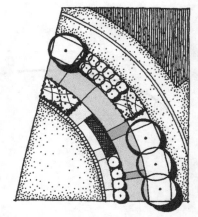

12.10 Above: Example of a design incorporating concentric arcs.

12.11 Left: Southern portion of the site plan for the Mesa Entertainment and Arts Center.

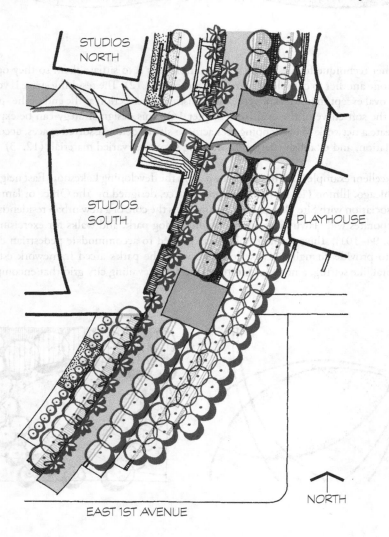

STUDIOS NORTH

STUDIOS SOUTH

PLAYHOUSE

NORTH

EAST 1ST AVENUE

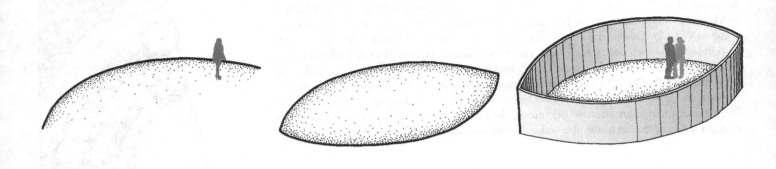

12.12 Transformation of a single arc into an enclosure of multiple arcs.

Another technique for designing with multiple arcs is to situate them so they oppose and cross one another to completely surround an area (12.12). The resulting space is very similar to an oval except that sides converge into a distinct intersection at the end of the space rather than the soft curve of the oval (see Chapter 14). This design strategy can be expanded on to create a network of overlapping arcs across a site to define assorted spaces, accommodate circulation, and establish energetic, sweeping strokes of varied materials (12.13).

An excellent example is the design of the park in the developing Lakeshore East neighborhood in Chicago, Illinois (12.14–15). This green space, designed by The Office of James Burnett in association with Site Design Group Limited is the core of a new urban residential area and incorporates wide lawn areas, a playground, a dog park, and walks for exercising (Martin 2006, 94–101). The sweeping walks were located to accommodate pedestrian desire lines and to provide changing vistas along the way. The park's arced framework establishes a pastoral like setting, a notable counterpart to the prevailing city grid that encompasses it.

12.13 Example of multiple arcs surrounding and extending through a space.

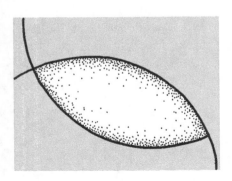
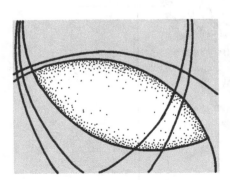
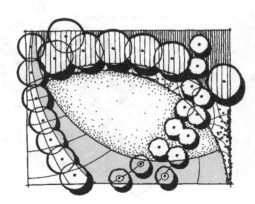

EAST SOUTH WATER STREET

NORTH PARK DRIVE

NORTH WESTSHORE DRIVE

EAST BENTON PLACE

NORTH

12.14 Above: Site plan of Lakeshore East Park.
12.15 Below: Images of Lakeshore East Park.

12.16 Above: Examples of the arc's ability to capture and direct the eye.

Direct the Eye

Like all lines, the arc's one-dimensional quality inherently captures the eye and leads it along its length (12.16). The distinction of this allure is its grace and elegance, a notable departure from the authoritative straight line and the unsettled angled line. When standing directly on an arc and looking along its length, one's attention is lithely taken along its curve in a manner that simultaneously draws the eye into the distance and laterally across the landscape (12.17). How much one's awareness is ushered horizontally across a scene depends on the degree of the arc's curvature. A differentiating consequence of the arc's curvature is that its terminus may be out of view because of the degree of the arc's bend and/ or the height of vertical elements along its length. When this occurs, the arc instills curiosity and mystery in the landscape (12.18).

STRAIGHT LINE

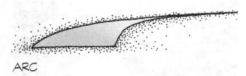

ARC

12.17 Above: The arc takes the eye laterally as well as in depth.

12.18 Right: The arc can create mystery when it disappears.

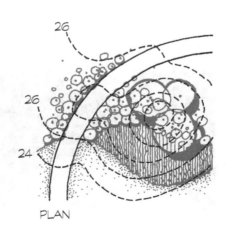

PLAN

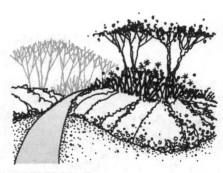

PERSPECTIVE

12.19 Left: Examples of arcing walks through the landscape.

12.20 Below: The arc directs views outward to the adjoining landscape.

Accommodate Movement

The arc can similarly serve as a conduit for physical movement through the landscape and possesses three notable traits while doing so. First, advancement along an arc is flowing and graceful, thus appropriate for a contemplative and reflective stroll through a setting. This attribute is particularly evident when the arc's degree of curvature is gentle and extends over a protracted distance (12.19). The second quality of circulation on an arc is one's attention is focused to the outside of the line, not down its center (12.20 and 12.28) (also see Design Guidelines). Consequently, a person walking along an arc is exposed to an ever-evolving scene. Passage is measured by the transforming views to outside of the arc, not just the perceived distance to its end. Lastly, the arc is well suited for gradually and fluidly changing the direction of movement from one orientation to another (12.21). Few other geometric typologies have the ability to effortlessly alter the course of circulation.

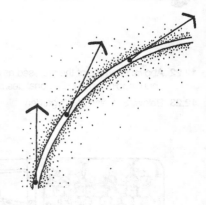

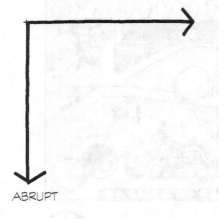

ABRUPT

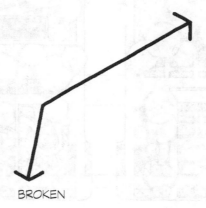

BROKEN

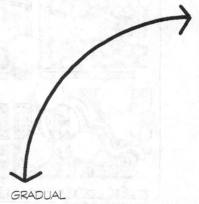

GRADUAL

12.21 The arc escorts movement via a gradual change in direction.

265

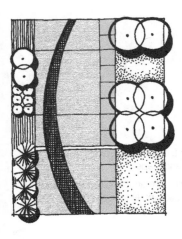

Visual Counterpoint

The arc, whether defined as a single line or a collection of many curves, is a visual counterpoint to orthogonal and angular geometries. The interjection of a single arc into a straight-lined design structure forges a striking disparity within a site between the curve's feminine spirit and the prevailing blunt edges and emphatic corners (8.38, 12.22). Moreover, the juxtaposition of the dissimilar geometries tends to emphasize the idiosyncratic qualities of each. The straight-edged configuration appears more rigid in such a setting while the serene aspect of the arc is likewise manifested. This design strategy energizes the entire design and alleviates potential monotony from over use of a single configuration. However, this concept also runs the risk that the arc will be perceived as an uncoordinated and alien element that is out of place with its setting.

A landscape architectural project that includes an arc as a counterpoint is the design of the Citygarden in St. Louis, Missouri, designed by Nelson Byrd Woltz Landscape Architects (12.23). Envisioned as a key component of the Gateway Mall that extends around the State Capital and through the core of downtown St. Louis, City Park is intended to be a setting for sculpture and to recall the geology and plant habitats of the Mississippi and Missouri rivers (Hazelrigg 2008, 152–155) (Hazelrigg 2010, 126–127). The arc is defined by a wall that suggests the shape of the rivers' edges and is a demarcation between different levels and habit zones within the park. The arc is also a notable foil to the orthogonal structure of the site and its context.

12.22 Above: Example of the arc used as a counterpoint to an orthogonal design.

12.23 Below: Site plan of Citygarden.

CHESTNUT STREET

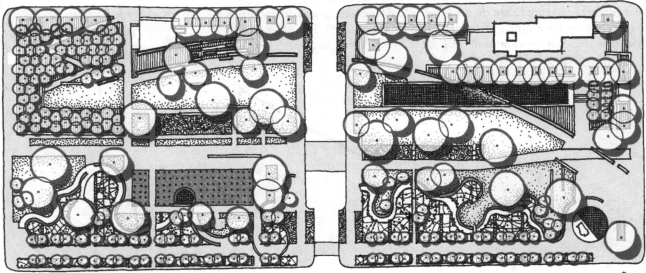

MARKET STREET

NORTH

DESIGN WITH
ENTRAPPING CORNER

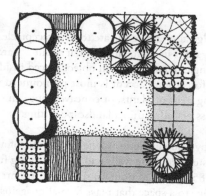

DESIGN WITH ARC

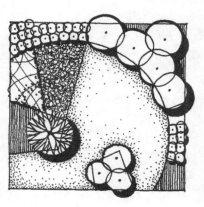

Mask Corners

The arc is an excellent design form for disguising problem corners of a space or site. The corners of an orthogonal space, especially when defined by walls, fences, or lines of plants that follow the site edges, inherently arrest the eye and retain it like a visual snare (4.5 and top left 12.24). The sides of a space that step back into or are angled toward a corner likewise grasp attention (top right 12.24). Placing an arc that is reinforced in the third dimension across a corner alleviates these potential predicaments (bottom 12.24). The arc smoothly and effortlessly carries the eye from one side of the space to the next and merges a scene that would otherwise be fragmented by the corner.

12.24 The arch can eliminate entrapping corners.

View Receptacle

The arc's alcove-like qualities that generate a spatial edge also enable the arc to be a receptacle for views in the landscape. That is, the arc's curvature holds and frames views that are directed toward it in a similar way that a half-square or semicircle does (12.25). The arc's gentle curve also functions like the converging sides of a triangle to emphasize an object placed inside it although without the triangle's assertive force. The arc's subtle containment and framing of a foreground accent is most pronounced when the arc is three-dimensional so that it conceals whatever is behind it. An arced wall, sweeping mass of plants, or concave slope can each be an effective receptacle at the far edge of a space, a terminus to an axis, or an individual recess placed within a landscape setting.

A residential garden in Hanover, Germany, designed by Ludwig Gerns is a good example of an arc employed as a view receptacle (12.26). Here, a series of arced terraces defined by low, rusted steel retaining walls and mass planting function as a subtle enfolding terminus at the end of a rectangular pool (Cooper and Taylor 1996, 85–89). Additionally, the arcs concentrate attention toward the apex where a water feature is strategically located. The arcs are a fitting edge to a space that plays formality against informality.

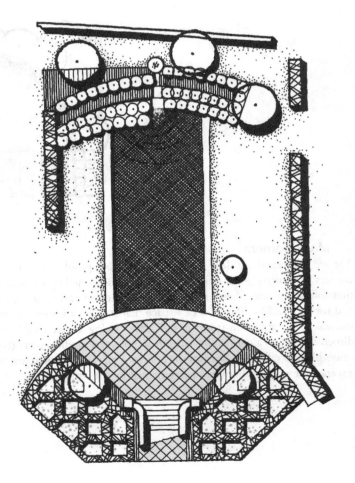

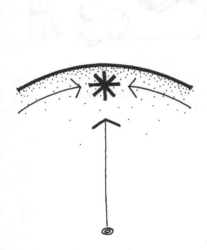

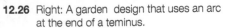

12.25 Above: Concept of the arc's ability to subtly capture views.

12.26 Right: A garden design that uses an arc at the end of a teminus.

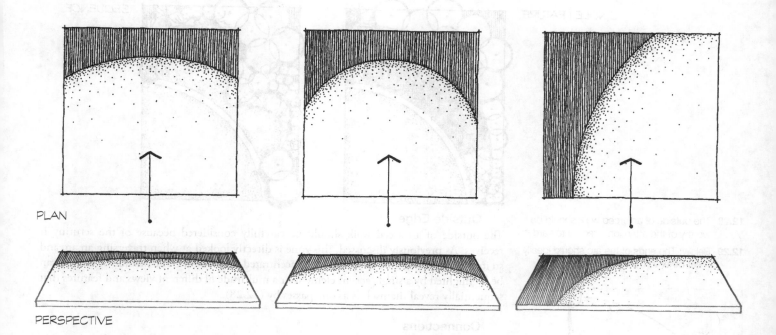

PLAN

PERSPECTIVE

One's vantage point and the degree of curvature should be carefully considered.

Design Guidelines

The arc is a relatively simple geometric form to design with in the landscape if fundamental principles of composition are adhered to. The most essential standards are discussed below and should be observed when designing with one or more arcs.

Curvature and Length

It is recommended that an arc's degree of curvature and its length be carefully examined in the early design phases because these variables have a direct influence on perceiving the arc in the landscape. It is advisable to first determine how the arc will be seen. Remember that an arc's curve is relatively flat when it is viewed from the side and consequently must be pronounced enough if the intent is to discern the arc's bend (left and middle 12.27).

By comparison, the arc's degree of curvature is more easily recognized when it is viewed along its length and so its curvature can be gentler if desired (right 12.27). In addition, one should examine whether the arc should be seen along its entire extent or whether it should bend out of view (see Landscape Uses). Both the arc's length and placement of three-dimensional elements along the arc need to be studied to achieve the desired result.

SINGLE FEATURE

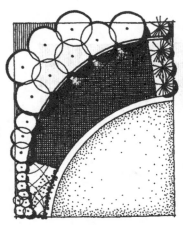

SEQUENCE

12.28 The outside of an arced walk should be worthy of the attention directed toward it.

12.29 Below: The ends of the arc should ideally meet other forms at 90 degrees.

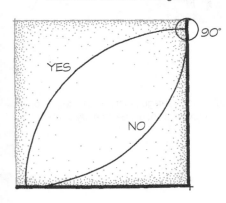

Outside Edge

The outside of an arced walk should be carefully considered because of the scrutiny it receives. As previously discussed, this zone is directly looked at when traversing an arc and so its makeup should be deserving of concentrated observation. The outside of the arc can be highlighted by a single accent element or a multitude of different views and features that sequentially reveal themselves as one passes by (12.28).

Connections

It is important to pay close attention to how the arc meets and joins other forms in landscape just as it is with all curved shapes. The ends of an arc should ideally connect to adjoining forms at a right angle to establish the most structurally and compositionally stable attachment (12.29). When this is not possible or desirable, the end of an arc should not meet another edge at less than a forty-five degree angle to avoid the potential problems associated with acute angles (see Chapter 10). Similar guidelines also apply to how the arc intersects other forms along its length. Ideally, adjoining lines should coincide with radii extended from the arc to its center point (left 12.30). Lines that meet the arc at an obtuse

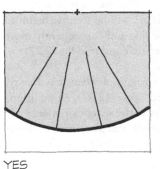

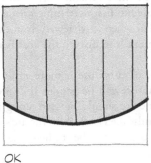

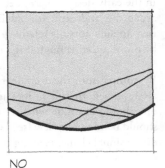

YES

OK

NO

12.30 Adjoining lines should be radii extended from the arc's center point.

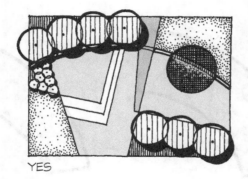
YES

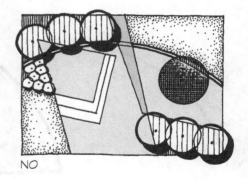
NO

12.31 The arch should not cut off areas or create awkward connections.

angle are also acceptable and lines that meet at an acute angle are to be avoided (middle and right 12.30). Similarly, an arc should be situated so that it passes through the interior of material areas and spaces rather than merely touching edges or awkwardly cutting off corners and small sectors of areas (12.31).

Third Dimension

The arc's fundamental relationship to the ground plane should also be considered because the arc's curvature creates a range of design possibilities that are not feasible with a straight line. It will be recalled that a straight line best fulfills its potential landscape uses when it is situated on level ground (3.24). This is not necessarily so with the arc. An arced walk, for instance, can gradually move higher or lower in elevation as it moves through the landscape, a gesture that accentuates its fluidity and the experience of moving along it (left 12.32). An arc can likewise be adapted to inclined topography or a mound by gracefully sliding up or down a convex landform (right 12.32). All in all, it is essential to think three-dimensionally when designing with the arc.

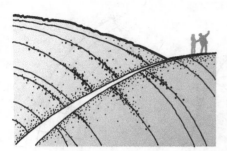

12.32 An arc is easily adapted to and reinforces rolling topography.

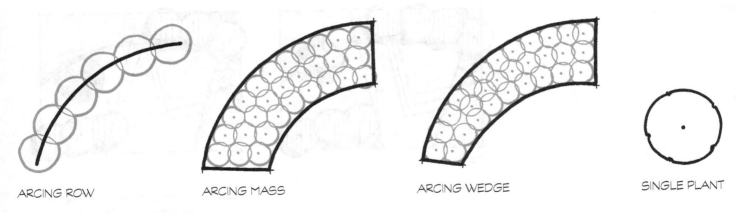

ARCING ROW   ARCING MASS   ARCING WEDGE   SINGLE PLANT

12.33 Vocabuary of organizing structures for plant materials along an arc.

Material Coordination

All materials and elements associated with an arc should reinforce and/or echo its curvature with sweeping gestures that express energy and movement. For plant materials, this translates into a vocabulary of four possible arrangements: arcing rows, arcing masses, wedges, and single plants (12.33). Arcing rows are the most simplistic method and directly echo the linearity of an arc. Arcing masses and wedges provide depth and weight to a planting, allowing a design to expand beyond a single line or edge. Furthermore, arcing masses and wedges provide an opportunity to exploit variations in height, foliage color, and texture as one mass of plants extends into or by another. As in all genres of form, the single plant is normally used as an accent at strategic points within the design.

Structural elements and materials should be organized in similar formats. Three-dimensional elements like walls are linear and directly emulate the arc. Steps, planters, water bodies, pavement areas, and other ground materials have width and may be placed within arcing shapes that have parallel sides or diverging sides like those in wedges of plants. Lines and elements within these areas can be parallel and/or perpendicular to the arced sides (12.34).

12.34 Alternative methods for organizing lines and elements within pavement areas.

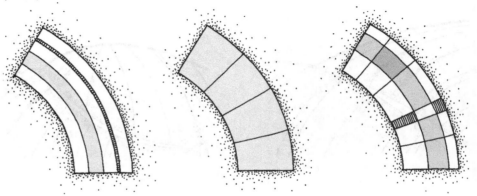

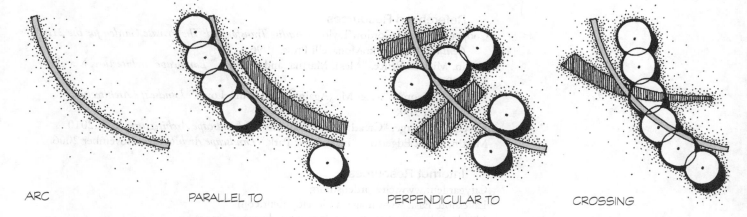

ARC   PARALLEL TO   PERPENDICULAR TO   CROSSING

There are three general tactics for organizing materials and elements along an arc. The first is to directly parallel the arc by locating plant materials and structural elements in concentric rings (12.8–11 and middle left 12.35). This elementary concept can be as simple as one element or as complex as multiple layers of elements and materials. However it is expressed, this design scheme generates sweeping movement. The second method for placing elements and materials in association with an arc is to locate them perpendicular to the arc (middle right 12.35). Such a placement aligns the elements with the center point of the arc and can be used to create a cadence along the arc. The third strategy for organizing elements and materials is to allow them to cross in a fabric of interwoven arcing lines (12.13–14 and right 12.35). This is a more sophisticated method of organizing elements, allowing for spatial enclosure and an intertwining of materials. These alternative strategies for designing with an arc can be employed by themselves or synthesized in a creative manner that takes advantage of the inherent qualities of each (12.36).

12.35 Alternative technques for organizing elements in relation to an arc.

12.36 Example of a design that synthesizes alternative ways to organize elements and materials.

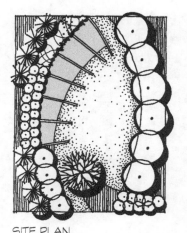

SITE PLAN

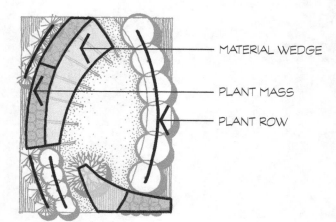

STRUCTURING ARCS   MATERIAL AREAS

MATERIAL WEDGE

PLANT MASS

PLANT ROW

Referenced Resources

Cooper, Guy, and Gordon Taylor. *Paradise Transformed: The Private Garden for the 21st Century.* New York: Monacelli Press, 1996.

Dollin, Michael Bruce. "Mesa, Martha, and the Mac." *Landscape Architecture*, March 2007.

Hazelrigg, George. "Meet Me (Again) in St. Louis, Louis." *Landscape Architecture*, October 2008.

Hazelrigg, George. "Creating an Urban Oasis." *Landscape Architecture*, April 2010.

Martin, Frank Edgerton. "Preemptive Park." *Landscape Architecture*, November 2006.

Internet Resources

Citygarden: www.citygardenstl.org

Lakeshore East: www.magellandevelopment.com

Martha Schwartz Partners: www.marthaschwartz.com

Nelson Byrd Woltz: www.nbwla.com

The Office of James Burnett: www.ojb.com

The Circle 13

Like the square and the triangle, the circle is one of the primary shapes that are elegantly simple and the genesis for other forms in their genre. Yet the circle is unlike the other primary shapes because it is the only one that is curved, thus lacking straight sides and corners. The circle's continuity and purity are idiosyncratic among all forms. Furthermore, the circle is seen in nature in the shape of the sun, moon, various flowers, fruits, stones, and so forth. The intertwining of simplicity and potential complexity make the circle a compelling form to work with as evidenced by its broad use in all design fields including landscape architectural site design during virtually all time periods. This chapter examines various aspects of the circle including:

- Geometric Qualities
- Landscape Uses
- Design Guidelines

Geometric Qualities

The circle is defined as a set of points that are an equal distance from a fixed point on the same plane (13.1). Collectively, the points create a continuous circumference that sweeps 360 degrees to enclose the area within the circle. The circle is further distinguished by the following geometric qualities.

Components

There are a number of inherent components that comprise the circle. Among these, the center and circumference are the most apparent and critical to the circle's delineation (also see Center). A chord is a line that connects any two points on the circle's circumference while the diameter is a special type of chord that connects two opposite points as it passes through the circle's center (left 13.2). The radius is half a diameter or a line that connects one point on the circle's circumference to the center point.

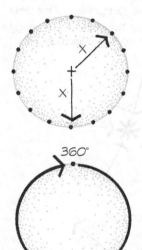

13.1 A circle is a set of points that are an equal distance from a fixed center.

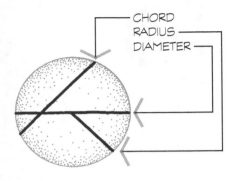

CHORD
RADIUS
DIAMETER

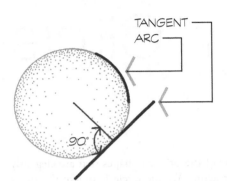

TANGENT
ARC

90°

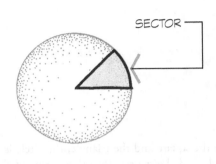

SECTOR

13.2 Above: Components of the circle.

13.3 Below: The center directs energy and attention inward and outward.

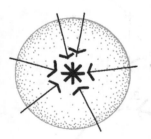

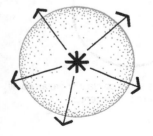

There are two types of lines associated with the circle's circumference. The first is the arc, a segment of the circle's perimeter that was studied in the previous chapter (12.1 and middle 13.2). A tangent is a straight line that touches the outside of circle's circumference. It may be any length and orientation although it always makes a 90-degree angle to the radius at the point where it connects to the circle.

Finally, a sector is a pie-shaped area of the circle formed by two radii and an arc on the circle's circumference (right 13.2). A sector is one way of subdividing the internal area of circle and can be used to define different material and use areas within the confines of circle as discussed in more detail in a following section, the Single Space.

Center
The circle's center is comparable to the square's although perhaps more significant because the circle's entire presence revolves around its midpoint. The center is literally and figuratively the nucleus of the circle and dominates all aspects of the circle. Each of the just-defined components relates to and is subordinate to the circle's midpoint with some passing through the center while others are generated in direct relation to the center. Visual and symbolic energy simultaneously emanates from and gravitates to the circle's center (13.3). The core cannot be denied and so is often explicitly acknowledged by accenting the center or implicitly with elements that are organized around /or extending from the center (13.4).

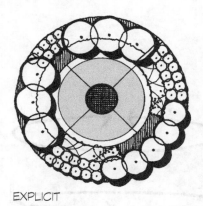

EXPLICIT

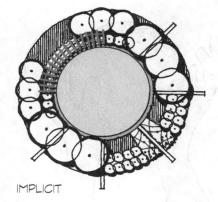

IMPLICIT

13.4 Left: The circle's center may be explicitly or implicitly expressed.

13.5 Below: The circle's edge is a continuous line unlike the other primary shapes.

Continuum

One of the most distinguishing qualities of the circle is its uninterrupted circumference (13.5). Unlike the square or triangle that have distinct sides and corners, the circle has no separate edges or junctions between them. The circle's perimeter is one endless line that is forever connected and unified. While it is possible to define opposite sides or points that have different orientations on the circle, they are nevertheless on the same line and thus share a common relationship. All the points are also the same distance from the center, further reinforcing their parity. In simple terms, the circle establishes integration and consolidation (see Landscape Uses).

Landscape Uses

As previously suggested, the circle is a widely used form in design and can be employed for a number of interrelated landscape uses. Some of the most noteworthy are: spatial foundation, compositional accent, compositional unifier, gathering node, focus and dispersal, fit natural settings, and symbolic meanings.

Spatial Foundation

A principal function of the circle in landscape architectural design is to be the armature for single spaces and an aggregation of multiple spaces. While potentially diverse in type and temperament, all circular spaces share an ever-present center, an embracing sense of enclosure, a comparatively graceful disposition, and the lack of hard corners.

Single Space. An independent circular space is a self-contained entity whose design is confined within its circumference. An entry courtyard, urban plaza, public green space, garden, or circular site area are all potential locations for a single circle in the landscape. In addition, a circular space can be one entity in the context of many other spaces. A solitary circular space may be forged simply to envelop space and/or to fulfill other potential uses such as a compositional accent, gathering node, or a suggestion of unity and equality (see other Landscape Uses).

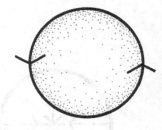

277

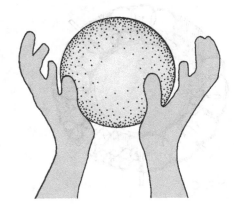

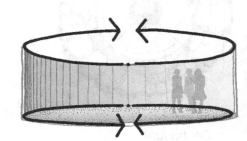

13.6 Right: The circle's continuous perimeter creates an embracing, cocoon-like space.

13.7 Below: Typology of single circular spaces.

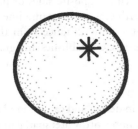

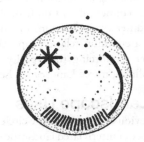

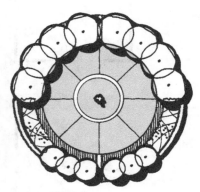

SYMMETRICAL
VOLUMETRIC SPACE

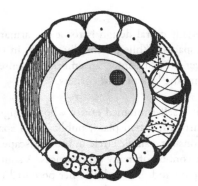

ASYMMETRICAL
VOLUMETRIC SPACE

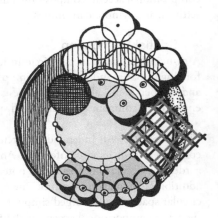

CUBIST SPACE

Like square and triangular volumes, a single circular space can be volumetric or cubist depending on the continuity of its edge and treatment of its interior. The most distinguishing quality of volumetric spaces is the continuous, comparatively soft boundary that is amiable and passive in temper. The circle's smooth, unbroken perimeter creates a cocoon-like volume that gently surrounds and embraces a space in the third dimension (10.8, 13.6). To "circle" is to enclose. The eye moves uninterrupted around the outer plane of a circle and returns gracefully toward the viewer without being literally and figuratively trapped in corners.

The interior of a circular volumetric space may be structured symmetrically or asymmetrically depending on design circumstances. The symmetrical organization is the most apropos to a volumetric space with an explicit, accentuated center and ground patterns defined by radii and/or concentric rings (left 13.7). Such a space is appropriate as the hub for converging axes in a symmetrical context, an open gathering node, and/or place intended to engender reverence for a notable element in the middle. An asymmetrical layout lacks the discipline of its symmetrical counterpart and may be composed of assorted elements that collectively create enclosure (middle 13.7). This type of space is appropriate for informal design settings, as an area of convergence for divergent circulation routes, and/or to express originality on the ground plane.

A single cubist space based on the circle lacks the spatial clarity and simplicity of a volumetric enclosure (right 13.7). The circumference is typically composed of multiple elements positioned in proximity, but not necessary on the perimeter itself. The interior of the space is interrupted by strategically placed two and three-dimensional elements. The overall organization of a cubist space often does not explicitly rely on or directly express the circle's internal geometry. Instead, it uses these components as references and emulates their character rather than their actual location.

Both volumetric and cubist spaces must routinely be subdivided into different use and material areas within their borders. One way for doing this is by utilizing concentric circles and radii. Concentric circles and radii are to the circle what axes and its associated grid are to the square (4.1–2). That is, these internal geometric components are the basis for subdividing the circle into smaller areas that are intrinsically related to their parent shape. Concentric circles are a series of strata-like rings that are centered on the circle's midpoint. In the landscape, concentric circles are defined by two-dimensional materials placed between them and/or three-dimensional elements located along them (13.8). The spacing of the concentric circles and the distribution of materials and elements within them in relation to the circle's center are factors that can be manipulated to meet program needs and fit existing site conditions. The commonality of all concentric circle configurations is the duality of enveloping enclosure and rotational energy along each ring.

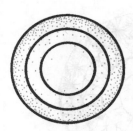

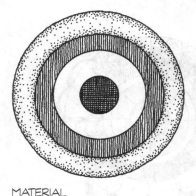

MATERIAL

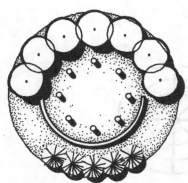

3D ELEMENTS

13.8 The circle may be subdivided on the basis of concentric circles.

279

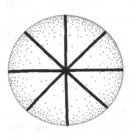

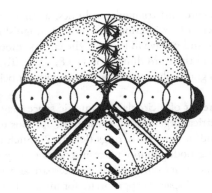

SECTOR EXPRESSED   RADII EXPRESSED

13.9 The circle may be subdivided on the basis of radii.

The circle's radii can be engaged in two ways to subdivide the circle. One is to use the radii as edges between materials, thereby defining sectors or pie-shaped wedges that expand outward from the circle's center to its circumference (middle 13.9). Size, spacing, and balance of content around the center point are design variables. A second strategy for designing with the circle's radii is to explicitly define them by placing three-dimensional elements or narrow bands of contrasting ground material directly on the radii (right 13.9). Again, the spacing and content of the radii are factors that can be choreographed as desired. The overriding aspect of this "spokes of a wheel" motif is the undeniable visual energy to and from the circle's center, a factor that must be kept in mind when engaging radii. Concentric circles and radii can be also integrated with each other as the foundation of a design within a circle (13.10). This is a more complex method than the previous techniques but is generally the most preferable because of the numerous design possibilities it yields. In essence, the combination of concentric circles and radii creates a web of arcing and straight lines that is like a grid that is warped around the circle's midpoint.

13.10 Examples of circles subdivided via concentric circles and radii.

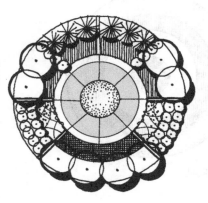

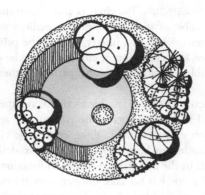

NONCONCENTRIC CIRCLES

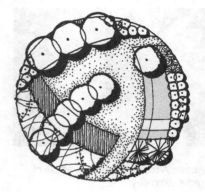

ARCS

A second general means for designing within a circle is to use nonconcentric circles and/or arcs to establish use and materials areas, a strategy that emulates the character of the circle without relying in its internal geometry. One method is to incorporate overlapping circles of varying sized circles that are partially and/or completely placed inside the parent circle (left 13.11). Similarly, arcs whose center points are located outside the circle can subdivide its interior area (right 13.11). This scheme generates the impression that selected segments of the circle's circumference have been transposed to its interior (also see Chapter 11).

The third comprehensive method for designing within a circle is to incorporate straight lines or geometric forms based on them (13.12). This design scheme creates the greatest contrast to the circle and treats the circle as merely a frame around a self-contained composition. Deference for the circle is less important in this strategy than creating a design that performs by itself. Nevertheless, caution must be exercised where the straight lines of these disparate geometries connect to the circle's circumference (see Design Guidelines).

13.11 Examples of circles subdivided via nonconcentric circles and arcs.

13.12 Examples of circles subdivided via straight lines.

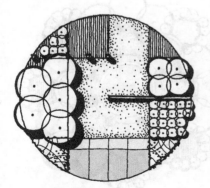

ORTHOGONAL FORMS

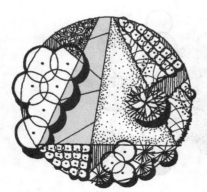

TRIANGULAR FORMS

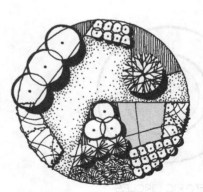

POLYGONAL FORMS

281

Multiple Spaces. The circle is also a form that can be replicated numerous times to forge an ensemble of spaces. The most expedient ways of configuring such designs is by means of symmetry and asymmetry, two of the principal organizational structures discussed in Chapter 1. A collection of circles can also be organized on a grid, but the results are most applicable for two-dimensional patterns rather than the framework of landscape space.

Symmetry. The most feasible tactic for symmetrically assembling circles is radial symmetry (1.44, 13.13). This organizational structure appends spaces to a principal circle by placing them on extended radii, along concentric circles around the outside of the circle, or a combination of both (13.14). Thus, the design expands outward to whatever extend is desired. In the first strategy, the radii function as axes similar to an orthogonal design. The second tactic has no axes, only an overall symmetrical arrangement. In all circumstances, the core circle should be the foremost space in both use and visual prominence because of its pivotal position in the entire design.

13.13 Above: A flower that is an example of radial symmetry.

13.14 Below: Alternative concepts of radial symmetry.

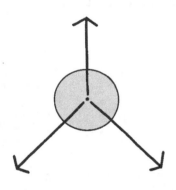

RADII

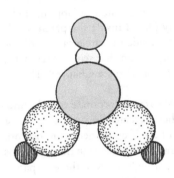

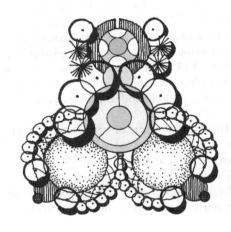

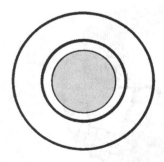

CONCENTRIC CIRCLES

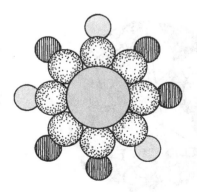

Asymmetry. The second primary organizational structure for multiple circular spaces is asymmetry, a design configuration that can be established in several ways. This first is via interlocking additive transformation that produces a series of layered spaces that collectively imply a swirling vortex of intertwined motions and cycles (13.15). The circle's inherent ability to return on itself proliferates with numerous circles that interlace one another with overlapping arced gestures (13.16). The overlapping circles also produce an interlocking chain of arcs around the exterior, an effect that is particularly evident when the perimeters of the circles are extruded into the third dimension with a similar element. The perimeter's scalloped silhouette is an amicable connection to the area outside the circles and permits a structure of overlapping circles to settle into its surroundings.

Face-to-face additive transformation is not feasible with circles because of the tenuous connections created between immediately adjoining circles (see Design Guidelines).

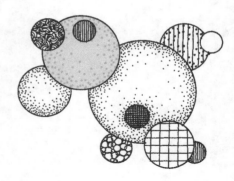

13.15 Above: Abstract example of interlocking circles.

13.16 Left: Example of a design based on interlocking circles.

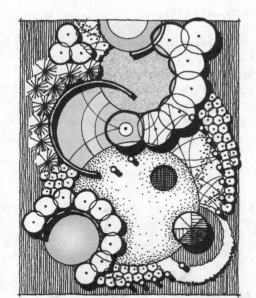

PLAN

CONCEPT

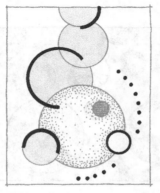

STRUCTURES

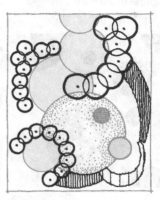

PLANT MATERIALS

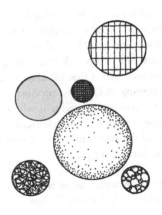

13.17 Above: Example of a circular design based on spatial tension.

A second principal method for establishing multiple circular spaces is by means of spatial tension. The intervening negative space produces distinct and separate spaces that are concurrently isolated by distance and unified by similarity of form (13.17). The sense of autonomy is further reinforced by the gravitation towards the center of each circle and the curved circumference that visually repels nearby circles (13.18).

Another unique aspect of circles organized by means of spatial tension is that the negative space is truly a reverse figure, looking very much like a slice of Swiss cheese punctuated by holes (left 13.19). The intertwined background web is an effective consolidating element when defined with one ground material and is well suited for circulation that must simultaneously accommodate many divergent directions (middle and right 13.19). Circulation is also preferable in the surrounding interstitial space when the circles contain uses that cannot be bisected with disruptive movement.

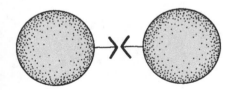

13.18 Above: The circle's circumference visually repels other circles.

13.19 Below: Example of using the interstitial space for multidirectional circulation.

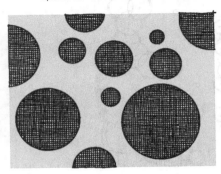

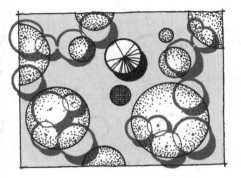

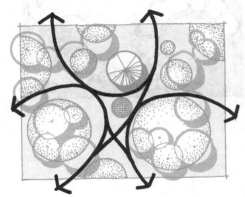

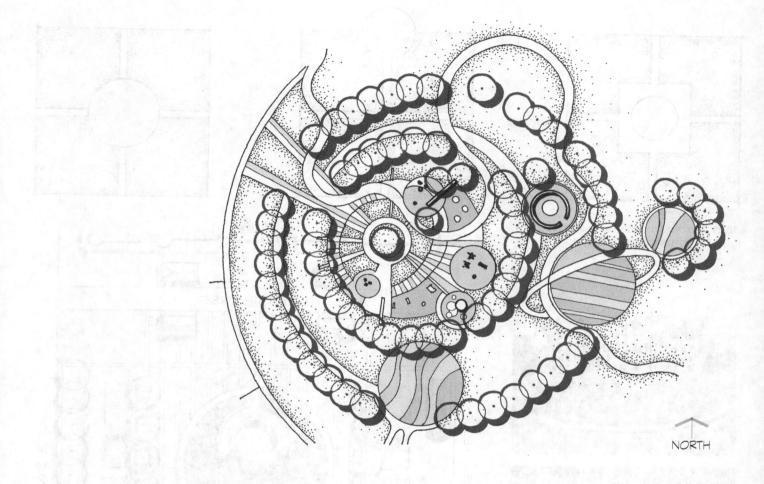

NORTH

13.20 Site plan of Discovery Frontier.

All the assorted means of creating multiple circular spaces can be applied as outlined in the previous pages or synthesized to provide the designer with many more options and avenues for creativity. One example fusing different circular structures is Discovery Frontier, an adventure playground in Grove City, Ohio, designed by the landscape architectural firm MSI (13.20). Here, multiple circular spaces have been located by means of interlocking addition and spatial tension on both a symmetrical and asymmetrical foundation. The circles in this design portray planets of the solar system, thus implying an exciting journey through a series of unique play spaces. The planetary theme is carried out with the choice of play equipment, pavement patterns, and sculpting of the ground plane. The circles are appropriate organizing shapes because they provide a semisoft structure appropriate for the spontaneous nature of children's play.

285

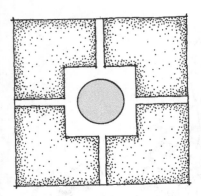
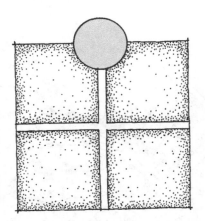
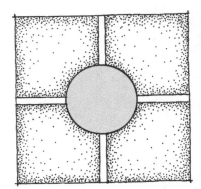

13.21 The circle is readily used as an accent in a symmetrical design organization.

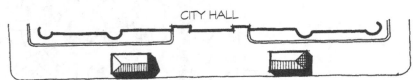

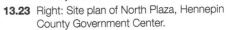

13.22 Above: Photos of North Plaza, Hennepin County Government Center.

13.23 Right: Site plan of North Plaza, Hennepin County Government Center.

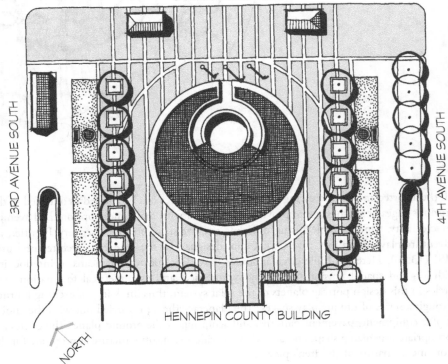

Compositional Accent

The simplicity and uniqueness of a single circle makes it easily detected when strategically positioned among other forms and accordingly an effective compositional focal point. This use of the circle has broad applications. In a symmetrical design, a circle is appropriately used as an accent at the junction of two or more axes or at the terminus of a single axis (13.21). In either location, a circle may describe the overall configuration of the space or be an element within a space as defined by a pavement design, planting area, water feature, or three-dimensional element (7.19). Examples of this use include the lower parterre garden at Villa Lante (7.3) and the North Plaza of the Hennepin County Government Center in Minneapolis, Minnesota (13.22–23).

In addition, the circle can be an alluring accent in asymmetrical spaces, especially in orthogonal and angular designs where its shape contrasts the prevailing straight lines. The circle can be set apart to highlight its individuality or integrated as a less obvious, though nevertheless strategic element (13.24, 13.28). A single circle can also function as a notable feature in designs dominated by curvilinear and arcing lines like the pool does in a desert hillside landscape designed by Thomas Church (13.25).

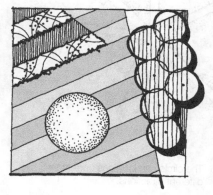

13.24 Above: Example of a circle used as an accent within a contrasting design structure.

13.25 Below: A circular pool that is a simple accent in a hillside desert garden.

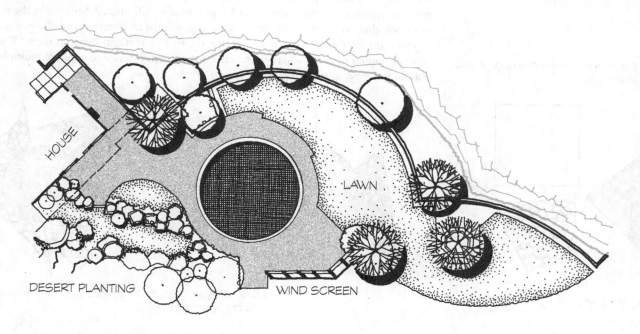

HOUSE

LAWN

DESERT PLANTING

WIND SCREEN

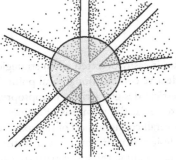

13.26 The circle can join lines from many different directions.

Compositional Unifier

The circle's homogeneity and lack of corners makes it ideal to connect other lines and forms that have no apparent alignment or relation to each other. The circle permits disparate forms to be fastened and hinged together in one synchronized configuration. One application of this use of the circle is to join intersecting lines that are at random angles to each other as often occurs with crossing paths in a park or campus (13.26). The circle's center is placed at the point of the lines' intersection and creates a central space that all the lines uniformly attach to. This technique not only creates a joint among the paths, but also celebrates the point of intersection with a space that has potential significance. Additionally, the presence of a circle eliminates the possibility of acute angles at the intersection and allows circulation to move among the paths without wearing the surface material between them. This same concept applies to roads where traffic circles are a useful device to connect multiple roads that do not meet at right angles.

13.27 The circle can be a uniting hinge among other forms.

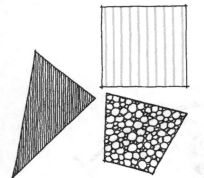

UNRELATED FORMS

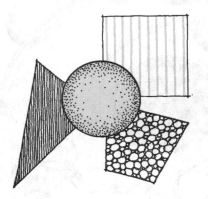

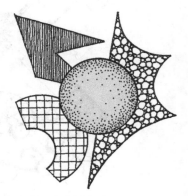

CIRCLE Is a HINGE THAT UNITES
UNRELATED FORMS

Moreover, the circle is an excellent form to resolve awkward connections among adjoining or closely spaced surface areas that are mismatched in shape and alignment (13.27). The circle is strategically located and sized so that the edges of the nearby forms meet the circle's circumference at a right angle, a technique that is easily accomplished when all the areas are being configured at the same time but more difficult to do if some or all of the areas already exist. The circle compositionally integrates the neighboring forms and simultaneously generates a common space that potentially serves as a central meeting point (13.28).

The circle can likewise be an integrating element when placed in a landscape comprised of diverse elements, materials, and architectural styles as occurs in urban locals. An illustration of this use is the proposed renovation of Mining Circle on the campus of the University of California Berkley designed by Sasaki Associates (13.29). Mining Circle moderates the diversity of the surrounding academic buildings, serves as junction for converging circulation routes, and is a shared gathering space (see Gathering Node on the next page).

13.28 Above: Example of the circle used as a compositional hinge among other spaces.

13.29 Left: Proposed site plan for Mining Circle.

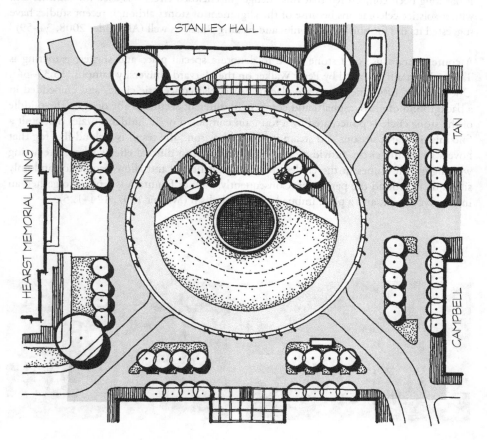

STANLEY HALL

HEARST MEMORIAL MINING

TAN

CAMPBELL

NORTH

289

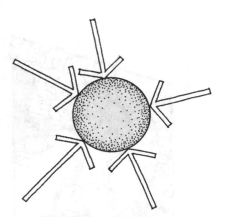

13.30 The circle inherently serves as a gathering node.

Gathering Node

The circle, like the square discussed in Chapter 4, is an ideal form for gathering although the circle's inherent internal focus and lack of corners make it even more opportune for convergence. The circle's continuously uniform curvature implies that people from all directions are equally welcome (13.30). Once assembled, the circle accommodates facial contact and conversation for those around the perimeter assuming the circle is not too large. The capacity to readily see other people around the circle and to focus attention on a person or activity at its center promotes a sense of family and community. This use of the circle also nurtures a sense of accord among those gathered and is epitomized in the phrase "circle of friends" (also see Symbolic Meanings).

The use of the circle for gathering has a long history as evidenced by numerous ancient stone circles throughout Europe where prehistoric peoples used them for religious gatherings, burial grounds, and astrological observatories. Stonehenge with its monolithic Sarsen stones on the Salisbury Plains in England is perhaps the most famous among these (13.31–32). It has long been conjectured that this "henge" or enclosed circle was used for summer and winter solstice celebrations because of the alignment of stones although recent studies have suggested its use for burial ceremonies and healing rituals as well (Alexander 2008, 34–59).

A contemporary use of a stone circle to denote a special place and suggest gathering is Tanner Fountain designed by Peter Walker on the Harvard University campus (13.33–34). One hundred fifty-nine stones are placed in irregular concentric circles and embedded in a background of grass, asphalt, and concrete in different sectors of the design. The middle of the stone circle is punctuated by a fountain composed of 32 hidden nozzles that emit a fine mist in warm seasons and steam in the cold season. The result is a cloud-like fog that hovers above the circle, providing different seasonal and diurnal effects when interacting with light. The stones in the circles are about seat height and allow people to randomly sit on them around the perimeter. Consequently, Tanner Fountain is a place to gather, an interactive accent, and a place imbued with symbolism (Walker 1997, 124–125).

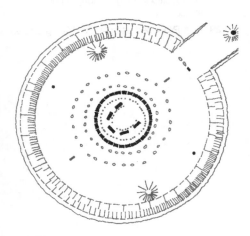

13.31 Above: Plan of Stonehenge as it was envisioned to have been.

13.32 Right: Images of Stonehenge.

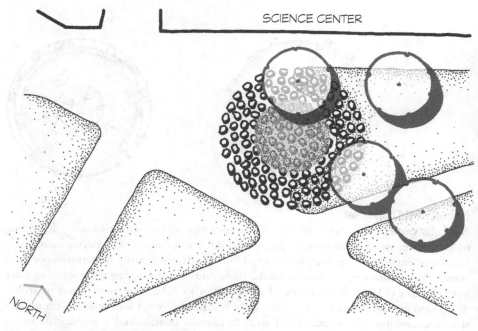

SCIENCE CENTER

13.33 Left: Site plan of Tanner Fountain.

13.34 Above: Images of Tanner Fountain.

The many historic precedents of the circle's use as a structure for gathering have been the inspiration for similar uses in landscape architectural design. One of the most notable examples is Jens Jensen's "council ring" which is a hallmark of his park and estate designs in the Midwest. The council ring was defined by a low stonewall or stone bench encircling a fire pit and was normally located at the edge of a wooded area with views looking outward (13.35). The purpose of the council ring was to provide a setting where people could gather to talk in a democratic atmosphere of equality, listen to poetry, watch a small performance, or contemplate the natural surroundings (Grese 1992, 176–178). The circle similarly lends itself to spaces for backyard family gatherings, meeting areas in a camp, instructional areas in learning gardens, social spaces outside restaurants, reading circles associated with schools or libraries, and so on.

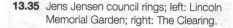

13.35 Jens Jensen council rings; left: Lincoln Memorial Garden; right: The Clearing.

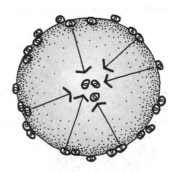
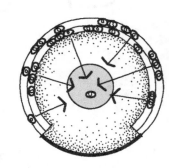

13.36 Right: The circle inherently supports viewing activity within itself.

Focus and Dispersal

A circular space can be a venue of inward focus or a place of outward orientation depending on the treatment of its interior, degree of enclosure, and context. The circle's inescapable interior orientation makes it an ideal spatial form to view an activity or performance at its center. People sitting or standing around a circle cannot escape seeing what is taking place in the middle (13.36). Furthermore, the circle affords similar views to everyone regardless of location around the circle. A circular space is intrinsically apt for outdoor performance spaces, classrooms, and so on. A half circle has similar benefits and is appropriate where the central activity is best seen from one general vantage point or where there is sloped topography as is frequently needed for an outdoor amphitheater (13.37).

A completely opposite quality of the circle is its centrifugal inclination as suggested by the outward curvature of its circumference (left 13.38). While this is not the most obvious or compelling trait, it is nevertheless a characteristic that can be harnessed to disperse views and movement away from the circle. Thus, a circular space is appropriate for observing the immediately surrounding landscape or providing a platform for panoramic views to an expansive landscape beyond (right 13.38). A more focused orientation is established when

13.37 Above: Examples of amphitheaters based on a circular form.

13.38 Right: The circle can provide an outward orientation to the surrounding landscape.

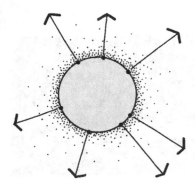

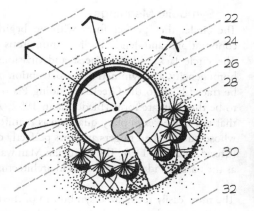

13.39 The circle can thrust attention and movement outward into the surrounding landscape.

one side of the circle is enclosed thereby directing observation to the open side (13.39). Like the triangle, both a full circle and a half circle are also apropos to disperse pedestrian circulation into a relatively spacious landscape especially when situated at the end of restricted walk or an axis (also see Landscape Uses, Chapter 10).

Fit Natural Settings

The circle is additionally suitable for accommodating different functions and spaces in an undisturbed rural landscape. A collection of circular spaces is particularly fitting in sites characterized by rolling topography, clumps and drifts of vegetation, and/or meandering water bodies. In these settings, circles echo tree trunks, flowers, round rocks, globular leaves, ripples of water, and so on to establish a simpatico relationship with the natural environment. Furthermore, asymmetrical arrangements of circles can be inserted into these locations with minimal impact because of their adaptable structure as mentioned before (13.40). Yet, the circle remains anthropomorphic with distinct edges and potentially structural materials to express the presence of people. Multiple circles are, therefore, ideal to visually and symbolically knit the natural and human worlds together.

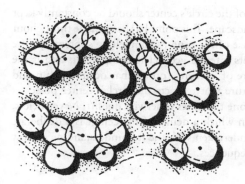
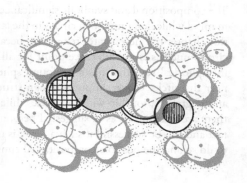

13.40 Circular spaces fit naturalistic landscapes of rolling topography and clumps of trees.

293

13.41 Leonardo da Vinci's Vitruvian Man.

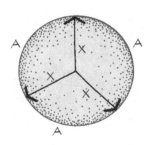

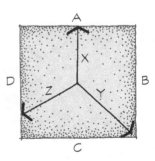

13.42 Comparison between the equality created by the circle and square.

Symbolic Meanings

The circle, the "perfect form with no beginning and no ending," is rich in symbolic connotations and lends itself to numerous affiliated interpretations in the landscape. The circle lacks sides, corners, and divisions, thus making it a paragon of simplicity, homogeneity, and symmetry. The perception of the circle being the consummate figure can be traced back to the Greeks including Plato and his followers who considered the circle to be the ultimate form (Biedermann 1992, 70). During the Renaissance, it was believed that the circle's exemplary quality was manifested by Leonardo da Vinci's Vitruvian Man whose outstretched fingers and toes perfectly coincide with a circle's circumference (13.41) (Tresidder 2005, 119). The Vitruvian Man was employed during the Renaissance and since as the basis for ideal proportions in architecture and design.

The most easily recognized symbolism of the circle is its intertwined implications of unity, equality, completeness, wholeness, and eternity. All the points on the circle's circumference share an identical relation to the center and coexist on a single line. No one point is dominant or subordinate to any other; all locations on the circumference merge in absolute equality. This trait was exploited during the Paris Peace Accords held in the late 1960s to end the Vietnam War. After initial debates, it was agreed to make the negotiating table round so that all the representative parties would be interpreted as being equal to each other in both position and distance (13.42). A square or rectangular table would have established distinct sides and a hierarchy of importance to those who sat at the table. Similarly, this same concept of assembling people in a circle to promote consensus is sometimes used in town meetings, classes, religious assemblies, therapy sessions, and so on.

Design Guidelines

The circle requires special attention to address various design challenges created by its rounded shape. The following design guidelines are offered as a way to handle these possible issues and to assure the circle achieves its maximum potential as a structuring form in the landscape.

Center

The compositional and symbolic significance of the circle's center should be constantly kept in mind while designing with circles in the landscape. This point has been made throughout this chapter but necessitates reiteration because of the center's compelling supremacy. The circle's nucleus is the reference point for all its internal geometric components and is the metaphorical soul that has a profound sphere of influence on all that occurs within and near the circle. Quite simply, a design structure that respects the circle's center possesses an integral relationship with the circle while one that does otherwise doesn't. Nevertheless, there are circumstances as suggested before in which a denial of the center is a deliberate tact and can be successful if such a move is undertaken with the full understanding of how to do so and the possible compositional consequences.

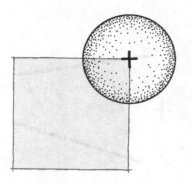 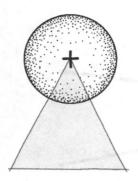 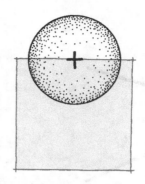 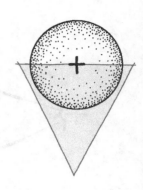

CENTERED on CORNER   CENTERED on EDGE

Connections

The circle's soft edge is gentle in temperament and yet problematic when trying to relate it to other forms. The curvature of the circle's perimeter does not accommodate the continuous surface-to-surface attachment between abutting forms that are possible with orthogonal shapes and triangles (4.6, 10.45). The circle is able to "touch" adjacent forms only at a single point and so does not forge a strong design configuration (1.19). Such a connection produces acute angles in the negative space, a situation that should be avoided for a number of compositional and practical reasons (see Design Guidelines, Chapter 10).

Consequently, the circle should be separated from a nearby form with a space or it should overlap the other form (13.15 and 13.17). The ideal connection between a circle and another form is to place the center of the circle directly on the side or corner of the adjoining shape (13.43). This assures that the point of intersection between the circle's circumference and the other area will be a right angle. If this is not feasible, then the amount of overlap should not be too little or too much.

13.43 Ideal connections between the circle and the other primary forms.

13.44 Design examples illustrating inappropriate and appropriate connections to a circle.

NO

YES

295

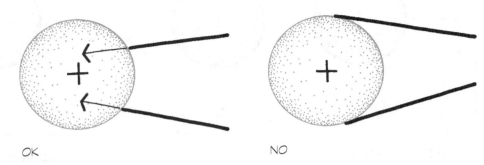

IDEAL OK NO

13.45 Adjoining lines should ideally align with the circle's center point.

It should be noted that when the circle's center is located on the edge of an adjoining orthogonal or triangular form that the circle's radius coincides with the sides of the attached form. Any line or edge that directly corresponds with an extended radius establishes a stable connection with the circle (13.45) (also see Compositional Unifier in Landscape Uses).

Relation to Site

Similarly, circles should not touch a site edge especially if it is a structural element like a building, site wall, walk, and so on (13.46). There are three strategies to avoid this. The first is to reduce the size of the circles so that they are completely contained within the site and defined by on-site elements. Extended radii or gentle arcs that curve from the site edge to the circle can provide linear connections to the exterior for circulation (left 13.47). A second tactic is to enlarge the circles so that they overlap the boundary. This strategy implies a larger area than expressed and instills intrigue because the completion of the circles is unresolved (right 13.47). The third tactic is to use other forms as a transition to the site edge.

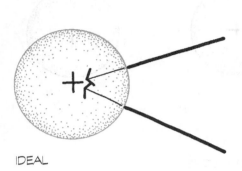

13.46 Above: This type of connection between a circle and adjoining structure should be avoided.

13.47 Right: Alternative strategies for relating circular spaces to the site edge.

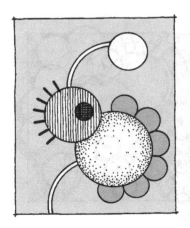
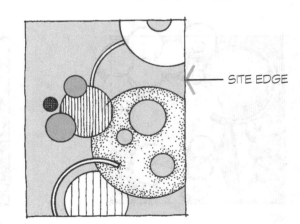

SITE EDGE

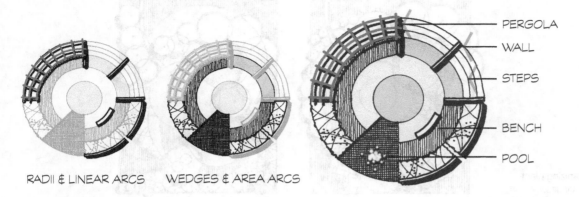

PERGOLA
WALL
STEPS
BENCH
POOL

RADII & LINEAR ARCS   WEDGES & AREA ARCS

Material Coordination

The arrangement of materials and elements like pavement, pools of water, walls, steps, pergolas, and other site structures inside and around a circle should correspond to one of the methods previously described for designing within a single space (see Spatial Foundation). Among these methodologies, the circle's radii and implied internal concentric circles are the most critical components to employ as guides. When combined, radii and concentric circles produce a vocabulary of four shapes that materials and elements fit within: radii, linear arcs, wedge, and area arc (13.48). These shapes can be used singularly or combined with one another to create complex configurations of materials and elements within a circle.

The organization of woody plant materials in a circular design depends on the number of circles. For a single circle or a design dominated by one circle, linear arrangements or rows of plants should be placed on the circle's radii and/or in arcs around the center. Areas or mass of plants should be configured in area arcs and/or wedges (13.49).

13.48 Vocabulary of shapes for structuring materials and elements within a circle.

13.49 Plant materials should ideally be placed in the same configurations as other materials.

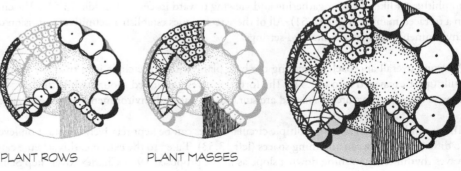

PLANT ROWS   PLANT MASSES

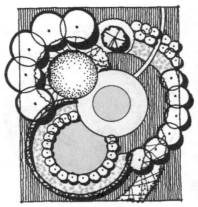

13.50 Alternative tactics for organizing plant materials around multiple circles.

CONCENTRIC BANDS   SWEEPING ARCS

There are two broad approaches for organizing plants around multiple circular spaces. The first is to follow the guidelines for a single circle by extending plants out from the circle along radii and/or in circular bands (left 13.50). This simple approach is effective from within any given circle, but is less successful from the outside because the bands of plants potentially conflict with one another. Furthermore, the outer layers of concentric circles do not integrate with an orthogonal site and potentially meet the site boundaries at awkward angles. To resolve these issues, an alternative technique is to arrange plant materials in arcing lines or drifts that sweep toward or against the circles of the design (right 13.50). This echoes the temperament of the circles without exactly duplicating them and visually opens the inner core of the design to unite with the surrounding site.

Topography

There are a number of options for addressing the ground plane within a circular space. One is to treat the base plane as flat surface, an approach that maintains its integrity as a basic geometric form like the square and triangle (see Design Guidelines, Chapters 4 and 10). This approach maximizes the usable area and is preferable when the circle is an occupied space. Another concept is to create hard-edged steps and terraces using the circle's suggestive concentric rings and/or radii as the foundation. Concentric circles can step up to form a visual accent and place from which to look outward to the surrounding landscape (left 13.51). Or the rings of circles can step downward to create an amphitheater like space for gathering and viewing toward its center (middle 13.51). The circle's radii likewise can suggest elevation changes in a terraced manner (right 13.51). All of these techniques establish a definitive expression of elevation change and are appropriate in urban environments or tightly controlled settings.

A second overall approach to grading the base plane within the circle is to treat the ground plane as soft, pliable earth that can be gently built up or excavated into (13.52). The former creates a rounded mound while the later forges a bowl like space. Both approaches should express the supple nature of soil and are suitable for pastoral environments where earth and vegetation prevail.

The ground elevation among multiple circular spaces can be kept relatively constant on level sites or terraced to fit into a moderate slope or to differentiate between adjoining spaces (left 13.53). Taken to the extreme, this scheme can create a cascading series of terraces that suggest waves rhythmically washing down a slope as in the proposed 1974 Charles River Step Sculpture by Athena Tacha (right 13.53).

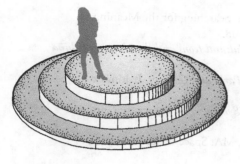

STEP UP

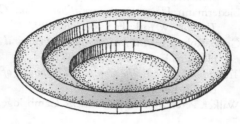

STEP DOWN

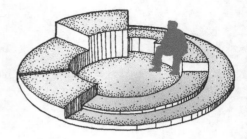

COMBINATION

13.51 Above: Techniques for working with elevation change within a circle.

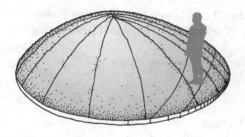

MOUND

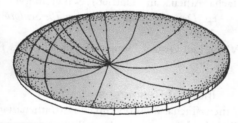

DEPRESSION

13.52 Left: The ground within a circle can be graded in a soft mounds or depressions.

13.53 Below: Multiple circles can be terraced up and down a slope.

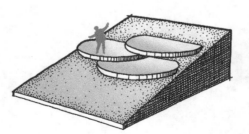

SIMPLE TERRACING

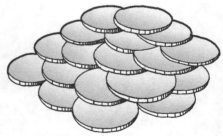

WAVE EFFECT

Referenced Resources

Alexander, Caroline. "If the Stone Could Speak: Searching for the Meaning of Stonehenge." *National Geographic*, June 2008.

Biedermann, Hans. *Dictionary of Symbolism: Cultural Icons and the Meaning Behind Them*. New York: Facts on File, 1992.

Grese, Robert E. *Jens Jensen: Maker of Natural Parks and Gardens*. Baltimore: Johns Hopkins University Press, 1992.

Tresidder, Jack, ed. *The Complete Dictionary of Symbols*. San Francisco: Chronicle Books, LLC, 2005.

Walker, Peter. *Minimalist Gardens*. Cambridge, MA: Spacemaker Press, 1997.

Further Resources

Church, Thomas D., Grace Hall, and Michael Laurie. *Gardens Are for People*, 2nd edition. New York: McGraw-Hill, 1983.

Flanagan, Regina M. "Rhythm as Form, Rhythm as Place." *Landscape Architecture*, March 2007.

Tacha, Athena. "Rhythm as Form." *Landscape Architecture*, May 1978.

Tacha, Athena, and Harriet F. Senie; interview by Glenn Harper; James Grayson Trulove, ed. *Dancing in the Landscape: The Sculpture of Athena Tacha*. London: Hi Marketing, 2000.

Viani, Lisa Owens. "Reweaving the Campus Tapestry." *Landscape Architecture*, September 2005.

Internet Resources

Athena Tacha: www.oberlin.edu/art/athena/tacha.html

Berkeley Landscape Heritage Plan: www.cp.berkeley.edu/lhp/index_flash.html

MSI: www.msidesign.com

Peter Walker and Partners: www.pwpla.com

Sasaki Associates: www.sasaki.com

Stonehenge: www.sacred-destinations.com/england/stonehenge

Tanner Fountain: http://epd372.blogspot.com/2008/05/tanner-fountain.html

The Oval 14

The oval, a seductively elegant jewel among shapes, is another genre of curved geometry that can be employed to structure the landscape. Equally appropriate in a timeless symmetrical design as a cutting edge contemporary landscape, the oval is a muted, yet energetic form with numerous idiosyncrasies and design possibilities. This chapter examines the following aspects of the oval in landscape architectural site design:

- Geometric Qualities
- Landscape Uses
- Design Guidelines

Geometric Qualities

An oval is an oblong, egg-like shape, most easily composed of arcs from four overlapping circles that collectively define a continuous, flowing, and symmetrical enclosure (14.1). While this concept of overlapping circles serves well for defining most ovals in the landscape, it should be noted that the oval can also be fabricated from more than four simple arcs, some of which may be compound in nature (14.8). In whatever manner it is created, the oval is always longer than wide and encircled by a smooth, fluid edge. The oval possesses many geometric qualities of the circle, rectangle, and triangle, yet remains its own distinct form. The following paragraphs detail the traits that are similar to these other forms as well as those that are specific to the oval itself.

Symmetry

Most ovals possesses one principal axis that is centered along its long dimension (left 14.2). This commanding line asserts its authority over all aspects of the oval, defines a bilateral symmetrical shape with two mirrored sides, and directs attention and energy along its course. An oval often possesses a second axis that is perpendicular to the first, thus making it symmetrical in two directions (middle 14.2). Center points for the oval's enclosing arcs typically coincide with the axes although the arcs themselves may not always be the same size (right 14.2 and 14.8).

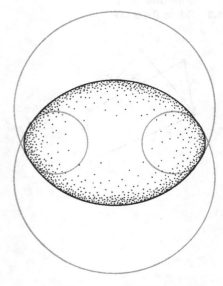

14.1 An oval composed of four overlapping circles.

PRIMARY AXIS

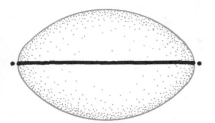

CROSS-AXIS

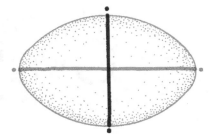

CENTER POINTS

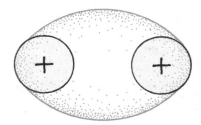

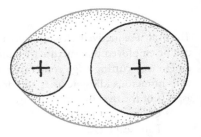

14.2 Above: Principal geometric oomponents of the oval.

14.3 Below: The ellipse.

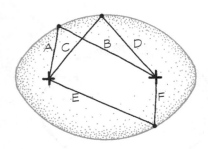

One special type of oval that is symmetrically balanced on the two perpendicular axes is the ellipse. An ellipse is defined as a series of points in a plane that each have the same total distance to two fixed points on an axis (14.3). The sum of A and B is equal to the sum of C and D, the sum of E and F, or the sum of any other two lines connecting a perimeter point to the two fixed points on the axis. The terms *oval* and *ellipse* are sometimes interchanged to mean the same thing. Although an ellipse is an oval, the reverse is not always true.

Directionality and Focus

The oval may be thought of as a circle that is elongated along one dimension, integrating the directionality of the rectangle with the controlled focus of the triangle. The oval's extended length gives it a distinct sense of direction and movement in comparison to the static quality of the circle. When viewed along the its length, the oval has a greater perception of distance in relation to the circle which actually appears to be an oval itself with its length stretched perpendicular to the line of sight (left and middle 14.4). The opposite is true when viewing across the short dimension of the oval (right 14.4). From this vantage point, the impression of distance is foreshortened and the curved arc on the opposite side visually flattens out. It should be noted that the curvature of the oval's "flat" sides may not be noticed at all if the degree of curvature is too gentle.

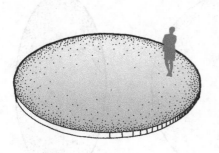

VIEW ACROSS CIRCLE

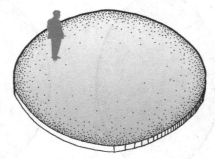
VIEW ALONG OVAL

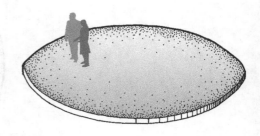
VIEW ACROSS OVAL

The oval's length also guides attention toward its ends, especially when the perimeter is an enclosed vertical plane. While this effect is similar to a rectangle, the focus in an oval tends to be even more pronounced because its sides converge toward the end point like a triangle (14.5; compare to 10.3). However, the curvature of the oval's end is "soft" and provides a restful backdrop to a focal point placed in front of it or a gentle gesture to an accent beyond (bottom 14.5).

Implied Sides

One other consequence of the oval's elongated profile is the formation of sides even though there are no corners or intersections along the periphery. Once again, the integrated qualities of the circle and rectangle are evident. The perception of sides results from the presence of an axis and the two long outer perimeters (left 14.6). The sense of sides is less apparent when the two long edges are more rounded and/or the end arcs are less sharp, causing the circumference to appear more circular (right 14.6).

14.4 Above: The oval's length gives it an exaggerated sense of depth.

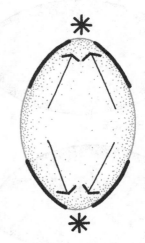

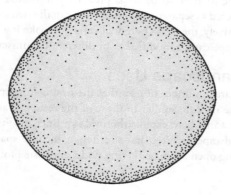

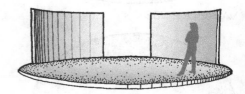

14.5 Above: The oval guides attention toward its ends.

14.6 Left: An oval has implied sides.

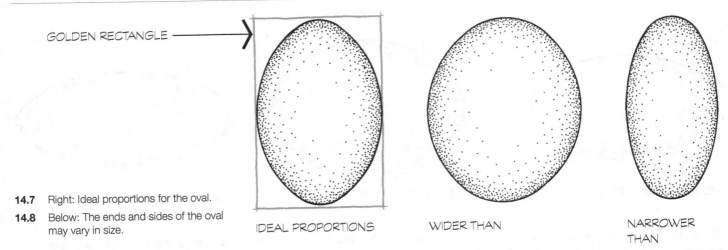

GOLDEN RECTANGLE

IDEAL PROPORTIONS   WIDER THAN   NARROWER THAN

14.7 Right: Ideal proportions for the oval.

14.8 Below: The ends and sides of the oval may vary in size.

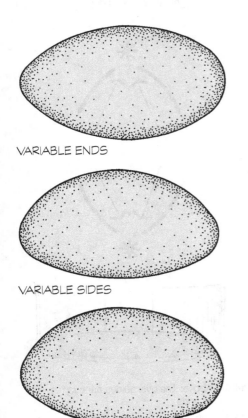

VARIABLE ENDS

VARIABLE SIDES

COMBINATION

Variability

One idiosyncratic quality of the oval in comparison to the circle and square is the oval's potential variability. The circle and square are constant shapes that can fluctuate only in size while the oval may alter in two additional ways: (1) relative proportion of width to length and (2) comparative size of arcs on the opposite side of the oval. As with a rectangle, the width and length of an oval can be whatever dimensions are desired to best fit a given situation. Although any width to length proportion is possible, the ideal ratio of the oval is 1:1.61803398874, the same as it is for the golden rectangle (5.4 and left 14.7). An oval that is much wider than this ratio begins to replicate a circle while an oval that is narrower than the golden section appears cigar shape (middle and right 14.7).

The second variable of an oval is the relative size of the arcs on opposite sides of the figure. The common notion of an oval is that opposite arcs have the same dimensions although this doesn't have to be so as previously indicated (right 14.2). The two end arcs can be considered as separate components as can the two side arcs, each with its own radius (14.8). Collectively, the oval's potential variables make it a highly flexible form whose proportions and shape can be modified to fit different circumstances.

Landscape Uses

There are a number of uses that the oval is inherently suitable for in the landscape. Some of these uses are similar to those of the rectangle and circle although the applications that are set forth here exploit the oval's distinct qualities. The fundamental uses for the oval in landscape architectural site design include spatial foundation, compositional accent, unifying open space, gathering node, and visual foil.

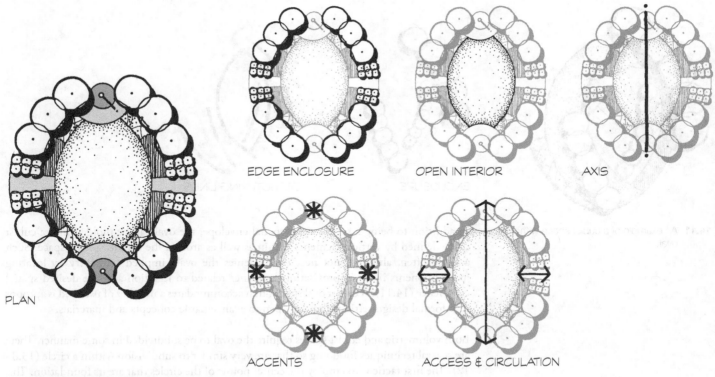

PLAN

EDGE ENCLOSURE

OPEN INTERIOR

AXIS

ACCENTS

ACCESS & CIRCULATION

Spatial Foundation

As with all the previously discussed forms, one of the foremost uses of the oval in the landscape is the underpinning of outdoor space. Historically, the oval has been primarily used as the foundation of single spaces that are intended to be places of special note in the landscape. More recently, some designers have explored using multiple ovals as the basis of more complex spatial configurations. Both are examined in the following paragraphs.

Single Space. The oval's inherent symmetry lends itself to a simple, elegant volumetric space that is delineated by vertical elements aligned along the oval's perimeter (14.9). The resulting spatial envelope shares qualities of circular and rectangular spaces. Like the circle, the oval's enclosure is unbroken, sweeping the eye effortless around the space. The oval's curvature imparts a gentle, embracing, expansive sense of enclosure that is innately comfortable to be in. Like the rectangle, the oval is elongated along a central axis, thus furnishing formality, depth, and focus toward the ends of the space as previously discussed. The axis also governs the distribution of elements along the oval's edges, defines the location of entry/exits points, regulates through-circulation, and suggests the placement of accents within the space. Despite its implied formality, a volumetric oval space is a welcoming one that is a synthesis of symmetry's authority and the curve's femininity (14.10). A single volumetric oval space is suitable as a compositional accent, a unifier among other spaces and elements, and/or to direct movement and views as discussed in othe parts of this section.

14.9 Above: Qualities of a volumetric oval space.

14.10 Below: View into a volumetric oval space.

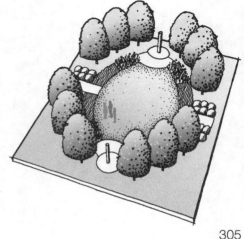

305

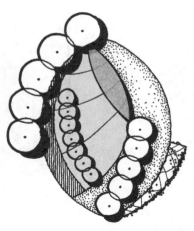

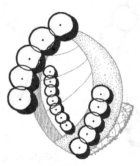

ENCLOSURE

STRUCTURING LINES

14.11 An example of a cubist space within the oval.

In addition to being a simple open spatial envelope, the oval can be molded into a cubist space defined by vertical elements within as well as around the exterior of the space. Such a space often, although not necessarily, denies the oval's implied symmetry by locating its components in an improvisational manner related to function and the desired spatial experience (14.11). A cubist oval space often accommodates a number of uses and is apropos in informal design settings that are open to avant-guarde concepts and materials.

Both volumetric and cubist spaces require the oval to be subdivided in some manner. There are several techniques for doing so that are very similar to subdivision within a circle (13.8–12). The first tactic is to employ the center points of the circles that are its foundation. This is accomplished by delineating portions of concentric circles around the four center points, resulting in a series of overlapping arcs that mimic the oval's perimeter (top left 14.12). Designs that are based on these arcs have a pronounced visual relationship between the oval's edge and its interior (top right 14.12).

A second strategy for defining subspaces and material areas within an oval is to utilize the radii of its underlying circles. Radii can be extended across the oval from any of the center points to create a simple pattern of radiating lines (middle left 14.12) or overlaid on top of one another to create a more complex network. As with the circle, this approach focuses attention on the chosen center point, thus making this spot inherently prominent within the design (middle right (14.12).

The third method for designing within the oval is to emulate its curved periphery without directly replicating it. In essence, the oval is treated as a boundary around an internal design scheme that is distinctly flowing and asymmetrical. One way to achieve this is with one or more arcs that sweep through the oval (bottom middle 14.12; also see Chapter 12). This creates a design with compelling movement. Another technique is to employ curvilinear geometry with multiple curves, embracing spatial alcoves, and drifts of plant materials (bottom right 14.12; also see Chapter 15).

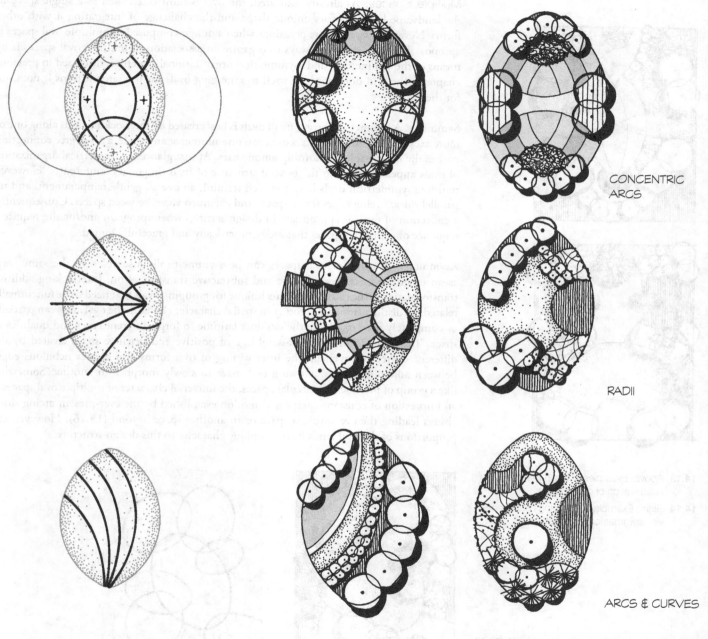

CONCENTRIC
ARCS

RADII

ARCS & CURVES

14.12 Alternative strategies for subdividing and designing within an oval.

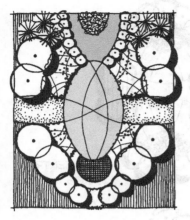

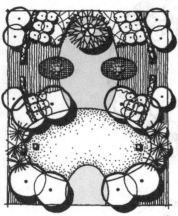

Multiple Spaces. As already indicated, the oval is most often used as a single space in the landscape because of its unique shape and the challenge of integrating it with other forms. Nevertheless, there are occasions when a design composed of multiple oval spaces is apropos. The most common ways to organize an association of multiple oval spaces is by means of the symmetrical and asymmetrical organizational structures discussed in previous chapters. The grid does not lend itself to arranging ovals for the same reasons it does not for the circle.

Symmetry. A symmetrical structure of ovals is best created by interlocking ovals along one or more axes (14.13). Although axes can cross one another at any angle, a 90-degree connection creates the most stable relationship among axes. At first glance, a symmetrical organization of ovals appears similar to the general structure of its orthogonal counterparts. However, multiple symmetrical ovals have rounded termini, an overall gentle temperament, and no parallel sides. Arcing edges frame spaces and extended views between spaces. Consequently, a collection of ovals is appropriate in design settings where program and/or site require a sequence of elongated spaces that are symmetrically and gracefully joined.

Asymmetry. A group of oval spaces can be asymmetrically assembled in the same ways as an ensemble of circles: additive and subtractive transformation. Interlocking additive transformation is the most suitable technique for grouping ovals that need to be functionally related yet distinct from one another in spatial character (14.14). The oval areas can partially or completely overlap, giving the designer latitude to forge different types and qualities of space. The result is an organic assemblage of positive and negative space created by the different degrees of overlap. The intertwining of oval forms also creates nebulous edges between adjoining spaces, allowing one space to slowly morph into another. Somewhat like a group of interlocking circular spaces, the universal character of multiple oval spaces is an impression of constant energy and motion established by the ever-present arcing sides, always leading the eye within a space or to another space beyond (13.16). However, the proportions of the oval lends its own unique character to this design structure.

14.13 Above: Examples of a symmetrical organization of oval spaces.

14.14 Right: Example of grouping oval spaces via asymmetrical organization.

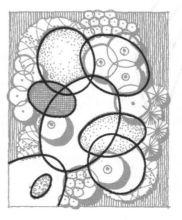

Like polygons and circles, multiple ovals may also be subtracted from a site to create an interlacing network of negative space that is apropos for circulation in parks, campuses, and so forth. The oval is particularly favorable to this concept because it is perfectly sculpted to permit moving air, water, or people to effortlessly pass around its boundary. Its aerodynamic profile resembles a river stone that has been washed and eroded over thousands of years to allow the water to efficiently move around it (14.15). An example of using a collection of ovals dispersed in a field of circulation occurs in the proposal of Perk Park in Cleveland, Ohio, designed by Thomas Balsley Associates (14.16; compare to 13.19). The underlying notion of this design is to forge a "forest and meadow" metaphor with the forest being composed primarily of large existing trees (Balsley Associates). A series of oval mounds in this space create a network of paths that weave through and among the trees, providing shady strolling and sitting areas. The multiple ovals are well suited to generate a passive atmosphere and flowing routes of travel. Note too the use of an oval mound in the lawn area that serves an accent and subtle promontory.

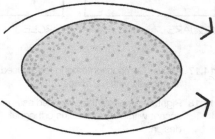

14.15 Above: An oval is similar to a stone worn by flowing water.

14.16 Left: Site plan of Perk Park.

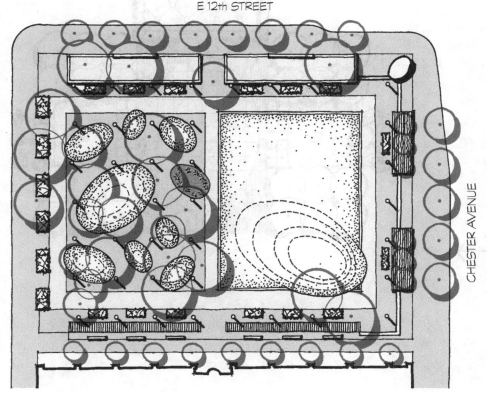

E 12th STREET

CHESTER AVENUE

NORTH

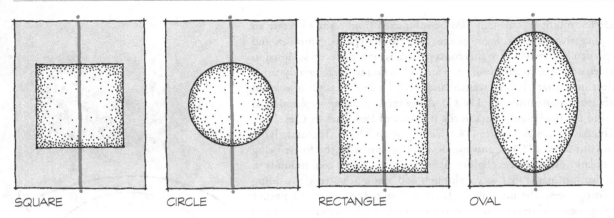

SQUARE CIRCLE RECTANGLE OVAL

14.17 Above: Comparison among forms used as accents within a space.

14.18 Right: Example of the oval used as an accent within an symmetric orthognal design.

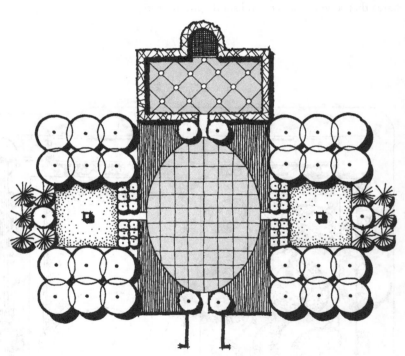

14.19 Alternative ways of using the oval as a terminus space.

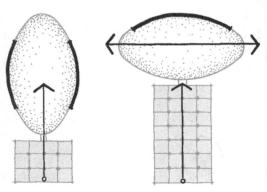

310

Compositional Accent

The oval, as an alluring singular form, is inherently suited to serve as an accent in the landscape, especially in classic designs where the oval's intrinsic symmetry makes it predisposed as a centerpiece located along the axis of a design or as featured element at the end of an axis. While the square, rectangle, and circle can also be emphatic elements on an axis, the oval's use in this regard is best for proportionally long site areas where there is a desire for fluid formality (14.17). Only an oval is able to create a muted, relaxed form that highlights extent along an axis. An oval can be a focal point in numerous contexts and often serves this intent best when it is in an orthogonal design structure that makes the oval's gentle curvature more pronounced by virtue of contrast (14.18).

Another use of the oval as an accent is at the end of an axis where it can capture and retain the attention directed to it (14.19). Here, the oval's orientation can create divergent effects. When located parallel to the axis, the oval extends the sense of depth and focuses attention toward its far end (left 14.19). When placed perpendicular to the axis, the oval provides a soft terminus and turns the primary attention 90 degrees to either side, creating two termini that may be revealed only upon entering the oval space (right 14.19).

Finally, the oval may also be used as an accent in a nonsymmetrical landscape where it is usually situated as a lone element within an open setting. An excellent illustration of this is Enterprise Plaza in Houston, Texas, designed by the Office of James Burnett (14.20). The oval, defined as terraced fountain basin, encloses a sitting/gathering space and the primary circulation path to and from the adjoining office building. The water feature is highlighted by a series of jets to create a choreographed display of water. The oval's distinction is amplified by its askew orientation to the buildings, streets, and grid pavement pattern.

14.20 Site plan of Enterprise Plaza.

LOUISIANA STREET

LAMAR STREET

NORTH

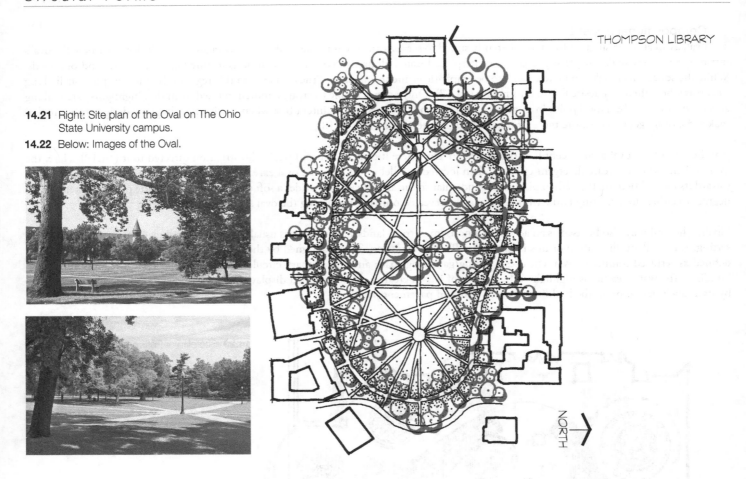

THOMPSON LIBRARY

14.21 Right: Site plan of the Oval on The Ohio State University campus.

14.22 Below: Images of the Oval.

NORTH

Unifying Open Space

The oval is an apt form to use in the landscape as a unifying open space where the site is elongated and the surrounding context is composed of varied elements and materials. The oval's uninterrupted and comprehensible curvature visually consolidates diverse uses and buildings along its edge to frame a predominant open space where people can congregate. Examples include the Oval within the University Circle area in Cleveland, the Campus Green at Kennesaw State University in Georgia, and the Oval at The Ohio State University. The latter is the literal and figurative heart of the campus where informal and formal assemblies of people occur (14.21–22). Additionally, the oval form compositionally unifies the many buildings encircling the open space, provides an understated structure for the casual Olmstedian planting, and celebrates the authority of the William Oxley Thompson Library located at the west end of the space. A recent master plan completed by Michael Van Valkenburgh Associates, Inc. attempts to restore the clarity of the Oval by strengthening the massing of trees around the Oval's perimeter and removing the visual clutter in front of the enclosing buildings. Furthermore, the central east-west pedestrian spine is visually strengthened, thus allowing the many cross paths to seem less cluttered (compare to 9.26).

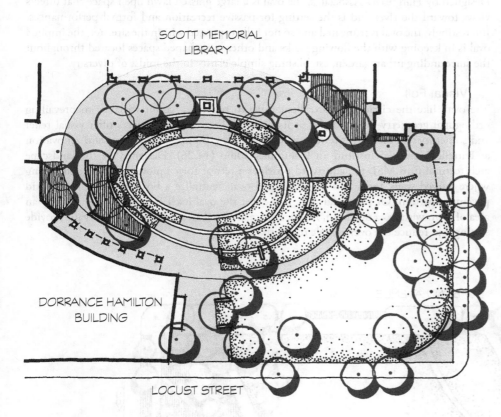

SCOTT MEMORIAL
LIBRARY

DORRANCE HAMILTON
BUILDING

LOCUST STREET

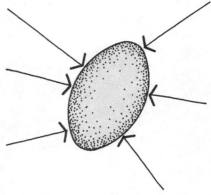

14.23 Above: The oval can coalesce and unite circulation routes from all directions.

14.24 Left: Thomas Jefferson University plaza.

NORTH

Gathering Node

Like the circle, the oval's gentle, arcing enclosure is the foundation for an amiable gathering space. The oval's curvature allows paths from many directions to deftly converge into one common area (14.23). Once within the space, the surrounding edges suggest an inward focus permitting users to sit along the outer edges and observe activity within. The periphery also creates an embracing space that encourages users to stop or sit within. One example is a new plaza on the campus of Thomas Jefferson University in Philadelphia, Pennsylvania, designed by the landscape architectural firm Andropogen (14.24). The plaza is conceived to be a new "heart" to the urban campus and is intended to be the location for various academic events and ceremonies (Andropogen). The plaza includes numerous seating opportunities, a café, and public art. In addition, the oval form is a response to the adjoining building, thus enhancing the relationship between architecture and site.

Another example of the oval serving as a core gathering space is found in Elizabeth Caruthers Park, a two-acre civic space located near the Willamette River in Portland, Oregon (14.25). Designed by Hargreaves Associates, the oval is a large grassed lawn open space that directs views toward the river and is the setting for passive recreation and formal performances. Interestingly, the oval is truncated and so not fully expressed within the site. Yet, the implied oval is in keeping with the flowing walks and other oval-shaped spaces located throughout the surrounding urban garden, establishing simple clarity in the midst of diversity.

Visual Foil

The oval, like the circle, is an excellent form to provide a counterbalance to prevailing orthogonal geometry within a site or its context. The oval's soft curves offer visual relief and sometimes an alcove for retreat as they do in the proposal for a courtyard renovation at Battelle Memorial Institute in Columbus, Ohio (14.26). Designed by the landscape architectural firm MSI, the courtyard provides a retreat for employees in a garden setting where curved walls and walks of an overlaid oval neutralize a boxlike space and its grid pavement pattern. Of particular note is the fact the oval itself is partially disguised by an area of lawn with trees overhead. A series of smaller oval areas within the courtyard provide seating and reduce the overall scale of the space.

14.25 Elizabeth Caruthers Park.

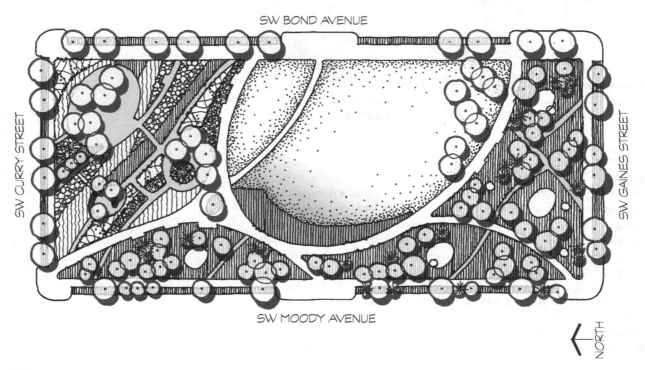

SW BOND AVENUE

SW CURRY STREET

SW GAINES STREET

SW MOODY AVENUE

NORTH

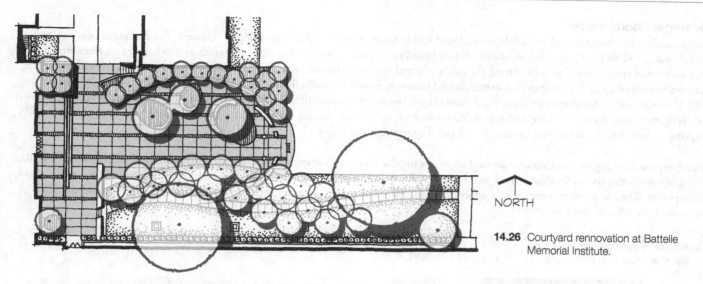

14.26 Courtyard rennovation at Battelle Memorial Institute.

NORTH

Design Guidelines

Given the similarities between the circle and the oval, it only stands to reason that many of the guidelines offered in previous chapter for the circle also apply to the oval. In particular, the design guidelines for connecting circles to other forms and how circular spaces should relate to the edge of a site directly apply to the oval. The reader is referred to Chapter 13 to review these guidelines. Additional recommendations for designing with the oval are offered in the following paragraphs.

End Termini

As previously discussed, the oval's elongated proportions and tapering ends guide views to either end when the oval is a simple open space (14.5). This function is most evident when the oval is symmetrically organized and has enclosed sides, thus containing and directing views to the narrower ends of the space. In these circumstances, a notable space or element worthy of attention should be located at the ends of the oval to capture the inherent energy directed there (14.27). As with the rectangle, the lack of such an accent neglects the oval's fundamental layout and form.

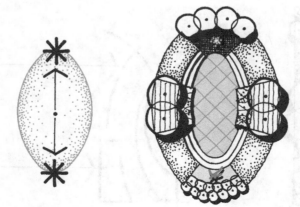

14.27 The ends of a symmetrical oval space should be properly highlighted.

315

Material Coordination

The organization of elements and materials around and inside an oval space varies depending on context, design intent, desired spatial character, scale, and so on. Nevertheless, there are two broad strategies for organizing plant materials and other design elements on the outside of an oval space. The first is to extend the oval's internal geometry beyond the oval as an organizing structure. As with the circle, this creates a vocabulary of four shapes that materials and elements fit within: radii, linear arcs, wedge, and area arc (top 14.28; compare to 13.48). The radii and wedge shapes push outward from the oval while the arcs parallel the sides of the oval. This tactic forges a configuration that directly reiterates the oval's shape and is suitable for formal, volumetric spaces. However, this scheme may encounter problems when attempting to associate the encircling elements with other spaces and site edges.

A second approach to organizing elements around an oval is to echo its general shape with arcing forms and material areas (bottom 14.28). This strategy replicates the oval's sides with a series of layered arcs, some expressed as sweeping lines and rows, others as arced wedges and drifts of plants. The use of structuring arcs is appropriate for informal spaces, creating broad gestures and layers that extend the sense of space beyond the edge of the oval itself.

14.28 Alternative strategies for organizing elements around an oval space.

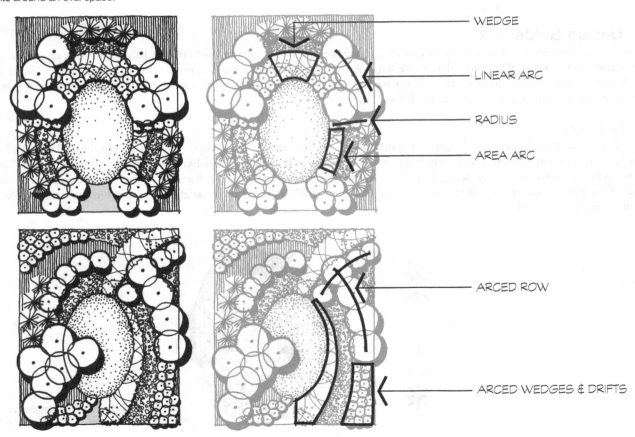

WEDGE

LINEAR ARC

RADIUS

AREA ARC

ARCED ROW

ARCED WEDGES & DRIFTS

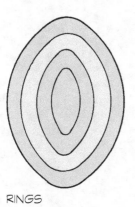

RINGS

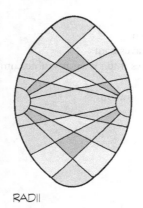

RADII

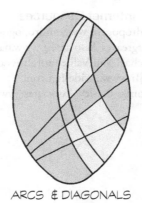

ARCS & DIAGONALS

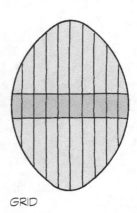

GRID

The methods of employing concentric arcs, radii, and curves presented earlier in the chapter are the most applicable for the guiding the placement of elements within the oval (14.12). Pavement patterns inside the oval can likewise comply to one of these tactics, a combination of them, an orthogonal grid, or other scheme depending on the preferred visual affect (14.29).

14.29 Possible pavement patterns within an oval.

Topography

The topographic treatment of the oval depends on whether or not the oval is a space or object in the landscape. The ground plane of the oval should be relatively level or uniformly sloped if the oval is an occupied space or an area that is continually traversed. Excavating into in the ground to create a gradually sloped depression can also generate a spatial void (left 14.30).

The topography of the oval is typically elevated when the oval is an object in the landscape. This can be accomplished by means of steps and/or terraces just like within a circle (13.51). Similarly, an oval can be mounded, often resembling a buried egg with soft contouring of the earth (middle 14.30). This concept lends itself well to creating a series of obstacles that gently direct movement through a space (14.16 and right 14.30).

14.30 The oval lends itelf to soft depressions and mounds.

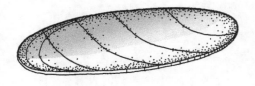

DEPRESSION

MOUND

Internet Resources
Andropogen: www.andropogon.com
Hargreaves Associates: www.hargreaves.com
Michael Van Valkenburgh Associates, Inc.: www.mvvainc.com
MSI: www.msidesign.com
Thomas Balsley Associates: www.tbany.com

The Curve 15

The last type of circular form is the sensuous genre of shapes composed of flowing, curved lines. Curvilinear shapes are the most lyrical of all the geometries discussed so far, appealing to the right brain's sense of feeling and intuition. Curvilinear geometry is the antithesis to orthogonal forms, embodying the unpredictable and the emotional. Moreover, curvilinear forms represent nature and occur in the environment where wind and water shape the earth (15.1, 16.8). Human created curved forms are inspired by nature and have been used in many landscapes including Chinese and Japanese gardens. In western culture, curved geometry emerged from the 18th-century English Landscape style and was epitomized by William Hogarth's statement "...the waving line is the way to beauty" (Mann 1993, 60). The modern design era witnessed the use of curved forms by such renowned landscape architects as Thomas Church and Roberto Burle Marx. Curvilinear geometry remains a widely employed structuring system in the contemporary landscape especially where earth, plant materials, and/or water prevail on residential sites, parks, naturalized landscapes, and the like. This chapter explores the following aspects of curvilinear forms in landscape architectural site design:

- Geometric Qualities
- Landscape Uses
- Design Guidelines

15.1 Examples of curved lines in nature.

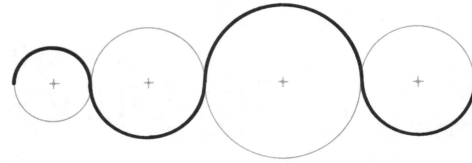

15.2 A curvilinear line is composed of multiple arcs centered on adjoining circles.

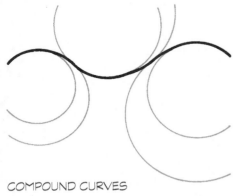

COMPOUND CURVES

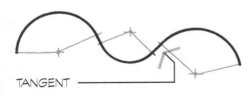

TANGENT

15.3 Above: A curvilinear line may be composed of compound arcs and tangents.

15.4 Right: Comparison between arcs and curvilinear lines.

Geometric Qualities

The basis of curvilinear geometry is the serpentine line composed of multiple arcs connected to each other in a continuously flowing gesture. In theory, each arc is a segment of a true circle drawn around a center point (15.2). In actuality, the composition of the curved line is often more complex and may include compound arcs and spiral curves that have variable degrees of curvature (top 15.3). These components mimic the actual curves found in nature and therefore give the curved line a less mechanical appearance. In addition, short tangents are sometimes inserted between the arcs as transitions between reverse curves (bottom 15.3).

A curved line may seem like the arc previously presented in Chapter 12. Indeed, there are similarities because both employ a bowed line, sometimes in multiples, as their foundation (15.4). However in arced geometry, the lines remain single gestures even though they may be placed near one another or even overlaid to forge complex configurations. In curvilinear forms, the lines are attached to each other in an ongoing series of "S" curves. Each individual curve is absorbed into the overall line and thus looses its singular identity.

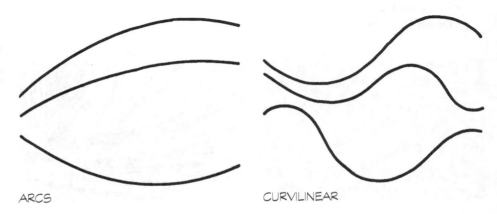

ARCS

CURVILINEAR

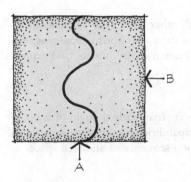

A

B

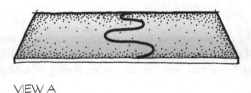

VIEW A

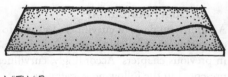

VIEW B

Despite the ability to draw a curved line with mechanical instruments or a computer program, the ideal method for constructing a curved line is by hand. This requires superb hand-eye coordination and an intuitive sense for what "feels" correct. The ability to create an appealing curved form isn't an innate skill and frequently requires developed practice. Nevertheless, a curved line drawn by hand will invariably be one that most closely resembles what is found in nature and that is intuitively most appealing to the eye. The Greeks knew this well and avoided absolute straight lines, circles, and curves derived from circles in their designs because they understood the artificiality of such forms (Grillo 1960, 38–39).

A curvilinear line is characterized by the ever-present push and pull along its length. This dichotomy of opposing forces generates an idiosyncratic pulsation that is spirited and captivating especially when viewed along its length (15.5). Even a view from the side reveals animation. Another consequence of the curvilinear line's undulation is that it takes a longer length of serpentine line to extend between points or to enclose an area compared to other forms (15.6). This can be a disadvantage if efficiency is important but a benefit if the objective is to create the maximum edge for a prolonged experience or display.

15.5 The expression of a curve varies from different vantage points.

15.6 A curvilinear edge is longer than that in comparable primary forms.

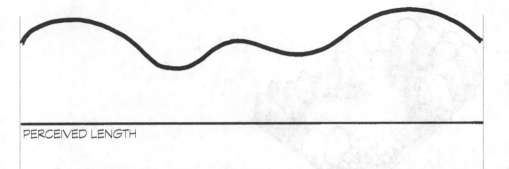

PERCEIVED LENGTH

ACTUAL LENGTH

321

Landscape Uses

Curvilinear forms are suitable for a wide range of uses in landscape architectural site design. As with other form typologies, many of these applications coincide with one another so that fulfilling one use often achieves others as well. The most noteworthy landscape uses of curvilinear forms are: spatial foundation, exploratory experience, emulate natural settings, balance human environments, and express sensuous fluidity.

Spatial Foundation

A fundamental use of curvilinear forms is to be the armature of landscape space. Although curved forms are frequently thought of as being the antithesis of anything structural, they in fact provide similar organizational and space delineating capabilities as other forms discussed in previous chapters. Accordingly, curvilinear forms can serve as the underpinning of a single space or a sequence of affiliated spaces as presented in the following paragraphs.

Single Space. A curved line and/or grouping of elements can gracefully enclose an individual volumetric space in the landscape (15.7). Such a space synthesizes the irregularity of an asymmetrical polygon with the curves of the circle and oval (15.8). The consequence is an asymmetrical, sensuous, relaxing, and nurturing space that appeals more to the emotions than the intellect. It is often comforting to be in a space defined by curved forms, particularly when they are defined with soft, pliable elements like vegetation and earth. A curvilinear space also lacks the predictable shape and proportions that are inherent in the primary shapes, an appealing quality for acclimating to a site with numerous restrictions.

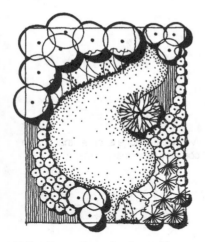

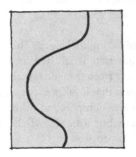
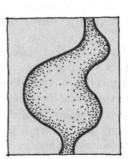

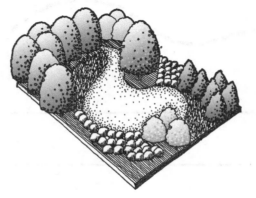

15.7 Above: Example of a curvilinear, volumetric space.

15.8 Right: View into a volumetric space.

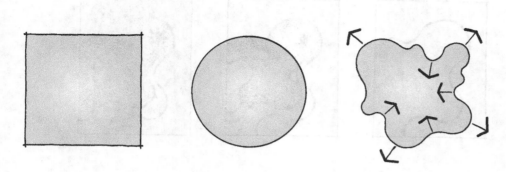

The curved edge, with its continuous push into and pull away from the interior of the space, forges a relatively complex space when directly compared to the simplicity and clarity of square and circular spaces (15.9). A curvilinear space is not as comprehensible and may not be fully understood from all vantage points. Like the asymmetrical polygon, the projections into the space can hide areas and consequently create an air of intrigue (15.10). Finally, the edge of the space yields a feeling of energy and movement that is rhythmic and pulsating, particularly when it possesses dramatic, sweeping curves.

The complexity of a single curvilinear space increases as the defining elements encroach into the interior to forge cubist space (15.11). The edge is less distinct in location and views through the space acquire a sense of depth as one must look through and around strategically placed elements. This type of space also invites movement because it cannot be easily comprehended from any one vantage point.

15.9   Comparison of the complexity in a curved form with the square and circle.

15.10   Some areas of curvilinear space may be hidden from view.

HIDDEN FROM VIEW ⟶

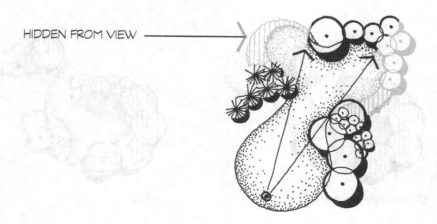

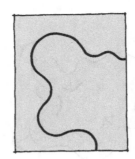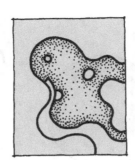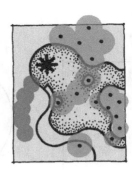

15.11 An example of a cubist space based on the curvilinear form.

Like other form typologies, most curvilinear spaces need to be subdivided or directly added on to in order to accommodate different use and material areas. But unlike all the previously discussed forms, the curvilinear space has no internal structure composed of axes, diagonals, extended edges, radii, and so on. This lack of an inner geometry gives the designer great flexibility although there are some tactics that are more advisable than others. The most prudent approach to partitioning a curvilinear space is by repeating the curvilinear form inside or along the outside of the space (left and middle 15.12). Care must be exercised in how the forms are joined (see Design Guidelines). A slightly different tactic is to use arcs and/or segments of circles that likewise replicate the general appearance and feeling of the curvilinear form (right 15.12). Straight sided forms can also be introduced, but with the understanding that they are contrary to the curve's temperament and so must be employed with the utmost care.

15.12 Alternative tactics for partitioning a curvilinear space.

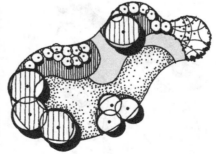

CURVILINEAR LINES

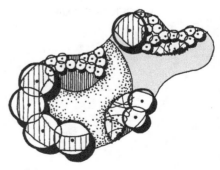
ARCS

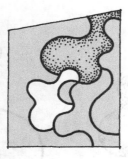

INTERLOCKING

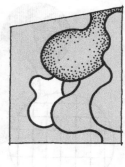

FACE-to-FACE

A single curvilinear space has many applications from being a calming place of reflection to one animated and filled with sweeping gestures. Regardless of particulars, all curvilinear spaces combine the control of the human hand with nature's variability. Moreover, the ability to reinforce curves with plants, earth, and water make curvilinear spaces an appealing solution in design circumstances where the inclusion of nature is desired to foil human control (see other Landscape Uses).

Multiple Spaces. The curvilinear form can also be employed to define multiple spaces in the landscape. Given the irregular and pliable nature of the curve, multiple curvilinear spaces are most appropriately coordinated on the basis of an asymmetrical organizational structure by means of additive or subtractive transformation. Associated curvilinear spaces can readily be fabricated by interlocking addition and spatial tension like other curved forms depending on the desired degree of connectivity (left 15.13). But unlike circles and ovals, related curvilinear spaces can also be attached by means of face-to-face addition (right 15.13). This is possible because the elastic nature of curved forms permits them to be joined along continuous, common edges like flat-side forms. The only compositional consideration of face-to-face connections is how the edges of the two spaces should meet one another at the point of junction (see Design Guidelines).

An association of curvilinear spaces can also be forged by means of subtraction, creating a design structure that includes an interwoven interstitial space very similar to that generated by circles and ovals (15.14; compare to 13.19 and 14.16). Again, the relative pliability of the curvilinear form permits it to be molded to exactly accommodate whatever paths of circulation occur through a site, whether they be direct, indirect, primary, or secondary. Another unique quality is that curvilinear forms can be shaped to create nodes and alcoves within the design fabric, thus providing for places to pause or meet others.

15.13 Above: Alternative ways to use addition to create multiple curvilinear spaces.

15.14 Below: An example of subtracting curvilinear forms as the basis of design.

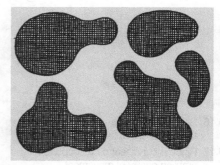

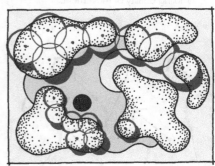

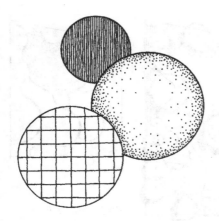
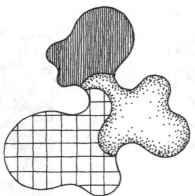
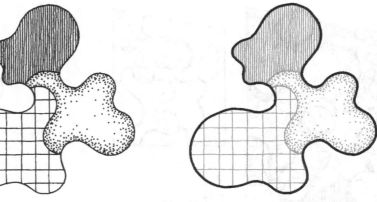

15.15 Connected curvilinear spaces are noted for the contunuity of the enclosing edge.

A group of curvilinear spaces share many of the same spatial qualities as single spaces: relaxing, undulating, adaptable, and suggestive of "nature." There is also one other idiosyncratic trait: flowing continuity among spaces. The uninterrupted nature of curved forms has been highlighted in previous chapters regarding both the circle and the oval. Yet these forms are self-contained and so create a clear separation between adjoining spaces even though each space is similar in form (left 15.15). By comparison, the edge that defines multiple curvilinear spaces is a continuous one that carries on from one space to the next (middle and right 15.15). The distinction between spaces is made by the relative size of thresholds and contrasting materials, but not by corners or divisions along the edge. The result is a sequence of spaces that smoothly course through the landscape.

Exploratory Experience

Curvilinear forms are ideal for fabricating an exploratory experience in the landscape by means of an undulating line and/or a sinuous space. It will be recalled that asymmetrical orthogonal and polygonal typologies likewise can be employed for the same purpose (8.18, 11.25). All these organization systems are the foundation for constantly altering views and spaces that engender the yearning to seek out the unknown just out of view.

15.16 Below: A curvilinear path directs attention to many areas of the landscape.

15.17 Right: A curvilinear path supports the ambling quality of movement.

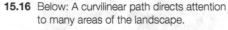

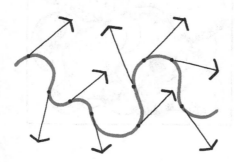

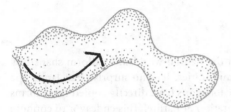 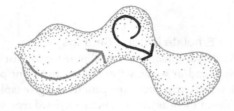 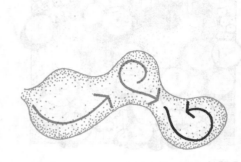

15.18 Movement through a curvilinear space is like water flowing in a stream.

What is unique about curvilinear forms is that they underpin the ambling, fluid quality of human movement. A curvilinear path through the landscape supports a casual, yet intentional direction of movement with fluctuating views in different directions. In one instant, a person's attention is directed to a given area of the landscape and in another moment to a new locality (15.16–17). Similarly, a person tends to move through a curvilinear space like water flowing through a stream, being guided in altering directions by the side of the space (15.18). All this occurs in a seamless and graceful manner with one scene melding into another. The concept of progressive or serial realization is inherent in a curvilinear design and only needs to be reinforced in the vertical planes of enclosure to sequentially conceal and reveal objects and scenes (15.19; compare to 7.35). Research studies have shown that people actually prefer curved walks to straight ones, especially when there is mystery with hints of what is yet to be fully seen (Kaplan 1998, 91).

15.19 A curvilinear design lends itself to progressive realization.

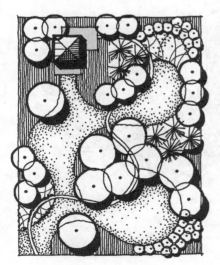 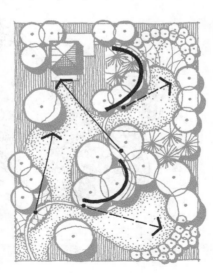

DESIRED VIEW
ALTERNATIVE VIEW
OBSTRUCTED VIEW

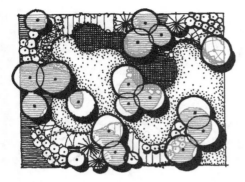

15.20 Example of design intended to suggest a natural setting.

Emulate Natural Settings

As already alluded to, curvilinear forms exist in the natural world in landform shaped by wind and/or water, water bodies, and plant communities. It is no surprise that landscape designers in various time periods and geographic locations have directly copied these forms or used them as inspiration in a stylized representation of nature. This endeavor to connote nature is particularly successful when the two-dimensional structure is reinforced with an undulating ground plane, drifts and clumps of plant materials, and fluid edges of water bodies (15.20).

The epitome of this design typology is the so called "beautiful" landscape style of softly undulating shapes that was popularized during the mid-1700s by some English Landscape style designers (15.21) (Symes 1993, 18). A representative example is Birkenhead Park in England designed by Joseph Paxton in 1843 (15.22). This verdant open space was the prototypical foundation for Central Park, Prospect Park, and similar green spaces designed by Fredrick Law Olmsted and his contemporaries in the late 1800s and early 1900s. In all of these examples, the underlying concept was to create an idealized Arcadian landscape of rounded and flowing forms evocative of a natural scene.

15.21 Above: Images of the English landscape style.

15.22 Right: Plan of Birkenhead Park (based on the original design).

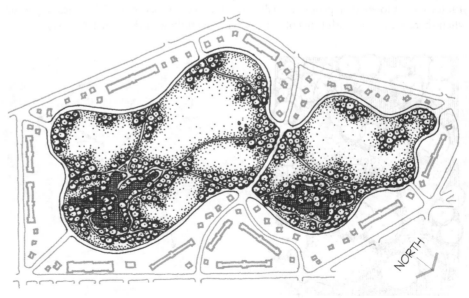

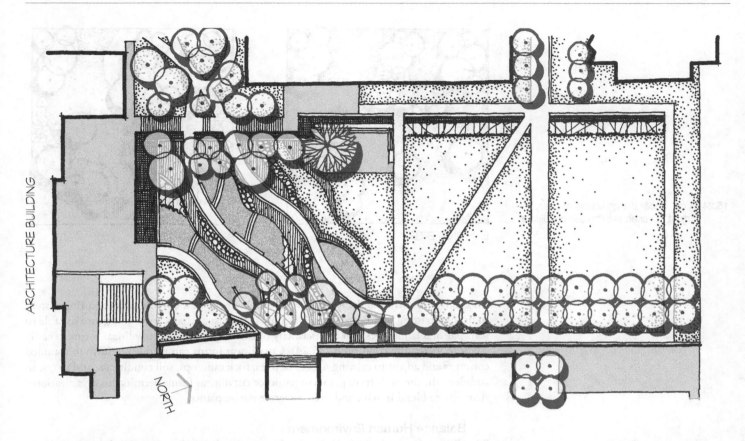

ARCHITECTURE BUILDING

NORTH

15.23 Site plan proposal for the Arts Commons.

The use of curvilinear forms to convey nature in a stylized, controlled manner is still valid in contemporary design. It should be noted that while a curvilinear design structure might suggest nature to many people, it is actually a human interpretation. Genuine representation of nature must go beyond form to include a broader concept of nature as a complex system of numerous integrated components and cycles. Many of the concepts and principles of sustainability are a way to more accurately replicate a naturally functioning environment rather than merely creating a visual impression of nature.

Nevertheless, the suggestion of nature is possible with curvilinear forms as long as its limitations are understood. Furthermore, curvilinear forms can be abstracted as they are in a proposal designed by the Olin Partnership for the Arts Commons at the University of Virginia (15.23). A series of interwoven curves were used to define walks, sitting/teaching spaces, and retaining walls that accommodate a significant grade change at the south end of the site. The curves also suggest eddies of water flowing across the site, interjecting a natural statement in direct contrast to the more conventional lawn area to the north (Martin 2004, 58–64).

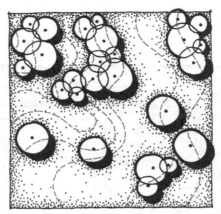
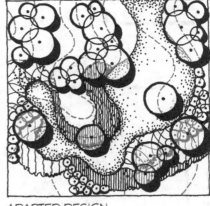

15.24 A curvilinear design is able to easily adjust to varied existing site conditions.

EXISTING SITE

ADAPTED DESIGN

An extension of this landscape use is the employment of a curvilinear structuring system to fit into existing natural settings. Not only is the visual character of this genre suitable to soft, pastoral landscapes, but the plasticity of the shapes permits curvilinear forms to easily adapt to varied site conditions (15.24). Curvilinear forms can readily conform to rounded contours and adjust to existing masses of trees, rock outcrops, soil conditions, and so on. In addition, the use of drifts of plants to reinforce curvilinear forms permits this organizational structure to blend in with and even integrate native plants.

Balance Human Environments

The ability of curvilinear forms to emulate nature also makes them ideal for neutralizing the human world, especially in urban settings. One way for doing this is to interject curvilinear forms into an otherwise orthogonal or angled design where they impart a soft, animated quality that is directly contrary to the remainder of the site (15.25). Similarly, curvilinear forms can be overlaid on an orthogonal structure as in the design of City Garden in St. Louis, Missouri, designed by Nelson Byrd Woltz Landscape Architects (12.23). The southern side of this design is a garden with a curvilinear path and wall that meander through an orthogonal patchwork of perennial beds and a series of linear hedges that demarcate historic property lines and former building foundations (Hazelrigg 2008, 152–155). Another approach is to create a design entirely composed of curvilinear forms in a site surrounded by an urban grid as occurs in Balsley Park in New York, New York, designed by Thomas Balsley Associates (15.26). Here, a series of curved walls based on the oval, free standing arced planes, and a soft mound collectively negate the prevailing city grid (Space Maker Press 2000, 70–71). The sinuous path and wall counterbalance the urbane setting with exuberance and energy.

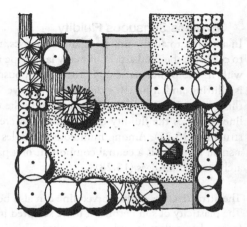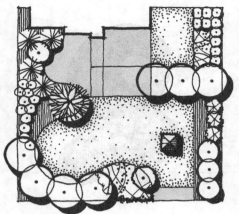

15.25 A curvilinear form can foil the stark, flat boundaries of an orthogonal site.

15.26 Below: Site plan of Balsley Park.

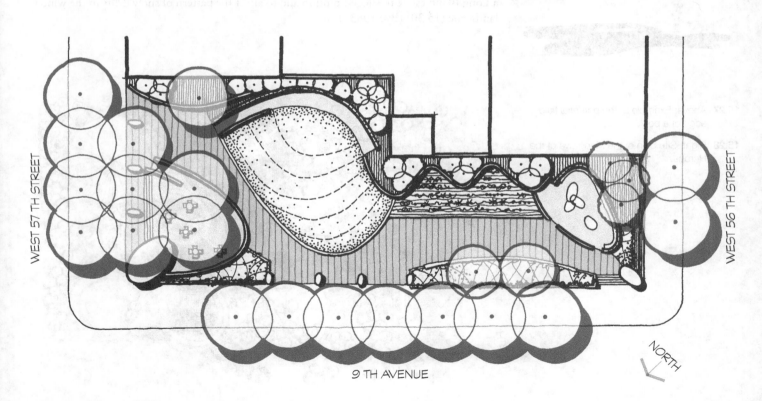

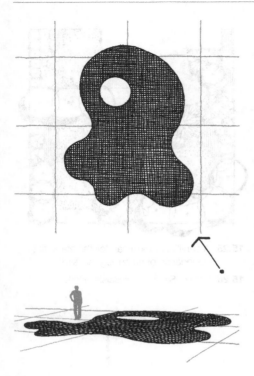

Express Sensuous Fluidity

In addition to all the previous landscape uses, the curvilinear design structure can be used to celebrate the fluid aspect of many landscape materials and, in doing so, appeal to the eye with its sculptural sensuality. The voluptuousness of rhythmically repeating curved lines is alluring and innately seductive to the eye in almost any setting. One context where this quality is suitably articulated is along the edge of a water body where the curvilinear line expresses the fluidity of the water and creates a visual transition between liquid and structure (15.27). Among numerous examples of this landscape use is the curved edge of a small lake that is a central component of a park in Belem, Brazil, designed by landscape architect Rosa Kliass (15.28).

The attractiveness of the curved line can also be expressed with supple, rolling topography. The plasticity of soil permits it to be sculpted into many shapes, especially soft, undulating forms that reflect its inherent quality. This is often best studied with clay models that permit the designer to mold the earth in sweeping gestures (15.29). Numerous landscape architects and artists have explored this aspect of earth including Edward Bye, who graded a Long Island estate to suggest motion and to affect the pattern of snow drifts in the winter landscape (15.30) (Bye 1983, 1–8).

15.27 Above: Example of the potential fluid edge of a pool.

15.28 Right: Site plan of the Mangrove of the Herons.

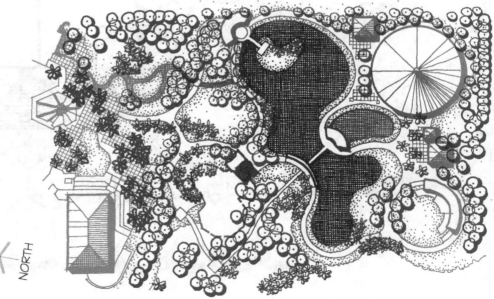

NORTH

15.29 Left: Student clay models showing the potential sculptural quality of earth.

15.30 Below: Grading plan for Soros estate.

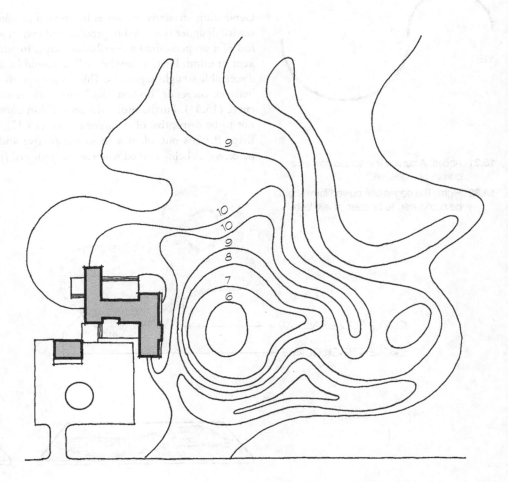

NORTH

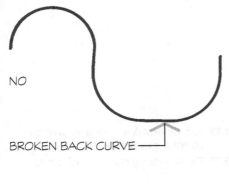

NO

BROKEN BACK CURVE

YES

15.31 Above: A curved line should flow as a continuous gesture.

15.32 Right: The edges of a curved form should be pronouced to be seen at eye level.

Design Guidelines

It is recommended that the following guidelines be taken into account when designing with the curvilinear design structure in the landscape. These suggestions should, of course, be exercised in the context of the numerous other considerations typical of any design setting.

Creating the Forms

As previous presented, it is advised that curvilinear forms be drawn by hand when designing with them so that they are visually appealing and akin to serpentine forms observed in nature. This suggestion is even advocated when the computer is the primary means of conveying a design. In this circumstance, curvilinear forms should be initially created by hand and then imported into a computer graphics program where they can be digitally traced.

Generating attractive curves is intuitive and takes skilled hand-eye coordination, so the novice designer is advised to practice and even trace successful landscape projects to get the feel of a properly drawn curvilinear shape. In addition, several other guidelines should be kept in mind. First, a curvilinear line should be a series of continuous curves without any discernible straight segments. This means that there should be no excessively long tangents between curves or "broken back" curves where a straight line is inserted in the middle of a curve (15.31). Furthermore, the arcs within curved forms should not be too flat in order not to be disruptive of their continuity (15.32). As noted in previous chapters, a curved shape flattens out when seen in perspective and so must be pronounced in plan to be perceived as being curved when actually viewed from eye level.

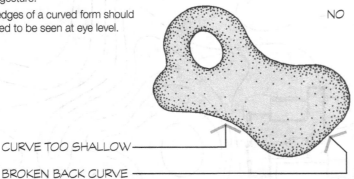

NO

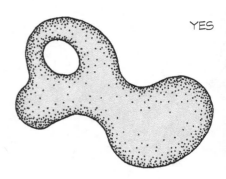

YES

CURVE TOO SHALLOW

BROKEN BACK CURVE

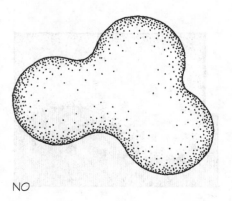

NO

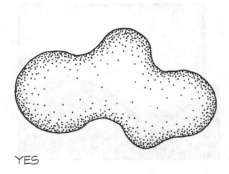

YES

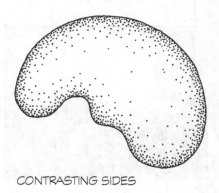

CONTRASTING SIDES

Another guideline is that the size and degree of curvature of the arcs comprising a curvilinear form should vary (left and middle 15.33). Arcs that are too similar to each other produce an edge that is static and mechanical in appearance, especially where a curvilinear line is the enclosing edge around a space or material area. Similarly, it is often preferable to contrast a set of complex curves against a simple curve on the opposite side of a space (right 15.33). Both these suggestions establish organic diversity. While variety and contrast are desirable, they must not be over exaggerated so as to create a design that is too busy (15.34). The fabrication of curvilinear shapes must always keep scale, use, and maintenance in mind so that the curvilinear edges of space are appropriate to how it is intended to function.

15.33 There enclosing curves should vary in size and location.

15.34 The size of the curves should relate to the scale of the space and site.

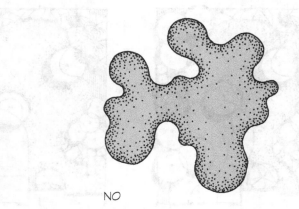

NO

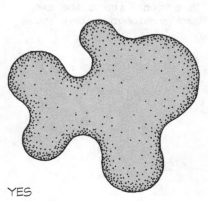

YES

335

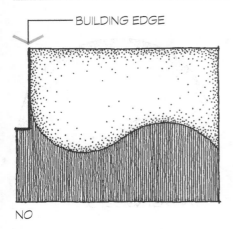

BUILDING EDGE

NO

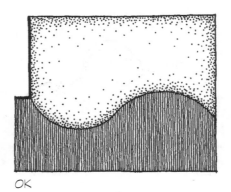

OK

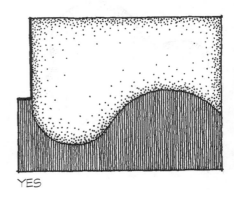

YES

15.35 Curved forms should meet the edge of adjoining elements at 90 degrees.

Connections

The interface of curvilinear shapes with other forms in the landscape needs special attention as it does with all circles and their derived geometries. Like all circles and arcs, curvilinear shapes should ideally connect to other forms and structures at a right angle. This is most critical where curved forms meet the straight edges of a site or building (15.35). In addition to the possibility of generating askew or even acute angles, haphazard intersections of curved forms with a building can create a weak association between structure and the landscape. That is, the building is apt to look unstable without straight lines to visually attach it to the surrounding ground plane. This was in fact a criticism of some English landscape designers who eradicated formal gardens in favor of an undulating landscape immediately adjacent to stately houses (Newton 1971, 214). So, there should often be a transition of short orthogonal lines inserted between a building and the landscape to create a proper interface between the two (15.36).

15.36 There shoud be a transtion between buildings and nearby curvilinear spaces.

NO TRANSITION

TRANSITION

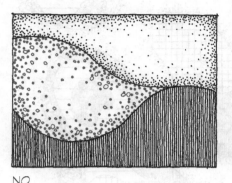

NO

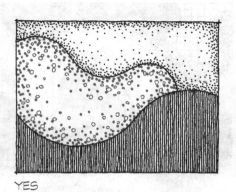

YES

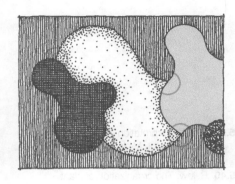

The same considerations should also be given to how curvilinear forms link to each other. A normal tendency when joining curved forms is to blend them together so that the edge of one gradually merges with the edge of another (left 15.37). This is easily achieved on paper and permits the adjoining lines to flow together in a continuous manner. However, such a relationship produces an increasingly smaller space between the lines that must be defined by an actual material in the landscape (10.39–41). The question that must be asked is: what material can fill this tiny space so that the intersection of the curved forms is defined? In reality, there is no such material except for carefully cut pavement and even that must be laterally supported to hold it in place. So, it is best to avoid such connections of curved forms by joining them at right angles or at least nonacute angles (middle and right 15.37). This requires the flow of some curved edges be stopped as they connect to other forms, an action that may seem counterintuitive, but is a realistic way of linking curvilinear forms in the landscape where weathering, frost heave, size of plants, and so on must all be taken into account.

15.37 Curved lines should not join in a way that forges acute angles.

Material Coordination

The use of materials in a curvilinear design organization offers opportunities and some limitations not present with other form typologies. For example, the curvilinear scheme provides the chance to organize plant materials in natural-looking masses, an occurrence that many find more appealing than arranging vegetation in rows or other architectural formations. There should nevertheless be a structure to plants in a curvilinear design even if it is not apparent to the untrained eye. Ideally, woody plants should reinforce the forms of a curvilinear design by being arranged in sweeping drifts (15.38). The shape of the plant drifts should repeat the forms elsewhere in the design with arcing gestures that are longer than wide. This tactic emulates the general temperament of the design and reinforces the movement inherent in curvilinear forms as it does in the planting scheme for the roof garden of the Ministry of Education and Health in Brazil designed by Roberto Burle Marx (15.39). Note how the individual planting areas all fit together like jigsaw puzzle pieces.

15.38 Woody plant materials should be organized in sweeping drifts.

337

15.39 Right. Interpretation of the planting design for the Ministry of Education and Health.

15.40 Below: The organization of plant materials should reinforce the "push-and-pull" quality of a curvilinear design.

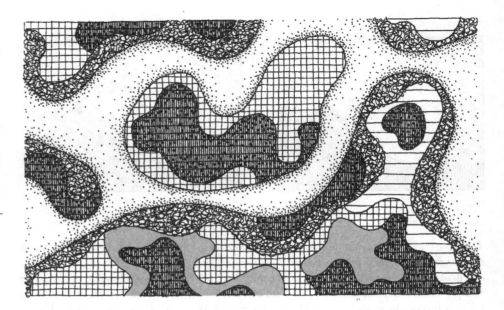

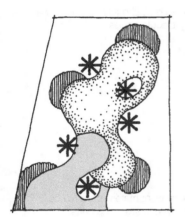

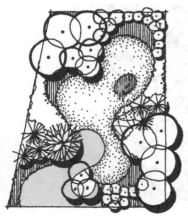

Another consideration in designing with plant materials in a curvilinear design organization is the placement of vegetative accents in relation to the undulating structure. As noted before, the curvilinear design genre possesses rounded projections that push out from an edge and recesses that move back. The peninsula-like projections are readily seen from many positions while the alcoves may be hidden from certain vantage points and framed from others. The organization of plant materials should relate to these varied conditions by placing accent plants like a sculptural tree, a splash of colorful perennials an/or annuals, and the like on the most prominent projections (15.40). The end of the recesses should also display special plants in those locations where the view is framed and focused toward them.

Pavement material and pattern should also be synchronized with the curvilinear design structure. In theory, the best pavement material for a curvilinear area is a plastic material like gravel, concrete, or asphalt because these materials easily conform to the shape in which they are placed. Modular pavement like stone, brick, or concrete pavers can also be laid within a curved form, but require cutting of each paving unit along the edge. This is possible to do with modern equipment that can cut pavement units into small pieces. Nevertheless, it should be kept in mind that sawing numerous individual pieces of pavement increases labor cost, sometimes substantially.

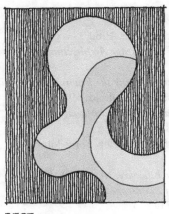

BEST

GOOD

OK

15.41 Above: Alternative patterns for expansion joints in concrete pavement.

15.42 Below: The grading of the ground plane should reinforce a curvilinear space.

From a compositional standpoint, it is best to create pavement patterns that reinforce the overall temperament of a curvilinear design with oscillating shapes and lines (15.12 and left 15.41). Again, this is achieved most easily with malleable materials although rigid modular materials can be used with the considerations already discussed regarding cutting. Concrete is an ideal pavement material because of its initial plasticity, but care must be given so that expansion joints intersect the edge of the pavement at a right angle (middle 15.41). This means that each expansion joint must be individually aligned rather than being positioned on the basis of an overall repeating pattern. Orthogonal and grid pavement patterns can also be used in a curvilinear design as a neutral, non-directional ground plane. However, these patterns have the potential to meet the curved edges at awkward angles that produce unstable units of pavement (right 15.41). Small individual pieces of brick, concrete pavers, and stone are structurally weak at the edge of a pavement area and must be held in place by mortar or with an edge material.

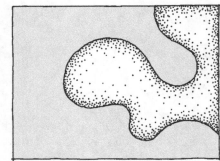

Topography

The grading of the ground plane has the most flexibility with a curvilinear design in comparison to other geometric typologies. The ground plane of curvilinear outdoor spaces where people are to walk, stand, or sit should be relatively level. However, the ground plane in other areas can be molded to whatever shape is desired assuming slopes are within limits for proper drainage, universal accessibility, and the given soil type. It is important that the contours reinforce the two-dimensional curvilinear shapes and be coordinated with plant massing (15.42).

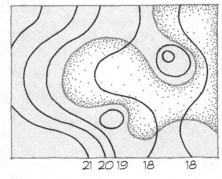

21 20 19   18   18

Referenced Resources

Bye, A. E. *Art Into Landscape*, 2nd edition. Mesa, AZ: PDA, 1983.

Grillo, Paul Jacques. *Form, Function, and Design*. New York: Dover, 1960.

Hazelrigg, George. "Meet Me (Again) in St. Louis, Louis." *Landscape Architecture*, October 2008.

Jellicoe, Geoffrey, and Susan Jellicoe. *The Landscape of Man: Shaping the Environment from Prehistory to the Present Day*. New York: Van Nostrand Reinhold, 1982.

Kaplan, Stephen, and Rachel Kaplan. *With People in Mind: Design and Management of Everyday Nature*. Washington, DC: Island Press, 1998.

Mann, William. *Space and Time in Landscape Architectural History*. New York: John Wiley & Sons, 1993.

Martin, Frank Edgerton. "Artistic Grounds." *Landscape Architecture*, March 2004.

Newton, Norman. *Design on the Land: The Development of Landscape Architecture*. Cambridge: Belknap Press of Harvard University, 1971.

Symes, Michael. *A Glossary of Garden History*. Buckinghamshire, UK: Shire Publications, 1993.

Space Maker Press. *Thomas Balsley: The Urban Landscape*. Berkeley: Space Maker Press, 2000.

Further Resources

Martignoni, Jimena. "Into the Mangroves." *Landscape Architecture*, April 2006.

Montero, Marta Iris. *Roberto Burle Marx: The Lyrical Landscape*. Berkeley: University of California Press, 2001.

Murphy, Pat. *By Nature's Design*. San Francisco: Chronicle Books, 1993.

Internet Resources

Thomas Balsley Associates: www.tbany.com

The Organic 16

The last typology of forms is the organic, a group of shapes that is derived from natural elements and patterns (16.1). Organic forms are the antithesis of orthogonal forms examined earlier in the book and are the least influenced by human guidance. Landscape site designs that incorporate organic forms do so by directly copying and integrating naturally occurring shapes or by abstracting them, using them more as a source of inspiration.

Organic forms have not been extensively used in the evolution of western gardens and landscape designs. In fact, it has been suggested that western cultures have often attempted to control and subdue nature by imposing human geometries on the landscape (McHarg 1971, 26, 70–71). The 17th-century English landscape style is perhaps one exception although this was a romanticized interpretation of nature (15.21). By comparison, organic forms have historically been the basis of Chinese and Japanese gardens by copying, abstracting, and sometimes miniaturizing natural landscapes. These gardens likewise represent a philosophy that the natural world is a source of knowledge and wisdom.

There is an increasing desire among contemporary landscape architects to incorporate organic forms in their designs. This no doubt results from the ever-expanding human, urban landscape and the simultaneous need to design environments that are sustainable and in sync with natural processes. This chapter studies the most prevalent natural forms and how they can be used as the basis of landscape architectural site design. The specific sections of this chapter are:

- Definition
- Typologies
- General Landscape Uses
- Typological Landscape Uses
- Transformation
- Design Guidelines

16.1 Examples of natural patterns and forms.

Definition

The term *organic* generally means that which is derived from, related to, or has the characteristics of living organisms. In the broadest sense, any element or pattern observed in a natural environment is organic and consequently the potential basis for form and space in landscape architectural design.

Organic forms tend to be thought of as irregular, rough, unrefined, and raw, being applied to design with minimum alteration by human intervention. Yet, the circle is also an organic form because it is seen in the sun, moon, flowers, water-washed stones, berries, and so forth. It will be recalled that the circle is frequently considered to be the most simple and pure of all forms, not at all rugged or crude. Other forms like various polygons, arcs, and curvilinear lines are also found in nature and can be accurately labelled *organic*. And the symmetrical design organization discussed throughout the previous chapters occurs in the structure of leaves, fruit, animals, and people.

So, the term organic must be applied thoughtfully because it encompasses a range of forms, many of which may initially seem to be more in the human realm than the natural one. This chapter concentrates on those organic forms that have not been previously addressed and are based on the typology of natural patterns discussed in the next section.

16.2 Sample pattern forms.

GROVE of TREES

CLOUDS

Typologies

Natural patterns and elements exist everywhere in the undisturbed landscape from the smallest of details to the macro features of a region. The landscape architect simply needs to be observant, directly copying what is seen or using it as inspiration in creating forms in a project. There are countless possibilities to draw from, making it potentially overwhelming to select. To make sense of the seemingly innumerable natural forms, several authors have attempted to categorize natural patterns and elements into typologies that can be used by designers and others. One such person is Richard L. Dubé who offers the broadest classification via a "library" of 48 pattern forms in the book *Natural Pattern Forms*. These pattern forms include a broad range of natural landscape elements and features like the island, mountain top, fissure, clouds, beach edge, grove of trees, and so on (16.2). The underlying premise is that each pattern can be the foundation for determining the overall design character and appropriate space defining elements within selected project types and features.

Two other authors offer a more succinct classification of forms by identifying recurring patterns found throughout nature: Pat Murphy in *By Natures' Design* and W. Gary Smith in *From Art to Landscape*. Murphy concisely presents six typologies into which all natural structures fall: (1) spirals and helixes, (2) meanders and ripples, (3) sheers and explosions, (4) branching, (5) packing and cracking, and (6) fractals. By comparison, Smith offers these groups of natural patterns: (1) scattered, (2) mosaic, (3) naturalistic drift, (4) serpentine, (5) spiral, (6) circle, (7) radial, (8) dendritic, and (9) fractured (Smith 2010, 33–57).

Although these two classifications of natural patterns employ slightly different terminologies, they are nevertheless very similar. Consequently, this text synthesizes Murphy's and Smith's categories as the basis for discussing the types and uses of organic forms in the landscape. A brief examination of each follows, proceeding from the least systematic and concluding with the perfection of the circle. Examples of the potential uses for each of these form categories follows in a later section of this chapter.

Scattered

The scattered pattern is composed of a repeated element dispersed across an area and separated by space. The spacing may appear random although it is usually not because the average distance between elements recurs throughout the pattern. The tighter the spacing, the more perceptible and cohesive the pattern appears. Fallen leaves below a tree or the distribution of shells on a beach are examples (16.3).

Mosaic

In art, a mosaic is a composition composed of many small individual pieces of glass, stone, or tile that collectively define an overall image. More broadly, a mosaic is an assemblage of many elements that are clumped together to create a complex configuration of material, color, and texture. A mosaic pattern is often noted for its diversity of parts, yet cohesiveness of its totality. Examples of a mosaic pattern are seen in native plant communities with an array of species coinciding with one another and the layering of foliage within a selected area (16.4).

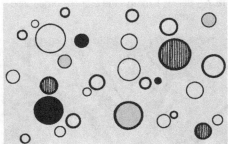

16.3 Above: Scattered pattern.

16.4 Left: Mosaic pattern.

16.5 Example of the cracked/fractured pattern.

16.6 Right Example of the fractal pattern.

16.7 Below: Example the branching/dendritic pattern.

Cracked/Fractured

This pattern results from pressures of expansion and contraction on an element or surface, often from drying or quick cooling. Cracks in a dried mud surface, stones, bark, or even old paint are examples (16.5). In nature, the tendency to crack often creates a network of lines that meet one another at 120 degrees. This is the most compact and efficient way of connecting lines and adjoining areas as manifested in the honeycomb (11.16) (Murphy 1993, 74–75).

Fractals

A fractal is a shape that has "self-similarity." That is, the shape of the details or smallest components of an object are the same as the overall form of the object. A magnified view is the same as the overall view. Fractals typically are complex, irregular shapes that seem to have no organization at first glance, yet reveal a recurring pattern when studied more closely. A fern branch is an excellent example of a fractal structure (16.6).

Branching/Dendritic

The branching or dendritic pattern is seen in the leaf, trunk, branch, and root structure of a tree (16.7). Many river networks and the human circulatory system also exhibit a dendritic configuration. A branching structure exists in nature as a conduit for gathering and/or dispersing a material from a broad area to a central one. It is a very efficient structure for connecting to a wide area with the least distance (Murphy 1993, 60–61).

Meandering Edge/Serpentine

The meandering edge or serpentine form is often created by wind and water moving through the landscape as evidenced in a flowing river, ripples of water, and the contours of sand dunes or by the edge and veining of leaves (16.8). This sensuous, dynamic form represents movement and energy and was discussed at length in the previous chapter.

Spiral

The spiral occurs in seashells, spider webs, the inner portion of sunflowers and daisies, and pine cones among others (16.9). This dynamic form represents outward expansion and growth from a single source. As the form enlarges, it does so in a manner that each additional increment has the same proportions as those from which it originated. It will be recalled from previous discussions of the rectangle that the spiral fits the proportions of the golden ratio and expresses the Fibonacci sequence (5.8).

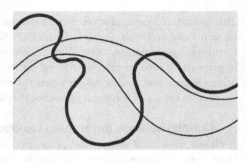

Circle/Radial

The circle was previously studied in Chapter 13 and is often described as the "most perfect" of forms. The sphere is a three dimensional expression of the circle and is a form that contains the most volume with the least surface area (Murphy 1993, 48). The dynamic transformation of a circle results in a radial pattern or explosion with components extending outward and around the center as revealed in flowers, leaf patterns, ripples of water, and many ocean organisms (16.10).

16.8 Above: Example of the meandering/serpentine pattern.

16.9 Left: Example of the spiral pattern.

16.10 Example of the circle/radial pattern.

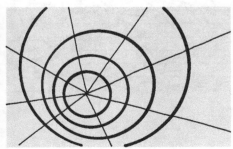

General Landscape Uses

All organic forms, regardless of type or origin, can potentially be employed as the basis of structuring space in landscape architectural site design as outlined in this section. The next section examines landscape uses based on specific organic form typologies.

Simulate Nature

Perhaps the most common use of organic forms in landscape architectural site design is to replicate nature by creating environments that appear to have little or no human influence. There are many reasons for undertaking this, including the desire to restore a degraded landscape to its indigenous condition, create a sustainable setting, provide a nurturing and healing environment, and/or forge a counterpoint to the human environment (see Counterbalance the Human Landscape below).

This can occur in several ways. First, a natural landscape can be diligently copied and then reproduced as carefully as possible with native elements and materials. Second, nature can offer an inspiring point of departure for various degrees abstraction. The end result uses organic forms to suggest nature. Many Eastern gardens are good examples, imitating and simplifying organic forms. Still another strategy is to insert a space into an existing natural setting, attempting to surround the space with a seemingly untouched environment. This often occurs in park and garden design where the need is to locate a human use area within an undisturbed landscape. In all cases, organic forms are used as means of forging a landscape that appears natural.

Counterbalance the Human Landscape

A closely associated second use of organic forms is to create landscapes that are a foil to the prevailing and ever-expanding human environment. The majority of the world's population lives in urban and suburban areas where there is frequently minimal contact with natural settings and their processes. Furthermore, many urban landscapes are ecological wastelands completely covered by buildings and pavement. The use of organic forms is one means for countering surroundings dominated by straight lines, flat planes, concrete, and glass (16.11). Organic forms sometimes provide the irregular, inconsistent, unplanned, unedited, and unprocessed. Furthermore, organic forms represent a symbolic connection to that which is beyond human capabilities.

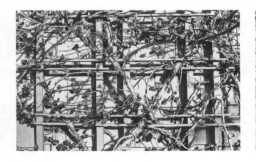 

16.11 Organic forms counterbalancing structural elements.

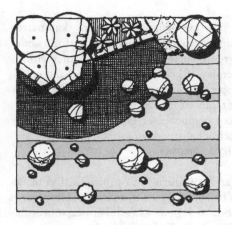 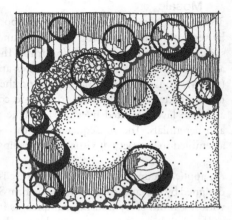

16.12 Left: Examples of designs incorporating scattered elements.

16.13 Below: A striking base plane can visually unite scattered elements.

Typological Landscape Uses

This section examines landscape uses associated with the organic form typologies previously outlined in this chapter. Because of the highly varied character of these typologies, it is difficult at best to comprehensively cover all potential uses. Rather, this section offers representative examples of each typology with the hopes that they provide a point of departure for additional exploration by the reader. And as with forms discussed in other chapters of this text, many of the landscape uses discussed here coexist with one another, allowing the designer to accomplish a number of landscape uses in one setting.

Scattered

The scattered organic pattern offers a challenge to many designers who are accustomed to grouping elements to create a cohesive design. It will be recalled from Chapter 1 that mass collection is one of the most fundamental organizational structures in design (1.30–31). Yet, the scattered concept does have uses, especially in forging cubist space. A splintered space can be created on an open site by randomly sprinkling elements about. An open field populated by dispersed trees or a plaza randomly filled with rocks are examples (left 16.12). The scattered elements function less as space enclosing elements as they do as objects within a space that is suitable for casually passing through. Another use of the scattered structure is in planting design where a selected plant species can be located sporadically throughout the design (right 16.12).

A key to all these design examples is the visual strength of the ground plane. A base plane that is defined by a striking material or pattern extending below all the dispersed elements will create a common, pronounced background that visually links the separate elements together. Without the unifying base plane, the design is apt to appear chaotic and unplanned.

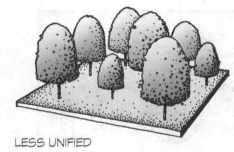

LESS UNIFIED

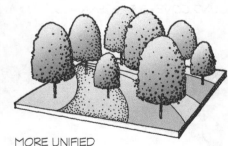

MORE UNIFIED

347

Mosaic

The mosaic pattern is particularly apropos for planting design and gardens dominated by vegetation. In organizing plants, the underlying concept is to mass plants of the same species together in clumps and/or drifts. These groups are then assembled together within a planting area in a manner that creates an interplay of height, form, texture, and color (16.14). Thus, the individual plants and their respective clumps are the basis of the overall mosaic pattern. Furthermore, this same concept can be extended vertically with shrub and tree layers located over a base-plane pattern composed of ground cover, annuals, and perennials. The consequence is a three-dimensional tapestry of many plants that are assembled in a variety of visual relationships with one another.

An applied example of a mosaic structure is Charlotte Garden in Copenhagen, Denmark designed by the landscape architecture firm SLA (16.15). The garden, an enclosed courtyard within a multi-story housing complex, is intended to suggest a beach landscape because of the site's historic proximity to the sea (Lee 2007, 127). To fulfill this objective, clumps of different varieties of grasses and fescues are organized in a mosaic pattern, suggesting a puzzle-piece-like arrangement of diverse plant colors and textures.

16.14 A planting design based on the moasic structure.

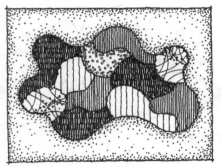
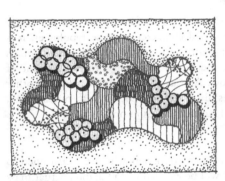
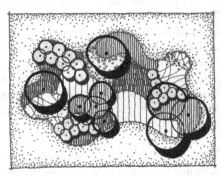

GROUND COVERS & PERENNIALS   SHRUBS   TREES

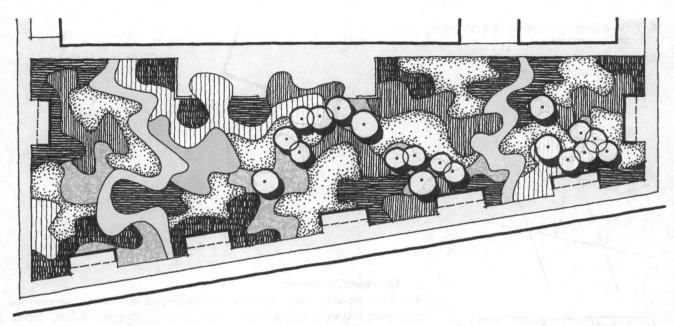

The mosaic concept can also be applied to landscape designs that are composed of a range of materials, not just plants. Again, the intent is to orchestrate diverse materials and elements laterally and vertically through a space, creating engaging juxtapositions among the constituent parts (16.16). This is best achieved by means of an interlocking organization that suggests layers much like what is seen in the juxtaposition of foliage on many plants. The challenge of a mosaic design is to establish an overall sense of cohesiveness despite the inclusion of numerous elements and strata of the design. This is often realized by careful repetition of selected elements and/or materials throughout the design.

16.15 Site plan of Charlotte garden.

16.16 An example of a design based on the mosaic structure.

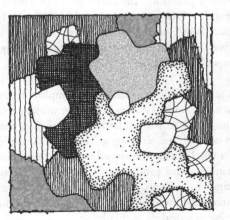

GROUND MATERIALS

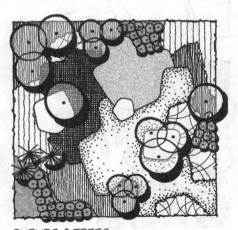

SHRUBS & TREES

16.17 Right: Comparison between the polygon and fractured forms.

16.18 Below: Transformation of a site area into a fractured configuration.

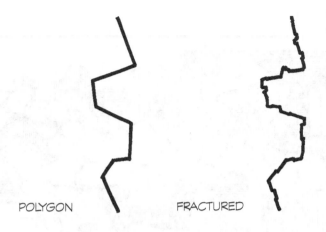

POLYGON   FRACTURED

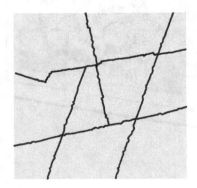

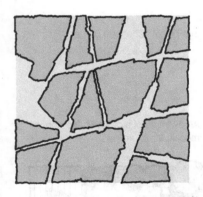

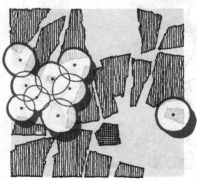

Cracked/Fractured

This form typology shares some characteristics and uses of the asymmetrical polygon previously discussed in Chapter 11. Both convey the irregular, broken, uneven, crooked, and rutted. The cracked form, however, is more erratic with its imperfect and misshaped profile (16.17). The cracked/fractured pattern can be used as the basis of site design in a number of ways. First, it can be created by means transformation that progressively partitions an entire site area into fragmented pieces (16.18). This process is akin to the movement of the earth's tectonic plates that has yielded detached continental masses. As presented in earlier chapters, subdivision frequently forges a series of positive masses separated by an intertwined negative or interstitial space (13.19, 14.16, 15.14). When conceived as cracking, the transformation creates a ruff, craggy space in which the fractured pattern permeates the entire site, not simply the edge. An illustration of this concept is found in Elisengarten designed by SLA (16.19). Located in Aachen, Germany, this open space is intended to evoke a river delta with walks that divide a series of lawn areas like a river that is cutting through and fragmenting the sediment deposited as it empties into a larger body of water (SLA).

A second tactic of cracking also employs a transformation process to fracture an entire site area. However it differs in that the initial partitioning is based on straight and/or repetitive lines (16.20). The resultant pieces are then progressively moved and rotated at varied angles to one another, creating a haphazard arrangement of positive and negative space. It is as if a whole shape was tossed up into the air and then shattered when it hit the ground. The results of this process can vary widely depending on the size, shape, and spacing of the fragmented pieces. Care must be given to assure that the resultant space accommodates the intended function because it is easy to produce a configuration that is so fractured as to make practical use difficult.

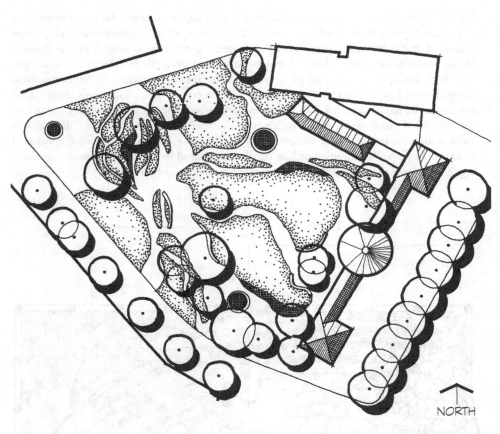

NORTH

16.19 Above: Site plan of Elisengarten.

16.20 Below: Transformation of a repetitive form into a fractured design structure.

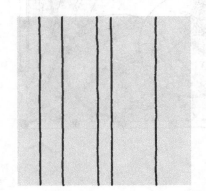  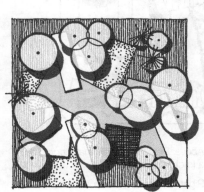

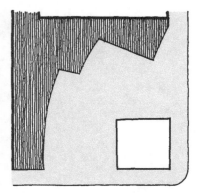

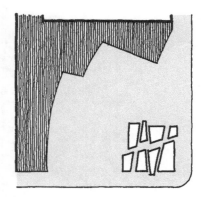

A third method for generating a cracked/fractured design is to apply the previous strategy to a selected area or element within a site (16.21). Consequently, the transformation process is focused and only alters a segment of the design. The resulting fractured area or element readily serves as an accent when it is notably divergent from the remainder of the design. One built example of this concept is found in the Tahari courtyards in Millburn, New Jersey, designed by Michael Van Valkenburgh Associates, Inc. These courtyards are intended as tableaus of nature inserted into a large suburban building, offering workers contact to natural and seasonal cycles otherwise absent from their work environment (Michael Van Valkenburgh Associates). The concept of fracturing was incorporated into the wooded courtyards by a walk composed of logs cut flat and placed in an irregular pattern, perhaps suggesting a tree that has fallen and fragmented on the forest floor. (16.22).

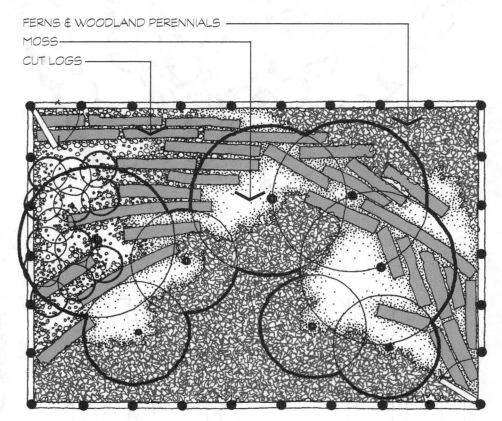

FERNS & WOODLAND PERENNIALS

MOSS

CUT LOGS

NORTH

16.21 Above: Design example that incorporates a fractured element.

16.22 Right: Plan of a Tahari courtyard.

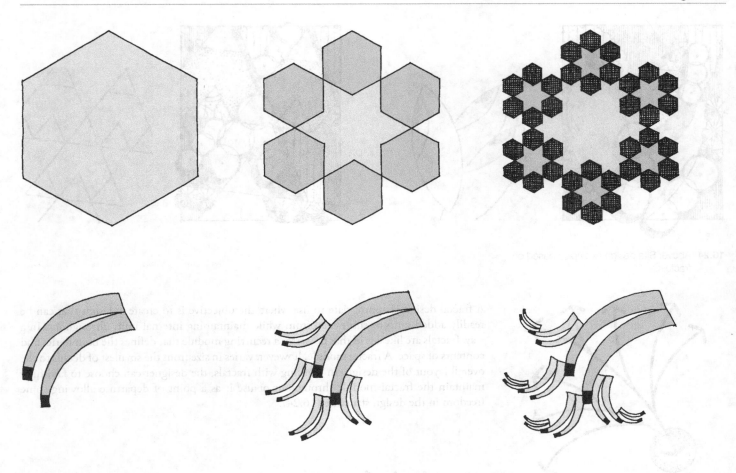

Fractals

The use of fractals as the basis of landscape architectural site design is a relatively new and
evolving area of interest. While a number of both theoretical and built projects exist within
allied fields like architecture and computer-aided design, few examples are present within
the body of work completed by landscape architects. Nevertheless, the use of fractals as a
potential foundation of form and space holds intriguing possibilities.

As indicated before, the basis of fractal design is a line, form, or pattern that lends itself to
repetitive replication, resulting in a composition that exhibits the original source in both
the detail and the overall configuration (16.23). It is important to note that a fractal design
can incorporate primary forms, polygonal forms, and more irregular naturalistic forms.
Despite its source, the aspect of the organic is exhibited by the ability of the design to
endlessly expand or contract in a crystalline-like manner.

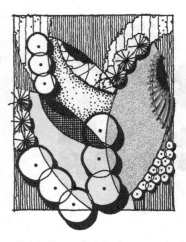

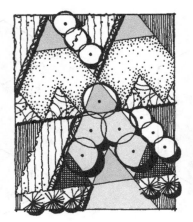

16.24 Above: Site design examples based on fractals.

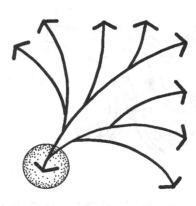

A fractal design is appropriate to use where the objective is to create a design that can be readily added onto or subtracted from while maintaining internal unity throughout. In a way, fractals are like a grid that possesses a recurring module that defines the boundaries and contents of space. A fractal module, however, varies in size from the smallest of details to the overall layout of the design. In working with fractals, the designer can choose to faithfully maintain the fractal module throughout or use it as a point of departure allowing some freedom in the design structure (16.24).

16.25 Above: The branching structure is apropos to direct movement between confined and expansive areas.

16.26 Right: Varied structural qualities of a branching structure.

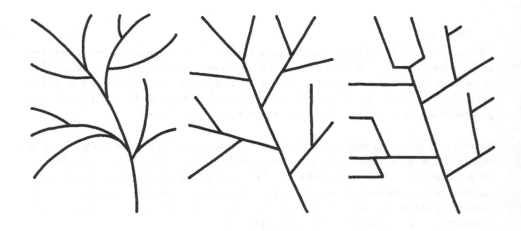

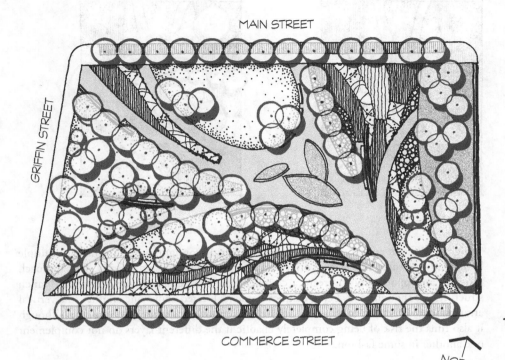

MAIN STREET

GRIFFIN STREET

COMMERCE STREET

NORTH

16.27 Site plan proposal for Belo Park.

Branching/Dendritic

As in nature, this organizational structure is most suited for guiding movement through the landscape, often to or from a point of concentration to a relatively large adjoining area (16.25). Such a system is apropos for large green spaces like parks, arboreta, campuses, and so forth, but not well disposed for spaces intended for congregation, sitting, and the like. Wherever it is employed, there are several variables that should be kept in mind. The first is the shape of the "branches" which can be straight, arced, angled, and so on depending on the desired quality of movement along them (16.26). Secondly, the width of the branches can also vary to accommodate different uses and materials within the design. A project example that demonstrates some of these possibilities is the proposal for Belo Park in Dallas, Texas, designed by Hargreaves Associates (16.27; compare to 14.25). A sweeping walk system is the primary armature for the plan, extending across the site in a series of "branches" from a point of origin in the southeast corner. Complementary shaded groves and perennial gardens are treated as additional branches that extend from the curved walks. The selection of materials and the implication of a river/stream corridor are collectively intended to reflect the regional Texas landscape.

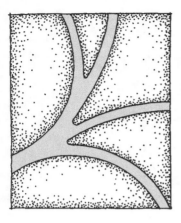

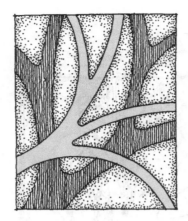

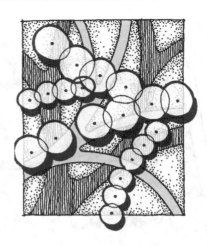

16.28 A design can be composed of multiple branches in layers.

A slightly different concept of the branching/dendritic configuration is to employ multiple branching structures, one layered on top another within one design (16.28). This approach provides an opportunity to create a complex design especially if the individual branch structures are thought of as being distinct elements located above one another in a vertical arrangement. This strategy forges a diversity of juxtapositions among the elements although it also runs the risk of being completely chaotic if the different layers do not complement one another in some fashion.

Meandering Edge/Serpentine
The meandering edge or serpentine form was discussed in depth in the previous chapter, and will not be given additional attention here. The reader is referred back to Chapter 15.

16.29 A spiral contracts space and directs movement to an internal terminus.

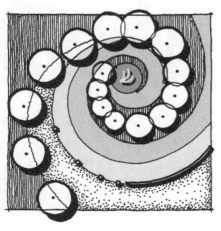

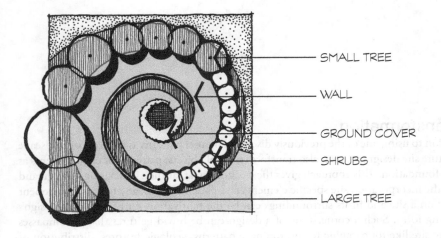

— SMALL TREE

— WALL

— GROUND COVER

— SHRUBS

— LARGE TREE

16.30 Left: The size of the space defining elements may also gradate.

16.31 Below: The spiral can suggest an explosive movement to and from a space.

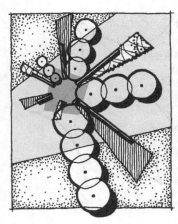

Spiral

The spiral potentially fulfills three distinct functions in landscape architectural site design. The first is to employ it for its symbolic associations such as evolution, continuity, and extension. In a like manner, the spiral suggests the cyclical aspect of breathing, the seasons, and birth and death (Tresidder 2005, 448–449). These are similar to the metaphorical meanings of the circle which also implies continuity and eternity (see Landscape Uses, Chapter 13). Yet, the spiral does not close back on itself like the circle but rather continues to extend itself in an ever-enlarging coil. This gradation of size is expressive of a sustained force and an exploding energy that is not possible with the circle.

A second use of the spiral is to generate a contracting, arced space that leads to a terminus (16.29). The spiral's unfolding edge creates an opening that invites the exterior to enter an ever-evolving space that gradually focuses attention on its end point. An accent is sometimes located at this strategic point to celebrate the spiral's resolution and the layered, encompassing envelopment. A spiral space can be delineated in a number of ways. For sizable spaces, large elements can be used along the edge at the opening, but are usually replaced by progressively smaller and thinner elements as the spiral approaches its innermost point (16.30). For smaller scaled spaces with limited area, low walls, ground cover, pavement patterns, and so forth are often employed to define an oval.

A third use of the spiral in site design is to express an energetic movement to or from a space. In this instance, the spiral is not completely expressed but rather intimated by repetitive gestures that peel away from the primary space (16.31). Collectively, these formations function like the sides of a spiral but without being connected along a continuum.

Circle/Radial

The reader is referred to Chapter 13 where the circle was previously discussed in length.

Transformation

In addition to using one of the previously discussed natural patterns as the basis of landscape architecture site design, one can also transform natural objects, patterns, or environments as a design foundation. This approach gives the designer great latitude in devising a design and permits the incorporation site specific elements and patterns. Thus, any natural component observed on a site and in its surroundings can be the motivation for generating a design's structuring form. Such a cornerstone of a design can be broad gestures that encompasses the entire site like topographic forms, drainage patterns, geologic features, distribution of different plant species, and so forth. Or the smallest of details like cracks in stones, bark, flowers, the shape of water moving around a rock, and the like can be used as the catalyst for a design.

In some situations the shape of the selected element, like a circle seen in a flower or fruit, can be directly applied to the site organization with little modification to the shape itself. However in many other cases, it is better to use the chosen element as a point of departure by abstracting and transforming it into a form that merely suggests it origin. This approach allows the designer to more freely adjust the form to fit the site, required program uses, and serve as the armature of space. An example is the transformation of a maple leaf into the foundation of a design (16.32–33, 16.34). Here the intersecting arcs of the leaf's edge are separated from the leaf, simplified, and then permitted to change size as a means of creating an organizational structure. In the end, the resultant design resembles the maple leaf's general character without being a direct copy of it.

16.32 Above: The inspiration: a maple leaf.
16.33 Below: Tranformation of the maple leaf.

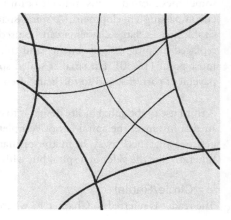

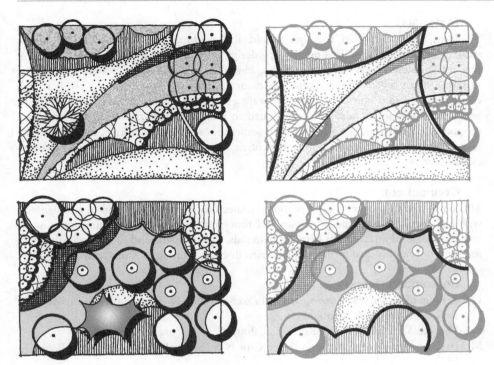

16.34 Design examples based on the transformation of the maple leaf.

Design Guidelines

Given the diversity of organic forms, it is difficult to offer concise design guidelines for each of them. Nevertheless, there are a number of general suggestions that pertain to all.

Relation to Function

The adage that "form follows function" applies to all forms used as the basis of site design. Nevertheless, it is a principle that should be constantly kept in mind when working with organic forms because it is easy to allow shape to become the most important aspect of a design in attempt to make it feel "natural" and perhaps representative of a naturally occurring element as previously discussed. When this occurs, basic requirements such as necessary spatial size, desired proportions, maintenance needs, and so forth are sometimes given incidental consideration or forgotten altogether. Thus, a critical challenge in working with organic shapes is to select a structuring form that relates to and supports the functional needs of a project. An organic design where form is given first priority may ultimately fail even though it possesses an engaging and innovative configuration.

Consider Spatial Experience

The need to think three-dimensionally and to design an encompassing spatial experience is likewise a truism for all landscape architectural designs. But again, it is sometimes easy to forget this basic requirement when designing with organic forms. A common mistake of novice designers is to create organic compositions that represent a natural object or pattern in plan view while forgetting about how the design will actually be experienced by a person within the design. To be successful, an organic design must convey its intended character at eye level as well as from above.

Materials

Similarly, the materials of a design should also reinforce the overall character of the structuring forms. The desired quality of a design should permeate all aspects of a design, not just the shapes seen from from above. However, this does not necessarily mean that materials of an organic design must be "natural." They can be when they are practical, cost effective, and support the desire to create a sustainable landscape. But many human-generated materials can also be incorporated so long as their character and composition supports the desired design persona. This sometimes requires innovative, unconventional uses of common materials, a notion that often requires creativity and the willingness to experiment.

Connections

Much was said in previous chapters about connections among forms within a design and with site edges. These same principles and thoughts also apply to organic forms. Acute angles, haphazard attachments between materials, tight corners, and so forth should all be minimized if not avoided for the same reasons discussed throughout this text.

Referenced Resources

Dubé, Richard L. *Natural Pattern Forms: A Practical Sourcebook for Landscape Design*. New York: Van Nostrand, Reinhold, 1997.

Lee, Uje, ed. *SLA*. Seoul, South Korea: C3, 2007.

McHarg, Ian. *Design with Nature*. Garden City, NY: Doubleday Natural History Press, 1971.

Murphy, Pat. *By Natures' Design*. San Francisco: Chronicle Books, 1993.

Smith, W. Gary. *From Art to Landscape: Unleashing Creativity in Garden Design*. Portland: Timber Press, 2010.

Tresidder, Jack, ed. *The Complete Dictionary of Symbols*. San Francisco: Chronicle Books, 2005.

Further Resources

Haeckel, Ernst. *Art Forms from the Ocean*. New York: Prestel, 2005.

Internet Resources

Hargreaves Associates: www.hargreaves.com

Michael VanValkenburgh Associates: www.mvvainc.com

SLA: www.sla.dk

Credits

Photographs

Figure 11.16 is from iStockphoto: #11006417. All other photographs are by the author.

Illustrations

Scale figures in selected illustrations are taken from All Silhouettes: http://all-silhouettes.com/people-silhouette/

Index